The 1912 Yale Peruvian Scientific Expedition Collections from Machu Picchu

YALE UNIVERSITY PUBLICATIONS IN ANTHROPOLOGY

EDITORIAL COMMITTEE

Richard L. Burger
Curatorial Editor-in-Chief
Charles J. MacCurdy Professor of Anthropology
Chair, Council on Archaeological Studies

Andrew Hill
J. Clayton Stephenson Professor of Anthropology

Roderick J. McIntosh
Professor of Anthropology

The Yale University Publications in Anthropology series, published by the Yale University Department of Anthropology and the Peabody Museum of Natural History at Yale University, is supported by the Theodore and Ruth Wilmanns Lidz Endowment Fund for Excellence in Scholarly Publications, dedicated to the dissemination of scholarly research and study of the world and its cultures.

The Yale University Publications in Anthropology series embodies the results of researches in the general field of anthropology directly conducted or sponsored by the Yale University Department of Anthropology and the Yale Peabody Museum of Natural History Division of Anthropology. Occasionally other manuscripts of outstanding quality that deal with subjects of special interest to the faculty of the Department of Anthropology may also be included.

For a complete list of available titles in this series visit www.yalebooks.com.

The 1912 Yale Peruvian Scientific Expedition Collections from Machu Picchu

Metal Artifacts

Edited by
Richard L. Burger
and Lucy C. Salazar

NUMBER 91

Published by
the Yale University Department of Anthropology
and the Yale Peabody Museum of Natural History

Distributed by
Yale University Press
NEW HAVEN AND LONDON

Yale

YALE UNIVERSITY PUBLICATIONS IN ANTHROPOLOGY
Number 91

Rosemary Volpe, *Publications Manager*

Nancy Moore Hulnick, *Project Editor*

Index by Aardvark Indexing

Distributed by Yale University Press
New Haven and London | www.yalebooks.com

Cover: A straight knife with a modeled fisherman (bronze, ANT.017973).
© Yale University. Photograph by William K. Sacco.

Copyright © 2012 Yale University. All rights reserved.

This book may not be reproduced, in whole or in part, including illustrations, in any form (beyond that copying permitted by Sections 107 and 108 of the U.S. Copyright Law and except by reviewers for the public press), without the written permission of the publishers.

For submission guidelines visit peabody.yale.edu or send inquiries to:
Publications Office, Peabody Museum of Natural History, Yale University,
P. O. Box 208118, New Haven CT 06520-8118 USA; peabody.publications@yale.edu

ISBN 978-0-913516-27-0
ISSN 1535-7082
Printed in the U.S.A.

Library of Congress Cataloging-in-Publication Data

The 1912 Yale Peruvian scientific expedition collections from Machu Picchu : metal artifacts / edited by Richard L. Burger and Lucy C. Salazar.
   p. cm. -- (Yale University publications in anthropology number 91)
 Includes bibliographical references and index.
   ISBN 978-0-913516-27-0 (pbk. : alk. paper)
1. Machu Picchu Site (Peru) 2. Yale Peruvian Expedition (1912) 3. Incas--Implements. 4. Incas--Antiquities. 5. Metal-work--Peru. 6. Metallurgy--Peru. 7. Peru--Antiquities. I. Burger, Richard L. II. Salazar, Lucy C.
 F3429.1.M3A18 2012
 985.06'31--dc23
                                                                                 2012032318

This paper meets the requirements of ANSI/NISO Z39.48-1992 (Permanence of Paper).

10 9 8 7 6 5 4 3 2 1

Contents

xi Preface
xiii Introduction

1 ONE • Metal Artifacts from the 1911–1912 Yale Expeditions to Peru
Robert B. Gordon, *Yale University*

    1 Previous Research on the Collection
    3 Research Methods
    7 Classification and Description of the Artifacts
  11 Research Results
  56 Significance of the Collection
  71 Acknowledgments

73 TWO • The Meanings of Metals: The Inca and Regional Contexts of Quotidian Metals from Machu Picchu
Bruce D. Owen, *Sonoma State University*

    75 The Comparative Data
    77 Variation in Late Horizon Metal Assemblages
    85 Regional Patterns in Andean Metalworking
  102 Cuzqueño and General Andean Types at Machu Picchu
  108 Exotics and Cosmopolitanism at Machu Picchu
  121 Life Histories of Quotidian Metal Artifacts
  138 Summary and Conclusions
  141 Acknowledgments
  142 Distribution Maps

191 Appendix A: Technical Descriptions of Selected Artifacts
211 Appendix B: Micrograph Locations
219 Appendix C: Catalog of Metal Artifacts in the Collection of the 1911–1912 Yale Peruvian Scientific Expeditions
249 Appendix D: Artifact Descriptions
255 Appendix E: Artifact Data Sources
261 Appendix F: Metal Artifact Typology
279 Appendix G: Illustrations of Selected Metal Artifact Types

Color plates follow page 202.

295 References

305 Index

Figures

Section One

- 8   Figure 1.1. Silver alloy shawl pin *(tupu)* ANT.018431.
- 9   Figure 1.2. Bronze knife *(tumi)* ANT.017855.
- 10 Figure 1.3. Bronze axe (ANT.017902).
- 11 Figure 1.4. Bronze chisel (ANT.017907).
- 12 Figure 1.5. Example of artisan's work in progress (ANT.017972).
- 13 Figure 1.6. Bronze pendant (ANT.017876).
- 14 Figure 1.7. Histogram showing the distribution of tin content in the bronze artifacts.
- 27 Figure 1.8. As-cast, dendritic structure of bronze in the head of a lime spoon (ANT.017970).
- 29 Figure 1.9. Microstructure of bronze that has been lightly deformed and then annealed.
- 31 Figure 1.10. Metal in the top of axe (ANT.017908).
- 32 Figure 1.11. Micrograph of alloy containing 76% silver and 34% copper.
- 33 Figure 1.12. Section of the stem of a shawl pin (ANT.017821).
- 34 Figure 1.13. Llama-head knife (ANT.017962).
- 35 Figure 1.14. Section through the head of a knife (ANT.017962).
- 36 Figure 1.15. Large pores due to gas release during solidification in the bronze crowbar (ANT.018478).
- 37 Figure 1.16. The gross casting defect in the broken axe blade (ANT.017974).
- 38 Figure 1.17. Large gas porosity in a broken axe blade (ANT.017969).
- 39 Figure 1.18. Bronze knife (ANT.017904).
- 41 Figure 1.19. Microstructure of an axe (ANT.017898).
- 43 Figure 1.20. Elongated sulfide inclusions near the tip of a bronze axe (ANT.017898).
- 44 Figure 1.21. Strain lines and elongated sulfide inclusions near the tip of a bronze chisel (ANT.017964).
- 45 Figure 1.22. Structure of metal 7 mm from the tip of a chisel (ANT.017964).
- 47 Figure 1.23. The upper part of the bronze stem of the llama-head knife (ANT.017962).
- 48 Figure 1.24. Microstructure of a silver-copper alloy forged bar (ANT.018449).
- 49 Figure 1.25. Interior microstructure of a copper-silver alloy headband (ANT.017872).
- 50 Figure 1.26. Surface of a bronze bar (ANT.017913).
- 51 Figure 1.27. Microstructure of a silver alloy spangle (ANT.018400).
- 53 Figure 1.28. Histogram of thickness measurements along the length of a silver alloy headband (ANT.017872).

54 FIGURE 1.29. Bronze disc (ANT.018480).
56 FIGURE 1.30. Alloy of copper plus 76% silver.
57 FIGURE 1.31. Alloy of copper plus 25% silver.
58 FIGURE 1.32. Edge of artifact ANT.018449.
59 FIGURE 1.33. Oblique cross section of a silver headband (ANT.017872).
60 FIGURE 1.34. Section of the tip of an axe (ANT.017898).
61 FIGURE 1.35. Edge of an axe (ANT.017902).
62 FIGURE 1.36. Edge of a chisel (ANT.017975).
63 FIGURE 1.37. Cross section of the tip of a chisel (ANT.017975).
64 FIGURE 1.38. Section of the top surface of a chisel (ANT.017907).
65 FIGURE 1.39. Section of the tip of a broken axe blade (ANT.017969).
66 FIGURE 1.40. Section of the tip of an axe (ANT.017900).

SECTION TWO

143 FIGURE 2.1. Distribution maps of the entire metals database, regional metalworking traditions, Late Horizon assemblages, and tupus.
144 FIGURE 2.2. Distribution maps of tupus.
145 FIGURE 2.3. Distribution maps of tupus.
146 FIGURE 2.4. Distribution maps of tupus.
147 FIGURE 2.5. Distribution maps of tupus.
148 FIGURE 2.6. Distribution maps of tupus.
149 FIGURE 2.7. Distribution maps of tupus.
150 FIGURE 2.8. Distribution maps of worn tupus, oversize tupu-like objects, and possible lime dippers.
151 FIGURE 2.9. Distribution maps of T-shaped tumis.
152 FIGURE 2.10. Distribution maps of T-shaped tumis.
153 FIGURE 2.11. Distribution maps of T-shaped tumis.
154 FIGURE 2.12. Distribution maps of flat tumis.
155 FIGURE 2.13. Distribution maps of Guayas tumis, handleless transverse knives, and rectangular knives with hole(s) near the back.
156 FIGURE 2.14. Distribution maps of long oval knives, chisels, and other tools.
157 FIGURE 2.15. Distribution maps of heavy chisels, celts, and axes.
158 FIGURE 2.16. Distribution maps of axe hafting features.
159 FIGURE 2.17. Distribution maps of axe blade shapes.
160 FIGURE 2.18. Distribution maps of axe blade shapes, "classic" axes, and "ancla" axes.
161 FIGURE 2.19. Distribution maps of socketed axes with tail flap, "yauri" forms, axes with side bars, and axes with hooks.
162 FIGURE 2.20. Distribution maps of regional axe types.
163 FIGURE 2.21. Distribution maps of mace heads.
164 FIGURE 2.22. Distribution maps of star-shaped mace heads.
165 FIGURE 2.23. Distribution maps of metal projectile points.
166 FIGURE 2.24. Distribution maps of all metal projectile points, atlatl parts, and bola weights.

167 FIGURE 2.25. Distribution maps of bola weights and suspension holes with crossbars.
168 FIGURE 2.26. Distribution maps of needles and tiny spoons.
169 FIGURE 2.27. Distribution maps of tweezers.
170 FIGURE 2.28. Distribution maps of tweezers.
171 FIGURE 2.29. Distribution maps of tweezers.
172 FIGURE 2.30. Distribution maps of tweezers.
173 FIGURE 2.31. Distribution maps of tweezers, earspools, and nose ornaments.
174 FIGURE 2.32. Distribution maps of lirpus and finger rings.
175 FIGURE 2.33. Distribution maps of cone "bells" and Titicaca figurine hair pendants.
176 FIGURE 2.34. Distribution maps of split bells and cup bells.
177 FIGURE 2.35. Distribution maps of headdress frontals.
178 FIGURE 2.36. Distribution maps of headdress frontals and structure, gauntlets, and "brazales."
179 FIGURE 2.37. Distribution maps of plain, flat, thin sheet metal discs.
180 FIGURE 2.38. Distribution maps of thin sheet metal discs.
181 FIGURE 2.39. Distribution maps of strips, metal vessels, plume holders, and mummy masks.
182 FIGURE 2.40. Distribution maps of traced decoration.
183 FIGURE 2.41. Distribution maps of traced decoration, repoussé, sheet metal fabricated with tabs, slots, and so on, and sheet metal fragments.
184 FIGURE 2.42. Distribution maps of bangles, spiral motifs, upset (mushrooming), and intentional destruction.
185 FIGURE 2.43. Distribution maps of axe-monies, socketed points, North Coast tumis, and metal spindle whorls.
186 FIGURE 2.44. Distribution maps of Atacama "earrings," "manoplas," "tokis," and "tincullpas."
187 FIGURE 2.45. Distribution maps of crowbars and production materials.
188 FIGURE 2.46. Distribution maps of "sea anchors," copper, silver, and gold.
189 FIGURE 2.47. Distribution maps of lead and tin.

Tables

Section One

Page	Table	Description
6	Table 1.1.	Distribution of items.
6	Table 1.2.	Silver alloy items.
16	Table 1.3.	Sources of metal artifacts.
18	Table 1.4.	Items examined in the laboratory.
20	Table 1.5.	Bulk compositions of artifacts using wet chemical, semi-quantitative analyses.
22	Table 1.6.	Composition of inclusions in bronze for copper, sulfur, and iron.
23	Table 1.7.	Microprobe analyses of bronze axes.
24	Table 1.8.	Trace element analysis of bronze axe ANT.017898.
25	Table 1.9.	Microprobe analyses of silver alloy artifacts.
26	Table 1.10.	Microprobe analyses of tin artifacts.
26	Table 1.11.	Examples of work in progress.
26	Table 1.12.	Metals used by Machu Picchu artisans.
28	Table 1.13.	Examples of bronze artifacts retaining as-cast microstructures.
30	Table 1.14.	Inca bronze artifacts cast to shape and then forged.
40	Table 1.15.	Examples of bronze artifacts forged to shape.
42	Table 1.16.	Inca items with edges shaped by forging.
46	Table 1.17.	Hardness gradients in bronze tools.
52	Table 1.18.	Silver alloy sheet artifacts.
68	Table 1.19.	Evidence of tool use.

Section Two

Page	Table	Description
79	Table 2.1.	Late Horizon metal assemblages.
86	Table 2.2.	Interpretation of geographic distributions of artifacts.
88	Table 2.3.	Meanings of some potentially Inca metal object types.
104	Table 2.4.	Metal artifacts from Machu Picchu that would not have appeared exotic there.
110	Table 2.5.	Metal artifacts and features of artifacts from Machu Picchu that would have referred to some other region.
120	Table 2.6.	Machu Picchu contexts that contained multiple metal objects.
124	Table 2.7.	Evidence of use of tupus at Machu Picchu.
125	Table 2.8.	Evidence of use of T-shaped tumis at Machu Picchu.
126	Table 2.9.	Evidence of use of axes, celts, and chisels in the entire database.
127	Table 2.10.	Evidence of use of axes, celts, and chisels at Machu Picchu.
133	Table 2.11.	Evidence of intentional destruction and repair at Machu Picchu.
134	Table 2.12.	Contexts of intentional destruction in UMARP excavations.
136	Table 2.13.	Contexts of quotidian metal artifacts at Machu Picchu.
137	Table 2.14.	Contexts of quotidian metal artifacts in Late Intermediate Period and Late Horizon contexts excavated by UMARP.

Preface

This book is the second in a series of Yale University Publications in Anthropology (YUPA) volumes devoted to the materials that were excavated in 1912 at the famous site of Machu Picchu by the Yale Peruvian Scientific Expedition under the direction of Hiram Bingham III. The first was dedicated to the human and animal remains recovered at Pachacuti's country palace, while this study focuses on the nearly 200 metal objects that were recovered. These metal objects were sent along with other archaeological materials to the Yale Peabody Museum of Natural History with permission from the Peruvian government for research and conservation, and they have been stored there for almost a century. As part of a recent agreement with the government of Peru, they are being returned to Cusco for storage, conservation, and study at the Universidad Nacional de San Antonio Abad del Cusco.

Among the pioneers of Andean archaeology, Bingham was exceptional in recognizing the research potential of archaeological collections and the need to involve specialists in the analysis of archaeological remains in order to extract as much information as possible from their study. Some of these specialists, such as the osteologist George Eaton, accompanied Bingham on the 1912 expedition, while others were consulted after his return to Yale University. In the case of the metal artifacts discovered at Machu Picchu, Bingham sought out C. H. Mathewson, a recently hired assistant professor of metallurgy at Yale University. Mathewson had studied metallography at Göttingen in Germany and was at the cutting edge of metallurgical research when he joined Yale in 1911. His work on the Machu Picchu collections produced numerous groundbreaking conclusions, many of which are accepted to this day. His study was presented in a 1915 article, "A Metallographic Description of Some Ancient Peruvian Bronzes from Machu Picchu," in the *American Journal of Science*. As indicated by the title, Mathewson did not conduct research on silver artifacts from Machu Picchu. His work served as the basis of knowledge concerning the metals of Machu Picchu over the next 65 years. Bingham drew heavily on Mathewson's study and incorporated its results into his 1930 monograph *Machu Picchu: Citadel of the Incas*.

When we arrived at Yale University in 1981, we made it a priority to reinitiate study of the Machu Picchu collections, which had not received attention from investigators for many decades. In 1982, we involved Robert Gordon, a professor in the Yale Department of Geology and Geophysics, in the study of the metals. Gordon had taught a course in archaeometallurgy at Yale for many decades and had conducted pioneering research on African and historical metallurgy. He was enthusiastic about having the opportunity to work on Inca metals, particularly since they represent the culmination of a distinctive native American metalworking tradition that spanned over two millennia. Gordon has made numerous discoveries concerning the Machu Picchu metals and published them in a series of articles in technical journals. Many Yale undergraduate and graduate students have become involved in the research on the Machu Picchu collections. Under Gordon's guidance, graduate student John Rutledge prepared a master's thesis consisting of a preliminary catalog of the Machu Picchu metals. Gordon's contribution provides the first comprehensive catalog of the Machu Picchu metals recovered by Bingham, as well as a presentation of the results of the studies he has carried out over the past two decades. These studies address the silver objects along with the bronze and copper artifacts. Gordon's findings reflect both the advances in knowledge of ancient metallurgy since Mathewson's time and the improved techniques available to study metal artifacts.

Great progress also has been made in understanding the nature of the Inca empire, or Tawantinsuyu, and the role of objects in exercising imperial power within this ethnically and linguistically diverse realm. This knowledge is essential for understanding the Machu Picchu metals. At a Dumbarton Oaks conference in 1997 Lucy Salazar argued that much of the ethnic composition of Machu Picchu can be explained by the presence at the country palace of specialized metalworkers from the provinces. For this volume we felt it essential to complement Gordon's contribution, from its metallurgical perspective, with an essay reflecting the advances in anthropological archaeology in order to provide a more complete understanding of the cultural and social context in which the metal artifacts from Machu Picchu functioned. While an undergraduate student in Yale College, Bruce Owen was exposed to the Machu Picchu collections and in 1986 wrote his master's thesis at the University of California, Los Angeles, on the role of common metal objects in the Inca state. He kindly agreed to expand and update this research for his contribution to this book.

As do the contributors to the YUPA volume on human and animal remains, Gordon and Owen strive to meet the goal of illuminating the Machu Picchu collections with new theoretical insights and analytical techniques. Through technical publications of this kind, public exhibitions, and web-based dissemination of the findings, the new research on the Bingham collection carried out at the Yale Peabody Museum of Natural History can reach the multitude of specialists and nonspecialists fascinated with the site of Machu Picchu.

As part of our role as editors, we have reviewed the provenience information for all the artifacts that are described and analyzed in this volume to ensure that all of them were recovered during Bingham's investigations at Machu Picchu. In some cases, some of these artifacts had been incorrectly attributed to Machu Picchu because of confusion in the recordkeeping over the last century. The current list of metal objects from Machu Picchu presented here should be considered the definitive listing of the metal finds.

Richard L. Burger
Charles J. MacCurdy Professor of Anthropology,
Yale University

Lucy C. Salazar
Research Associate,
Department of Anthropology, Yale University

Introduction

In July 1911 Yale University professors Hiram Bingham and Harry Foote were making their way down the Urubamba River into the remote interior of Peru in search of Vilcabamba, the site of the last Inca capital. While they camped for the night, a local farmer's son offered to show them some interesting ruins high on a neighboring mountain. Bingham made the climb while Foote remained below to continue his work as the biologist of the Yale Peruvian Scientific Expedition. Bingham spent two hours taking pictures of the ruins on the saddle between two mountain peaks. Later, in September, Bingham sent two members back to map the ruins that we now know as Machu Picchu. A year later members of the second Yale expedition to Peru dug trenches and explored burial caves in search of pottery, bones, and other artifacts that would help reveal the history of Machu Picchu. The material they collected included nearly 200 metal objects. Under an agreement with the Peruvian government Bingham sent these artifacts to Yale's Peabody Museum of Natural History in New Haven for analysis and study (Bingham 1930).

The metal artifacts the 1912 expedition found at Machu Picchu constitute one of the few collections of pre-Columbian metals from a precisely known site in the Andes of South America, the region where American Indians developed the most sophisticated metallurgical techniques found in the pre-Columbian New World. The collection from Machu Picchu is particularly significant because many South American metal artifacts now in museums are the product of extensive looting of archaeological sites throughout the Andean region, so that their provenience can never be established. Additionally, Machu Picchu was occupied for only about 80 years, from the start of construction sometime after A.D. 1450 to its abandonment by A.D. 1572 (Wright and Zegarra 2000:1). Hence, the collection is a record of the final stage of pre-Columbian metallurgical technology in the central Andean region of South America.

Shortly after the return of the 1912 expedition, C. H. Mathewson at Yale completed a detailed study of some of the bronze artifacts from Machu Picchu. His paper, published in the *American Journal of Science*, is also notable as one of the first applications of metallurgical science to the study of archaeological materials. After Mathewson's research, the Machu Picchu artifacts remained in the collections of the Yale Peabody Museum until a revival of interest in South American metallurgy and initial planning for a new exhibition on Machu Picchu led John W. Rutledge, Bruce D. Owen, and several other Yale students to reexamine the collection in 1982. By that year, analytical methods unavailable to Mathewson in 1912 could be used to reveal new information about the artifacts. In addition to improved metallographic techniques and photography, the electron microscope and microprobe permitted determination of the chemical compositions of individual constituents with the metal structure. The results of the renewed study of the Machu Picchu metal artifacts are reported here. While this research was under way from 1982 through 1985, many of the artifacts were taken in hand for conservation and preparation for the exhibition. Many of these are described in the book prepared in conjunction with the traveling exhibit *Machu Picchu: Unveiling the Mystery of the Incas* (Burger and Salazar 2004). The results of some new analyses, metallography, and recent research on replica alloys are also summarized here.

In the past, several different numbering systems were used to identify items in the collection of Machu Picchu artifacts. Here we use the current six-digit Yale Peabody Museum Division of Anthropology (YPM ANT) catalog numbers.

SECTION ONE

Metal Artifacts from the 1911-1912 Yale Expeditions to Peru

Robert B. Gordon

Previous Research on the Collection

After leaving Machu Picchu and on his way into the remote Peruvian interior in the summer of 1911, Hiram Bingham purchased two bronze axes and a chisel offered to him by local farmers. On his return to New Haven Bingham turned over these artifacts to Harry W. Foote, his companion in the search for Vilcabamba, and William H. Buell for study (Foote and Buell 1912). Foote was professor of chemistry in the Sheffield Scientific School at Yale University, and Buell, a graduate of that school, supervised the chemical laboratory at the Winchester Repeating Arms Company factory in New Haven (Williamson 1952:144). Foote and Buell analyzed metal taken from each artifact by drilling to determine its composition, measured the hardness on fresh surfaces they prepared, and examined the microstructure. They found one axe (ANT.017898) of particular interest because of the recrystallized microstructure of the bronze and decided that, despite its high tin content (12%), it had been forged to shape. They found a bar of 12% tin bronze that they made too brittle to forge. After quenching the bar from a temperature of about 500 °C, they were able to forge it into a close replica of the Peruvian axe. However, their conclusion that Peruvian artisans forged rather than cast high-tin bronzes to final shape, and therefore needed this heat-treating technique, has not been substantiated by subsequent research.

Shortly after the return of the 1912 Yale Peruvian Expedition, Bingham asked Champion H. Mathewson to undertake a laboratory study of a selection of the bronze artifacts recovered at Machu Picchu. Mathewson, a 1902 Yale graduate, had completed his doctoral dissertation in metallurgy at Göttingen with Gustav Tammann in 1906. Yale appointed Mathewson assistant professor of metallurgy in 1911. Tammann was one of the leading practitioners of the then new science of metallography, the study of the structure and properties of metals and alloys, and Mathewson initiated this line of research at Yale. Over the next 30 years Mathewson made Yale's Hammond Laboratory, along with the Massachusetts and Carnegie institutes of technology, one of the three leading places in the United States for the study of physical metallurgy. Since brass mills in Connecticut's Naugatuck Valley were the nation's principal suppliers of copper-base alloys in 1911, Mathewson was able to garner students and support from this local industry. Bingham's request gave Mathewson an opportunity to do original research on the physical metallurgy while he examined the artifacts from Machu Picchu. One reason for his interest was that the age of the Inca artifacts could help him study the then unresolved question of whether or not structural changes would take place in bronze over a duration of hundreds of years at ambient temperatures.

Metallographers in 1912 used the techniques of examining the microstructure of metals and alloys with optical microscopes pioneered in 1864 by Henry C. Sorby in Sheffield, England. Metallurgists had ignored Sorby's techniques for 20 years, until John Percy and Henry Bessemer promoted their potential for resolving questions about metals that chemical analysis alone could not provide (Smith 1960:169–185). Mathewson was among the few scientists who brought to the United States the methods developed in Europe for studying the processes involved in the casting, working, and heat-treating of metals. The methods developed in Mathewson's time remain a mainstay of modern materials science today. Before 1912, laboratory studies of metal artifacts had consisted largely of chemical analyses of samples taken by drilling or otherwise removing material from the object examined. These studies revealed little about the processes by which an artifact was made or how it was subsequently used.

Mathewson convinced Bingham that metallography could reveal new information on:
—casting technique, including cooling rates and mold designs;
—evidence of shaping by cold or hot forging;
—subsequent annealing;
—the strength properties attained by these techniques; and
—defects and imperfections.

This would be information rarely if ever found previously in the study of metal artifacts. Bingham consulted with William H. Holmes of the United States National Museum (at the Smithsonian Institution), who had done research on Maya sites in Mexico. The result was that "we determined it would be wise" to take advantage of the fact that the exact source of the artifacts was known—and that few were rare or of unusual design—to do a metallographic study, "even if it meant their complete destruction" (Bingham 1915a:10).

Mathewson completed a study of 33 artifacts, of which 21 were sectioned for examination of their microstructures, and published the results in a lengthy paper in the *American Journal of Science* (Mathewson 1915). As part of this project, Mathewson completed original research on strength properties, mechanical working, and annealing of copper-tin bronzes with 150 specimens of laboratory-made alloy. Thus, his paper is a report on the Machu Picchu bronzes and on the then new results in physical metallurgy. The paper is, in fact, a landmark in archaeometallurgy. Since he did not study any of the silver artifacts in the collection from Machu Picchu, Mathewson missed an opportunity to discover one of the most remarkable aspects of South American metallurgy, the technique of depletion silvering used to put a nearly pure silver surface on items made of silver-copper alloy.

We have not been able to find Mathewson's original notes and photographs. Fortunately, the 97 illustrations in his paper include prints of many of his micrographs. Although reproduced too small to reveal all that he was able to see, these micrographs do allow us to reexamine much of his original data.

Mathewson's research led him to several conclusions, most of which have stood the test of time and subsequent research. He found that tin is the alloying agent in all the bronze items, and that iron and sulfur are the only impurities present in quantities sufficient to influence their properties. Because the artifacts included some pieces of pure tin, he concluded that the Inca metalsmiths formulated their bronze alloys at Machu Picchu. He also concluded that the tin content of the bronze artifacts was unrelated to their apparent functions, and suggested that the Inca metalsmiths chose a high tin content to help retain fine detail in their more intricate castings. Most items were cast to near their final shape and then finished by forging. Even when little forging was required, the Inca artisans preferred to anneal their final products. The strength properties of the metal items were generally low because of excessive porosity in the castings. Whenever an artifact had a hole in it, the hole was part of the original casting rather than made later by punching or drilling. This implied that the Inca artisans lacked tools for piercing metals. Mathewson concluded that the Inca artisans did not understand how high-tin bronzes could be heat-treated to facilitate forging. Today we see this conclusion as irrelevant, since any high-tin bronze artifacts in the collection were cast rather than forged to shape.

Although the metallographic technique relied on examination of cut sections, this did not result in the destruction of the artifacts studied. In most cases Mathewson reassembled the sections so as to restore the artifacts to nearly their original form. Consequently, in many cases the sections Mathewson prepared were available for further study. However, some material was destroyed in his mechanical experiments and in the analysis of two small silver discs.

Mathewson did not mark the items he studied with his identification numbers. Consequently, we had to identify these items in the collection by comparisons with his descriptions. This led to positive identifications in most cases. It also revealed that two of the items he studied were missing from the collection in 1982.

Research Methods

By 1982 the Machu Picchu artifacts had been in storage for 70 years. Many were still covered with soil mixed with corrosion products. The only cleaning attempted was washing with soap and water to remove loose debris. This sufficed to expose the underlying metal in many of the artifacts. Where this was not the case, no attempt was made to remove attached corrosion products or materials such as cloth debris contained in the corrosion layers. Each artifact was photographed. Surface features that required some magnification for study were photographed with a Zeiss Neophot metallograph on 3.5 × 4.5-inch Polaroid film.

Metallography

Most of the metallographic examination was carried out on sections that exposed the interior structures of the artifacts (see Appendix B for locations of the micrographs). Many of the sections prepared during Mathewson's earlier study were available for reexamination. Where additional sections were needed, these were removed with thin saw blades to minimize the material lost to cuttings. Later these sections were replaced in the artifacts. In some cases, where samples could not be taken, small areas on the surface of artifacts were polished and etched for study.

Metallographic samples were mounted, polished, and etched using standard methods. Specimens were first examined in the as-polished condition. No further treatment was needed for most of the silver-copper specimens. To reveal grain structure of the bronze specimens, we used either the ferric chloride or hydrogen peroxide standard etches for copper-base alloys. Microstructures were photographed with the Zeiss Neophot metallograph on 3.5 × 4.5-inch Polaroid film. Some microstructures were rephotographed in 2005–2007 with a digital camera (see color plates). Back scatter electron images were made of specimens whose compositions were determined by microprobe analysis.

The hydrogen peroxide etch reveals small composition differences in bronze through varying degrees of darkening of the structure. The action of the ferric chloride etch is sensitive to grain orientation and so is better for revealing grain structure. For example, in specimens ANT.017898, ANT.017966, ANT.017970, and ANT.017974 the hydrogen peroxide etch used either by Mathewson or in our laboratory showed residual coring that the application of ferric chloride etch did not reveal.

Chemical Composition

Mathewson (1915) sampled 31 of the bronze artifacts by drilling and determined the composition of the chips by wet chemical, quantitative analysis. The analyst reported copper, tin, iron, and sulfur as the principal constituents, and silver and zinc when found. Arsenic was not reported, but we do not know whether it was sought.

From 1981 to 1985 Alan Pooley determined compositions of many of the metallographic specimens with the energy dispersive X-ray spectrometer on the Yale Peabody Museum of Natural History's scanning electron microscope. He used the Tracor-Northern Standardless Semiquantitative (SSQ) analysis program to reduce the data. The results of this program were calibrated against laboratory-made copper-tin and copper-silver alloys so that they could be used for approximate quantitative determination of tin and silver contents. Count times of 100 or 200 sec and a 20 kV accelerating voltage were used for these analyses. Areas of 20 to 60 mm^2 were scanned in these calibrations and subsequent measurements. The reproducibility of the data is shown by the following analyses for copper (Cu), tin (Sn), silver (Ag), sulfur (S), and iron (Fe) made several hours apart at the same 27 mm^2 area on specimen ANT.017900 from Rosalina (Owen 1983):

Analysis 1:	92.9% Cu	5.9% Sn	0.84% Ag	0.12% S	0.27% Fe
Analysis 2:	92.8	5.9	0.85	0.15	0.30

When the scanning electron microscopy standardless semiquantitative (SEM–SSQ) analyses were intended for use as an aid in identifying microstructural constituents, they were made with the electron beam focused on the feature of interest. Comparison with earlier wet chemical, quantitative analyses indicates that the copper-tin calibration is reliable. For example, the average tin content found in five analyses on adjacent 27 mm^2 areas of specimen ANT.017898 from Espiritu Pampa is 12.2%. The wet chemical, quantitative analysis Foote and Buell (1912) reported for this artifact is 12.0% tin.

Inhomogeneity is a more significant concern than instrumental reproducibility in determining the composition of the artifacts. Etching revealed composition variations within even the most homogeneous-appearing artifacts. The SEM–SSQ analyses confirmed these gradients in composition. There will always be some uncertainty in bulk compositions, since large volumes of artifacts have not been sampled.

In 2004 and 2005 James Eckert undertook additional analyses of some of the metallographic specimens prepared earlier with the JEOL JKA-8600 microprobe in the Yale University Department of Geology and Geophysics. Wavelength spectroscopy was used with a 15 kV accelerating voltage, 20 nA beam current, and 5 μ beam size for the quantitative measurements. The bulk compositions of the two-phase copper-silver alloys were determined by first measuring the compositions of the copper-rich and silver-rich phases. The overall composition was then found from the proportions of these phases, determined by point counts on micrographs of representative areas.

The Northern Analytical Laboratory, Inc., of Merrimack, New Hampshire, USA, made a trace element analysis on one bronze artifact using glow discharge mass spectrometry.

Hardness

We used a Leitz microhardness tester to determine Vickers hardness (HV), also known as the diamond pyramid hardness (DPH), on several of the metallographic specimens. Both Foote and Buell (1912) and Mathewson (1915) reported the rebound hardness for some of the specimens they studied. They measured rebound hardness with a sclerscope, a device then popular but now obsolete (Kehl 1949:249). To establish a comparison with their sclerscope readings and the Vickers hardness, we took data on a series of laboratory-made tin-bronze alloys. We used a sclerscope found among the old instruments left at the Hammond Laboratory, which could have been the one used by Mathewson. Data on these alloys were also taken on Rockwell B and Vickers scales.

Experimental Metallurgy

Several issues arose in the study of the artifacts from Machu Picchu that required research on laboratory-prepared alloys to resolve. Because many of the bronze

TABLE 1.1. Distribution of items.

Item	Total [a]	Number examined [b]
Awls	1	1
Axes	13	9
Bracelets	3	0
Chisels	3	3
Crowbars	1	1
Earspools	4	0
Finger rings	2	0
Gravers	1	1
Knives	28	5
Metal stock	11	8
Necklaces	1	1
Needles	4	1
Other	7	2
Pendants, solid	5	1
Pendants, disc	11	1
Plumb bobs or balls	4	1
Shawl pins	56	3
Lime spoons	2	1
Tweezers	9	1
Work in progress	5	4

[a] Number of items in the collection.
[b] Items studied in the laboratory, 1982–1985. Bronze and silver alloy items are included here.

TABLE 1.2. Silver alloy items.

Item	Number examined
Shawl pins	26
Headbands	1
Bracelets	2
Rings	2
Work in progress, probably pin stems	2
Pendants	1
Finials	1
Knives	1
Set of spangles	1
Balls, perhaps silver	1

artifacts appear to be still in the as-cast form but have the constituent metal fully recrystallized, we undertook study of a series of laboratory-made bronze alloys in 2004 to find the minimum amount of deformation that would result in recrystallization. We did a similar set of experiments on a bronze prepared with sulfur and iron impurity added to the compositions found in some of the Machu Picchu bronze artifacts. Strength properties of these alloys were measured (Gordon and Knopf 2006).

In 2004 and 2005 we made several silver-copper alloys that duplicated the compositions of the silver artifacts studied. These were used to determine strength properties, along with the forging and annealing schedule needed to reproduce the dimensions and structures of the artifacts from Machu Picchu (Gordon and Knopf 2007).

Classification and Description of the Artifacts

The shape of most of the 171 items in the collection suggests an apparent function or use that can serve as a basis for classification (Table 1.1). Visual inspection usually shows whether an artifact is made of silver-copper alloy (Table 1.2), bronze, or tin—the only types of metal found by the Yale Peruvian expedition at Machu Picchu. In terms of numbers, shawl pins (*tupus*; Figure 1.1), constituting 34% of the collection, dominate. Bronze and silver alloy pins are present in about equal numbers. Knives with arc-shaped blades (*tumis*; Figure 1.2) are the next most abundant type of artifact. With one possible exception, the knives are made of bronze. Their abundance suggests that they served utilitarian purposes such as cutting or chopping in the preparation of food or other light domestic tasks. These two classes of apparently domestic items, the shawl pins and knives, together make up 52% of the collection. Of the remaining items, 24% are clearly related to the work of artisans. These include axes (Figure 1.3), chisels (Figure 1.4), and work in progress (Figure 1.5). Most of the rest of the collection comprises an assortment of items for personal adornment (Figure 1.6) or domestic use, such as tweezers and needles.

Bingham's team of excavators at Machu Picchu were struck by, and perhaps disappointed at, the absence of gold from what they took to be a royal estate. Since the 1912 expedition, in which the metal artifacts were collected, only one gold object has been reported at Machu Picchu, a bracelet excavated next to an abandoned wall in the Eastern Urban sector (Wright and Zegarra 2000:43).

Weapons are remarkably absent in the collection: there are none of the spear points, knives, daggers, swords, or halberds that make up many of the collections of bronze artifacts from the Old World. Only one weapon, a mace head (Astete 2001:103), uses properties of bronze that could not be duplicated with stone, bone, or wood. Its weight and toughness would make it a formidable weapon when mounted on the end of a staff. Although the Inca did not rely much on metal weapons (Lechtman 1984), their absence from Machu Picchu suggests that whatever military force was there was not housed within the palace walls.

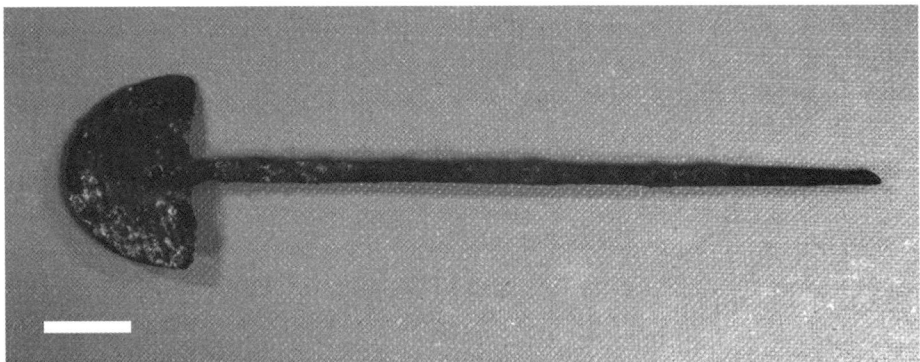

Figure 1.1. Silver alloy shawl pin (*tupu*), ANT.018431, 24 × 91 mm. This pin was photographed in 1982 while still in its as-recovered, corroded condition. Length of scale bar 1 cm.

Sounding devices such as bells, cymbals, or gongs, instruments for which bronze is a particularly appropriate material, are absent from the collection, and with one possible exception: the pendants (ANT.018427 and ANT.018428) may have been small bells (Burger and Salazar 2004:186). There are no metal vessels such as the bowls made by casting or from sheet metal that are often found at archaeological sites elsewhere in the world. Nor are there metal fittings for the management of animals. Tools, metal stock, and metalwork in progress dominate the collection in weight. However, they are quite limited in variety. Most of the tools are percussion implements such as axes and chisels that were evidently pounded on by hammerstones, since no metal hammers were found. Nor are there saws or chisels suitable for fine working of wood or bone.

Thus, nearly all the items in the collection have an easily identifiable, more or less prosaic use. In the modern interpretation of Machu Picchu developed by Richard Burger and Lucy Salazar (2004), the dead of the Inca ruling and religious elite were taken elsewhere for burial and the remaining resident members of these elite groups took their precious metal possessions with them when they departed for the final time. With few exceptions, we can visualize the items in the collection as originally associated with the retainers and artisans who served the ruling and religious leaders of the Inca empire during their residence at Machu Picchu. The abundance of silver alloy pins shows that this metal was sufficiently common that the families of artisans and retainers could own items of this material. Because most of these pins had cloth embedded in the encrusting corrosion when found, we know that they were worn with clothing at burial if not in everyday life.

Provenience at Machu Picchu
Rutledge (1984) compared each item in the collection with the expedition notes and publications to determine where each was found within Machu Picchu. He was able to fix the sources of 53 of the approximately 165 items in the collection (Table 1.3). He found that the shawl pins all came from caves and that, with one exception, items found in the caves and graves were all of the decorative or domestic type.

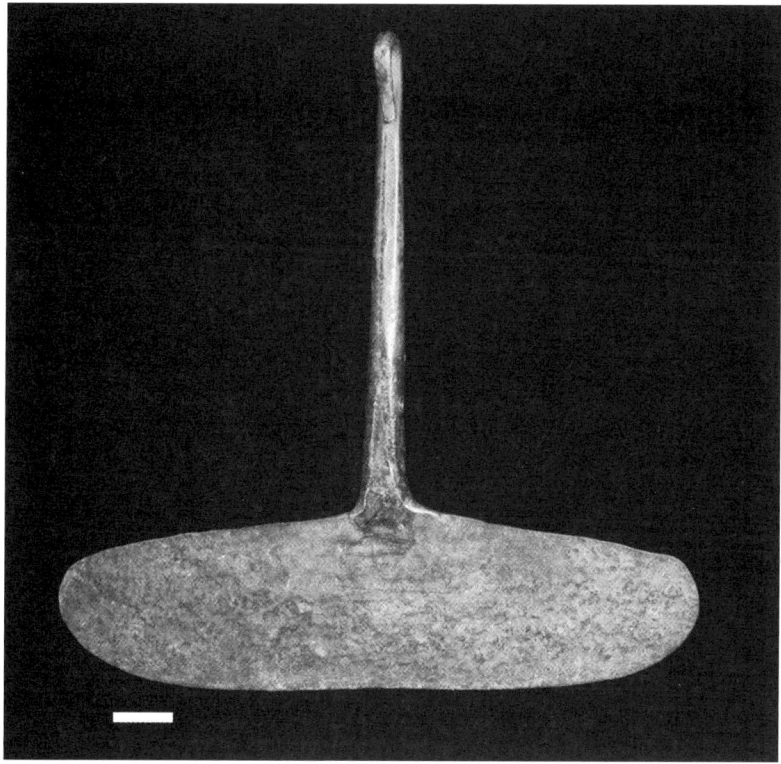

FIGURE 1.2. Bronze knife (*tumi*), ANT.017855, 110 × 110 mm. This is one of the artifacts analyzed by Mathewson (1915). Photographed in 1982. Length of scale bar 1 cm.

Both of the llama-head knives came from one cave (Cave 54). Most of the tools and metal stock are from sections 40, 41, and 44 of the site.

We can positively identify items in the collection that are scrap or residues from melting and casting, or were stock for formulating alloys, as the work of artisans in residence at Machu Picchu rather than materials that may have been brought in from elsewhere in the Inca empire. We find nothing about these items that distinguishes them from the others in the collection. While many of the items found at Machu Picchu may have been made there, we lack any way of distinguishing these from finished artifacts that may have been brought to the site. However, the absence of any items made of copper-arsenic alloy suggests that few products of northern Peru reached Machu Picchu.

Standardization of Design

Many of the items in the collection are of a generally standard design. The most common form of shawl pin has a flat, half-round head pierced with one hole near a thin, round stem (see Figure 1.1). Less common variants include pins larger than the common size, circular rather than half-round heads, and a very few examples of more complex shapes (Burger and Salazar 2004:181). The typical knife design

Figure 1.3. Bronze axe (ANT.017902), 130 × 109 mm. Surface markings on this axe indicate that it had been used in artisan's work. Photographed in 1982.

has an inverted "T" shape consisting of a thin stem ending in a flat blade with an arc-shaped edge (see Figure 1.2). The shape suggests a tool useful in chopping, as in food preparation, rather than for tasks such as cutting or carving wood.

Although they are made to a relatively small number of general patterns, few of the items are exact duplicates that would indicate perfectly standardized production techniques. Examples of items that are near identical matches are groups of shawl pins (Rutledge 1984): two bronze pins (ANT.017820 and ANT.017838) have head dimensions that match to within 1 mm. Two other bronze pins (ANT.017823 and ANT.017829) are also nearly identical. Nearly identical shapes are found in the pair of large pins (ANT.017845 and ANT.017846) and the pair of axes blades (ANT.017967 and ANT.017969). Thus, it seems that the artisans making most of the artifacts found at Machu Picchu worked to generally accepted designs and did not need to achieve a standard of uniformity in the shape and size of their products fixed by patterns or models.

Selection of Artifacts for Study
Items were selected for detailed study from among the different classes of objects (see Table 1.1). Since most of the shawl pins and knives have a common design and were apparently made by a common method of fabrication, only representative examples were selected. We focused attention on several unusual items, and on

Figure 1.4. Bronze chisel (ANT.017907), 65 × 40 mm. Surface markings on this chisel indicate that it had been used in artisan's work. Photographed in 1982. Length of scale bar approx. 1 cm.

the work in progress, since these could reveal evidence of artisans' skills and techniques. Items that seem to be tools were studied for evidence of the way they were used. Forty-six items (Table 1.4) were subjected to detailed laboratory examination in either Mathewson's research, from 1982 to 1985, or the studies during 2004 and 2005. They include 35 objects made of bronze and 4 made of silver-copper alloy. One item studied by Mathewson, a tweezers, lacks a catalog number and could not be found in 1982.

Research Results

Metals and Alloys
No evidence that artisans smelted metals from their ores at Machu Picchu has been found. While some of the artifacts found at Machu Picchu are known to have been made elsewhere, the unfinished products, metal scrap, hammerstones, and stone anvils found by the Bingham expedition show that artisans at Machu Picchu formulated alloys and produced finished artifacts (Rutledge and Gordon 1987). The small total weight of the collection, about 10 kg, suggests that the amount of metal carried up to Machu Picchu was small compared to other things brought from the valley below. Alloy preparation and artifact fabrication, much less fuel intensive than smelting, would have been relatively easy to carry out at

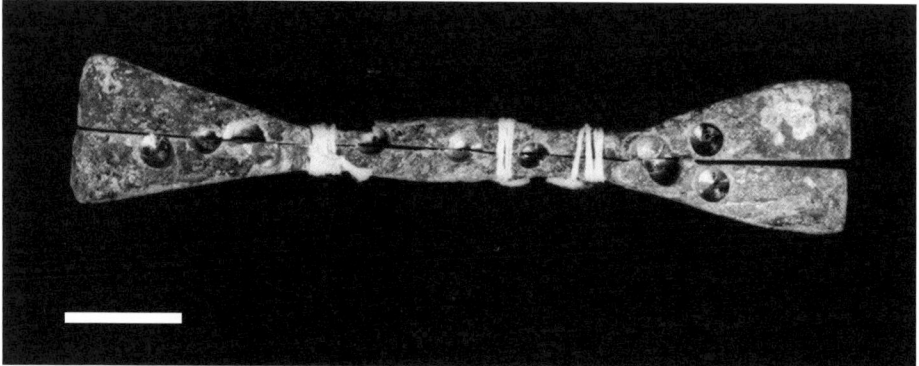

FIGURE 1.5. Example of artisan's work in progress (ANT.017972), 65 × 12 mm, bronze. This is interpreted as a partially forged blank that would have been later formed into a pair of tweezers. It was sectioned longitudinally for study of its cross section by Mathewson (1915), who designated it as No. 13 in his Table I and removed metal samples by drilling for chemical analysis. Photographed in 1982. Length of scale bar approx. 1 cm.

Machu Picchu and less likely to impose smoke and fumes on elite persons when in residence. The princely and religious denizens of this royal estate would have found it a convenience to have artisans at hand to make items as they desired them for gifts or their own use.

ALLOY PREPARATION AND COMPOSITION

The excavators at Machu Picchu found four pieces of pure tin: two in the form of sheets (ANT.017978 and ANT.017979) and two as rough lumps (ANT.017982a and ANT.017982b). Because no finished products made of tin have been found here or elsewhere in Inca contexts, this tin must have been used in making bronze alloys. The presence of chisel marks on the largest sheet of tin (ANT.017979) suggests that artisans cut off the small pieces they needed to make up the desired tin content in a crucible-size melt of bronze. The tin would have been brought to Machu Picchu from the southern reaches of the Inca empire in Bolivia.

The pieces of bronze found at Machu Picchu that solidified either in a crucible bottom or after being spilled on the ground (ANT.017988, ANT.018461, and ANT.018481) show that artisans there melted and cast alloys. To make bronze and the silver-copper alloys, artisans at Machu Picchu would melt copper with tin or silver in the proportions they needed to get the desired alloy composition. No copper or silver stock has been found at Machu Picchu. Since copper and silver minerals were common throughout the Andes, these metals could have been obtained from different places within the regions controlled by the Inca. The Machu Picchu artisans had to have ceramic crucibles that could withstand high heat, along with tools for cutting up metal stock. They needed a way of blowing air into a charcoal fire to attain a temperature at least as high as 1100 °C to melt the copper. They also needed tongs or other devices for handling the red-hot crucibles, and molds to pour the molten alloy into. No remains of this equipment have been found yet

FIGURE 1.6. Bronze pendant (ANT.017876), 97 × 56 mm. This pendant was apparently intended to be worn suspended from its center loop. Photographed in 1982.

at Machu Picchu. Of course, if the artisans here used withies for handling hot crucibles, such as those used by Egyptian bronze workers during the reign of Tutmosis III (Coghlan 1975:69), it is unlikely that any trace of them would have survived into the twentieth century.

All of the analyses of metal compositions that have been performed on the artifacts in the collection in this and previous research are listed here (Tables 1.5 through 1.10). The compositions reported by Mathewson were obtained by wet chemical, quantitative analyses using techniques that had been well standardized by 1912. The elements sought and determined in the SEM–SSQ analyses—copper, tin, arsenic, and silver—are the principal alloying constituents, along with the common impurities, sulfur and iron. The additional microprobe analyses done in 2004 and 2005 sought all metallic elements that the instrument could detect. An analysis for trace metals was done on a bronze axe (ANT.017898).

Evidence for the presence of arsenic and lead was sought in the SEM–SSQ analyses. Arsenic was the alloying element of choice for making bronze through Late Horizon times in northern Peru (Lechtman 1991). Elsewhere in the world, additions of lead to tin bronze were common by Middle and Late Bronze Age times. Neither arsenic nor lead was found in the metals from Machu Picchu in levels that would indicate their use in formulating alloys. The most common alloys used in the Machu Picchu artifacts are copper-tin bronze containing 3% to 6% tin, and silver-copper alloys ranging from 25% to 80% silver. Three items among those studied (ANT.017908, ANT.017971, and ANT.018453) are made of unalloyed copper.

BRONZE ALLOYS

The histogram here shows the distribution of tin concentrations in the bronzes (Figure 1.7). The peak of the distribution at 5% to 6% tin suggests that this was the preferred bronze composition, while the breadth of the peak suggests that the Inca

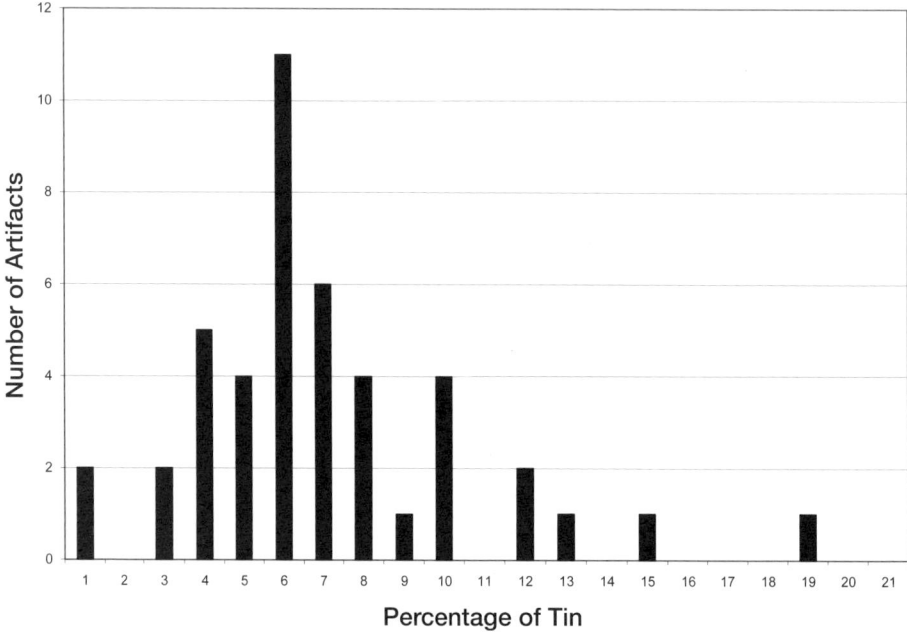

FIGURE 1.7. Histogram showing the distribution of tin content in the bronze artifacts.

artisans maintained control over the compositions of the alloys they made to within a few percent. The items falling on the high-tin tail of the distribution probably represent intentional formulation of alloys for particular purposes.

Mathewson suggested that the Inca artisans chose high tin content for castings that had fine detail to reproduce, such as the bird-head lime spoon (ANT.017970), and low-tin alloy for items that required extensive forging to finish. However, some of the items cast with high tin content, such as the "T" axe (ANT.017898), lack fine detail or, like the tweezers blank (ANT.017972, see Figure 1.5), required extensive forging to final shape. The star-head pin (ANT.017841), which does have fine detail, is a low-tin bronze. An alternative explanation of Inca alloy choice is that artisans used a high tin content when they wanted artifacts to have lighter color for particular prestige items. The pendant (ANT.017876, see Figure 1.6), with 18% tin, is not an unusually intricate casting, but has a distinctive near-gold color. Light color also may have been wanted for the bird-head lime spoon (ANT.017970), which contains 13% tin. Interest in experimentation with alloys to achieve distinctive color is a probable explanation for the unusual copper-tin-bismuth alloy used to cast a llama-head top to the bronze knife (ANT.017962) (Gordon and Rutledge 1984).

Impurities and Inclusions. Sulfur is the principal impurity present in the Machu Picchu bronzes. It is present as dispersed, nonmetallic inclusions. Analyses of these inclusions (Tables 1.6 and 1.7) identifies them as copper sulfide (Cu_2S), which contains 80% copper and 20% sulfur, sometimes with small amounts of iron also present. Mathewson (1915) observed Cu_2S inclusions in every bronze microstructure he examined, even when not reported in the chemical analysis, and noted that metallography is a sensitive detector of sulfur in bronze, because one part of sulfur yields five parts of Cu_2S. Sulfide inclusions are found in the additional bronze artifacts examined since Mathewson's study.

The items in the collection that are copper rather than bronze contain inclusions of copper oxide with the composition Cu_2O. Mathewson found these in the copper knife (ANT.017971). The characteristic structure of the Cu–Cu_2O eutectic is found in the axe (ANT.017908, see Appendix A).

Metallic impurities in amounts between 0.1% and 1% were found in many of the bronzes analyzed. Iron was detected in 11, and silver in 9, of the bronze artifacts. One artifact had a trace of antimony and 2 artifacts had traces of zinc. Because the tin used to make the bronzes was quite pure, and the charcoal fuel in the melting furnaces is sulfur-free, the sulfur and metallic impurities must have entered the bronzes from the copper metal stock used. These variations in composition suggest that the copper used at Machu Picchu, or that the artifacts themselves, may have come from different sources within the Inca empire.

Iron can enter copper during the smelting of copper minerals such as chalcopyrite, or from the iron oxide flux used in the smelting process. The gases in a copper smelting furnace can become sufficiently rich in carbon monoxide to reduce some metallic iron from the ore or flux along with the copper. When highly selected ore is smelted in a simple furnace that does not allow for tapping off excess slag, the copper typically contains 0.03% to 0.05% iron. When less pure ore is used, a larger volume of slag is formed. The copper may then contain up to several percent iron. To be a useful metal, copper containing this much iron must be fire-refined to reduce its iron content to 0.5% or less (Craddock and Meeks 1987). At this concentration most of the iron present is dissolved in the copper and in any sulfide inclusions that may be present. Dissolved, it does not degrade the properties of the copper. Iron at the level detectable in the SSQ analysis is absent from 37 of the bronze artifacts (see Table 1.5), indicating that, if present, its concentration is less than 0.1% in these items. This is another indication that the artifacts and the metal supplied to the artisans at Machu Picchu may have come from several copper sources, only some of which were smelting ore sufficiently impure to form large volumes of slag. The ratio of iron to sulfur in copper smelted from sulfide ores is about one, while for oxide ores it is about five (Tylecote, Ghaznani, and Boydell 1977). Thus, the suppliers of bronze artifacts and copper to the Machu Picchu artisans were probably smelting sulfide ores.

Copper-arsenic alloys were used throughout the northern Andes in pre-Inca times. Mathewson did not report arsenic in his wet chemical analyses. Since 1.1% arsenic was found in the bronze axe (ANT.017900) from the Urubamba Valley (see Table 1.7) but was not reported by Mathewson, it may be that arsenic was not sought in the wet chemical analyses. However, it seems that copper-arsenic alloys were not used in the artifacts from Machu Picchu and environs.

TABLE 1.3. Sources of metal artifacts. Objects are made of bronze (B), tin (Sn), or silver-copper alloy (Ag–Cu). After Rutledge (1984).

Source	Catalog number	Item	Material
Cave 2A	ANT.017871	Necklace	B
Cave 13	ANT.017830	Shawl pin	B
Cave 14	ANT.016678	Knife	B
Cave 29	ANT.016680	Shawl pin	Ag–Cu
Cave 37	ANT.016681	Shawl pin	Ag–Cu
	ANT.016682	Ear pendant	B
	ANT.016684	Tweezers	B
	ANT.018482	Shawl pin shaft	B
Cave 38	ANT.016679	Shawl pins (2)	Ag–Cu
	ANT.016685	Knife, heavy	B
Cave 52	ANT.018481	Ingot	B
Cave 53	ANT.017874	Finger ring	Ag–Cu
Cave 3A	ANT.017868	Small knife with llama head	B
	ANT.017913	Thin bar of bronze	B
Cave 57	ANT.018427/018428	Bells	B
Cave 62	ANT.017822	Shawl pin	Ag–Cu
Cave 63	ANT.018439	Pendant	B
Cave 66	ANT.017970	Bird-head spatula	
Cave 68	ANT.017829	Shawl pin	B
Cave 76	ANT.017831	Shawl pin	Ag–Cu
Cave 91	ANT.018433	Needle	
Cave 97	ANT.018437	Pendant	B
Cave 103	ANT.017880	Shawl pin	Ag–Cu
Cave 106	—	Finial	B
Grave 26	ANT.016683	Pin	B
	ANT.017890	Bird-head small spatula	B
	ANT.017893	Tweezers	B
	ANT.018480	Pendant disc	B
Grave 63	ANT.017819	Pin	B
Room 24A	ANT.017967	Axe	B
	ANT.017973	Fisher-boy knife	B
Room 26A	ANT.017979	Arc	Sn
Room 34A	ANT.017873	Bracelet	Ag–Cu
	ANT.017974	Axe blade, broken	B
Room 48A	ANT.017913	Bar or work piece	B
Room 64A	ANT.017891	Pendant	B
	ANT.018436	Bracelet fragment	B

TABLE 1.3 CONTINUED.

Source	Catalog number	Item	Material
Section 40A (between room 24A and caves 4A, 5A, 6A)	ANT.017912	Bracelet	Ag–Cu
Section 40A	ANT.017966	Chisel, broken	B
	ANT.017975	Chisel, broken	B
Section 41A	ANT.017850	Disc	Ag–Cu
	ANT.017978	Tin, crumpled	Sn
	ANT.018626	Needle, large	B
Section 44A	ANT.017854	Knife	B
	ANT.018478/018479	Crowbar	B
Station 9A at Snake Rock	ANT.017863	Knife	B
	ANT.018454	Pendant disc	B
Terrace north of main stairway	ANT.017875	Ring	Ag–Cu
Espiritu Pampa, Conservidoyac River	ANT.017898	Axe	B
Rosalina, Urubamba River	ANT.017900	Axe	B

Silver impurity is detected in eight of the bronze artifacts. Copper and silver minerals occur together in the Andean region, and are easily co-smelted. Thus the presence of silver in some of the artifacts is a further indication that the Inca artisans who supplied Machu Picchu used copper from varied sources. The axe (ANT.017900) purchased by the Yale Peruvian Expedition near Rosalina is unique in the collection because of its content of 1.6% silver and 1.1% arsenic. These additional elements are responsible for its unusual microstructure (see Appendix A).

Trace Elements. A small sample of metal from axe ANT.017898, purchased by Bingham in 1911 at Espiritu Pampa and similar to those found at Machu Picchu, was available for trace element analysis (Table 1.8). The principal trace elements present at levels between 400 and 100 ppm are arsenic, silver, antimony, and lead. These, along with bismuth (at 30 ppm), are commonly found in minerals associated with copper ores in the Andes and are easily reduced during copper smelting. Their low concentration shows that the Inca artisans were skilled in doing mineral separations before smelting their ores. Other metals are present only at concentrations of less than 10 ppm.

SILVER ALLOYS

Mathewson (1915) reported two spangles he analyzed to be essentially pure silver. New analyses of four artifacts in the collection (Table 1.9) show them to be silver-copper alloys containing 25% to 80% silver. Artisans in the northern Andean region used silver-copper alloys with compositions from a few percent to 30% silver in

TABLE 1.4. Items examined in the laboratory. Of a total of 46 objects, 35 are bronze (B) (32 of these have structural information), 4 are silver alloy (Ag), 3 are tin (Sn), 2 are copper (Cu), 1 is bronze or copper, 1 is bronze-bismuth (B–Bi), and 1 is missing.

Catalog number	Item	Material
ANT.016685	Small knife [a]	B
ANT.017821	Shawl pin	Ag
ANT.017823	Shawl pin [a]	B
ANT.017841	Star-head pin [a]	B
ANT.017844	Pin or awl, surface features only	B
ANT.017851	Pin in process, analysis and surface features	B
ANT.017872	Headband	Ag
ANT.017876	Gorget, analysis only	B (high tin)
ANT.017879	Molder's or potter's slick, surface features only	B or Cu
ANT.017882	Bar in process, a analysis only, surface features	B
ANT.017893	Tweezers, surface features only	B
ANT.017898	"T" axe [b]	B (high tin)
ANT.017899	"T" axe	B (low tin)
ANT.017900	"T" axe [b]	B
ANT.017902	"T" axe	B
ANT.017907	Chisel	B
ANT.017908	Axe or celt	Cu
ANT.017913	Bar in process	B
ANT.017962	Llama-head cast on knife	B–Bi
ANT.017963	Knife, heavy [a]	B
ANT.017964	Chisel, long	B
ANT.017965	Ball [a]	B
ANT.017966	Chisel, broken and twisted	
ANT.017967	"T" axe with broken corner	B
ANT.017969	Axe blade, broken	B
ANT.017970	Bird-head lime spoon	
ANT.017971	Knife [a]	Cu
ANT.017972	Tweezers blank	B
ANT.017973	Fisherman knife, a analysis only	B
ANT.017974	Broken part of axe blade	
ANT.017975	Chisel	B
ANT.017978	Tin stock	Sn
ANT.017979	Tin stock	Sn
ANT.017980	Bar fragment	B
ANT.017982	Tin lumps	Sn
ANT.017988	Button residue	B
ANT.018400–018404	Spangles, analysis only	Ag

TABLE 1.4 CONTINUED.

Catalog number	Item	Material
ANT.018449	Work piece or metal stock silver	Ag
ANT.018453	In-process low-tin bronze, analysis only	B (low tin)
ANT.018460	Sheet stock, analysis only	B
ANT.018461	Spilled bronze	B
ANT.018478/018479	Crowbar	B
ANT.018480	Pendant, soldered, possibly silver plate	B (Ag?)
ANT.018481	Bronze residue	B
ANT.018626	Needle [a]	B
	Tweezers [a] (missing)	

[a] Mathewson (1915).
[b] Foote and Buell (1912).

the Early Intermediate period. These alloys were extensively used in the Late Intermediate period (Lechtman 1980:291), and evidently adopted by Late Horizon Inca artisans, sometimes with higher silver contents.

Since these compositions (see Table 1.9) fall outside the solid solubility limits of copper in silver and of silver in copper, the metal in these artifacts is composed of two constituents, a silver-rich and a copper-rich phase. Additional elements detected are tin (up to 2%), lead, iron, and arsenic. Antimony was sought, but not found. Arsenic in the amounts present is soluble in both copper and silver, but it concentrates in the copper-rich phase in these alloys. Tin partitions preferentially into the silver-rich phase. Lead is insoluble in copper and slightly soluble in silver. It is found only in the silver-rich phase.

Inca artisans could have made copper-silver alloys directly by smelting the copper ores containing silver minerals that are common in the Peruvian Andes. The resulting alloys would have contained less than 20% silver along with the antimony that commonly accompanies the silver minerals in these ores (Lechtman 1980:292). The higher silver content of the artifacts analyzed and the absence of antimony argues against direct alloy production. More likely, Inca artisans melted silver and copper stock together in the desired proportions.

The silver stock used by the Inca metalworkers could have been smelted from silver ores containing minerals such as cerargyrite (AgCl) and argentite (Ag_2S). If these ores were free of lead, the resulting silver would have a lead content of less than 0.05%. The lead content of the α-phase in the artifacts analyzed is as high as 0.89%. Lead was commonly used as a solvent in silver smelting (Percy 1880:504; Barba 1923:209). Additionally, silver may have been smelted from silver-rich lead ores containing such minerals as cerussite ($PbCO_3$) or galena (PbS). Cupellation to recover the silver from the lead would result in a residual lead content of 0.2% or more in the product (Meyers 2003). Silver smelted at sites in the Mantaro Val-

TABLE 1.5. Bulk compositions of artifacts using wet chemical, semiquantitative analyses. CHM object numbers are from Mathewson (1915).

Catalog number	% Copper	% Tin	% Iron	% Sulfur	% Silver	% Other
ANT.016678 [a]	95.3	4.2		0.20		
ANT.016685 [a]	94.3	4.8	0.30	0.23		
ANT.017821 [b]	16.0				83.00	
ANT.017823 [a]	96.4	3.9				
ANT.017836 [b]	87.5	12.5				
ANT.017841 [a]	96.4	3.6				
ANT.017851 [b]	94.0	6.0				
ANT.017853 [a]	94.7	6.6		Trace		
ANT.017855 [a]	94.1	5.1	Trace	0.30	Trace	
ANT.017859 [a]	95.0	5.1		Trace	Trace	
ANT.017864 [a]	92.6	7.1		0.20	Trace	
ANT.017876 [b]	82.0	18.0				
ANT.017882 [a]	93.2	6.9				
ANT.017898 [c]	87.6	12.0	0.08	0.35B		
ANT.017898 [b]	86.0	12.0	1.00	1.10		
ANT.017899 [b]	98.7	0.6	Trace	0.70		
ANT.017900 [c]	93.7	5.6		0.10	0.60	
ANT.017900 [b]	94.0	5.0			0.80	
ANT.017902 [b]	94.0	5.0	0.30	0.40		
ANT.017907 [b]	93.0	6.0	0.50	0.40		
ANT.017908 [b]	100.0					
ANT.017913 [a]	92.1	7.3			0.31	
ANT.017914 [a]	91.2	8.9	Trace		0.37	0.37
ANT.017962 (head) [b]	73.0	9.0	0.30			18 Bi
ANT.017962 (blade) [b]	97.0	2.0		0.30	0.60	
ANT.017963 [a]	92.3	3.7		0.18	Trace	
ANT.017964 [a]	96.2	3.7				
ANT.017965 [a]	97.0	2.1			0.80	
ANT.017966 [a]	93.9	5.5	0.06	0.15		
ANT.017967 [a]	93.6	4.0		0.40	0.37	
ANT.017969 [a]	93.7	5.0	0.87	0.44		
ANT.017969 [b]	92.0	5.0	1.00	1.00		
ANT.017970 [a]	66.0	13.4				0.32 Zn

TABLE 1.5 CONTINUED.

Catalog number	% Copper	% Tin	% Iron	% Sulfur	% Silver	% Other
ANT.017971 [a]	99.7				Trace	
ANT.017972 [a]	90.1	9.7				
ANT.017973 [a]	88.0	9.4				0.17 Zn
ANT.017974 [a]	94.4	5.1		0.29		
ANT.017975 [b]	92.0	7.0		0.20		
ANT.017978 [b]		100.0				
ANT.017979 [a]		99.8				0.08 Sb
ANT.017980 [a]	94.4	6.0				
ANT.017982 [b]		100.0				
ANT.017988 [b]	88.0	11.0		0.20	0.40	
ANT.018400 [b]	29.0				71.00	
ANT.018453 [b]	99.0	0.3	0.40	0.20		
ANT.018460 [b]	97.0	3.0				Trace Sb
ANT.018461 [b]	91.0	7.0		0.20		1 Si
ANT.018478/018479 [a]	94.5	5.4		Trace		
ANT.018480 [a]	94.3	5.3				
ANT.018481 [a]	95.7	4.2				
ANT.018626 [a]	94.7	5.2				
CHM 19 [a]	94.7	5.5				
CHM 24 [a]	90.1	9.0		0.10	0.7	
CHM 29	93.2	6.9				
CHM 32 [a]					100.0	
CHM 33 [a]					99.5	Trace Pb

[a] Mathewson (1915), wet chemical analysis.
[b] SEM–SSQ, calibration corrections applied for tin and silver only.
[c] Foote and Buell (1912), wet chemical analysis.

ley of the Peruvian central highlands in Late Intermediate and Late Horizon times contains 0.2% to 1.6% lead (Howe and Peterson 1994). Howe and Peterson interpret this as evidence that artisans smelted lead-silver ores and refined the resulting silver by cupellation. Had the silver used in the Machu Picchu artifacts been made this way, it would be expected to have a much lower tin content than it does, since cupellation reduces the tin content to well below 0.2% (Meyers 2003). It is likely, then, that the tin and arsenic found in the artifacts entered the alloy with the copper used rather than with the silver.

TABLE 1.6. Composition of inclusions in bronze for copper, sulfur, and iron.

Catalog number	% Copper	% Sulfur	% Iron
ANT.017900	82	18	0
ANT.019702	81	17	2
ANT.017907	70	21	9
ANT.017969	70	20	9
ANT.017975	82	17	1
ANT.018481	83	17	0

Tin

Mathewson (1915) detected 0.08% antimony, barely at the detection limit, in the large tin sheet (ANT.017979). Antimony is one of the common impurities found in tin. Antimony—along with arsenic, copper, iron, nickel, cobalt, and silver, the other common impurities—is insoluble in tin. These impurities form intermetallic compounds (known as "hardhead") that are present as inclusions within the metal (see Plate 9). Compounds such as Sn_2Sb would have been dissolved in the wet chemical analysis procedure and detected if at a sufficiently high concentration. They might be overlooked in microprobe analysis of the metal alone.

In the tin lump (ANT.017982), inclusions were seen in both optical and electron micrographs and representative compositions determined with the microprobe (Table 1.10). The inclusion with the approximate composition $FeSn_2$ is an example of hardhead, common in impure tin. No inclusions were found in the microstructure of a crumpled sheet (ANT.017978) and no impurities were found at the limit of detection with the microprobe. The purity levels in the tin artifacts found at Machu Picchu are comparable to those found in tin from archaeological sites in Africa (Grant 1994) and Europe (Northover and Gillis 1999), and in tin made in reproduction smelting experiments (Timberlake 1994).

Fabrication of Artifacts

The examples of unfinished artifacts (Table 1.11) show that artisans at Machu Picchu fabricated metal products at the site. In pre-Inca times Andean artisans had relied primarily on techniques for shaping and joining sheet metal rather than casting. They cut metal with chisels and created patterns on the metal surface by embossing, repoussée, or chasing. Additionally, these artisans made deep objects such as bowls and crowns using the raising technique. In artifacts fabricated from several parts they joined the pieces mechanically with tabs or laces, or by soldering or welding (Tushingham, Franklin, and Toogood 1979). Few of these techniques were used in the artifacts excavated at Machu Picchu, because relatively few of them are made of sheet metal. Instead, the principal fabrication techniques represented in the collection are either casting or subsequent forging of cast blanks into finished products. These techniques are examined below.

TABLE 1.7. Microprobe analyses of bronze axes.

Catalog number	% Copper	% Tin	% Iron	% Sulfur	% Silver	% Arsenic
ANT.017898						
Metal	88.3 ± 0.9	11.5 ± 0.6	0.2	0.01		
Inclusions	75.0	0.02	3.6	22.00		
ANT.017900						
Metal	91.0	6.20	0.0	0.20	1.6	1.1
Inclusion I	6.8	9.40	0.0	0.00	82.3	1.1
Inclusion II	79.6	0.00	0.0	19.80	0.0	0.6
Inclusion III	64.9	31.50	0.0	0.00	3.0	0.5

SOURCE OF METALS

No distinctive characteristics that would permit identification of the specific sources of the metals used to make the artifacts in the collection have been found yet. Thirteen of the items in the collection are metal stock, unfinished products, or wastes from metalworking (Table 1.12). These are identified as materials used by the metalworkers at Machu Picchu. Nothing in the compositions of these metals differs significantly from those in other artifacts in the collection. This suggests that the metalworkers at Machu Picchu used the same range of alloys as those used by artisans elsewhere in the region from which the Inca acquired metal goods.

Casting Technology

Artisans in each of the Old World's Bronze Ages found it easier to make their products by casting bronze to its final form, or as near as possible to final form, instead of forging them. (Once bloomery iron was available, smiths relied on the forge to shape it.) Bronze smiths used forging techniques to make thin sheets, such as those used to fabricate vessels, or where forging could impart particular properties, as in cymbals and gongs. Artisans in the central Andes had developed their metalworking skills by forging and fabricating artifacts from thin sheets rather than by casting, and only later undertook casting objects to their final shape (Tushingham, Franklin, and Toogood 1979).

The metalsmiths at Machu Picchu melted copper with tin or silver to make their alloys. Once they had the molten alloy in a crucible, they could pour it into a mold shaped to the product they wanted. They might use the casting technique to make an object whose final form would have been difficult to make in any other way. They might cast metal to nearly its final form and rely on forging for final shaping. Or, they could cast a bar or plate to be later shaped by forging, perhaps by someone else. The extent to which the artisans at Machu Picchu preferred casting or forging techniques would be a distinctive aspect of their metallurgical traditions.

TABLE 1.8. Trace element analysis by glow discharge mass spectrometry of bronze axe ANT.017898. Reported in parts per million by weight (ppmw); elements present at concentrations of less than 0.1 ppmw are not reported.

Trace element	Concentration (ppmw)	Trace element	Concentration (ppmw)	Trace element	Concentration (ppmw)
H		Zn	0.80	Pr	
Li	0.016	Ga		Nd	
Be		Ge		Sm	
B	0.099	As	405.00	Eu	
C		Se	0.75	Gd	
N		Br		Tb	
O		Rb		Dy	
F		Sr		Ho	
Na	0.120	Y		Er	
Mg	0.042	Zr		Tm	
Al	0.280	Nb		Yb	
Si	7.400	Mo	0.89	Lu	
P	0.140	Ru		Hf	
S	5,000.000	Rh		Ta	
Cl	14.000	Pd		W	2.70
K	0.360	Ag	290.00	Re	
Ca	0.062	Cd	< 1	Os	
Sc		In	2.10	Ir	
Ti	0.052	Sn	Major	Pt	
V	0.058	Sb	100.00	Au	0.66
Cr	0.120	Te	0.13	Hg	
Mn	0.190	I		Tl	
Fe	2,300.000	Cs		Pb	105.00
Co	1.300	Ba		Bi	30.00
Ni	6.200	La		Th	
Cu	Major	Ce		U	

Evidence that an object was cast to its final form can be found in its shape or on its surface. Casting would have been the most convenient technique for making the bronze ball (ANT.017965), with its reentrant cavity and integral crossbar. The trace of a parting line left by a bivalve mold, as on one axe (ANT.017904), confirms that it was cast to final shape. Where such clear-cut surface evidence is absent—and it often is—we can examine the microstructure to determine the degree to which an artifact was brought to its final shape by casting or forging. Both the tin-bronze and the copper-silver alloys used by the Machu Picchu artisans develop distinctive cast microstructures as they solidify or are subsequently forged.

TABLE 1.9. Microprobe analyses of silver alloy artifacts. Except for the dress ornament (ANT.018400), which had two, eight analyses are reported here. The α-phase is a silver-rich phase; the β-phase is a copper-rich phase. Standard deviation (SD) is calculated in those cases in which enough repeat analyses were available.

	% Copper	% Silver	% Arsenic	% Tin	% Iron	% Lead	% Sulfur
Detection limits							
Silver-rich phase	0.14	0.10	0.07	0.11	0.06	0.13	0.060
Copper-rich phase	0.12	0.08	0.07	0.08	0.04	0.12	0.070
Alloy stock ANT.018449							
α-phase	6.4	92.3	0.00	2.9	0.00	0.89	0.070
SD	1.3	1.2	0.00	0.2	0.00	0.12	0.080
β-phase	92.8	5.5	0.09	2.05	0.01	0.05	0.030
SD	2.8	2.4	0.02	0.19	0.01	0.05	0.030
Bulk	68.6	29.4	0.06	2.20	0.20		
Headband ANT.017872							
α-phase	8.4	92.3	0.00	0.67	0.01	0.42	0.000
SD	1.5	2.1	0.00	0.09	0.02	0.07	0.000
β-phase	93.0	6.7	0.29	0.44	0.00	0.02	0.000
SD	1.4	1.4	0.08	0.06	0.00	0.02	0.005
Bulk	74.7	24.5	0.24	0.49	0.09		
Dress ornament ANT.018400							
α-phase	3.7	93.1	0.00	3.10	0.00	0.00	0.000
Shawl pin ANT.017821							
Bulk	19.0	81.0					

BRONZE ARTIFACTS

The solidification of bronze takes place over a temperature range of as much as 100 °C. In this interval, solid metal grows into the liquid with a tree-like, dendritic structure that is preserved in the fully solidified casting. Because the tin in the bronze tends to concentrate in the last metal to solidify, composition gradients (coring) in the artifact can be revealed in the microstructure by appropriate etches. The composition gradients that develop during the solidification of tin bronzes are best revealed by the hydrogen peroxide etch (see Figure 1.8), which indicates the metal structure of the bird-head lime spoon (ANT.017970). Cavities caused by the evolution of gas during solidification and undeformed sulfide inclusions are additional characteristic features of the as-cast microstructure.

Relatively few artifacts in the collection retain as-cast microstructure in whole or in part (Table 1.13). Among the artifacts whose microstructures were not examined, the bells (ANT.018427 and ANT.018428) and the balls seem to have been cast

TABLE 1.10. Microprobe analyses of tin artifacts.

Catalog number	% Tin	% Arsenic	% Copper	% Iron	% Nickel	% Cobalt	% Silver
ANT.017978							
Metal	100.0						
Metal	99.9						
ANT.017982							
Metal	99.6	0.4	0.1				
Metal	99.2	0.5	0.1				
Metal	99.9	0.1	0.0				
Inclusion I	89.0	1.0	1.0		7.6	0.4	0.2
Inclusion II	81.8	0.7		17.2			

TABLE 1.11. Examples of work in progress.

Catalog number	Item
ANT.017882	Bronze bar
ANT.017913	Bronze bar
ANT.017972	Tweezers blank
ANT.017980	Bronze blank
ANT.018449	Silver alloy bar
ANT.018460	Bronze sheet stock

TABLE 1.12. Metals used by Machu Picchu artisans.

Catalog number	% Copper	% Tin	% Silver
ANT.017851	94.0	6.0	
ANT.017913	92.1	7.3	
ANT.017972	90.1	9.7	
ANT.017978	100.0		
ANT.017979	99.8		
ANT.017980	94.4	6.0	
ANT.017982	99.6		
ANT.017988	88.0	11.0	
ANT.018449	69.0	2.2	30
ANT.018453	99.0	0.3	
ANT.018460	97.0	3.0	
ANT.018461	91.0	7.0	
ANT.018481	94.7	5.2	

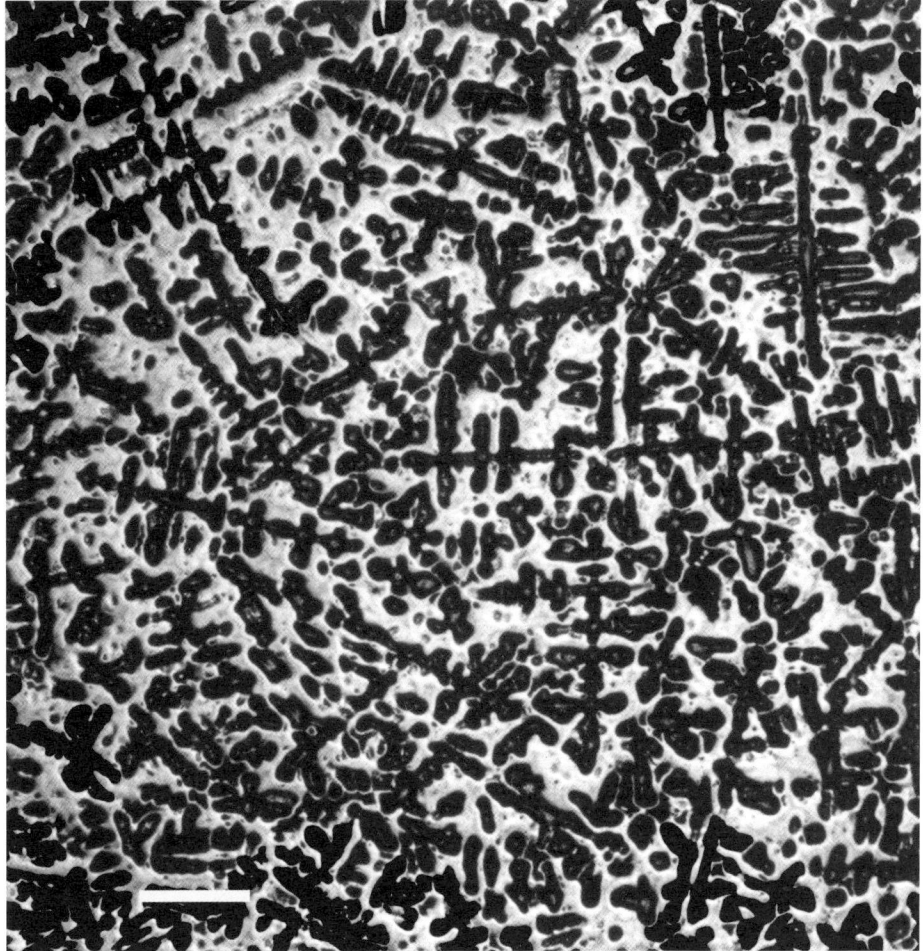

Figure 1.8. As-cast, dendritic structure of bronze in the head of a lime spoon (ANT.017970). Hydrogen peroxide etch; original magnification 50×. Length of scale bar 0.2 mm.

to final shape without further treatment. These are all relatively small objects and they make up a minority of the objects in the collection.

Mathewson's research showed that the Inca artisans made tumi knives by casting bronze blanks to the approximate shape they wanted, and then finishing them by forging. He examined one bronze shawl pin (ANT.017823) and found that it was made by casting a blank to near the final shape followed by forge-finishing that involved enough deformation to obliterate most traces of the as-cast structure after the pin was annealed. These examples of knives and shawl pins examined seem to be representative of the others in the collection.

The combination of casting followed by minor forging simplified the production process for knives and shawl pins. Artisans avoided the heavy labor of hammering out a knife blade or the disc on the end of a shawl pin. A simple open mold

TABLE 1.13. Examples of bronze artifacts retaining as-cast microstructures.

Catalog number	Item	Description
ANT.016685	Small knife	The cast structure is present in the thick sections of this knife.
ANT.017841	Star-head pin	The cast structure is present in the head only.
ANT.017876	Pendant	The high tin content of the bronze would have made forging impossible.
ANT.017962	Llama-head knife	The cast-on head retains its cast structure; the stem has been worked and recrystallized.
ANT.017965	Ball	The cast microstructure is retained throughout.
ANT.017970	Bird-head lime spoon	The bird-shaped head retains the as-cast microstructure; the stem was forged.
ANT.017973	Fisherman knife	Cast structure is retained in the decorated area, while there has been some forging of the area near the knife edge.
ANT.017988	Bronze residue of a bell	Coring and undeformed inclusions and pores are present.
ANT.018461	Bronze left over from a casting operation	Large porosity and grains with dendrites and coring are present.

could be used to cast the blank for a shawl pin. The stem of the blank would necessarily have a rectangular or half-round cross section, which could be subsequently rounded by light forging. Almost all the pins in the collection retain the hammer marks from this operation. To cast a pin with a round shank would have required use of a closed, bivalve mold.

The largest metal artifacts found at Machu Picchu—principally the axes and chisels—were cast to their final shape. Nevertheless, microstructural evidence shows that the Machu Picchu artisans then forged these items without significantly altering their shape, and then annealed them. Several artifacts were treated this way (Table 1.14). The evidence is illustrated by the fully recrystallized structure of the interior part of the chisel (ANT.017964, Figure 1.9). The retention of the porosity present in the original casting of the chisel and the undeformed inclusions of copper oxide found in the axe (ANT.017908, Figure 1.10) show that the forging done before the anneal did not reshape the artifact.

Experiments with laboratory-made bronze having the same tin content and impurities as the metal used at Machu Picchu show that the amount of deformation needed to induce recrystallization in a subsequent anneal is the equivalent of a 6% to 8% reduction in thickness (Gordon and Knopf 2006). This result could be attained with little remaining visible evidence of any alteration of the artifact's shape. The forging that was done on these artifacts did not close up the porosity of the original cast structure, and the hammered and annealed artifacts are no harder or stronger than they were when cast. It seems, then, that the forging and annealing procedure used by the Machu Picchu artisans was not intended to improve the strength properties of the cast artifacts. A possible explanation of this procedure is

FIGURE 1.9. Microstructure of bronze that has been lightly deformed and then annealed at a temperature of about 700 °C. The parallel-sided bands (annealing twins) are characteristic of recrystallized grains. Porosity from the original casting is retained. This structure is found 6 mm from the tip of chisel (ANT.017964). Ferric chloride etch; original magnification 100×. The copper sulfide inclusions are not resolved at this magnification. Length of scale bar 0.1 mm.

that the Machu Picchu artisans believed it to be a necessary part of the production process. This could represent a continuation of an established tradition derived from the forging technique, once dominant in Peruvian metalworking but no longer needed once the advantages of making products by casting were established. There are other examples of artisans working new materials with old, established techniques or of carrying out procedures that did not enhance the appearance or utility of a product. In Early Iron Age Europe, smiths forged iron to mimic cast bronze looped axes (Tylecote 1986:151). Early Iron Age Persian artisans (around 1000–800 BC) forged iron armlets and horse bits with forms characteristic of cast bronze (Allen and Gilmour 2000:478). In the Katanga region of Africa, metalworkers used iron-forging techniques on the new-to-them copper (Childs 1991). In the African Iron Age, smiths finished their forged iron products with an apparently unnecessary spheroidizing anneal (Gordon and van der Merwe 1984).

SILVER-COPPER ARTIFACTS

Casting silver-copper alloys with compositions comparable to those used at Machu

TABLE 1.14. Inca bronze artifacts cast to shape and then forged.

Catalog number	Item	Description
ANT.017898 *	"T" axe	Fully recrystallized; forging was limited to within about 20 mm of the tip; strain lines elsewhere in the structure are due to subsequent use.
ANT.017899	Copper "T" axe	Fully recrystallized, but with abundant large pores.
ANT.017900 *	"T" axe	Fully recrystallized, but retaining the original cored structure.
ANT.017902 *	"T" axe	Fully recrystallized; handle only examined; inclusions are undeformed and porosity is retained; strain lines are from use.
ANT.017907	Chisel	Fully recrystallized; top only examined; coring has been eliminated by anneals. There has been heavy deformation near the top surface due to use, but the sulfide inclusions in the interior are undeformed.
ANT.017908	Axe head	Fully recrystallized, with the eutectic structure of the oxide inclusions retained.
ANT.017962	Llama-head knife	The bronze stem is fully recrystallized, with porosity and traces of coring.
ANT.017964	Chisel	Fully recrystallized, with deformation confined to within about 10 mm of the tip.
ANT.017966	Chisel	Fully recrystallized; deformation of inclusions, confined to the very tip, is due to use.
ANT.017967	"T" axe	Fully recrystallized, with porosity and coring retained; strain lines due to use (handle only examined).
ANT.017969	Broken axe blade	Fully recrystallized with no deformation of inclusions; faint traces of coring survive anneal; deformation only at the point, from use.
ANT.017972	Tweezers blank	Fully recrystallized with traces of residual coring; good evidence on possible forging is lacking.
ANT.017974	Broken axe blade, edge piece	Fully recrystallized, but with undeformed inclusions.
ANT.017975	Broken chisel	Fully recrystallized; coring retained, sulfides undeformed.
ANT.018478	Crowbar	Fully recrystallized, with much retained porosity and traces of coring.
ANT.018480	Pendant	Undeformed inclusions; body fully recrystallized.

* Not from Machu Picchu.

Picchu is expected to yield characteristic microstructures consisting of dendrites of either the silver-rich (α) or copper-rich (β) solid solutions in a matrix of eutectic microconstituent, unless the alloy contains 72% silver, in which case the structure would be entirely eutectic (Figure 1.11). The silver-copper eutectic has a characteristic structure of lamellae of the β-phase in a matrix of the α-phase. In the silver

FIGURE 1.10. The metal in the top of this axe (ANT.017908) must have been plastically deformed and then annealed since it is fully recrystallized. Because the inclusions of copper oxide retain the characteristic eutectic structure formed on solidification, the amount of deformation prior to annealing was small. Ferric chloride etch; original magnification 200×. Length of scale bar 0.1 mm.

band (ANT.017872) and metal stock or work piece (ANT.018449) the silver content is less than 72% and dendrites of the β-phase formed on solidification. However, these dendrites are in a matrix of the α-phase rather than the eutectic that would ordinarily be expected. Laboratory experiments with alloys duplicating the compositions of these artifacts show that eutectic does not form on rapid solidification in the presence of β-phase dendrites (Gordon and Knopf 2007). Cooling in a small plaster, clay, or metal mold suffices to suppress the formation of eutectic structure. This indicates that the blank for the headband (ANT.017872) was probably cast in a shallow, open mold; it was subsequently heavily forged to its final thickness. The metal stock or work piece was similarly cast but not as extensively forged.

The shawl pin stem (ANT.017821) has a silver content (80%) greater than that of the eutectic. During solidification, growth of dendrites of the α-phase was followed by partial formation of the characteristic eutectic structure. The β-phase lamellae are short and very small, and some of the β-phase has formed in larger particles within the arms of the α-phase dendrites (Figure 1.12). Laboratory experiments with an alloy of the same composition show that use of either an open clay or plaster mold or a small, preheated metal mold results in the same structure.

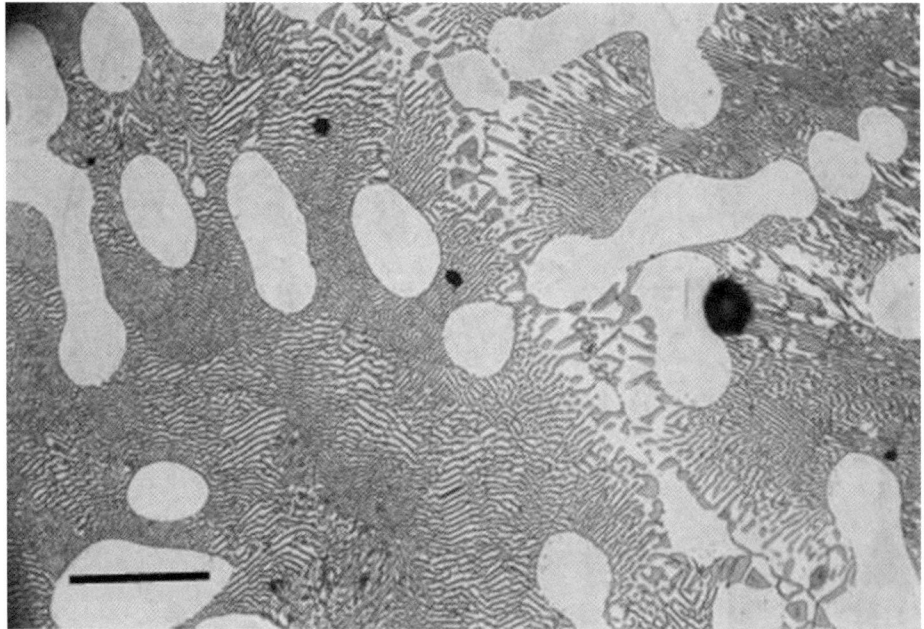

Figure 1.11. Micrograph of alloy containing 76% silver and 34% copper solidified slowly to develop the eutectic structure of lamella of the copper-rich β-phase in a matrix of silver-rich α-phase. The eutectic surrounds dendrites of the α-phase. Particles of the β-phase have formed at some dendrites and between some of the dendrite colonies. Ferric chloride etch; original magnification 300×. Length of scale bar 0.1 mm.

Hence it seems that the same casting technique used for the low-silver alloy items was used for this shawl pin.

Casting Techniques

Because so few traces of metalworkers' equipment have been found at Machu Picchu, our evidence of casting techniques used there must be gleaned from the artifacts themselves. The bronze and silver-copper alloys the Machu Picchu artisans used are liquid only at a bright red heat, 800 °C or higher. Iron tongs greatly facilitate the handling of a crucible of liquid metal this hot. We do not know what tools the metalsmiths at Machu Picchu used to pick up and pour the contents of crucibles containing molten metal into molds. Wet wooden withies similar to those shown in illustrations of the Egyptian artisans casting copper (Tylecote 1976:19) are one possibility. Alternatively, they may have placed molds beneath tap holes in their furnaces to allow molten metal to flow directly into the molds.

Pouring molten metal into an open stone mold would have been the easiest way for an artisan to produce a casting at Machu Picchu. An artifact cast this way retains the characteristic shape of the free surface of the liquid metal unless this surface has been removed by subsequent processing. The blanks for shawl pins and many of the knives could have been cast in open molds, and the evidence of this technique removed when these were finished on both sides. There is no evidence

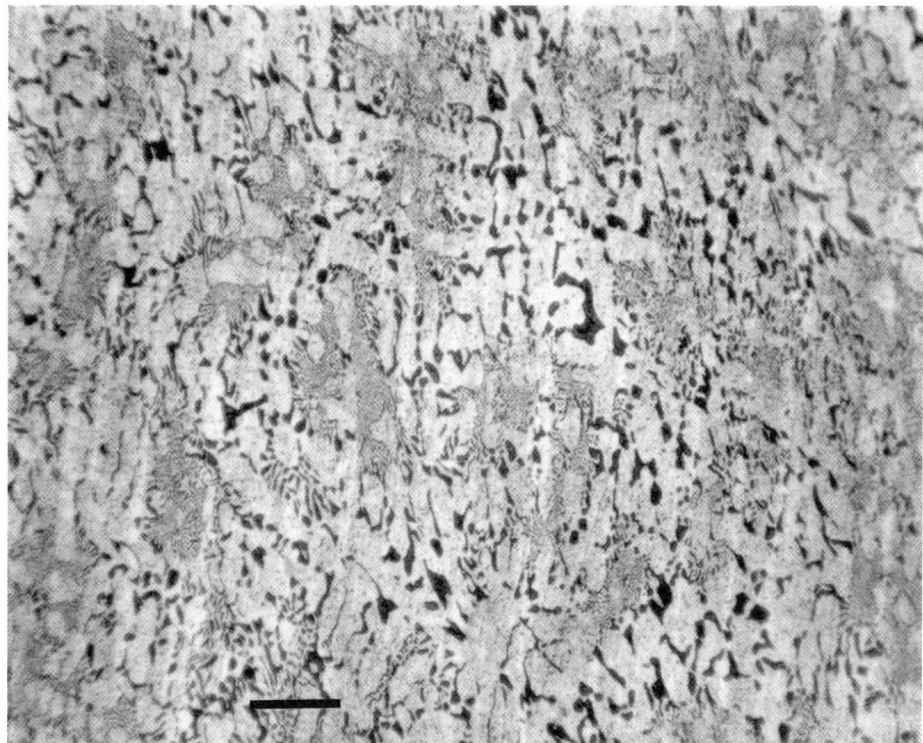

Figure 1.12. Section of the stem of a shawl pin (ANT.017821). Dendrites of silver-rich α-phase (bright) are surrounded by fine-scale eutectic. Some copper-rich β-phase has formed as massive particles on the α-phase dendrites. Ferric chloride etch; original magnification 500×. Length of scale bar 20 μ.

of a free surface on any of the Machu Picchu artifacts, although it is found on metal discarded from foundry work (such as on items ANT.018461 and ANT.018481).

There is evidence of parting lines left by bivalve molds on several artifacts (such as knife ANT.017904). Bivalve molds would have been convenient for making the large objects with a central plane of symmetry, like the axes and chisels. Subsequent finishing may have removed the flash formed at the parting line, leaving us without direct evidence of the mold design. Bivalve molds were probably made of clay, most conveniently with the aid of a pattern. Examples of retention of the imprint of the grain of a wood pattern in a bronze casting are found in European Bronze Age artifacts (Coghlan 1975:57). We do not find this evidence among the Machu Picchu artifacts. However, use of a pattern suggests that multiple objects of the same size and shape, such as the examples mentioned above, could have been produced.

Intricate objects such as the star-head and llama-head pins (ANT.017841 and ANT.017970) could have been made by the lost-wax casting technique. This technique would also have been the easiest way to make objects with cast-in holes, such as the small knife (ANT.016685). An artisan made a model of the desired object in wax, formed a clay mold around the model, and then melted and poured out the

Figure 1.13. Llama-head knife (ANT.017962) showing the head made of copper-bismuth-tin alloy cast on a tin-bronze stem. Length of scale bar 10 mm.

wax to leave a cavity that exactly reproduced the shape of the model. Since the mold had to be broken apart to extract the solidified casting, the process did not lend itself to the production of identical objects.

The llama-head knife (ANT.017962, shown in Figure 1.13) is an example of the use of a casting-on technique by the Inca artisans. They first cast the stem and blade of the knife with a hook shape at the top of the stem. They used an alloy of copper and 3% tin, giving this part a near-copper color. They then encased the top of the stem in another mold shaped like a llama head and poured a copper-tin-bismuth alloy, which has a distinctive color. The section (see Figure 1.14) indicates the join between the two castings (see Appendix A for a full description of this artifact).

Casting Problems and Difficulties

The Inca artisans successfully cast intricate shapes and complex designs, such as the llama-head tumi (ANT.017868), and very thin objects, like the disc (ANT.018480, see Figure 1.29). They encountered problems their technique could not fully address when they undertook the larger castings needed to make chisels and axes. It is difficult to make castings of tin bronze free of porosity. The molten bronze dissolves hydrogen drawn from hydrocarbons in the gases present in the melting furnace or from any impurities present in charcoal used to cover the molten metal. When a casting is poured, the stream of molten metal passing between the crucible and the mold dissolves oxygen from the air. As the bronze solidifies and the dissolved gases are expelled, the hydrogen and oxygen react to form steam. Some of this steam escapes and can make the solidifying metal spew from the mold. The remaining steam forms pores in the solid metal (Hull 1950).

Additionally, the bronze contracts 5% to 7% as it solidifies. The center and thicker parts of a casting are the last to harden. If there is no reserve supply of liquid during solidification, or no channel through which liquid can flow to the interior of the casting, additional porosity will result. Porosity decreases the density of the cast metal, reduces its tensile strength, and greatly lowers its ductility (Baker and Child 1944; Gordon and Knopf 2006). However, the overall shrinkage of the casting as seen at its surface may be small because of the included porosity. Hence, the metal

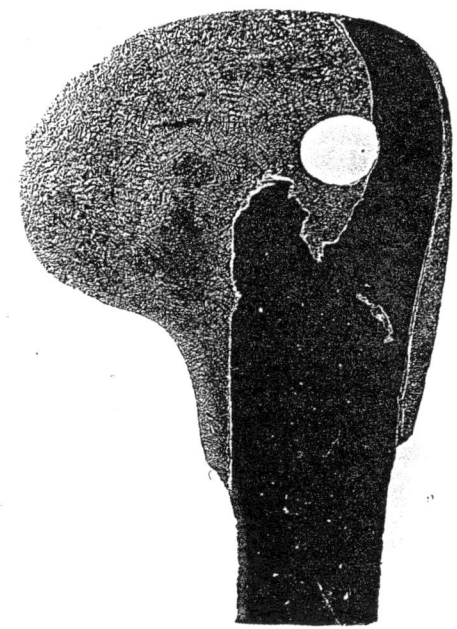

FIGURE 1.14. Section through the head of a knife (ANT.017962) showing the join between the bronze stem and the cast-on head of copper-tin-bismuth alloy.

may fill out a mold well and look sound from the outside even though it is riddled with pores inside (Baker, Child, and Glaisher 1944).

We do not know how many defective castings the Machu Picchu artisans simply remelted. Very few of the artifacts have gross casting defects. However, porosity is common in the Machu Picchu bronze castings and is particularly prominent in the large artifacts, such as the crowbar (ANT.018478, Figure 1.15). It is also common in the thick section of small objects, such as the bird-head lime spoon (ANT.017970). In objects such as the lime spoon, which do not have to sustain large forces when in use, interior porosity does not pose a problem for the user. However, the strength and toughness of a tool such as the crowbar (ANT.018478) are seriously degraded by its high porosity. Another casting problem, a misrun, is present in the broken axe blade (ANT.017974, Figure 1.16).

Concentrations of sulfide inclusions formed during solidification also degraded the physical properties of some of the bronze artifacts. Bands of these inclusions in a bronze bar (ANT.017913) caused the formation of cracks when the bar was forged. The breakage of the edge of an axe (ANT.017969; see Appendix A, Figure A16) is due to cracks traveling along paths defined by pores and sulfide inclusions (Figure 1.17). Mathewson found that a sample of metal he took from this axe was quite ductile when he passed it through a rolling mill. However, under tensile forces such as those caused by bending or twisting, an axe blade made of porous bronze is brittle. The fracture of a knife (ANT.017904, Figure 1.18) is due to this same cause. Examination of the fracture surface reveals metal weakened by abundant porosity.

Figure 1.15. Large pores due to gas release during solidification in the bronze crowbar (ANT.018478). Notice that the metal is fully recrystallized and that some of the porosity is in the form of cracks. Ferric chloride etch; original magnification 50×. Length of scale bar 0.2 mm.

Forging Technology

Both the bronze with less than 10% tin and the silver-copper alloys found in the artifacts from Machu Picchu are sufficiently ductile to allow artisans to hammer out finished products with the metal either cold or hot. Bronze with a tin content greater than about 10% is difficult to forge unless quenched from high temperature, a technique that Inca artisans did not use. The bronze objects in the collection with more than about 12% tin were cast, rather than forged to shape.

As an artisan worked either the low-tin bronze or the copper-silver alloy by hammering, the metal grew progressively harder. Eventually cracks would begin to form and the work piece would start to break up. The smith had to anneal the object he was making before this happened if he wanted to continue shaping it. Evidence of failure to anneal when required is found in some of the Machu Picchu artifacts, such as the crack formed near the junction of the stem and head of the silver-copper shawl pin (ANT.017821).

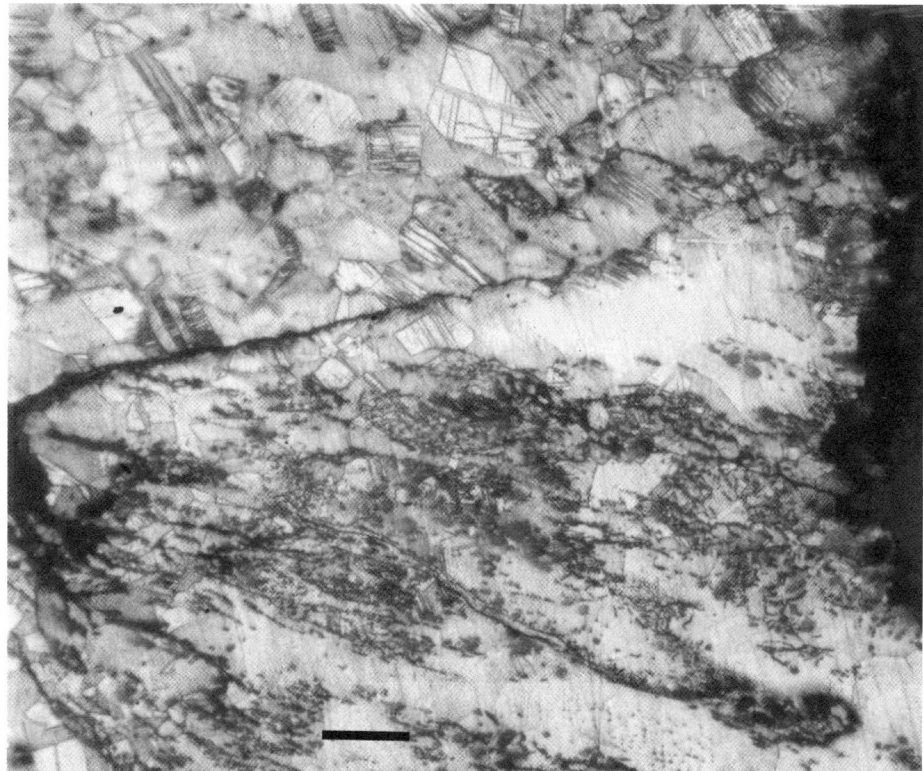

Figure 1.16. The gross casting defect in the broken axe blade (ANT.017974) was caused by a mis-run. Some metal splashed on the mold wall solidified prematurely and was later incorporated in the casting. Ferric chloride etch; original magnification 100×. Length of scale bar 0.1 mm.

In general, if the object being made was forged while red hot rather than cold, less labor was needed (because the metal was softer), and it did not require annealing, since this process went on while the forging progressed. However, a smith would have needed some way of holding the red-hot work piece that would allow him to manipulate it on the anvil as he hammered. The absence of evidence of tongs or other tool that artisans at Machu Picchu could have used for this task suggests that hot forging was not common practice there.

The artisans who made the artifacts found at Machu Picchu used forging techniques in four different ways. They forged some objects, such as those made of thin sheet metal, to their final form. More commonly, artisans cast a piece as close as possible to the final shape wanted and then finished it by light forge work. They made shawl pins and knives this way. The makers, or perhaps users, of some of their edge tools—knives, chisels, and axes—forged the working surfaces either to attain a desired edge profile or to harden the metal near the edge. Finally, artisans hammered and then annealed large objects without changing their shape, perhaps to express a belief about the need to forge all metal (see the discussion under "Bronze Artifacts" above).

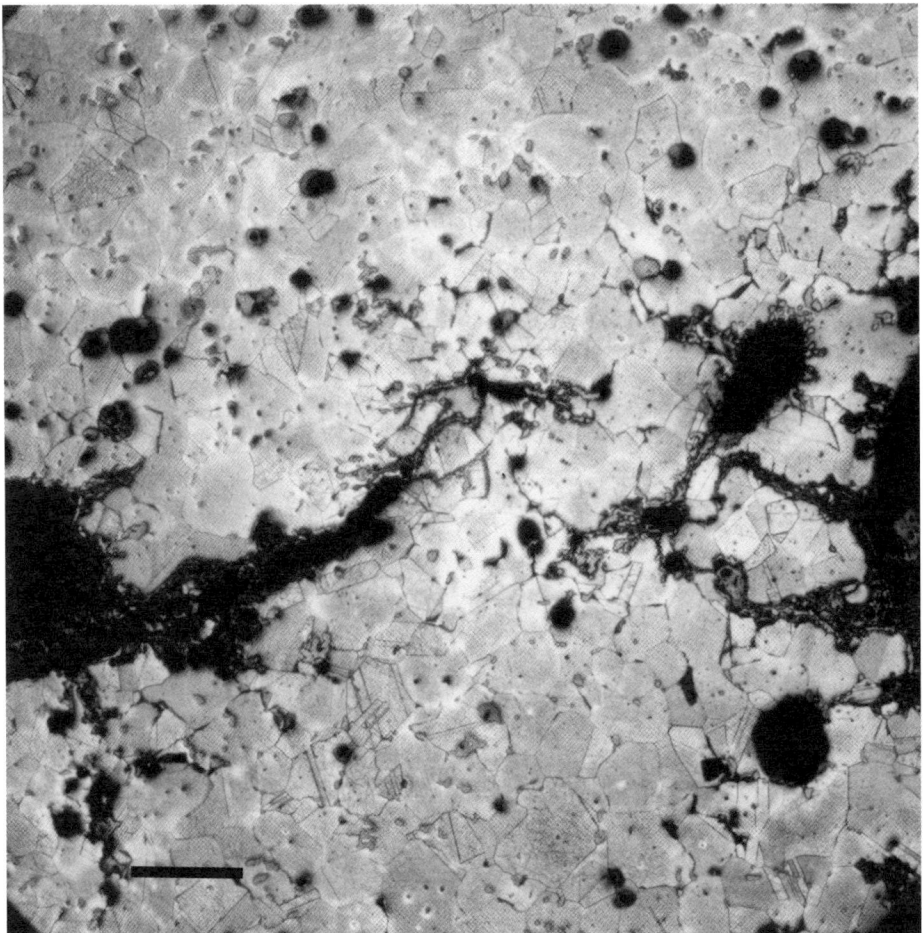

Figure 1.17. Large gas porosity in a broken axe blade (ANT.017969) embrittled the metal and led to the formation of the cracks seen in this micrograph. Ferric chloride etch; original magnification 50×. Length of scale bar 0.2 mm.

The form of some artifacts shows that artisans forged them to final shape. Tweezers (such as ANT.017893) would have been difficult to make in any other way. Indentations left by an artisan's hammer on the surface of a forged object and not removed in subsequent finishing operations show that forge work was done. Such indentations are found on the stems of nearly all the shawl pins and on many of the knives. At least 58 objects in the collection retain hammer marks or have a shape (such as that of the tweezers) that required forging to make. Evidence of forge work can also be found in the microstructures of both the bronze and silver alloy artifacts. Strain lines, revealed by etching, are a sensitive indicator of plastic deformation; the deformation caused by even a few light hammer blows can be discerned in the microstructure if there has been no subsequent anneal. The way in which metal flowed in heavier forging operations can be deduced from the distortion of both the metal grains and any copper sulfide or oxide inclusions that are present.

FIGURE 1.18. Bronze knife (ANT.017904), 120 × 92 mm. A high level of porosity in the bronze blade left it susceptible to easy breakage under moderate use.

Forging and Annealing Bronze

Strain lines and distortion of grains, easily seen in the microstructure, show that bronze in artifacts has undergone plastic deformation (Figure 1.19). Extensive deformation, such as might be used to shape an object from metal stock, can be recognized in the microstructure, even after annealing, by the elongation of the sulfide inclusions present in the bronze and by the disruption of the composition gradients (coring) left from the casting process (see Figure 1.19).

No heavily forged bronze item in the Machu Picchu collection whose microstructure was examined was left in the as-forged condition; all were annealed at a high enough temperature to fully recrystallize the metal. This annealing forms new, strain-free, recrystallized grains marked by parallel bands (annealing twins; see Figures 1.9 and 1.10). Because the recrystallized grains tend to be larger in proportion to the higher annealing temperature, the grain size in an annealed artifact can be used to estimate the temperature at which the metalsmith softened his work piece, as Mathewson (1915) demonstrated. If the metal in a bronze object that seems to have been cast to shape is recrystallized, it must have been at least lightly hammered, since as-cast metal will not recrystallize during an anneal (Gordon and Knopf 2006).

Artisans at Machu Picchu cast the bronze shawl pins and knives, which make up a large part of the collection, close to their final shapes and finished them by forging. Light forging sufficed to round the stems of the shawl pins. More extensive forging was used on some of the knives. Mathewson's (1915) micrograph shows greatly elongated sulfide inclusions in both the blade and handle of a knife (ANT.017963), where the metal is recrystallized. Strain lines show that the loop at the top of the handle was bent and then annealed. Elongated oxide inclusions in the blade of the copper knife (ANT.017971) show that the blade and handle had been partially shaped by forging.

TABLE 1.15. Examples of bronze artifacts forged to shape.

Catalog number	Item	Description
ANT.017851	Unfinished tool	Surface evidence of forging includes the flattened ends, irregular shape, and turned-over metal at one end that indicates incomplete shaping by hammering.
ANT.017871	Bronze discs	The 39 bronze discs, each about 11 mm in diameter and 0.2 to 0.3 mm thick, have holes punched in them to allow stringing as a necklace.
ANT.017879	Molder's or potter's slick	The surface evidence consists of circular indentations probably made by hammerstones, a flattened end, and turned-over metal that forms grooves on the surface.
ANT.017882	Bar	Irregular dimensions and surface indentations indicate forge work in progress; microstructure data are lacking.
ANT.017893/ 017895/017896	Tweezers	The shape, with its sharp bends and thin, curved section with sharp working edges, would have been formed from a blank-like item (such as ANT.017972).
ANT.017913	Rectangular bar	The microstructure shows heavy deformation; surface depressions correspond to the indentations made by hammerstones. The elliptical shape of a hole through the bar indicates elongation of at least 60%; the extension of the sulfide inclusions suggests even greater elongation of the bar by forging.
ANT.017972	Tweezers blank	Forming by forging is inferred from the shape, but the microstructural evidence is not conclusive. The high tin content might make cold-shaping difficult.
ANT.018453	Flat pin	The thin, wavy profile and irregular shape suggest forge work in progress.
ANT.018460	Sheet stock	At less than 1 mm thick, this is too thin to have been made without hammering out into sheet; the wavy form suggests the difficulty of keeping the metal flat while hammering it out. This item shows that artisans could make thin sheet from bronze as well as from the copper-silver alloy.
ANT.018626	Needle	This thin needle is covered with forge marks. Mathewson's (1915) micrograph shows deformation continued after a recrystallization anneal.

Of the comparatively few bronze artifacts in the collection forged to their final forms (Table 1.15), all are relatively small objects. The tweezers are the best examples of the forging skills of the Machu Picchu artisans. Metal in the center of

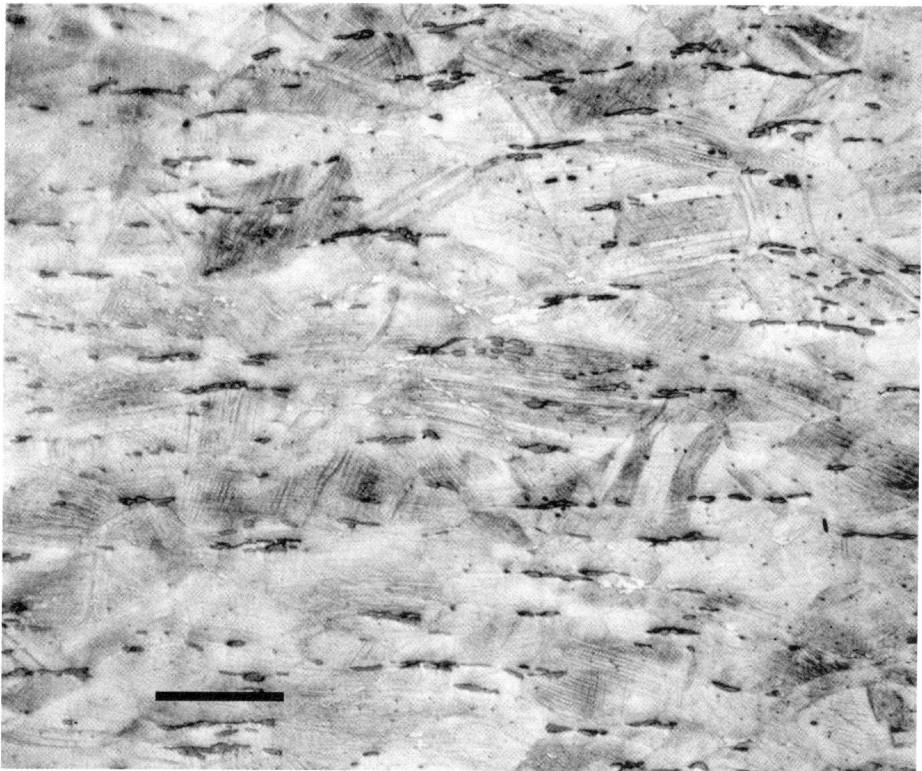

FIGURE 1.19. Microstructure of an axe (ANT.017898) 3.5 mm from the tip of the blade showing strain lines within the bronze grains and elongated sulfide inclusions. Hydrogen peroxide etch shows residual concentration gradients as delicate shading; original magnification 100×. Length of scale bar 0.1 mm.

the blank (see Figure 1.5) had to be reduced in width and the ends of the blank thinned and shaped into a complex curve for each blade. Making the two sharp bends needed to bring the forged blank to its final "U" shape would have been a particularly difficult task. Since the metal would be fully hardened at this stage of the process, it would have a very low strain-hardening rate. This would make it easier for the smith to make the necessary sharp bends.

Study of their microstructures shows that at least five items in the Yale Peruvian Expedition collection that were only lightly forged and then annealed were subjected to further, localized forge work (Table 1.16). In the "T" axe (ANT.017898) heavy forging at a working edge is revealed by the elongated inclusions (seen in Figure 1.20). If more forging were done after the last anneal, strain lines would be present in the recrystallized grains, as in the metal at the tip of the chisel from Machu Picchu (ANT.017964, seen in Figure 1.21). Deformation marks caused by use of the tool rather than by shaping an edge can be recognized by the direction of metal flow indicated in some of the tools (see the discussion under "Function and Use of Artifacts" below).

TABLE 1.16. Inca items with edges shaped by forging.

Catalog number	Item	Description
ANT.017898	"T" axe	After light forging and annealing, a 10 mm band at the edge of the blade tip was hammered to attain the desired blade profile.
ANT.017964	Chisel	After light forging and annealing, the tip of the chisel was formed by hot-forging to a depth of about 10 mm.
ANT.017966	Chisel	After light forging and annealing, the edge of the chisel was shaped by forging in a zone a few millimeters deep.
ANT.017970	Bird-head lime spoon	The end of the stem was forged and annealed, leaving the cast structure intact at the head. *
ANT.017975	Axe blade	After light forging and annealing, the blade was forged at the tip.

* Mathewson (1915).

Forging Temperatures. If an object is forged while red hot, deformation and recrystallization can occur simultaneously. Mathewson (1915) showed that if a bronze work piece is cooled quickly after the last hammer blow, its microstructure may contain a mixture of recrystallized and deformed grains. Only one example of hot forging has been found among the artifacts from Machu Picchu. The tip of a chisel (ANT.017964)was hot-forged (Figure 1.22). Because the forging was confined to a depth of less than 15 mm at the cutting edge and the chisel is 134 mm long, the smith may have been able to avoid the need for tongs by heating just the chisel tip. He could have wrapped the back end with wet cloth for a hand grip while he shaped the tip.

The sparse evidence of hot forging and the apparent absence of devices for holding hot objects suggests that the Inca artisans preferred to work metal cold and anneal it as required to overcome strain hardening.

Annealing Temperatures. Bronze containing the iron impurities and sulfide inclusions found in the artifacts from Machu Picchu can be fully annealed after light deformation at the dull-red heat, about 650 °C, easily attained with a charcoal fire. Artisans could have used braziers, such as the one Bingham found at Machu Picchu (Burger and Salazar 2004:146). Even a large hot wood fire will heat metal to about 700 °C (Coghlan 1975:28).

The α–δ eutectoid structure formed by coring during the solidification of bronze containing as little as 5% tin is often present in the microstructure of small castings. Estimates based on the diffusion rate of tin in copper indicate that any islands of α–δ eutectoid smaller than 0.1 mm would dissolve during annealing at a

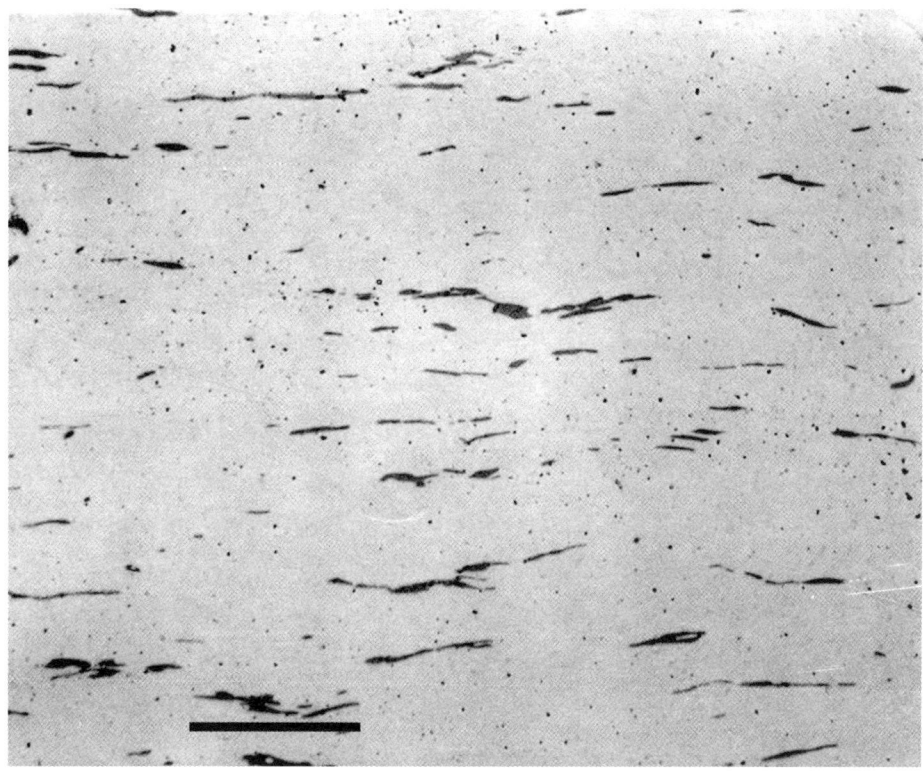

FIGURE 1.20. Elongated sulfide inclusions near the tip of a bronze axe (ANT.017898) show that the end of the axe blade was heavily forged. No etch, original magnification 200×. Length of scale bar 0.1 mm.

temperature of about 750 °C within an hour. Mathewson (1915) found that a short anneal at about 700 °C dissolved residual eutectoid in small bronze castings. The general absence of this structure in the Machu Picchu bronze tools suggests that the Inca artisans annealed their bronze at 700 °C or higher. A temperature of 850 °C rapidly homogenizes bronze as well as recrystallizing it. Since traces of composition gradients formed by coring are retained in most of the annealed bronze artifacts in the collection (Figure 1.23), it seems that the Machu Picchu artisans used annealing temperatures well below 850 °C.

Strain Hardening. Bronze with the tin content typical of the artifacts found at Machu Picchu can be cold-forged to hardness as high as HV 280, a hardness comparable to that often found in the bloomery iron used in the Iron Ages of Europe, Asia, and Africa. This property made bronze competitive with iron for use in tools and weapons in the Old World during the Early Iron Age, before artisans learned how to further harden iron by alloying it with carbon and heat-treating the resulting steel. We measured the hardness of the bronze in the tools found at Machu Picchu for evidence of deliberate strain hardening to see whether the Inca artisans took advantage of this property of bronze.

Figure 1.21. Strain lines and elongated sulfide inclusions near the tip of a bronze chisel (ANT.017964). Ferric chloride etch; original magnification 500×. Length of scale bar 0.02 mm.

We interpret strain hardening that extends only a few millimeters back from the working edge of a tool (Table 1.17) to be the result of tool use, because it would be difficult to strain-harden such a narrow zone by forging. Among four items (see Table 1.17), strain hardening extends as much as 20 mm back from the working edge only in the "T" axe (ANT.017898) and chisel (ANT.017964). There is no convincing evidence that the tips of any of the other tools were deliberately hardened. Thus, strain hardening to improve the properties of bronze tools does not seem to have been a common practice, if done at all, of the Inca smiths.

Forging and Annealing Silver

The combination of strength and ductility found in the silver-copper alloys used at Machu Picchu makes these materials ideal for metalworkers to shape by hammering. In making a product such as a thin sheet that required large deformation, the artisan needed to anneal the alloy one or more times. This could be accomplished at a somewhat lower temperature than needed for bronze artifacts.

The microstructural constituents present in the silver-copper alloys used at Machu Picchu have a distinctive shape in the as-cast condition. The primary α (silver-rich) or β (copper-rich) constituent is dendritic. In the eutectic, the β-phase

FIGURE 1.22. Structure of metal 7 mm from the tip of a chisel (ANT.017964) showing the simultaneous presence of deformed grains (marked by strain bands) and larger, undeformed grains characteristic of hot-forged bronze. Ferric chloride etch; original magnification 100×. Length of scale bar 0.1 mm.

is present as lamellae. The progress of forging and annealing can be followed in the successive shape changes of these constituents. Forging causes bending and kinking of the eutectic lamellae and shape changes in the dendrites. Subsequent annealing can spheroidize the lamellae, but retains the shape changes of the dendrites caused by the forging (Gordon and Knopf 2007).

All four of the artifacts whose microstructures were examined had been forged after casting. Forging had been started on the metal stock (ANT.018449) when it was abandoned. This resulted in spreading of the metal near the surface while leaving the original dendritic structure in the interior nearly unchanged (Figure 1.24). The distortion of the dendrites of the silver-rich phase in the stem of the shawl pin (ANT.017821) indicates a reduction in thickness of the original casting of 30% to at most 40%. The hammer marks found on other silver alloy shawl pins in the collection indicate that this final shaping after casting was the common practice of the Inca artisans who made these pins.

The large elongation of the copper-rich and silver-rich phases in the microstructures of the spangle (ANT.018400) and the headband (ANT.017872, Figure 1.25) shows that they were forged to reduction in thickness of as much as 90%. Laboratory experiments with duplicate alloys show that the Inca artisans probably

TABLE 1.17. Hardness gradients in bronze tools, with the results of measurements of the hardness profiles near the working edges of the tools. Vickers hardness (HV) microhardness measured with a 100 g load.

Catalog number	Item	Description
ANT.017898	Axe	Hardness decreases from HV 260 at the edge of the blade to HV 150 within 20 mm from the tip and thereafter remains constant. The tip of this axe had been forged to get a sharp oint and was further sharpened by rubbing it on stone. Strain-hardening would have made the relatively slender the tip of this tool useful for cutting wood. Deliberate hardening is therefore possible in this case.
ANT.017900	Axe	Hardness falls in a steep gradient from HV 270 at the tip to HV 115, 8 mm back from the tip of the blade.
ANT.017964	Chisel	Hardness ranges from HV 210 at the tip to HV 90, 200 mm back from the tip. The relatively light density of strain lines seen at 4 and 6 mm back from the edge indicates that there was no deliberate hardening of the chisel tip, and that it was damaged by subsequent use.
ANT.017974	Axe	No hardening of the tip was found.

annealed their work at least twice in the course of attaining such large reductions in thickness (Gordon and Knopf 2007).

METALWORKER'S TOOLS

The excavators at Machu Picchu found several hammerstones shaped for an easy grip, and at least one stone mortar that retains residue from metalworking (Burger and Salazar 2004:161, 168). Inca artisans used graded sizes of hammerstones in their masonry work (Protzen 1985; Menotti 1998). There is evidence of the use of a large, blunt hammerstone for heavy forging on the surface of the bronze bar (ANT.017913; see Appendix A, Figure A10), interpreted as work in progress. The indentations on the surface of this bar (Figure 1.26) show successive impacts such as would be made by a hand-size hammerstone having a gently curved, blunt working surface with a radius of curvature of about 10 to 15 mm. Such a tool would be appropriate for the rough forging of a bar intended to reduce its thickness and increase its length. Indentations left by smaller stones are common on the stems of the shawl pins, and are found on some of the knives. The impacts of the rounded ends of hammerstones leave characteristic circular patterns within the forged copper-silver alloy seen in a plane perpendicular to the hammer blows (Figure 1.27).

We lack evidence of the tools that would have been required for the complex shaping of objects such as the tweezers. Perhaps each artisan had a selection of hammerstones with shapes ranging from blunt to sharp.

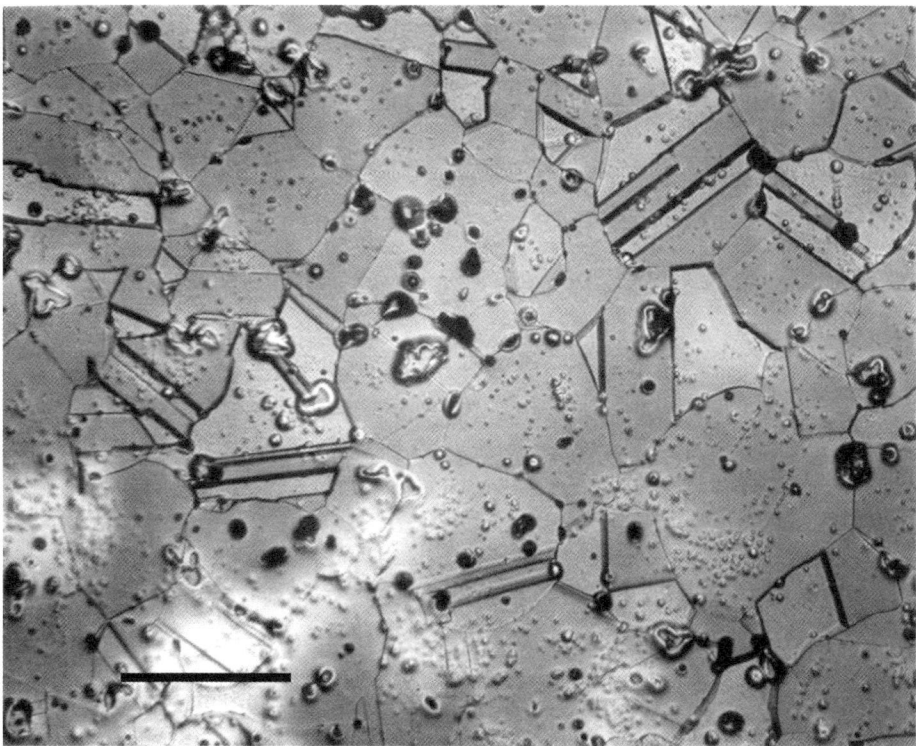

FIGURE 1.23. The upper part of the bronze stem of the llama-head knife (ANT.017962) has gradients in tin concentration retained from coring in the original casting. The hydrogen peroxide etch darkens the metal in proportion to the tin concentration; original magnification 200×. Length of scale bar 0.1 mm.

The rectilinear indentations on the tin sheet (ANT.017979) suggest that the Machu Picchu artisans had chisels with blunt ends that could be used to cut thin, soft metal (Rutledge and Gordon 1987). These would not have been suitable for fine work. The lack of symmetry in the openings cut into the headdress ornament (ANT.017878) (Burger and Salazar 2004:185) suggests that the artisan who made this item did not have the fine, sharp chisel needed for this kind of work.

Sheet Metal Fabrication

Making large pieces of thin metal sheet by hammering with stone tools was a particularly challenging task that Andean artisans had mastered centuries before Inca times. "Sheet" in this context is metal that is not cast to final thickness and is thin enough to be easily bent. Nine of the 165 items in the collection are sheet metal a few tenths of a millimeter thick. Two are bronze (see Table 1.15) and the rest silver-copper alloy (Table 1.18). Of the items found at Machu Picchu made of sheet metal, only the finger rings (ANT.017874 and ANT.017875), the plate handle (ANT.017897), and possibly the staff ornament (ANT.017912) include mechanical joints. The proportion of sheet metal goods among the artifacts in the Bingham collection is low in comparison with their dominance in collections of earlier

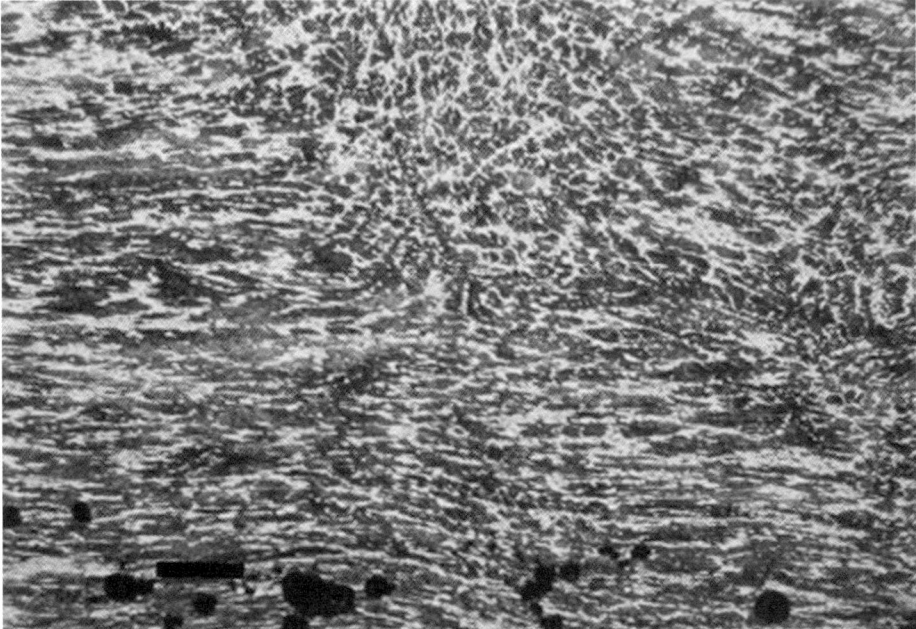

Figure 1.24. Microstructure of a silver-copper alloy forged bar (ANT.018449) showing the silver-rich (bright) and copper-rich (dark) solid solutions. In the forged part of the bar the original copper-rich dendrites have been elongated into bands; the lesser deformation near the center of the bar has left traces of the original dendritic structure. Original magnification 70×. Length of scale bar 0.2 mm. See also Plate 10.

Peruvian artifacts (Burger 1996). This may reflect the absence of high-status graves at Machu Picchu.

An alloy with a high rate of strain hardening facilitates an artisan's work in making sheet metal by hammering. The rapid hardening causes the metal that is thinned by a hammer impact to harden and thus resist further thinning. This helps the smith distribute his thinning blows uniformly along the working surface to produce a nearly uniform thickness. Both the bronze and silver-copper alloys used at Machu Picchu have high rates of strain hardening (Gordon and Knopf 2006, 2007). This would be particularly important in making a long, thin sheet such as the headband (ANT.017872). The histogram of the thickness profile (Figure 1.28) shows that artisans achieved a remarkable degree of control in the forging process. The strain-hardening characteristics of this alloy were essential to this control.

Surface Treatments and Decoration
Simplicity of shape and lack of decoration characterize most of the Machu Picchu metal artifacts. The most common decoration is a solid figure made as an integral part of a cast object. Examples include the decorated knife (ANT.017973), the lime spoons (ANT.017970 and ANT.017890), the llama-head knife (ANT.017962), scrolls

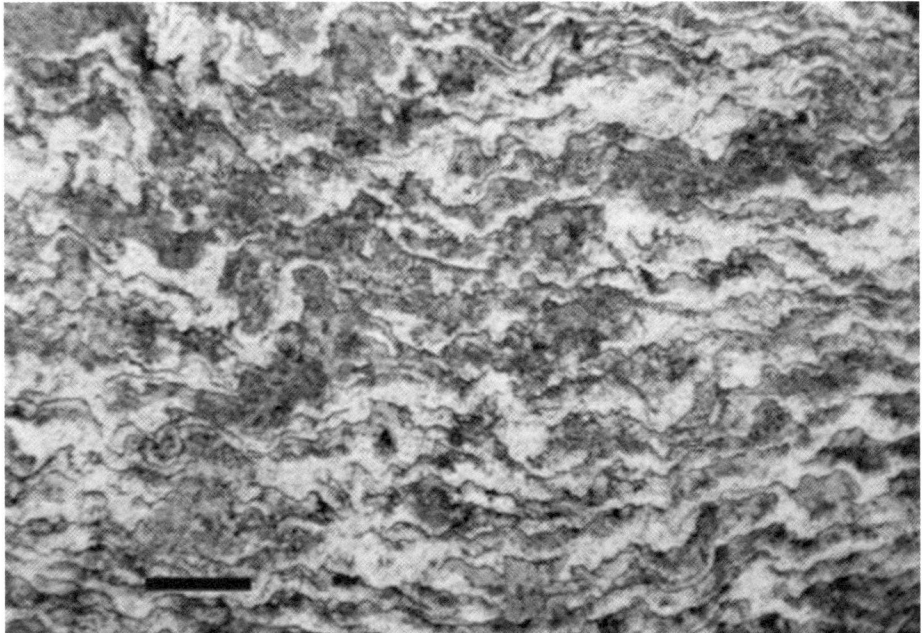

FIGURE 1.25. Interior microstructure of a copper-silver alloy headband (ANT.017872) showing the elongation of the original copper-rich dendrites (dark) resulting from the heavy forging used to convert a cast blank plate into a thin strip. Original magnification 700×. Length of scale bar 0.02 mm. See also Plate 1.

or loops on the pendant (ANT.017876), the knife (ANT.017868), the star-head pin (ANT.017841), and the finial with what seem to be long ears (ANT.017884). One only among the pins (ANT.017836), from the Peruvian Colonial period, has a circular head with a raised rim. Within the rim, and apparently formed in the original casting, is a figure suggesting a star on one side and a crescent on the other. The 12% tin content of the bronze suggests the deliberate use of a relatively high tin content to achieve a more yellow color than the usual run of low-tin bronzes in the collection.

Decoration cut into the metal surface of artifacts is found on only one of the pins, one knife, and a bracelet. The knife (ANT.017864) has a series of transverse lines apparently cut into its stem. The silver alloy bracelet (ANT.017873) has a pattern of triangles or diamonds scribed on its surface.

SURFACE COLOR

Surface treatments intended to achieve particular surface colors are a distinctive feature of pre-Columbian Peruvian metallurgy. From Early Intermediate Horizon times onward, Peruvian artisans devoted much effort to achieving special colors on the metal objects they made. They developed techniques for applying gold to the surface of copper articles by immersion in aqueous solutions (Lechtman, Erlij, and Barry 1982). They found ways to form silver or gold surfaces on copper-base alloys

FIGURE 1.26. Surface of a bronze bar (ANT.017913) photographed with oblique illumination at original magnification 15× showing indentations left by hammerstones. Length of scale bar 1 mm.

by the depletion technique (Lechtman 1973; Lechtman, Erlij, and Barry 1982). All of the silver-copper alloy artifacts found at Machu Picchu have the silver-enriched surfaces formed by depletion of their copper-rich constituents.

Only one among the bronze or copper artifacts from Machu Picchu—the disc ANT.018480—retains evidence of applied surface coloration. In his examination of this bronze disc (Figure 1.29) (Burger and Salazar 2004:187), Rutledge (1984) found evidence that this object had been plated with silver. Since Mathewson had sectioned this disc along its centerline in his 1915 study, as can be seen in the photograph (see Figure 1.29), further examination of the microstructure was possible in 1982. The section revealed that the disc has a concave-convex shape with a greater thickness of bronze in the center than at the edges. The microstructure showed that the disc had been cast to its final shape. Since the disc is 97 mm in diameter and nowhere more than 2.5 mm thick, it illustrates the Peruvian artisans' ability to make thin castings of good quality. When examined in 1982, traces of cloth fabric were present in the corrosion product that covered the entire artifact. When some of this corrosion was cleaned from half of the disc, patches of bright metal adhering to the bronze substrate were revealed. It was possible to place the entire half-disc in the scanning electron microscope, so Rutledge was able to show that the coating is pure silver. He found no evidence of a variation in thickness of the silver from top

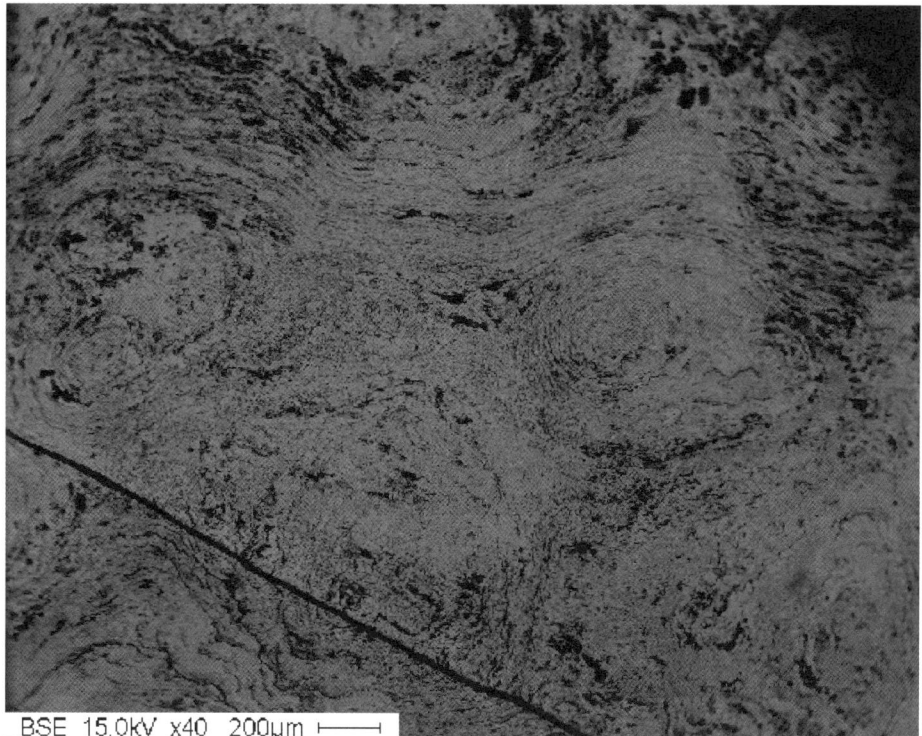

FIGURE 1.27. Microstructure of a silver alloy spangle (ANT.018400) showing the circular deformation pattern produced by hammerstone impacts. Original magnification 40×.

to bottom, such as would be expected if the disc had been dipped in molten silver. However, corrosion damage prevented seeing the finer details of the coating. It was likely applied by the method of deposition from aqueous solutions described by Lechtman, Erlij, and Barry (1982).

The silver-copper alloys developed by Peruvian artisans in the Early Intermediate period were widely used in the Middle Horizon to make artifacts of thin sheet metal. These alloys have a combination of strength and ductility well suited to hammering into thin sheets (Lechtman 1980:290–291). Heating these alloys while exposed to air, as in an annealing operation, results in preferential oxidation of the copper-rich phase at the surface. When the resulting copper oxide coating on the object is removed and the surface burnished, a silver surface color results. The depletion of copper from the surface can be further enhanced by treatment with solutions of corrosive salts. Japanese artisans used a similar technique to form a coating of pure silver on copper art objects alloyed with only 10% to 15% silver (Gowland 1910:14). The depletion technique was used to achieve the silver surface found on most of the silver alloy artifacts in the collection.

Middle Horizon artifacts have silver contents ranging from about 10% to 30% (Lechtman 1980:290; Howe and Peterson 1994). Two of the four Machu Picchu silver-copper alloy objects analyzed have substantially higher silver contents than are found

TABLE 1.18. Silver alloy sheet artifacts.

Catalog number	Item	Description
ANT.017850	Disc	This sheet metal, which may be bronze (analysis is lacking), is about 0.2 mm thick. It is thin and ductile enough to allow the disc to be folded over into a pattern of squares.
ANT.017872	Headband	Measures 658 × 37 mm, long.
ANT.017873	Bracelet	Measures 153 × 13 mm.
ANT.017875	Finger ring	A 66 × 18 mm strip bent into a circle.
ANT.017886/017888	Discs	Diameter 2.2 mm.
ANT.017897	Plate handle	Measures 48 × 15 mm, fabricated from several sheets.
ANT.018400	Dress ornament	Identified as spangles from a blouse or dress.

in the earlier artifacts. Perhaps the Inca artisans had access to more abundant supplies of silver than did their predecessors. Alternatively, they may have chosen the higher silver content to attain better surface finishes than are possible with the low-silver alloys (Gordon and Knopf 2007). The edge of a piece of laboratory-made silver-copper alloy containing 76% silver that was annealed at 625 °C for 30 minutes and then boiled in a solution of salt and 15% acetic acid for 1 hour formed a silver surface layer about 15 μ thick (Figure 1.30). The same treatment of an alloy containing only 25% silver created the porous surface layer, also about 15 μ thick (Figure 1.31).

The development of surface-depleted structures is seen in the microstructures of the headband (ANT.017872) and work piece (ANT.018449). The 3.3 mm diameter bar (ANT.018449) has the copper-rich constituent depleted to depths that range from 60 to 150 μ (Figure 1.32). The headband (ANT.017872), which has been hammered down to a thickness of 0.3 mm, has an average depletion depth of 33 μ (Figure 1.33). The anneals needed in the course of hammering out this band resulted in depletion of the copper-rich constituent to the irregular depths seen in the micrograph. Depletion of this artifact, which has a relatively low silver content, left it with a porous surface (see Figure 1.33). This would give the surface of the finished product a somewhat dull appearance similar to that found in sterling silver that has been annealed without protection from oxidation. Burnishing the surface would improve the appearance. Corrosion of the artifacts has removed evidence of any burnishing that may have been done.

Function and Use of Artifacts

For many of the artifacts in the collection, form indicates an intended function. Objects used for personal grooming—the tweezers (ANT.017893), for example—are also easily identified. Illustrations of Inca life give us additional evidence of the

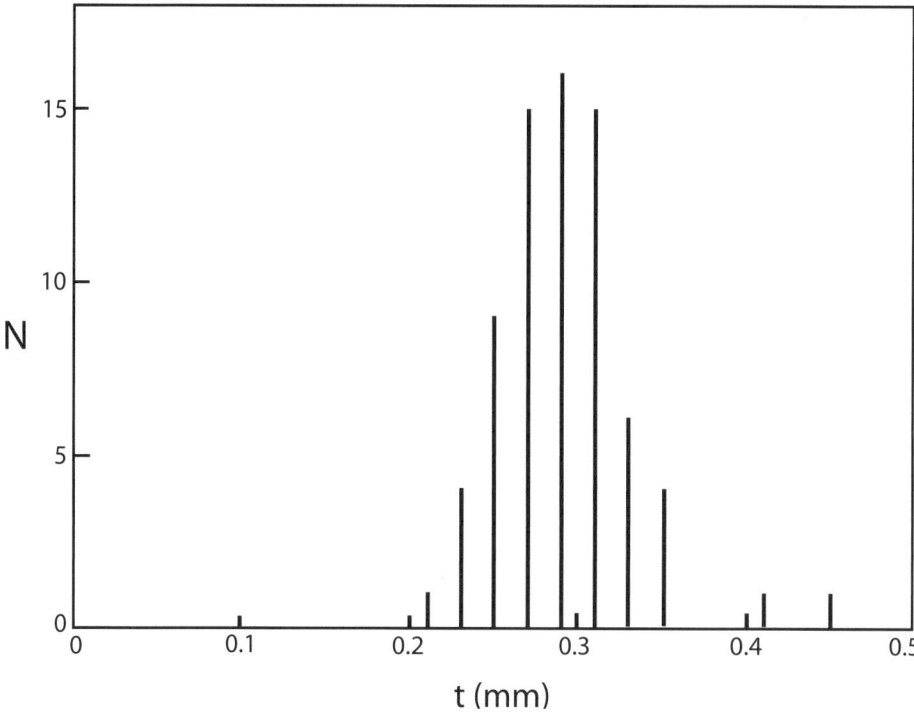

Figure 1.28. Histogram of thickness (t) measurements in millimeters along the length (N) of a silver alloy headband (ANT.017872).

intended function of many of the items. Guaman Poma's drawings, for example, show multitudes of women wearing shawl pins similar to those in the collection. In fact, most of the decorative items in the collection are easily identified.

Other items, such as the many knives, could have had either a symbolic or a utilitarian function, or both. We expect that items such as knives—if used only as symbols of power, authority, or the possession of particular skills by their owners—would be free of evidence of actual use. Nor would we expect artisans to go to the trouble of strain-hardening their edges. Not enough knives in the collection were studied in the laboratory to find conclusive evidence of their possible use as tools. However, the many axes and chisels found at Machu Picchu do carry such evidence.

Tool Design

Although tools made of stone can be used for cutting wood, they cannot easily be used for cutting or splitting tasks that require sustaining the impact of a hammer. Bronze with the tin content commonly found at Machu Picchu could be strain-hardened to a level greater than that of carbon-free iron, making it a useful material for woodworkers' cutting tools. The toughness of bronze makes it suitable for tools needed in fine stonework not easily accomplished with hammerstones, such as shaping deep recesses or sharp interior corners.

Figure 1.29. Bronze disc (ANT.018480), 97 × 80 mm. Photographed in 1982. Length of scale bar 1 cm.

The "T" axes are the largest single category of tool found at Machu Picchu. These may have had ritual or symbolic significance elsewhere, but the ones found at Machu Picchu were actually used as artisan's tools. The "T" shape suggests two alternative ways of using the tool. A worker intending to fell a tree could attach the axe to a handle with lashings passing around the crossbar. Alternatively, the blade could be held with one hand and pounded on with a hammerstone held in the user's other hand. The crossbar then aids the grip and protects the worker's fingers from misdirected blows by the hammer. The design is not unique to the Inca. Axes of similar design intended for use as cutting tools have been found in pre-Roman contexts in Egypt (Eaton 1912; Carpenter and Robertson 1930).

Shaping and fitting stone blocks was a major task for workers at Machu Picchu. Artisans selected blocks of granite of the desired size from the jumble of rock debris left by landslides and rockfalls at the quarry south of the Sacred Plaza (Wright and Zegarra 2000:70–71). Bronze pry bars would have been useful in exploiting the natural joints commonly present in this granite. Protzen (1985, 1986) has demonstrated how a set of hammerstones weighing from 0.5 to 10 kg make effective tools for shaping the flat surfaces and corners on granite blocks favored by the Inca masons. Small cracks that radiate from the point of impact of the rounded, blunt end of a hammerstone cause small bits of rock debris to flake off at each blow. The stone must be swung through an arc of about a third of a meter to achieve the requisite impact. The technique works well on the large, nearly flat surfaces that predominate in Inca stone construction. However, the blunt end of a hammerstone would not allow an artisan to cut a deep, narrow recess or a cylindrical hole in granite. While not numerous, there are examples of such features at Machu Picchu and elsewhere at Inca sites. A stone block intended for the water distribution system at Machu Picchu has a thin, curved channel (Wright and Zegarra 2000:35) that would have been difficult or impossible to cut with hammerstones alone. Thin slits and cylindrical holes in rhyolite found at Ollantaytambo (Protzen 1993) and the bas-reliefs found on a wall in Cuzco (Menotti 1998:67) could best be made by pounding or abrading with metal tools. In the absence of iron, only bronze would have the requisite toughness for a slender tool that could reach these recesses and re-entrants. Menotti (1998:31) quotes evidence presented by Heffernen and Zanabria of the use of bronze tools by Inca quarrymen and masons.

Evidence of Tool Use

The shape of a tool can suggest the task it was intended for. The blade of an axe (ANT.017898) has a slender profile (Figure 1.34) approximating that of a modern woodsman's axe. Since this cutting edge has been strain-hardened, it would be an effective tool for felling trees. The blunt edges of other "T" axes found at Machu Picchu would make them useless as tools for cutting wood or other soft materials, but effective in chipping rock. Evidence of this use can be found on tool surfaces and in the microstructures (Gordon 1985).

The impact of a bronze tool on a stone surface can leave an impression of the hard stone in the ductile metal. Thus, the indentations and striations on the working edge of axe ANT.017902 show that it has been pounded against a rough stone surface (Figure 1.35). Motion of a tool over the surface of a work piece can leave the characteristic surface markings formed as a hard material removes chips from the metal. These markings could arise from the use of a chisel in splitting stone, or by an artisan sharpening an edge of the tool by rubbing it against stone. The striations on the edge of the chisel ANT.017975 (Figure 1.36) probably arose this way, since the profile of this working edge (Figure 1.37) shows that metal was removed in a sharpening operation.

The metal microstructures of several of the tools record evidence of deformation caused by pounding on the tool with a hammerstone, or by impact of the working edge of the tool with hard material. There was deformation of the metal at the top surfaces of several of the axes and chisels (Figure 1.38). Working edges deformed (Figure 1.39) and damaged (Figure 1.40) are present. Evidence of use in heavy work is found in 11 of the 12 edge tools other than knives in the collection (Table 1.19).

FIGURE 1.30. Alloy of copper plus 76% silver heated in air to 625 °C for 30 minutes and then boiled in a solution of salt in 15% acetic acid for 60 minutes. A dense layer of silver has formed on the surface. Original magnification 700×. Length of scale bar 0.06 mm.

Among the axes and chisels only the celt-like object (ANT.017908) lacks evidence of heavy use. The few indentations in its blade could have resulted from domestic activities, such as food preparation. The absence of tin alloying would make it less useful than bronze tools for heavy work. Among the other items in this class, the axe (ANT.017898) and the chisel (ANT.017975) were probably used for cutting and splitting wood. The somewhat clumsy-looking axe (ANT.017899) could have been used for some relatively light task, perhaps butchering. The chisels (ANT.017964 and ANT.017966) were probably used for splitting stone. The most common use recorded on the tools themselves, however, is stone dressing by impact.

Since we lack information on the recovery rate of metal artifacts at Machu Picchu, we cannot judge how pervasive the use of metal was among the artisans and retainers whose possessions the collection appears to sample. The small variety of items, however, suggests a rather limited presence of metal in the material culture of Machu Picchu, where the most common materials were stone and ceramics.

Significance of the Collection

Andean Metallurgy before Machu Picchu

In the late eighteenth century Danish archaeologist Christian Thomsen proposed the concept of a Copper Age, three successive Bronze Ages, and an Iron Age to describe the sequence in which people made and used metals in northern Europe. As subsequent scholars found evidence for a similar sequence in southwest Asia, they began to see Thomsen's sequence as universal and as a consequence of the technological

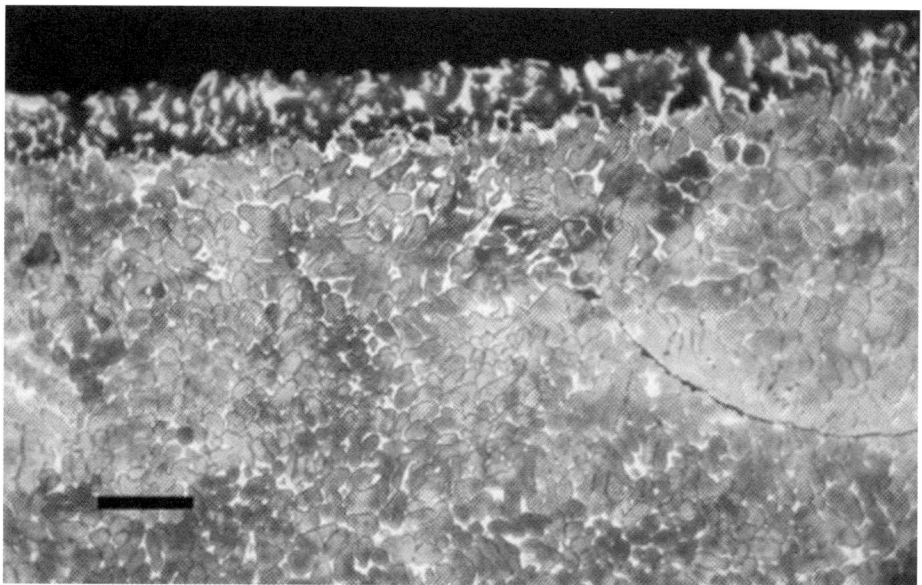

FIGURE 1.31. Alloy of copper plus 25% silver heated in air to 625 °C for 30 minutes and then boiled in a solution of salt in 15% acetic acid for 60 minutes. The silver layer that formed on the surface is porous. Original magnification 700×. Length of scale bar 0.03 mm.

difficulties that had to be overcome to advance from one stage to the next. Archaeologists and historians of technology embraced this concept, based on technological determinism, as the "Standard Model," applicable to a wider range of human experience with technology than just metallurgy. Research on the history of metallurgy in sub-Saharan Africa and South America, most done in the last third of the twentieth century, led scholars to realize that the Standard Model is not universal. Anthropologists found that in Africa copper smelting was not a necessary precondition for iron smelting. In South America, they found that the peoples of the Andes gained much expertise with gold and silver before shifting to the extensive use of copper. Unlike people in nearly all cultures in the Old World, the South Americans never smelted iron. The differences between Old and New World metallurgies, as reviewed by Lechtman (1980) and others, helped reveal the limitations of the concept of technological determinism that dominated early scholarship in the history of technology.

Anthropologists and archaeologists divide the chronology of the central Andes into three episodes of cultural integration, the Early, Middle, and Late Horizons, separated by two Intermediate periods. The approximate dates of these successive episodes of history are as follows:

—Late Horizon, AD 1476–1534;
—Late Intermediate period, AD 1000–1476;
—Middle Horizon, AD 600–1000;
—Early Intermediate period, 200 BC–AD 600;
—Early Horizon, 1000–200 BC; and
—Initial period, 1800–1000 BC.

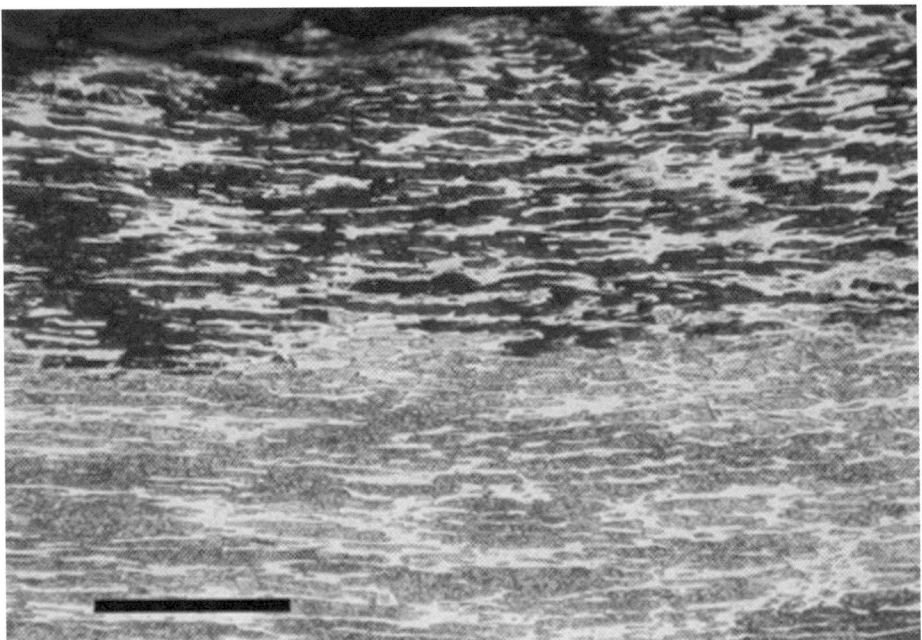

Figure 1.32. Edge of artifact ANT.018449 showing depletion of copper at the surface. The ferric chloride etch darkens the copper-rich phase. Original magnification 300×. Length of scale bar 0.1 mm. See also Plate 11.

Archaeologists have traced the use of metals in Peru back as far as about 1500 to 1400 BC. The evidence of the earliest use of metal by Andean people includes a goldsmith's set of stone tools found with some remnants of gold (Grossman 1972) and clay molds for casting artifacts (Rehren and Temme 1994). In the Old World, people gained their earliest experience with metals by collecting and shaping native copper. In South America the earliest evidence for the use of native copper is from about 1200 to 1090 BC (Burger and Gordon 1998). Thus, unlike the experience in the Old World, use of copper followed that of gold in South America. In middle Early Horizon times, perhaps around 500 BC, artisans in northern Bolivia began smelting copper (Lechtman 1980:280). Thereafter mining and smelting copper spread through the central highlands of Peru and became widespread in the years between about 200 BC and AD 1. Initially artisans made ornamental objects from copper. Later they began supplying people with copper for chisels, needles, spindle whorls, and occasionally for weapons.

The Chavín, the first widespread, organized civilization in the central Andes, made the production and display of gold artifacts an important way of demonstrating the power of its religious and political elite. From about 800 to 400 BC, Chavín people spread the use of gold throughout their area of influence. The Chavín artisans hammered gold into thin sheets that they then shaped into ceremonial and religious symbols (Burger 1996). Because gold occurs only as a native metal, Chavín artisans did not need smelting technology for this task. They used the high

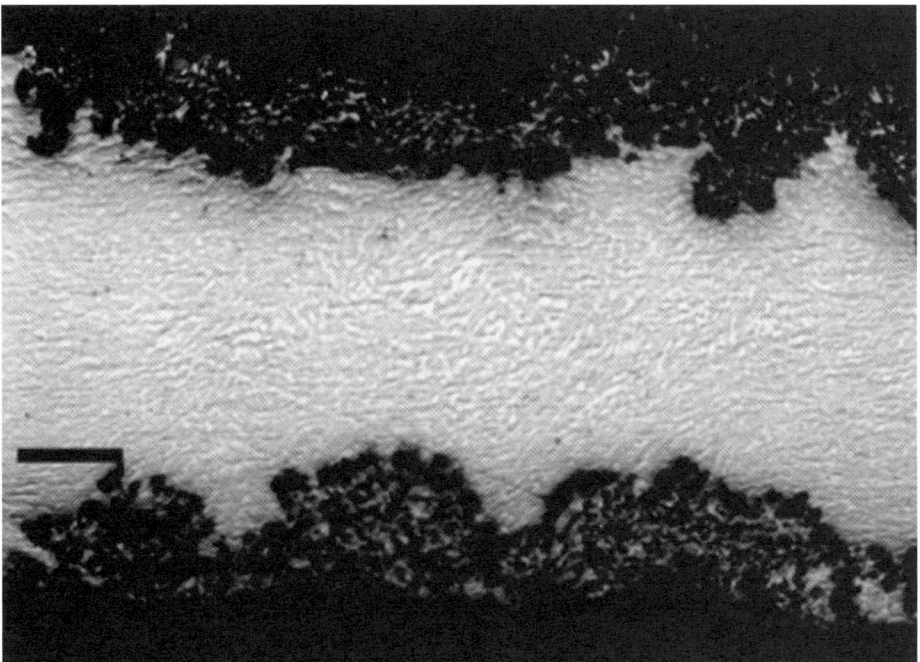

Figure 1.33. Oblique cross section of a silver headband (ANT.017872) showing the surface depletion layer. Unetched; original magnification 70×. Length of scale bar 0.2 mm.

ductility of gold to hammer placer nuggets into thin sheets that they could then raise or emboss with stone tools. By about 400 BC Chavín artisans had perfected techniques for joining thin sheets of gold alloys to make three-dimensional objects (Lechtman 1980:279). Since they worked with gold-silver-copper alloys that had to be formulated by melting the constituent metals, we know that they had learned to make crucibles that could withstand temperatures as high as the 1100 °C needed to melt these metals. They also had learned how to apply forced draft to charcoal fires to attain high temperatures. Chavín artisans apparently formulated alloys with successively lower melting points to use as solders for joining complex sheet metal components (Burger 1996). Thus, their skills probably included, in addition to smithing with stone tools, the capacity to formulate alloys for desired melting temperatures and colors. To date, we lack evidence of the source of the silver they used in making these alloys. However, since sources of native silver were not abundant in the Andes, smiths may have learned the art of smelting silver minerals.

Through the Early Intermediate period artisans of the Mochica culture in northern Peru added new metallurgical techniques, using copper, to those based primarily on gold, silver, and thin sheet metal inherited from earlier times. They began making castings with open stone molds and, later, by the lost-wax technique. Mochica artisans created a technique for forming a thin plating of silver or gold by deposition from aqueous solutions on objects made of sheet copper. They alloyed copper with silver to achieve a higher strength in the objects they made of sheet

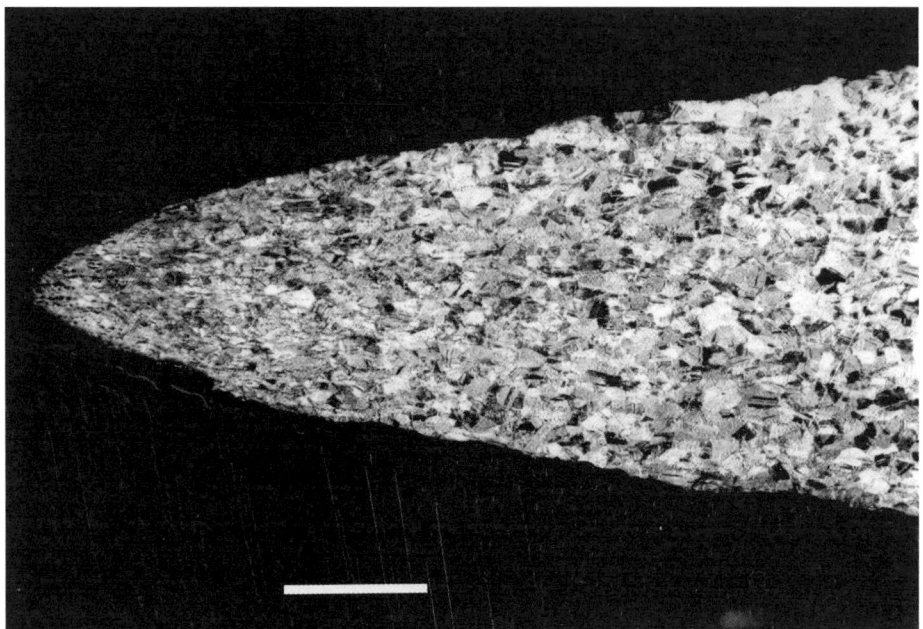

FIGURE 1.34. Section of the tip of an axe (ANT.017898) showing that it is slender enough to cut wood. Ferric chloride etch; original magnification 15×. Length of scale bar 1 mm.

metal, and to attain the colors they wanted on the surfaces of their products. They found that annealing an artifact made of copper-silver alloy resulted in depletion of copper from the artifact's surface, leaving a finished object that seemed to be made of silver when in fact it was an alloy with only modest silver content. They enlarged their use of the depletion technique to alloys of gold and silver, and of gold, silver, and copper, known as *tumbaga*, thereby creating a thin layer of gold on the surface of artifacts (Lechtman 1973; Lechtman, Erlij, and Barry 1982).

As in earlier times, prestige goods made of sheet metal were the dominant products of the Mochica artisans. By the Late Intermediate period, after about AD 1000, in the region of northern Peru controlled by the Chimú culture, artisans adopted a new alloy, copper deliberately combined with a few percent arsenic (Lechtman 1996a). (The presence of about 1% or less arsenic is generally considered accidental, the result of smelting copper ores that contained arsenic minerals as an impurity.) Arsenic-bearing ores were easily available in northern Peru and, alloyed with copper, made a material with sufficient strength to be useful in tools such as hoes, chisels, and spear points (Lechtman 1996a). Also during this period, the Chimú artisans learned how to smelt the much more abundant sulfide ores of copper found in the highlands in place of the less abundant oxide ores used by predecessors.

The increased scale of copper production combined with the technique of alloying for strength in the Late Intermediate period created the possibility of including metal implements in the materials of everyday life in northern Peru. Evidence

Figure 1.35. Edge of an axe (ANT.017902) showing indentations and striations caused by contact with stone. Original magnification 15×. Length of scale bar is 1 mm.

from a site in the Upper Mantaro Valley shows that the Wanka used lead smelted from lead ores to make utilitarian objects such as bolas (Costin et al. 1989:127) and silver-copper alloys hammered into thin sheet usually containing 10% to 30% copper. The silver contained 0.2% to 0.7% lead. Howe and Peterson (1994) interpret this as evidence that the silver was produced by the use of lead as a solvent in the smelting of impure silver ore followed by cupellation.

Field evidence of copper smelting techniques is sparse throughout the Andes, perhaps in part because frequent earthquakes and landslides in this geomorphically active region make poor conditions for the preservation of remains and structures. The most detailed information on smelting methods is from the Batán Grande site in north coastal Peru, where archaeologists have been able to recover furnace remains spanning the years from about AD 850 to 1532 (Shimada, Epstein, and Craig, 1982; Shimada 1994). The artisans here used the prill smelting technique. Copper metal formed as droplets in the semimolten slag in the smelting furnace. Smelters used the hammerstones, which archaeologists have found in abundance at the furnace sites, to break up the cold slag to release the copper prills. They then melted the prills in crucibles to get ingots of metal to work with.

We know less about the metallurgical history of the southern Andes than about the north. Abundant mineralization along the tin belt stretching south from

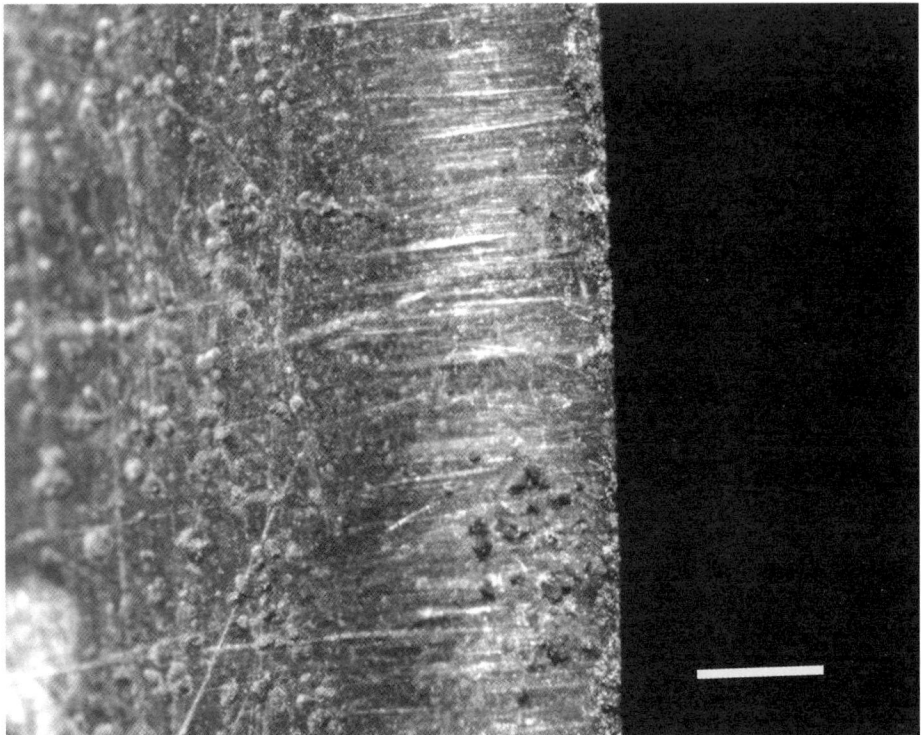

FIGURE 1.36. Edge of a chisel (ANT.017975) showing striations cut perpendicular to the edge. Original magnification 15×. Length of scale bar 1 mm.

the vicinity of Lake Titicaca to northwest Argentina had the potential to yield antimony, bismuth, lead, silver, and tin. The *huayrachina* or *guairas*, a distinctive shaft furnace perforated to admit air driven by the wind, was used by native artisans in Bolivia during Colonial times (Barba 1923:199). These furnaces were probably of indigenous origin, and have recently been studied in detail with the aid of archaeological evidence (Van Buren and Mills 2005). The copper-nickel-arsenic alloys used for cramps to secure stonework at Tiawanaku are evidence of metallurgical experimentation and innovation by artisans in the southern Andes by about AD 500 (Lechtman 1998). By about AD 800 they used tin bronze for most of their metal products (Lechtman 2003). Dated horizons in cores taken from a lake near Potosi suggest that large-scale production of silver and tin was under way there in the years around AD 1100 (Abbott and Wolfe 2003). For as long as bronze was used in the southern Andes, tin was the preferred alloying element. While artisans made arsenic bronze by co-smelting copper and arsenic minerals, they could make tin bronze by adding previously smelted tin to copper. Metallic tin could be carried about more easily than could tin minerals or tin ore. With a supply of tin delivered to them, artisans could formulate bronze alloys wherever copper and fuel were available. Properties comparable to, or in some cases better than, those of copper-arsenic alloys could be attained with tin as the alloying element.

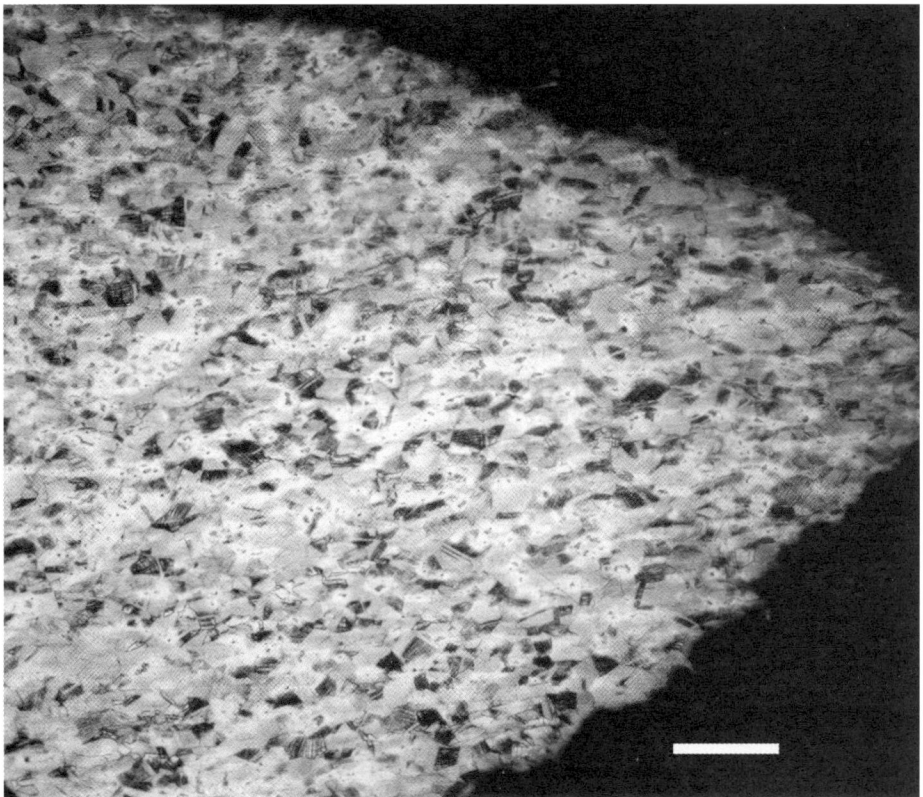

Figure 1.37. Cross section of the tip of a chisel (ANT.017975). There is no evidence that the tip was forged to shape. Instead, the surface cuts across structural features, indicating removal of metal by sharpening, as by rubbing on a rough stone surface. Ferric chloride etch; original magnification 50×. Length of scale bar 02 mm. See also Plates 7 and 8.

As the Inca established their empire in the fifteenth century, they incorporated peoples who participated in both the northern and southern Andean metallurgical traditions. The artifacts found at Machu Picchu represent both traditions. The silver-copper alloys with surface depletion coloring are from the northern tradition, while the exclusive use of tin bronze (in preference to northern-style copper-arsenic alloy) is an adoption of a southern technology. The Inca increased the scale of metal production beyond anything previously seen in the Andes. Lake cores record a second peak of tin and silver production near Potosi after the time of the Inca conquest (Abbott and Wolfe 2003). Lechtman (1980:315) has suggested that tin bronze may have been a state-imposed alloy choice intended to unify the diverse cultural groups conquered by the Inca. Control of tin production in Bolivia would have made this possible. The Inca increased metal production throughout their empire, but they added no new metallurgical techniques. One is reminded of the Romans, who drew on the metallurgical expertise of the territories they occupied, and organized it to increase the scale of metal production using existing techniques with little further innovation (Tylecote 1976:53).

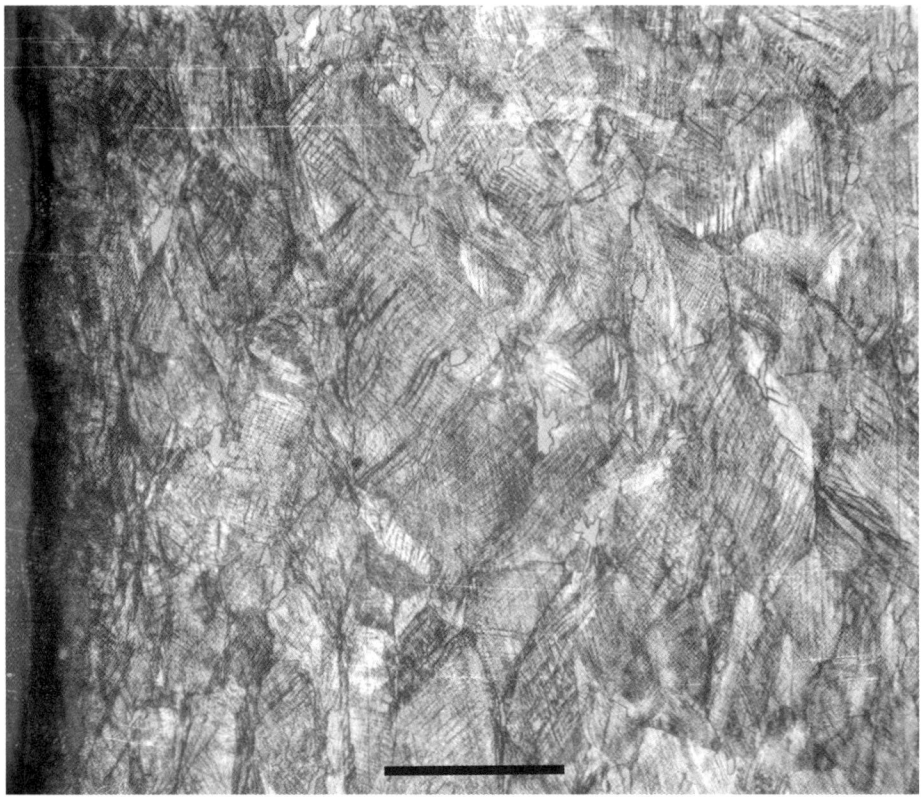

Figure 1.38. Section of the top surface of a chisel (ANT.017907). The heavy deformation decreasing in intensity downward shows that the chisel was hammered on in use. Ferric chloride etch; original magnification 200×. Length of scale bar 0.1 mm.

Skills and Innovation

The artifacts recovered at Machu Picchu are not high art or high-value prestige items. Their significance lies primarily in what they can tell us about the products supplied to the artisans and retainers who staffed Machu Picchu (Salazar 2007), and about the range of skills the Inca metalsmiths used to make these products.

The Machu Picchu metalsmiths had good-quality raw materials with which to formulate their alloys. The tin found at the site has purity greater than 99% (see Table 1.9). We must evaluate the quality of the copper and silver stock they used based on the purity of the alloys they made with it. Sulfur was the only impurity in the copper used at Machu Picchu that might have impaired the quality of bronze made there. The control of composition attained by the Inca artisans in formulating their bronze was sufficient to yield a generally uniform color and allowed them to increase the proportion of tin to get distinctive color when they wanted to make items for display. We lack enough analyses of the silver artifacts to be able to evaluate the composition control attained by the makers of these alloys, or to decide whether they intended to attain particular compositions.

FIGURE 1.39. Section of the tip of a broken axe blade (ANT.017969). The presence of twin bands shows that the bronze was forged and annealed. The deformation was light, because the sulfide inclusions are not deformed. Later use of the axe caused strain lines in the recrystallized grains. Ferric chloride etch; original magnification 200×. Length of scale bar 0.1 mm.

The artifacts from Machu Picchu show us that the Inca metalworkers had the basic skills of forging and annealing in hand. They also show that the Inca artisans had developed some particular techniques for shaping metals by hammering, as in the thin sheets of bronze and silver-copper alloy they made with nearly uniform thickness (see Figure 1.28). These techniques represent the accumulation of skills Peruvian artisans developed over a thousand years of experience with sheet metal work. Their understanding of functional design as well as their skills in fabrication are evident in the many tweezers (such as ANT.017893) found at Machu Picchu.

The Inca artisans at Machu Picchu were still learning the full range of casting skills needed for their work. To successfully cast bronze products, metalworkers needed to select mold materials and design molds with gates and risers that would allow proper filling of the mold cavity and the escape of gas released during solidification. The risers had to provide the reserve of liquid needed to compensate for shrinkage as the metal cooled. Once the mold was ready and the alloy melted in its crucible, the founder had to judge when the temperature of the molten metal was

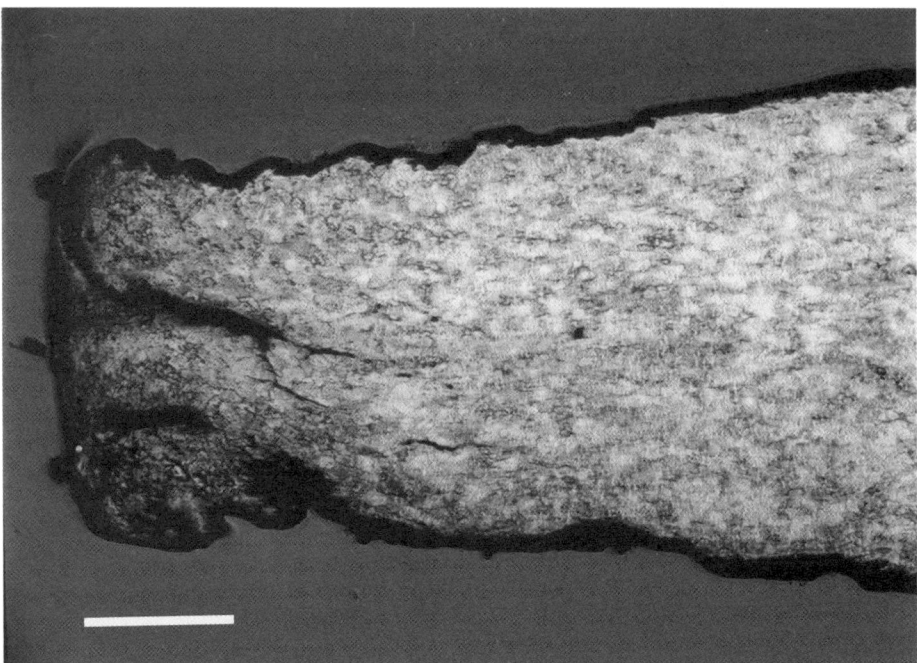

Figure 1.40. Section of the tip of an axe (ANT.017900) showing its blunt point and damage from heavy use. Ferric chloride etch; original magnification 15×. Length of scale bar 1 mm.

correct for pouring. It had to be hot enough to fill out a mold when poured without solidifying prematurely, but not so hot as to result in excess oxidation of the liquid. As an artisan poured the casting, he had to either remove any dross that formed on the metal on melting or keep the dross from being carried into the mold with the metal.

Many examples, such as the bird-head lime spoon (ANT.017970) and the cast-in recess with a crossbar in the ball (ANT.017965), show that the Inca artisans had mastered the art of molding to create intricate shapes. The collection of finished artifacts cannot tell us about the success rate in making these castings, since defective items could simply be remelted. Only one example of a misrun was found among the artifacts examined (see Figure 1.16). We have seen (in the discussion "Casting Problems and Difficulties" above) that the Machu Picchu artisans had not fully mastered the skills needed to pour large castings free of porosity, with the result that many had deficient strength properties. Making tools for artisans' work also seems to be a relatively new addition to the work of Inca metallurgical artisans. Lack of experience in making these tools is reflected in their poor metal quality.

The abundant shawl pins and arc-like tumi knives in the collection reflect routine production of common articles. Yet the Inca artisans serving Machu Picchu also had the opportunity for some innovation in addition to routine production. Some of this experimentation was directed toward attaining decorative coloring by alloying, such as the use of high tin content to achieve a more gold-like color in bronze articles. The addition of bismuth to the bronze cap on the llama-head knife (ANT.017962) can be interpreted as an experiment with coloration. Perhaps it was made very late in the history of Machu Picchu so that there was not opportunity for further exploitation of the success attained.

Machu Picchu Metallurgy in Context
Nearly all the metal artifacts found at Machu Picchu are plain, unadorned items for use in everyday life. They are not ceremonial or ritual objects and may have had only limited symbolic significance for their owners. The plebian character of the artifacts, and the absence of gold, suggests that metal goods were made for the artisans, retainers, and others who staffed Machu Picchu more or less permanently to provide food and services when the members of the royal household were in residence (Salazar 2004). The large-scale production and abundance of shawl pins and tumi knives shows that by Inca times metal, including silver, was sufficiently abundant that ownership of metal goods was no longer the province of the rich and powerful members of Inca society. While the metalworkers at Machu Picchu made utilitarian products for the artisans and retainers, they probably made high-value products for the royal and religious elite owners of the estate to use or to present as gifts to visitors. However, we lack direct evidence, since their owners left none of these high-quality products at Machu Picchu.

The metallurgical techniques practiced at Machu Picchu represent the culmination of 3,000 years of experience with the use of the metal resources of the Andean region. The metal artifacts found there show how the Inca selected some components of the earlier Andean metallurgical heritage for their own use and rejected others. They adopted the silver-base alloys developed in northern Peru, but with a richer silver content. They chose the copper-tin bronze that artisans in the south had pioneered, and rejected the copper-arsenic alloys used in the north. Lechtman (1980) has suggested that the exclusive use of tin bronze in Inca-controlled regions of the Andes is evidence of the imposition of tin as the alloying element of choice by the central authority of the empire (Lechtman 1980). Few lead artifacts were found at Machu Picchu even though lead had been used in Peru since AD 100 (Costin et al. 1989:127; Howe and Peterson 1994).

The artifacts found at Machu Picchu show that Inca artisans had moved away from the well-established north Andean methods of making items by hammering out sheet and then using the sheet stock to fabricate shapes by joining techniques such as crimping and soldering. Nearly all the artifacts found had first been cast to near final form and then finished by the forging methods that had been the mainstay of Andean metallurgy since its beginning. The Machu Picchu artisans reduced the amount of labor needed to make shawl pins and tumi knives by adopting casting technology. Yet these artisans continued to do some forging on cast products that did not need, or gain in quality, from this treatment, perhaps because of a metallurgical tradition or beliefs we do not know about.

TABLE 1.19. Evidence of tool use.

Catalog number	Item	Description
ANT.017898	"T" axe	This tool is heavily indented on its top surface, with strain lines in the microstructure, as from pounding with hammerstones. The tip of the tool has been work-hardened to an HV of 255 and is sufficiently sharp to cut wood. It is interpreted as a tool used for felling or shaping timber. (See also Appendix A.)
ANT.017899	"T" axe	Indentations on the top surface and deformation marking in the metal beneath show that this tool was pounded on. Striations on the edge suggest sharpening. The low alloy content and clumsy shape suggest unsuitability for heavy work. It might have been used in butchering. (See also Appendix A.)
ANT.017900	"T" axe	The piece broken out of the corner of the blade indicates heavy use in which the blade was twisted. Indentations on the top show it was pounded on. The blunt working edge has an HV of 255. Burrs have been turned over at the edge and deep striations show that there was sliding contact with a rough, hard surface, such as freshly split rock. Cracks extending into the metal have been initiated at the edge. It is interpreted as used for dressing stone. (See also Appendix A.)
ANT.017902	"T" axe	The top surface is depressed and indented by hammer blows, as are the ends of the crossbar, which seem to have been used for hammering. The blunt edge is heavily indented and one section was about ready to break off the last time the tool was used. This axe was used for heavy pounding without penetration of the work piece, as in dressing stone. (See also Appendix A.)
ANT.017904	Axe or knife	The indented and broken blade (see Figure 1.18) indicates use in hard work.
ANT.017907	Chisel	The top surface is heavily indented by hammer blows, some of which have produced lateral flow. Dense strain lines in the metal below the top surface confirm this usage. The cutting edge has been blunted by use against hard materials. (See also Appendix A.)
ANT.017964	Chisel	The blade of this chisel has been heavily damaged by use with burrs turned over and deep cracks initiated in the metal. The heavy damage and striations suggest use in splitting stone. (See also Appendix A.)
ANT.017966	Chisel	This tool is broken off above the tip and twisted. Deep gouges on the surface show sliding contact with rock. It is interpreted as used for splitting stone with penetration of the blade into the stone. A badly directed hammer blow applied to the inserted blade could have broken off the now missing top. (See also Appendix A.)
ANT.017967	"T" axe	The broken blade and hammer marks on the crossbar indicates hard use.

TABLE 1.19 CONTINUED.

Catalog number	Item	Description
ANT.017969	Axe blade	This is probably the bottom part of a "T" axe that was broken in use. Deep striations on the surface show sliding contact with a rough material. There are dense strain lines in the metal at the tip, which, while having been sharpened against stone, retains a blunt end. This tool was used for splitting or dressing stone. (See also Appendix A.)
ANT.017974	Axe blade	This is the tip broken off an axe blade. Mathewson concluded it had been used in working stone, but the evidence of use is slight. Casting defects caused this blade to break after limited use. (See also Appendix A.)
ANT.017975	Chisel	The top of this chisel has been broken off and is missing. The edge has been sharpened by rubbing on stone. Strain lines in the metal near the tip are sparse. Fine striations on the sides suggest use in splitting wood. (See also Appendix A.)

The Machu Picchu metalsmiths mastered the art of making small, intricate castings, and could cast blanks that they could then forge into relatively simple shapes. The abundance of bronze allowed them to begin making artisans' tools, which required much more metal than the domestic items. Inca masons and artisans were discovering new tasks they could undertake with these tools. The Inca were moving the use of metals from the symbolic and ritual sphere to the workaday realm of life at Machu Picchu. The metalworkers had successfully made small, decorative castings and blanks they could forge into household or decorative items. The demand for metal tools challenged them to learn the art of making large castings with the strength properties needed in a tool or weapon intended for hard use. They had not yet mastered this art at the time Machu Picchu was abandoned. The strength of the tools they made was undermined by gross porosity in their castings. The bronze crowbar found at Machu Picchu had a tensile strength of 192 MPa and an elongation of 6% (Mathewson 1915). Soundly cast bronze of the same composition would have had a tensile strength to 320 MPa and an elongation of 67% (Cook and Tallis 1941). The porosity in the casting reduced the strength and greatly diminished the ductility of the metal; this crowbar would have needed gentle handling by the artisan who used it.

Artisans in Bronze Age Europe, Britain, and Ireland cast flat axes nearly identical to those made 2,700 years later at Machu Picchu (such as axe ANT.017908). These artisans cast axes, chisels, halberds, spearheads, rapiers, dirks, and palstaves. They used higher tin content (8% to 12%) than the Inca artisans, forged their products more extensively, and, after annealing, usually strain-hardened the cutting edges. Inca artisans made little use of the strain-hardening properties of bronze in their tools. By the Late Bronze Age, European artisans generally included up to

8% to 10% lead in the tin-bronze alloys they used for casting (Allen, Britton, and Coghlan 1970), an innovation not seen in the Andes. Partly because lead facilitates making sound castings, the quality of the metal in the British and Irish Late Bronze Age castings was generally sound and free of the excess porosity common in the Machu Picchu bronzes. Nor did Andean artisans adopt two other metallurgical techniques practiced much earlier by peoples throughout the Old World: they did not smelt iron, and they did not use bellows to provide draft to their furnaces. Rehder (1994) has suggested that these factors may be related: as long as artisans used only blowpipes, they could not attain the furnace temperatures needed to smelt iron.

Compared to the uses made of metals in the Old World through medieval and renaissance times, metals had a rather limited place in the pre-Columbian culture of western South America (Lechtman 1980, 1984). The elite of successive cultures of this region, culminating with the Inca, used gold and silver in alloys with copper as symbols of their power and prestige. Utilitarian use of metals, as in the cramps for stonework at Tiawanaku or as tools at Machu Picchu, was infrequent and on a small scale. Consequently, exploitation of the rich mineral resources of the Andes was light in comparison with the intense mining and smelting activities characteristic of the following Colonial years. Not only was the quantity of metal produced small in relation to the population, it was restricted to a relatively narrow range of activities. The variety of artifacts made in the Andes was small compared to the range and quantity of metal products used in pre-industrial Old World contexts, even in Africa. The lack of iron, the peoples' metal in the Old World because of its abundance and cheapness relative to the nonferrous metals, foreclosed widespread use of metal implements and tools among Inca workers and agriculturalists. However, the Spanish miners, smelters, and artisans who followed Pizarro found much that was useful in the mining, milling, and smelting techniques practiced by the Inca whom they conquered.

The Spaniards' preoccupation with precious metals led them, after they confiscated the gold and silver held by the Inca elite, to undertake silver production with the mining and smelting methods used by the Inca artisans. Because we have few records and little archaeological evidence of Inca smelting methods, early Colonial records are a useful source of information on how Inca metallurgists made their primary materials.

Spanish colonists set Indians from the Inca mines and smelters at Porco, Bolivia, to work mining silver-lead ores from the huge volcanic stock at Potosi in 1545. They used fire-setting to fracture the rock of the silver veins, and then dug out the ore with tools of stone, hard wood, horn, copper, and bronze. After crushing the ore with rocking stones, the Inca artisans diverted water from streams to wash the lighter-gauge minerals away from the heavier silver ore. In the absence of furnaces provided with bellows to supply the needed forced-air draft, the principal furnace used in the Inca smelting technique was a 2 m high, wind-blown shaft furnace—the *guayra* or *huayrachina*—placed on a hillside exposed to the prevailing wind. This furnace produced a silver-lead alloy. The Inca artisans placed this alloy in perforated crucibles (also known as "muffles") that they heated in small furnaces, about 0.8 m in diameter, where the forced draft was supplied by blowpipes. In this furnace the lead was oxidized, as in the European process of cupellation, leaving fairly pure silver as the end product. To implement these processes, the Spanish colonists simply took over the artisans retained by the Inca elite and the Inca system of tribute labor to operate their metal production. Only after 35 years did they supplant the Inca system of extracting silver with the amalgamation technique used in Spain (Bakewell 1984).

Archaeological evidence of the merging of Indian and Spanish extraction techniques has been found in the province of La Paz, Bolivia, where production of silver continued to 1781. Remains of the ore concentrating plant and its water supply system survive here. The initial crushing of the ore was done with the *arrastra*. It has a 2 m diameter circular, paved track set in the ground with a socket for a central, vertical shaft that carried an arm from which drag stones were hung by chains. As mules dragged the arm around its circular path, the dependent stones ground the ore in a slurry of water. Amalgamation, the European extraction technique, was accomplished with the *quimbelate*, a crushing device similar to a mortar and pestle that used a rounded roller rocked back and forth in a mating cavity cut in stone (Mackay 1995).

Acknowledgments

Following an initiative by David Killick and Richard Burger, John W. Rutledge carried out the initial examination and cataloguing of the collection from 1982 to 1985. Killick assisted with the metallographic examination of selected artifacts. Alan Pooley determined composition with the semiquantitative analysis system installed in the Yale Peabody Museum of Natural History electron microscope at that time.

Robert Knopf prepared the metallographic specimens used in the 2004–2005 reexamination of certain artifacts, and carried out trials with reproduction alloys to determine the properties of the materials used by the artisans who made the objects the Yale expeditions collected. Heather Galli contributed her remarkable metallographic skills to the preparation of selected specimens for microphotography. James Eckert made the new microprobe analyses. Richard Guidoboni at the Northern Analytical Laboratory generously donated a glow discharge mass spectrometry analysis for trace elements in one of the bronze tools. Roger Colten, senior collections manager at the Yale Peabody Museum, undertook responsibility for locating and identifying specimens in the collection. Yuichi Matsumoto assisted in identifying photographs and reviewing the manuscript. Jason Nesbitt helped with the images and provided citations to recent research. Critical reading of the manuscript by an anonymous reviewer and by Bruce Owen was particularly helpful. Nevertheless, some unresolved issues of interpretation remain for future researchers to tackle.

Special thanks are due Richard Burger and Lucy Salazar for the assistance and guidance they have provided throughout the project.

SECTION TWO

The Meanings of Metals:
The Inca and Regional Contexts of Quotidian Metals from Machu Picchu

Bruce D. Owen

Fancy metal objects in the Inca world conveyed specific meanings about rank, office, and affiliation with the Inca state. It was so typical of nobles to wear showy earspools, often of gold or silver, that the Spanish *conquistadores* referred to this upper class as *orejones* ("big ears") (Guaman Poma 1615; Garcilaso de la Vega 1961:13; Cobo 1983:208). Inca diplomats used and strategically distributed silver and gold drinking vessels as political gifts that symbolized imperial support and local allegiance (Cieza de León 1959:157; Garcilaso de la Vega 1961:91, 152, 184; Cobo 1983:246–247; DeMarrais, Castillo, and Earle 1996; Cummins 2007). Rare and distinctive cast *yauri* pikes may have been insignia of specific high offices (Larrea 1941; Lechtman 2007), as were various sheet metal headdress ornaments (Guaman Poma 1615; Cobo 1983:245–246).

These sorts of objects are not found at the royal country estate of Machu Picchu. They would have returned to Cuzco with their visiting elite owners (Salazar 2004:44–46). Such objects are exceptional finds at any site. But what about the far more numerous, more quotidian metal artifacts of the "silent majority" (Salazar 2007) of the less elite who populated the Inca empire? Most or all of the population that we can detect archaeologically at Machu Picchu were *yanacona*, or retainers, drawn from multiple distant regions recently conquered by Machu Picchu's builder, Pachacuti Inca Yupanqui (Salazar 2001, 2004, 2007; Burger 2004). Their metal objects communicated meaning too. *Tupu* shawl pins signified the feminine (Lechtman 2007:332). Axes of particular shapes may have signified state military power and possibly offices, along with one style of star-shaped axe head and axe-maces found at other sites (Guaman Poma 1615; Lechtman 2007). The colors of metal objects in the tri-metal gold, silver, and copper system signified hierarchical positions in a variety of gender, political, and supernatural contexts (Lechtman 2007). Another dimension of meaning of quotidian metal objects was their reference to a geographic place or ethnicity of origin. Much as the multiethnic yanacona of Machu Picchu marked their identities of origin with heirloom ceramics (Salazar 2001, 2007), they also communicated messages through metal objects that referred to known, or unknown, places.

The pivotal known place would have been Cuzco, the capital of the Inca empire. Some types of quotidian pre-Columbian metal objects, from *tumi* knives and tupu pins to T-shaped bronze axe heads, are said to be in "imperial style" (Rowe 1996:301, 314) or even "emblems of the Inca state: silver shawl pins, tweezers, and plated bronze mirrors" (Salazar 2004:45). But tweezers, for example, are unlikely to have signified the Inca state; they are typical of certain provinces, not of the Inca heartland. Moreover, they are scarce or absent at most other royal or imperial Inca sites. One task of this section, then, is to reconstruct the geographic distributions of quotidian metal artifacts and regional metalworking traditions using a Geographic Information System (GIS) database of 10,120 metal objects found at known places in the Inca empire. This regional context is essential to an understanding of the Inca and provincial referents of quotidian metal artifacts from Machu Picchu and other late prehistoric Andean sites.

What exactly would an imperial style be? Rowe (1996:301) used "imperial" to describe a style of "objects of metal and wood, textiles, and pottery [that] were made by craft workers to government specifications and distributed to people in the provinces as gifts to reward loyal service." Moseley (2001:78–80) calls such styles "corporate." This corporate style would characterize Cuzqueño identity or political affiliation with the Inca state (Moseley 2001:79–80). Lechtman (2007:320, 345–346) refines the notion of an Inca style by following Murra's (1980) "distinction between manufactures for use by the crown (the emperor and members of the royal allyus) and those for the state (items produced for purposes of redistribution)."

Lechtman (2007:336–337) has shown that the fundamental features of distinctively Inca style in metals were technological: the combination of casting objects to shape and the use of tin bronze. The Inca took the tin bronze of the south-central Andes and made it the nearly universal bronze alloy used throughout the empire (Lechtman 2007:332–334). Yet the meaning of tin bronze as a material is difficult to assess (Owen 1986; Lechtman 2007:332) and it was widely used for objects of otherwise local, non-Inca style (Owen 1986; Lechtman 2007:342).

In practice, the style of Inca metals was not tightly controlled, even among those objects that were "essentially 'state issue'" (Lechtman 2007:337). The data in this section bear that out. Given the variability in even corporate-style metals, it may be more correct to visualize the meanings of quotidian metal artifacts as falling along a continuum of "Inca-ness." At one extreme fall artifacts that had no connection at all to the Inca state or ethnicity. These include objects that were broadly Andean, as well as objects that clearly referred to some other region or ethnicity. Toward the middle of the continuum are objects that were characteristic of ethnic Inca or Cuzqueño material culture, which Cuzqueños would have used because they were familiar and signified their natal identity. According to the distinction used by Lechtman and Murra, items made "for use by the crown (the emperor and members of the royal allyus)" (Lechtman 2007:320, 345–346) would be the finest examples of these ethnically Inca or Cuzqueño goods. Finally, at the other extreme are artifacts in an Inca corporate style that explicitly conveyed affiliation with the

Inca state. Access to these items may have been controlled for imperial ends. These corporate-style artifacts would be the ones made "for the state (items produced for purposes of redistribution)" (Lechtman 2007:320, 345–346).

Which, if any, quotidian metal artifacts fell toward the "imperial Inca" or corporate-style end of the continuum? Aside from the nearly universal adoption of tin bronze, and the cross-cutting meanings of gold, silver, and copper as materials, what constituted an Inca style of everyday metal artifacts, if one existed at all? Before examining the broader regional context, this section compares the assemblages of quotidian metal objects from several excavated and well-attributed Inca contexts, including Machu Picchu. The goal is to determine which artifacts or features of artifacts these assemblages have in common, that is, to discover a shared Inca style of commonplace metals. Combining these comparisons of Inca assemblages with the broad context of regional traditions, it turns out that in daily life among the less-than-noble, metal objects were indeed freighted with meaning, but few referred directly to the Inca state.

The rest of this section develops these ethnic and geographic contexts and comparisons. The results allow us to better read the meanings of late prehistoric quotidian metals in the Andes in general, and at Machu Picchu in particular. They clarify the roles of such objects in the Inca state, as well as their other meanings. These comparisons also illuminate the life histories of everyday metal objects (Hoffman 1999:119), from production through exchange, use, destruction, restoration, and burial. In so doing, they shed light on the lives of the Inca subjects who owned them.

The Comparative Data

Much of this section is based on a large database of mostly quotidian metal artifacts with geographic provenience specific enough to plot on a small-scale map of the Andes. Some of the objects were recorded in association with excavation projects, especially the Upper Mantaro Archaeological Research Project (Earle et al. 1987; D'Altroy and Hastorf 2001; Owen 2001). Others were studied in museums, including the Machu Picchu material at Yale University's Peabody Museum of Natural History, the Phoebe A. Hearst Museum at the University of California at Berkeley, the American Museum of Natural History (AMNH), the Field Museum of Natural History (FMNH), and the Museo Contisuyo in Moquegua, Peru. Many additional artifacts were recorded from digital photographs and catalog data provided by Patrick Williams of the Field Museum, and from catalog cards provided by Bruce Smith of the Smithsonian Institution. More were culled from publications. Eugen Mayer's monumental compilations of metal weapons, tools, and derived forms such as axe monies (Mayer 1986, 1992, 1994, 1998) were added last, with care to avoid duplications. Including Mayer's voluminous material biases the database towards the types of artifacts that he recorded, so one cannot use this data to judge the relative commonness of weapons or tools versus personal implements such as tupus or tweezers that are not included in his compilations. (See Appendix E for sources and the number of objects contributed by each.) The quality of the objects' provenience ranges widely, from good excavated associations to purchases and donations. A known geographic origin at least as specific as a province, department, or valley was the only requirement for inclusion. Objects of uncertain provenience, or from regions as broad as "north coast of Peru" or "Bolivia," were excluded. While the emphasis was on artifacts from the Late Intermediate Period and Late Horizon, many earlier, and a few later, artifacts are clearly included, most notably among the artifacts from Vicus, Sipán, and other north coast localities. Unique and precious objects, especially of gold and silver, were not sought, and are underrepresented in the database, because the emphasis is on ordinary objects that are common enough to form clear geographic patterns and to be found at least occasionally in excavations.

Although beads were recorded, they are excluded from this analysis to avoid skewing the results, because beads are often found in large lots. It is not clear how to quantitatively compare a large number of beads from one necklace, for example, with a single bead or a single object of another kind. It is rarely possible to tell how many beaded items might be represented by a large lot of beads, or whether several beads from nearby contexts represent a single item or several. For similar reasons, four large lots of sheet metal objects that apparently decorated textiles from Ica, Chepen, and Sillustani are also excluded. Although similar arguments could be made concerning other sheet metal discs and bangles, sheet metal fragments, and perhaps other object types, none of these would skew the results to a comparable degree. Counts represent the original number of intact artifacts, regardless of breakage into fragments. When a meaningful count was not possible, as with many collections of sheet metal fragments, a count of one was recorded. The resulting 10,120 artifacts, including 180 from Machu Picchu, constitute the analyzed sample. While more objects could be added with further museum work and from additional publications, this sample should be large enough to suggest the geographic patterning of quotidian metal artifacts in the Andes.

Typology and Variables
In addition to provenience, catalog data, and time periods indicated by ceramic associations where available, the principal information recorded about each artifact is its type, according to a typology of forms developed from the thousands of drawings and photographs used in this project. Additional variables describe form and technical details, evidence of use wear, and so on. Some objects were measured, but metric data play little role in the present analysis except for the classification of discs into size ranges. A guess about the principal metal present and possible depletion gilding or silvering (Lechtman 1996b) was recorded, based on color and appearance of corrosion products when possible, or on statements in publications. No attempt was made to distinguish copper from bronzes. Most of the objects in the database bear the green corrosion products of copper or copper alloys. Without instrumental analyses, these estimates are poor approximations at best (Lechtman

1973, note 7). Because these estimates of composition are unreliable and different alloys were frequently made into identical forms, most of this analysis ignores the material composition and considers only artifact types and attributes of form. (See Appendix F for brief descriptions of the types, identified by arbitrary four-digit numerical codes, and the other variables in the database. See Appendix G for schematic illustrations of representative examples of many of the types.)

A Note about Types of Tumi Knives

Several different kinds of objects have been called "tumis." In this typology, types 2840 through 2849 are called T-shaped tumis (see Appendix G, Figures G8 and G9). T-shaped tumis have an inverted T shape with a wide blade and a narrow perpendicular handle rising from the center back edge of the blade. Shapes differ considerably, and many show signs of sharpening or wear from cutting or scraping, or both. Many have a loop or hole near the end of the handle, parallel to the cutting edge, so that if strung on a necklace the blade would lie flat against the wearer's chest. Well-preserved coastal examples suggest that the handles were often covered by wood or fiber hafting and often bore short loops of cord more suited to pass around the user's wrist than his or her neck.

Types 5100 through 5119 are called "flat tumis" here. These have wider, and often shorter, handles of roughly the same thickness as the blade. The whole tumi resembles a cutout from sheet metal, although they were not necessarily made that way. They often have a hole cut through the sheet-like handle, perpendicular to the cutting edge. If strung, these flat tumis would not naturally lie flat. Even more than T-shaped tumis, flat tumis often show heavy use wear.

These two general types are clearly variants of the same functional concept, as are the "Guayas tumis" identified by Mayer (1992), with their distinctive blade shape and thick handles without holes. All of these contrast with a category of artifact that has also been called a tumi, here called a "North Coast tumi" (types 5000 to 5080). North Coast tumis are uniform in thickness, like sheet metal cutouts, with very wide handles and relatively narrower blades. Some have elaborate decorations on the handles, but most are plain. The wide, flat handles and thin blades virtually preclude practical use. They rarely, if ever, show signs of sharpening or use wear. These seem to be stylized representations of cutting implements, rather than functional tools. North Coast tumis are found primarily on the north coast of Peru, often in caches of many tumis. They may have been stores of wealth, comparable to axe monies (Hosler, Lechtman, and Holm 1990).

Variation in Late Horizon Metal Assemblages

A "Cuzco" or "Inca" style of quotidian metal objects has been noted, albeit not well described, since the early days of Andean archaeological research (Dorsey 1901:256, 280; Uhle 1912:33; Nordenskiöld 1921:37-43, 48-59; Root 1949:34). Nevertheless, a comparison of 740 metal artifacts from eight substantial Late Horizon assemblages and several smaller ones (Table 2.1) indicates that, while a few commonplace metal object types were typical of the Inca heartland and were probably disseminated by activities of the empire, few are found widely or consistently enough in Inca contexts to suggest that they constituted a corporate style that was regularly intended to signify affiliation with the Inca state. There is no typical Inca metal assemblage.

Finely decorated Inca ceramics functioned as explicit symbols of the Inca state (Julien 1983:8, passim; D'Altroy 1992:180–183; see Moseley 2001:79–80). Although people typically continued to use their local styles of ceramics after they were incorporated into the empire, imperial administration usually added an Inca component that is often easy to recognize in even small surface collections. The same is not true for quotidian metals. There was apparently no standard Late Horizon commonplace metal object or assemblage that was regularly transplanted into conquered provinces. Local metalworkers gained access to tin and switched comprehensively to tin bronze (Owen 1986; Costin et al. 1989; Bezur and Owen 1996; Lechtman 2007:341), but in virtually all other respects the great bulk of the metals used in any given place during the Late Horizon reflected local metalworking traditions with little obvious Inca influence. Any explicitly Inca quotidian metal artifacts must have been so scarce that they cannot be easily recognized. Metal objects such as earspools and certain headdress ornaments were insignia of status or office, but these were rare, belonging to a few nobles. No common types or features of metal objects seem to have functioned as explicit symbols of the state, because none was used consistently at Inca facilities or in regions under Inca rule.

If any Late Horizon metal assemblage could represent Inca norms, it would be the one from Pachacuti Inca Yupanqui's royal country estate at Machu Picchu, along with the smaller collections excavated from another of his estates at Ollantaytambo (Niles 2004:50) and the ritual center of Sacsawaman, near Cuzco. Yet even these three metal assemblages from the Inca heartland differ sharply from each other, and other, more distant Late Horizon assemblages differ even more.

The differences among sites and regions are dramatic (see Table 2.1). Tupus, for example, range from about 73% of the Late Horizon metals assemblage in the area northeast of Titicaca, to about 23% at Machu Picchu, to none in the Ica and Lambayeque assemblages. While some variant of round-headed and half-round-headed tupus is found in all of the Late Horizon assemblages except Ica and Lambayeque, no other type of tupu is found in more than three of the eight assemblages, and most are found in only one. The small, flat discs with a single hole (type 5422) that are common at Machu Picchu and around Jauja are rare at Sacsawaman and Ollantaytambo, and absent from the other four assemblages. Some of the types of tweezers found at Machu Picchu also appear at Sacsawaman, but rarely or never in any other Late Horizon assemblage. Six axes of various types account for more than 3% of the Machu Picchu assemblage (and a much higher percentage of the total by weight of metal), yet there is not a single axe in five of the other Late Horizon assemblages. The star-shaped mace heads (type 2760) that constitute more than 4% of the metal objects from Sacsawaman are absent from all the other large Late

TABLE 2.1. Late Horizon metal assemblages, showing the types of metal objects found in eight notable Late Horizon assemblages, including Machu Picchu, plus several smaller ones lumped into the totals.

Description	Type	Machu Picchu[a] #	%[j]	%[k]	Sacsa-waman[b] #	%	Ollantay-tambo[c] #	%	La Plata Island[d] #	%	Jauja area[e] #	%	Ica area[f] #	%[j]	%[k]	NE of Titicaca[g] #	%	Lambay-eque[h] #	%	All Late Horizon[i] #	%[j]	%[k]
Total objects (n):		180			98		31		29		90		184			70		29		740		
Tupu																						
Half-round	1010	14	7.8	9.8	14	14.3	2	6.5	4	13.8	1	1.1	—	—	—	3	4.3	—	—	38	5.1	5.9
Round (some have decoration)	1001	8	4.4	5.6	17	17.3	3	9.7	—	—	2	2.2	—	—	—	6	8.6	—	—	36	4.9	5.6
Thin head, indeterminate shape	1037	4	2.2	2.8	1	1.0	1	3.2	3	10.3	—	—	—	—	—	1	1.4	—	—	11	1.5	1.7
Half-round > semicircular	1012	4	2.2	2.8	9	9.2	3	9.7	1	3.4	—	—	—	—	—	—	—	—	—	17	2.3	2.6
Half-round, head thick as shaft	1011	3	1.7	2.1	3	3.1	—	—	2	6.9	—	—	—	—	—	—	—	—	—	8	1.1	1.2
Half-round or drooping, (indeterminate)	1015	2	1.1	1.4	—	—	—	—	—	—	1	1.1	—	—	—	—	—	—	—	3	0.4	0.5
Star-shaped mace form, small, no hole	1083	1	0.6	0.7	—	—	—	—	—	—	—	—	—	—	—	—	—	—	—	1	0.1	0.2
Half-round transitional	1007	1	0.6	0.7	—	—	—	—	—	—	—	—	—	—	—	—	—	—	—	1	0.1	0.2
Cone, double, with loop	1062	1	0.6	0.7	—	—	—	—	—	—	—	—	—	—	—	—	—	—	—	1	0.1	0.2
Drooping	1014	1	0.6	0.7	1	1.0	1	3.2	—	—	—	—	—	—	—	2	2.9	—	—	5	0.7	0.8
Cone, single, with loop	1061	—	—	—	1	1.0	—	—	—	—	—	—	—	—	—	—	—	—	—	1	0.1	0.2
Round, small bump	1022	—	—	—	1	1.0	2	6.5	—	—	2	2.2	—	—	—	—	—	—	—	5	0.7	0.8
Round, spirals	1024	—	—	—	—	—	—	—	—	—	2	2.2	—	—	—	—	—	—	—	2	0.3	0.3
Round, crude	1005	—	—	—	—	—	—	—	—	—	1	1.1	—	—	—	—	—	—	—	1	0.1	0.2
Loop	1048	—	—	—	—	—	—	—	—	—	1	1.1	—	—	—	—	—	—	—	1	0.1	0.2
Cast animal head: llama with ears	1055	—	—	—	—	—	—	—	—	—	1	1.1	—	—	—	—	—	—	—	1	0.1	0.2
Cast standing anthropomorphic figure	1060	—	—	—	—	—	—	—	—	—	1	1.1	—	—	—	—	—	—	—	1	0.1	0.2
Miscellaneous cast in the round	1089	—	—	—	—	—	—	—	—	—	1	1.1	—	—	—	1	1.4	—	—	2	0.3	0.3
Long taper	1006	—	—	—	—	—	—	—	—	—	1	1.1	—	—	—	3	4.3	—	—	4	0.5	0.6
Rattles (one to three, plain or elaborate)	1086	—	—	—	—	—	—	—	—	—	—	—	—	—	—	19	27.1	—	—	19	2.6	2.9
Round to half-round, neck lobe	1020	—	—	—	—	—	—	—	—	—	—	—	—	—	—	3	4.3	—	—	3	0.4	0.5
2-piece flat mold, llama head	1050	—	—	—	—	—	—	—	—	—	—	—	—	—	—	3	4.3	—	—	3	0.4	0.5
Bolivian bifurcated cast types	1087	—	—	—	—	—	—	—	—	—	—	—	—	—	—	3	4.3	—	—	3	0.4	0.5
Round, neck step	1002	—	—	—	—	—	—	—	—	—	—	—	—	—	—	2	2.9	—	—	2	0.3	0.3
Flat narrow head (may be needle)	1029	—	—	—	—	—	—	—	—	—	—	—	—	—	—	1	1.4	—	—	1	0.1	0.2
Flat figural wire-relief	1090	—	—	—	—	—	—	—	—	—	—	—	—	—	—	1	1.4	—	—	1	0.1	0.2
Applied spirals	1091	—	—	—	—	—	—	—	—	—	—	—	—	—	—	1	1.4	—	—	1	0.1	0.2
Probably colonial	1097	—	—	—	—	—	—	—	—	—	—	—	—	—	—	1	1.4	—	—	1	0.1	0.2
Two spirals	1027	—	—	—	—	—	—	—	—	—	—	—	—	—	—	—	—	—	—	0	0.0	0.0
Other and indeterminate type		—	—	—	—	—	3	9.7	—	—	—	—	—	—	—	—	—	—	—	5	0.7	0.8
All		39	21.7	27.3	47	48.0	15	48.4	10	34.5	14	15.6	—	—	—	50	71.4	—	—	178	24.1	27.6
Any tupu with worn or sharpened edge		7	3.9	4.9	2	2.0	—	—	—	—	1	1.1	—	—	—	6	8.6	—	—	16	2.2	2.5

Continued.

TABLE 2.1 CONTINUED.

Description	Type	Machu Picchu[a] #	%[j]	%[k]	Sacsa-waman[b] #	%	Ollantay-tambo[c] #	%	La Plata Island[d] #	%	Jauja area[e] #	%	Ica area[f] #	%[j]	%[k]	NE of Titicaca[g] #	%	Lambay-eque[h] #	%	All Late Horizon[i] #	%[j]	%[k]
Disc																							
Plain, convex, 1 hole near center, >100 mm diameter	5466	—	—	—	1	1.0	—	—	—	—	—	—	—	—	—	—	—	—	—	1	0.1	0.2
Plain, flat, 1 hole near edge, 40–100 mm diameter	5423	1	0.6	0.7	1	1.0	—	—	—	—	—	—	—	—	—	—	—	—	—	2	0.3	0.3
Plain, flat, 1 hole near edge, <40 mm diameter	5422	40	22.2	2.1	2	2.0	1	3.2	—	—	10	11.1	—	—	—	—	—	—	—	53	7.2	2.5
Plain, flat, no hole, <40 mm diameter	5412	—	—	—	1	1.0	—	—	—	—	1	1.1	—	—	—	—	—	—	—	2	0.3	0.3
Plain, flat, indeterminate hole, <40 mm diameter	5402	—	—	—	—	—	—	—	—	—	4	4.4	—	—	—	—	—	—	—	4	0.5	0.6
Multiple (conjoined discs in one piece)	5670	—	—	—	—	—	—	—	—	—	1	1.1	—	—	—	—	—	—	—	1	0.1	0.2
Plain, convex, 2 opposed holes near edge, <40 mm diameter	5482	—	—	—	—	—	—	—	—	—	—	—	59	32.1	1.6	—	—	—	—	59	8.0	0.3
Plain, flat, indeterminate hole, 40–100 mm diameter	5403	—	—	—	—	—	—	—	—	—	—	—	2	1.1	1.6	—	—	—	—	2	0.3	0.3
Plain, flat, 2 close holes near edge, 40–100 mm diameter	5433	—	—	—	—	—	—	—	—	—	—	—	1	0.5	0.8	—	—	—	—	1	0.1	0.2
Plain, flat, 2 holes close near edge, <40 mm diameter	5432	—	—	—	—	—	—	—	—	—	—	—	—	—	—	—	—	—	—	1	0.1	0.2
All		41	22.8	2.8	4	4.1	1	3.2	—	—	16	17.8	62	33.7	3.9	—	—	—	—	125	16.9	4.8
Tweezer																							
Triangular	1101	2	1.1	1.4	1	1.0	—	—	—	—	—	—	—	—	—	—	—	—	—	4	0.5	0.6
Straight transitional	1109	1	0.6	0.7	1	1.0	—	—	—	—	—	—	—	—	—	—	—	2	6.9	4	0.5	0.6
Pointed	1115	1	0.6	0.7	2	2.0	—	—	—	—	2	2.2	—	—	—	—	—	—	—	5	0.7	0.8
Teardrop transitional	1104	2	1.1	1.4	—	—	—	—	—	—	—	—	—	—	—	—	—	—	—	2	0.3	0.3
Miscellaneous symmetrical valve style	1121	1	0.6	0.7	—	—	—	—	—	—	—	—	—	—	—	—	—	—	—	1	0.1	0.2
Flaring	1111	1	0.6	0.7	—	—	—	—	—	—	—	—	1	0.5	0.8	—	—	—	—	2	0.3	0.3
Spiral-armed	1122	—	—	—	—	—	—	—	—	—	—	—	11	6.0	8.7	—	—	—	—	11	1.5	1.7
Indeterminate type	1100	—	—	—	—	—	—	—	—	—	—	—	1	0.5	0.8	—	—	2	6.9	3	0.4	0.5
Teardrop	1103	1	0.6	0.7	—	—	—	—	—	—	—	—	—	—	—	1	3.4	—	—	2	0.3	0.3
Circular, flaring neck	1105	—	—	—	—	—	—	—	—	—	—	—	—	—	—	1	3.4	—	—	1	0.1	0.2
All		9	5.0	6.3	4	4.1	—	—	—	—	2	2.2	13	7.1	10.2	—	—	6	20.7	35	4.7	5.4
Axe																							
Rectangular tangs, no hole, trapezoidal blade ("classic")	4250	2	1.1	1.4	—	—	1	3.2	—	—	—	—	—	—	—	—	—	—	—	3	0.4	0.5
Curved tangs, no hole, wide crescent blade ("ancla")	4470	1	0.6	0.7	—	—	—	—	—	—	—	—	—	—	—	—	—	—	—	1	0.1	0.2
Rectangular tangs, no hole, wide crescent blade (atypical)	4270	1	0.6	0.7	—	—	—	—	—	—	—	—	—	—	—	—	—	—	—	1	0.1	0.2

Continued.

TABLE 2.1 CONTINUED.

Description	Type	Machu Picchu[a] #	%[j]	%[k]	Sacsa-waman[b] #	%	Ollantay-tambo[c] #	%	La Plata Island[d] #	%	Jauja area[e] #	%	Ica area[f] #	%[j]	%[k]	NE of Titicaca[g] #	%	Lambay-eque[h] #	%	All Late Horizon[i] #	%[j]	%[k]
Indeterminate haft, trapezoidal blade	4750	1	0.6	0.7	—	—	—	—	—	—	—	—	—	—	—	—	—	—	—	1	0.1	0.2
Indeterminate haft, indeterminate blade shape	4701	1	0.6	0.7	—	—	—	—	—	—	—	—	—	—	—	—	—	—	—	1	0.1	0.2
Indeterminate haft, long rectangular blade	4720	—	—	—	—	—	—	—	—	—	—	—	1	1.1	—	—	—	—	—	1	0.1	0.2
All		6	3.3	4.2	—	—	1	3.2	—	—	1	1.1	—	—	—	—	—	—	—	8	1.1	1.2

Other tool or weapon

Description	Type	#	%[j]	%[k]	#	%	#	%	#	%	#	%	#	%[j]	%[k]	#	%	#	%	#	%[j]	%[k]
Weapon: star-shaped mace head	2760	—	—	—	4	4.1	—	—	—	—	—	—	2	1.1	1.6	—	—	—	—	7	0.9	1.1
Chisel: fine	2700	3	1.7	2.1	2	2.0	—	—	—	—	2	2.2	—	—	—	—	—	—	—	7	0.9	1.1
Bola weight: spheroid with suspension hole	1801	3	1.7	2.1	2	2.0	—	—	1	3.4	4	4.4	—	—	—	2	2.9	—	—	12	1.6	1.9
Celt: all		4	2.2	2.8	2	2.0	—	—	—	—	—	—	—	—	—	1	1.4	—	—	7	0.9	1.1
Tool: plumb bob	2740	1	0.6	0.7	1	1.0	—	—	—	—	—	—	—	—	—	—	—	—	—	2	0.3	0.3
Tool: crowbar	2750	1	0.6	0.7	1	1.0	—	—	—	—	—	—	—	—	—	—	—	—	—	2	0.3	0.3
Chisel: heavy	2710	1	0.6	0.7	—	—	—	—	—	—	—	—	—	—	—	—	—	—	—	2	0.3	0.3
Knife: handleless transverse	2830	1	0.6	0.7	—	—	—	—	—	—	—	—	—	—	—	—	—	—	—	1	0.1	0.2
Tool: spindle whorl (some may be beads)	2720	—	—	—	—	—	—	—	—	—	1	1.1	—	—	—	—	—	2	6.9	3	0.4	0.5
Tool: ladle	2735	—	—	—	—	—	—	—	—	—	—	—	—	—	—	—	—	1	3.4	1	0.1	0.2
Tool: other tool, spatula, punch, and others	2715	—	—	—	—	—	—	—	—	—	—	—	—	—	—	—	—	—	—	1	0.1	0.2
All		14	7.8	9.8	12	12.2	—	—	1	3.4	7	7.8	2	1.1	1.6	3	4.3	3	10.3	31	4.2	4.8

Ornament or personal implement

Description	Type	#	%[j]	%[k]	#	%	#	%	#	%	#	%	#	%[j]	%[k]	#	%	#	%	#	%[j]	%[k]
Headdress: concave-sided frontal	5311	—	—	—	1	1.0	1	3.2	—	—	—	—	—	—	—	—	—	—	—	2	0.3	0.3
Lirpu: disc with pierced tab for suspension	5610	3	1.7	2.1	4	4.1	1	3.2	—	—	1	1.1	—	—	—	—	—	—	—	9	1.2	1.4
Other: strip (may be bracelets, headbands, and others)	3190	3	1.7	2.1	1	1.0	—	—	—	—	1	1.1	5	2.7	3.9	—	—	—	—	10	1.4	1.5
Conical "bell" (probably hair ornament): all		4	2.2	2.8	—	—	—	—	3	10.3	—	—	—	—	—	—	—	—	—	7	0.9	1.1
Split bell: all		3	1.7	2.1	—	—	—	—	—	—	—	—	—	—	—	—	—	—	—	3	0.4	0.5
Tiny spoon: bird finial	1701	2	1.1	1.4	—	—	—	—	—	—	—	—	—	—	—	—	—	—	—	2	0.3	0.3
Ring: all		2	1.1	1.4	—	—	—	—	—	—	—	—	—	—	—	—	—	4	13.8	6	0.8	0.9
Nose ornament: sheet	2202	—	—	—	—	—	—	—	—	—	—	—	—	—	—	—	—	1	3.4	1	0.1	0.2
Other: rectangular folded-up tray/plaque/ornament	3120	—	—	—	—	—	—	—	—	—	—	—	—	—	—	—	—	9	31.0	9	1.2	1.4
Knife: possible long oval blade	2839	1	0.6	0.7	—	—	—	—	—	—	—	—	—	—	—	—	—	—	—	1	0.1	0.2
Other: plume holder cone	3110	1	0.6	0.7	—	—	—	—	—	—	—	—	5	2.7	3.9	—	—	—	—	6	0.8	0.9
Bangle	3020	1	0.6	0.7	—	—	—	—	—	—	—	—	21	11.4	16.5	—	—	—	—	22	3.0	3.4
Other ornament types		3	1.7	2.1	1	1.0	—	—	—	—	—	—	3	1.6	2.4	—	—	—	—	7	0.9	1.1
Ear spool: all types		—	—	—	—	—	—	—	—	—	—	—	14	7.6	11.0	—	—	—	—	14	1.9	2.2
Sheet sheathing: all types		—	—	—	—	—	—	—	—	—	—	—	18	9.8	14.2	—	—	—	—	18	2.4	2.8
All		23	12.8	16.1	7	7.1	2	6.5	3	10.3	2	2.2	66	35.9	52.0	—	—	14	48.3	117	15.8	18.1

Continued.

TABLE 2.1 CONTINUED.

Description	Type	Machu Picchu[a] #	%[j]	%[k]	Sacsa- waman[b] #	%	Ollantay -tambo[c] #	%	La Plata Island[d] #	%	Jauja area[e] #	%	Ica area[f] #	%[j]	%[k]	NE of Titicaca[g] #	%	Lambay- eque[h] #	%	All Late Horizon[i] #	%[j]	%[k]
Possible lime dipper or tiny tupu																						
Other head cast in the round, various	2439	1	0.6	0.7	—	—	1	3.2	—	—	—	—	—	—	—	1	1.4	—	—	3	0.4	0.5
Biconical club-shaped head, no hole	2430	1	0.6	0.7	—	—	—	—	—	—	—	—	—	—	—	—	—	—	—	1	0.1	0.2
Cast cone head with loop, single	2410	—	—	—	—	—	—	—	—	—	—	—	—	—	—	—	—	—	—	3	0.4	0.5
All		2	1.1	1.4	—	—	1	3.2	—	—	—	—	—	—	—	1	3.3	—	—	7	0.9	1.1
T-shaped tumi																						
Backswept blade	2846	—	—	—	2	2.1	—	—	—	—	—	—	—	—	—	1	1.4	—	—	4	0.5	0.6
Straight back	2840	17	9.4	11.9	5	5.1	3	9.7	—	—	1	1.1	—	—	—	4	5.7	—	—	31	4.2	4.8
Slightly flaring back	2841	4	2.2	2.8	2	2.0	—	—	—	—	—	—	—	—	—	4	5.7	—	—	10	1.4	1.5
Tiny cast blade	2849	1	0.6	0.7	—	—	—	—	—	—	—	—	—	—	—	—	—	—	—	1	0.1	0.2
All		22	12.2	15.4	7	7.1	3	9.7	—	—	1	1.1	—	—	—	8	11.4	—	—	42	5.7	6.5
Any with fancy cast head		2	1.1	1.4	—	—	—	—	—	—	—	—	—	—	—	1	1.4	—	—	3	0.4	0.5
Needle																						
Loop-eye, all types		2	1.1	1.4	—	—	—	—	—	—	5	5.6	—	—	—	—	—	—	—	7	0.9	1.1
Pierced-eye, all types		2	1.1	1.4	—	—	—	—	—	—	11	12.2	—	—	—	1	1.4	—	—	18	2.4	2.8
Simple bent loop (flapless loop-eye)	1207	1	0.6	0.7	—	—	—	—	—	—	—	—	—	—	—	—	—	—	—	1	0.1	0.2
Indeterminate type	1200	—	—	—	—	—	1	3.2	—	—	—	—	—	—	—	—	—	—	—	1	0.1	0.2
All		5	2.8	3.5	—	—	1	3.2	—	—	16	17.8	—	—	—	1	1.4	—	—	27	3.6	4.2
Vessel																						
Sculptural *vaso retrato*	1402	—	—	—	—	—	—	—	—	—	6	3.3	4.7	—	—	—	—	—	6	0.8	0.9
Carinated pan	1404	—	—	—	—	—	—	—	—	—	6	3.3	4.7	—	—	—	—	—	6	0.8	0.9
Indeterminate type	1400	—	—	—	—	—	—	—	—	—	2	1.1	1.6	—	—	—	—	—	2	0.3	0.3
Kero	1401	—	—	—	—	—	2	6.5	—	—	—	—	5	2.7	3.9	—	—	—	—	7	0.9	1.1
Cast	1407	—	—	—	—	—	—	—	1	3.4	—	—	—	—	—	1	1.4	—	—	2	0.3	0.3
Rounded bowl	1405	—	—	—	—	—	—	—	1	3.4	—	—	—	—	—	—	—	—	—	1	0.1	0.2
Handled plate	1412	1	0.6	0.7	—	—	—	—	—	—	—	—	—	—	—	—	—	—	—	1	0.1	0.2
All		1	0.6	0.7	—	—	2	6.5	2	6.9	—	—	19	10.3	15.0	1	1.4	—	—	25	3.4	3.9
Production																						
Smelting or refining product, excess from melting	2920	5	2.8	3.5	1	1.0	—	—	—	—	6	6.7	—	—	—	—	—	—	—	12	1.6	1.9
Sheet scrap (cutmarked, jagged, folded, stacked, and others)	2933	3	1.7	2.1	—	—	—	—	—	—	4	4.4	—	—	—	—	—	—	—	7	0.9	1.1
Ingot	2930	1	0.6	0.7	—	—	—	—	—	—	—	—	—	—	—	—	—	—	—	1	0.1	0.2
All		9	5.0	6.3	1	1.0	—	—	—	—	10	11.1	—	—	—	—	—	—	—	20	2.7	3.1
Figurine																						
Standing nude female, hands on torso, Inca style	1514	—	—	—	3	3.1	—	—	3	10.3	—	—	—	—	—	—	—	—	—	6	0.8	0.9
Other types		1	0.6	0.7	—	—	—	—	—	—	—	—	2	1.1	1.6	—	—	—	—	4	0.5	0.6
All		1	0.6	0.7	3	3.1	—	—	3	10.3	—	—	2	1.1	1.6	—	—	—	—	10	1.4	1.5

Continued.

TABLE 2.1 CONTINUED.

Description	Type	Machu Picchu[a] #	%[j]	%[k]	Sacsa-waman[b] #	%	Ollantay-tambo[c] #	%	La Plata Island[d] #	%	Jauja area[e] #	%	Ica area[f] #	%[j]	%[k]	NE of Titicaca[g] #	%	Lambay-eque[h] #	%	All Late Horizon[i] #	%[j]	%[k]
Probable store of wealth																						
Axe monies: feathers[l]	3107	—	—	—	—	—	—	—	—	—	—	—	—	—	—	—	—	1	3.4	1	0.1	0.2
North Coast tumi: rectangular handle, semicircular blade, plain	5010	—	—	—	—	—	—	—	—	—	—	—	—	—	—	—	—	1	3.4	1	0.1	0.2
All		—	—	—	—	—	—	—	—	—	—	—	—	—	—	—	—	2	6.9	2	0.3	0.3
Fragment, other, miscellaneous																						
Indeterminate: sheet fragment	3210	2	1.1	1.4	—	—	—	—	4	13.8	5	5.6	19	10.3	15.0	3	4.3	3	10.3	39	5.3	6.0
Indeterminate: shaft fragment	3200	2	1.1	1.4	2	2.0	—	—	6	20.7	12	13.3	—	—	—	2	2.9	1	3.4	25	3.4	3.9
Indeterminate, rare types, bar, wire, and others		4	2.2	2.8	11	11.2	5	16.1	—	—	4	4.4	1	0.5	0.8	1	1.4	—	—	35	4.7	5.4
All		8	4.4	5.6	13	13.3	5	16.1	10	34.5	21	23.3	20	10.9	15.7	6	8.6	4	13.8	99	13.4	15.4

[a] Mostly from burials, some from occupation deposits. Excludes one bead as explained in the text. See Appendix D for lists of included and excluded objects. (Foote and Buell 1912; Bingham 1915c, 1930, 1948; Mathewson 1915; Eaton 1916; Rutledge 1984; Burger and Salazar 2004).

[b] Mostly from burials, possibly buried offerings, and possibly construction fill. Primarily from Valcárcel's published excavations, plus five objects at the Phoebe A. Hearst Museum collected by Max Uhle, one gold figurine now at the Field Museum of Natural History, and one tumi from a burial published by Valencia Zegarra (1970) (cited in Mayer 1998). Excludes one evidently colonial bronze object that resembles a pestle (Valcárcel 1934a:33.59) (Valcárcel 1934a, 1934b, 1935a, 1935b; Mayer 1998; Julien 2004).

[c] From construction fill and burials (Llanos 1936), plus one axe now at the British Museum (Mayer 1998).

[d] Objects at the Field Museum of Natural History, collected by George Dorsey from a burial and other contexts (Ecuador) (Dorsey 1901).

[e] Objects from Late Horizon domestic areas and burials in the Jauja area, collected by the Upper Mantaro Archaeological Research Project at sites J1 (Pancan), J2 (Hatunmarca), J54 (Marca), J66, and J70 (Earle et al. 1980, 1987; Costin et al. 1989; Bezur and Owen 1996; Owen 2001).

[f] Objects in the Phoebe A. Hearst Museum from burials at Ica sites T and Z (Kroeber and Strong 1924b; Root 1949; Menzel 1976).

[g] Objects at the American Museum of Natural History, collected by Adolph Bandelier from burials in the area northeast of Lake Titicaca, at the sites of Ka-ata, Kalachaca, Kasapata, and Chocaripa-pata (Chapin 1961).

[h] Objects at the American Museum of Natural History, excavated by Wendell Bennett from burials at Purgatorio TU-1 and Lambayeque 2 (Bennett 1939).

[i] Includes all the columns shown, plus 29 items from smaller Late Horizon assemblages at the following sites: Armatambo, Cerro Morro Solar, Lima (Díaz and Vallejo 2002); Cerro Azoguini, Puno (Julien 1982); Coquimbo, Chile (Ampuero Brito 1969); Maranga, tombs CVI-CIX, Huaca I (Jijon y Caamaño 1949); Maukallaqta (Bauer 2004); Muyuntasita, Bolivia (Helsley-Marchbanks 2004); Quebrada de la Vaca (Phoebe A. Hearst Museum 4-8317); and Atacama A (Latcham 1938).

[j] The percentages in this column count all discs as separate items, as shown in the "#" column.

[k] The percentages in this column count three large sets of matching discs that probably each represent a single decorated textile as a single item each. These sets comprise 38 discs found near Snake Rock at Machu Picchu (YPM ANT.017871); 32 discs from Grave A at Ica site T, and 27 discs from Grave K at Ica site T.

[l] Hosler, Lechtman, and Holm 1990.

Horizon assemblages except Ica, with two. The metalworking debris and materials so notable at Machu Picchu are matched only in the Late Horizon assemblage from around Jauja, plus a single piece of casting waste from Sacsawaman. The geographic patterning discussed below suggests that T-shaped tumis (types 2840 to 2849) are one of the better candidates for a type of metal artifact spread by Inca expansion and administration. Nevertheless, T-shaped tumis of any variety occur in just over half of the eight Late Horizon assemblages.

Some object types are common enough in these Late Horizon assemblages that they might have been spread around the empire by the Inca, albeit not in the consistent way that Inca ceramics were. Types that were spread by the Inca empire should be present in the Inca core (for example, in at least one of the three heartland assemblages) and reasonably common across the empire (for example, in at least half of the eight major assemblages). Using these criteria, we find that types that might have been spread in at least an inconsistent way by the empire include: several variants of half-round-headed tupus (types 1010, 1011, 1012); plain round-headed tupus (type 1001); drooping tupus (type 1014); small, flat discs with a single hole near the edge (type 5422); larger discs with a pierced suspension tab, called *lirpus* and discussed below (type 5610); T-shaped tumis of various kinds (types 2840 to 2849); and spheroid bola weights (type 1801). Sheet strips (type 3190) meet the criteria, but this catch-all category probably includes too many different kinds of objects to be meaningful in itself. Nevertheless, in all four of the Late Horizon assemblages in which strips are found, at least one example is the possible headband subtype. The discussion about geographic distributions of artifacts will evaluate all these candidates, and others.

Some other quotidian metal artifact types are sometimes considered to be characteristically Inca, including: the triangular tweezers (type 1101) emphasized by Mathewson (1915), Nordenskiöld (1921), and Rutledge and Gordon (1987, figs. 7, 8); teardrop-shaped tweezers (type 1103); a characteristic type of cast conical or bell-shaped ornament (types 1900 to 1903); and star-shaped mace heads (type 2760). None of these types turn up consistently in these Late Horizon assemblages. It would be difficult to argue on archaeological grounds that any of them were part of a consistently deployed package of Inca symbols, although their geographic distributions suggest that some were spread in less formal and consistent ways through Inca state activities.

Ethnohistorical sources such as Garcilaso de la Vega (1961:13) and Cobo (1983:208) say that only people of high status had the privilege of wearing large earspools. Guaman Poma (1615) routinely depicts Inca nobles and officials with earspools. He notes that the first Inca noble, Manco Capac, wore ear ornaments of gold (Guaman Poma 1615:87). Metal earspools were evidently symbols of nobility, office, and perhaps the state. Yet metal earspools (types 1300 to 1311) are found among the Late Horizon assemblages only in Ica, and the geographic data presented in the following discussion confirm that they come almost exclusively from the coast, typically from burials. Metal earspools are scarce in Late Horizon assemblages, probably because most excavations simply do not sample burials of people of high enough status. This is clearly the case at Machu Picchu, where most artifacts apparently pertain to yanacona retainers (Salazar 2004:27, 30, 44–45). Metal earspools were probably too rare in use, and even more so in archaeological contexts, to show the expected geographic patterns. Nevertheless, the strong coastal bias of the ones that have been recovered begs for some explanation.

Similarly, Guaman Poma (1615) illustrates Inca rulers and some officials holding maces with star-shaped heads that were probably metallic, although this form was also made in stone (Verneau and Rivet 1912; Salazar and Burger 2004a:163–164). Cobo (1983:246) describes gold-colored *champi*, probably star-shaped maces, that were both a category of weapon and insignia of the Inca ruler. Using Mayer's publications (1986, 1992, 1994, 1998), Lechtman (2007:336–341) identifies star-shaped mace heads as imperial "standard issue" shiny metal arms or insignia distributed by the Inca, in part for their visual impact. Nevertheless, metal star-shaped mace heads are scarce in the sample of known Late Horizon metal assemblages, appearing only at Sacsawaman, Ica, and a small Late Horizon collection from Quebrada de la Vaca. At least five of the star-shaped mace heads in the database came from burials. Star-shaped maces were more widely distributed than metal earspools, but they were still only inconsistently part of quotidian Late Horizon metal assemblages.

In short, these Late Horizon assemblages suggest that no metal objects or sets of objects for everyday use were consistently typical of Inca occupations. Ethnohistorical sources suggest that a few types, such as earspools, headdress frontals, and yauri pikes, were imperial symbols, but they were so rare and presumably prized that they rarely entered the archaeological deposits sampled here. They certainly were not part of daily life for anyone but the high nobility. Several more quotidian types were probably characteristic of the Cuzco area or the Inca ethnicity, but they were not consistently used as markers of ethnicity or Inca state affiliation in the way that decorated ceramics were. Late Horizon metal assemblages such as that of Machu Picchu have to be assessed in comparison to assemblages from specific regions, such as the Inca heartland, or by comparison to specific sites, because there was no broad Inca imperial standard for commonplace metalwork.

Regional Patterns in Andean Metalworking

While the comparison of Late Horizon assemblages is based on fewer than 800 artifacts with good associations for dating, all 10,120 artifacts in the database can contribute to geographic distribution maps (Figures 2.1 through 2.47, page 142). In these maps, the sizes of the symbols are proportional to the number of objects at each location, "MP" indicates the location of Machu Picchu, and locations within 10 km of each other are lumped for better visibility. The geographic coverage of the full sample (Figure 2.1A) corresponds roughly to the maximum extent of the Inca empire, while the coverage of artifacts with documented Late Horizon associations (Figure 2.1C) is more limited. Comparisons of many maps of different metal artifacts suggest 17 regions of contrasting metal artifact assemblages (Figure 2.1B). Despite some subjectivity and gaps in the underlying data, these regions should approximate the regional metalworking traditions of the Late Intermediate and Late Horizon periods. They correspond roughly to broad cultural regions defined primarily by ceramics (Lumbreras 1974:2).

These maps present the geographic distributions of many types of metal artifacts, loosely grouped by similarity and the regions in which they are concentrated. They provide the regional context necessary for interpreting metal assemblages such as the one from Machu Picchu.

TABLE 2.2. Interpretation of geographic distributions of artifacts.

Inca heartland	Periphery	Interpretation	Inca style?
Scarce	Concentrated	Provincial	No
Present, not concentrated	Widespread	General Andean	No
Concentrated	Scarce	Cuzqueño	Yes
Concentrated	Widespread	Cuzqueño or corporate Inca	Yes

Possible Inca Types

Which, if any, quotidian metal artifacts signified a connection to the Inca empire? The geographic distribution maps suggest some answers. Metal objects would have been exchanged and carried from place to place by their owners, most notably by *mitimaes*, settlers moved by the state from their homeland to colonize some other location, and yanaconas, permanent servants or retainers of the elite, who were also frequently relocated by the Inca (Niles 2004:58). The Inca moved metalsmiths from many different regions to Cuzco and other places (Lechtman 2007:320), where they probably made at least some objects in their home styles. Smiths may have emulated or adopted styles from other regions, including an Inca style. Despite this complexity, the geographic distributions of commonplace metal artifacts are often clear.

Four kinds of patterns help in identifying Inca-style artifacts (Table 2.2). First, many types of artifacts are relatively scarce in the Inca heartland around Cuzco and concentrated in a peripheral region of the empire. These styles, presumably not Inca, are provincial and specific to non-Inca ethnicities. Second, other artifacts are uniformly widespread throughout the Andes, without any particular concentration in the Inca heartland. These, too, are probably not Inca in style, but rather broadly Andean. These types might be particularly old or might have spread from an earlier originating center such as Huari or Tiwanaku, after which centuries of continuing manufacture and exchange in peripheral areas obscured the pattern of concentration at the original source. Third, a few artifact types are concentrated in the Inca heartland and are scarce or patchy outside it. These artifacts are probably Inca in style but were not spread by the expansion of the Inca state. They fall toward the middle of the continuum of Inca-ness, reflecting Cuzqueño material culture, and they were apparently not manufactured and distributed regularly for imperial purposes. Finally, some artifacts are concentrated in the Inca heartland and also well distributed throughout much of the empire. These are probably Inca-style objects that were spread, intentionally or incidentally, by the empire. They could be markers of Cuzqueño identity that were dispersed along with Inca administrators, or by other people adopting signifiers of the politically dominant ethnicity. In principle, these artifacts could also be components of an Inca corporate style, dispersed as part of an imperial strategy. However, since the comparison of Late Horizon assemblages suggests that there was no consistent corporate Inca style of quotidian metal artifacts, this pattern indicates only a dispersed Cuzqueño, not imperial, style.

Using similar reasoning, we can identify several bronze object types that were widespread enough to suggest that their distribution resulted from, or was facilitated by, activities of the Inca state: tupus with half-round heads, tupus and T-shaped tumis with animal heads, T-shaped tumis in general, bola weights with suspension holes with crossbars, "classic" star-shaped mace heads, "classic" T-shaped axes, "ancla" axes, and "axe-maces," which replaced one point of a star-shaped mace head with a small axe blade (Mayer 1986, 1992, 1994, 1998; Lechtman 2007:336–337). Lechtman calls several of these "essentially 'state issue.'" These objects were visual markers of association with the Inca state or Cuzqeño ethnicity, although they were not as standardized as were cumbi cloth or fine ceramics (Lechtman 2007:336–337), and were not consistently deployed in the way that ceramics were. The following discussions reconstruct some possible meanings of quotidian metal objects by combining conclusions from the comparison of dated Late Horizon assemblages, regional patterning (shown in Figures 2.1 through 2.47), and, in some cases, ethnohistorical sources. The results are summarized in Table 2.3.

Tupus

Tupu pins were ubiquitous throughout most of the study area (see Figure 2.1D; all these maps should be evaluated relative to the distribution of the entire database, plotted in Figure 2.1A, B). Compared to the whole sample, tupus are more concentrated in the Inca core, the region northeast of Titicaca, and the southern Titicaca region, that is, in the south-central highlands. Conversely, tupus are relatively scarcer on the Peruvian coast. The concentration of tupus in the south-central highlands could be a matter of material culture style, or it might be a functional response to the colder highlands weather and corresponding dress, since tupus served, among other things, to secure women's clothing (Guaman Poma 1615; Lechtman 2007:332).

A clearer picture emerges from looking at specific types of tupus. The discussion of Late Horizon assemblages suggested that several variants of half-round-headed tupus might have been associated with Inca ethnicity or the state. The geographic distribution of half-round-headed tupu types 1010, 1011, and 1012 (Figures 2.2B, C, D and 2.3A) tends to confirm that. Half-round-headed tupus are concentrated in the Inca core area, with a thin but broad scattering throughout much of the rest of the empire. These tupus are far from ubiquitous in the sampled Late Horizon assemblages, which suggests that they were not a necessary or vital component of intrusive Inca material culture. It seems likely, however, that they reached many regions outside the Inca core through the people serving Cuzco.

The only other tupu types with a distribution that suggests a possible link to the Inca empire are a range of rare types topped by cast heads of camelids, felines, and perhaps other animals (types 1055 to 1058; Figure 2.3B). Lechtman (2007:336) identifies tumi knives with these animal heads as an imperial Inca type, as does Rowe (1996:314). While lost-wax casting was practiced in some places long before

TABLE 2.3. Meanings of some potentially Inca metal object types.

Type	Late Horizon assemblages	Geographic distribution	Meaning: regional reference
Ear spool	One peripheral assemblage: Ica	Concentrated on coast, very scarce in Inca core	Ethnohistory suggests explicit symbol
Yauri	None of the assemblages	Concentrated in Inca core, almost exclusively	Possibly explicit symbol[b]
Axe-mace[a]	None of the assemblages	Concentrated in Inca core, very scarce in periphery	Possibly explicit symbol[c]
Frontal: concave-sided	Two Inca core assemblages	Concentrated in Inca core, very scarce in periphery	Possibly explicit symbol[d]
Star-shaped mace head: "classic"[a]	Two Inca core, two peripheral	Concentrated in Inca core, widespread and moderately common in periphery	Cuzqueño identity? Military role?
Axe: "classic" T-shaped[a]	Two Inca core, no peripheral	Concentrated in Inca core, widespread and moderately common in periphery	Cuzqueño identity?
Axe: "ancla" form	One Inca core: Machu Picchu	Concentrated in Inca core, widespread but not common in periphery	Cuzqueño identity?
T-shaped tumi in general	Three Inca core, two peripheral	Concentrated in Inca core and south of Titicaca, widespread and common in periphery	Cuzqueño identity or affiliation?
T-shaped tumi: animal-head[a]	One Inca core, one peripheral	Concentrated in Inca core, widespread and marginally common in periphery	Cuzqueño identity?
T-shaped tumi: disc head	None of the assemblages	Concentrated in Inca core, widespread but very scarce in periphery	Cuzqueño identity?
Tupu: animal-head	One peripheral: Jauja	Concentrated in Inca core, widespread but scarce in periphery	Cuzqueño identity?
Tupu: half-round, all variants	Three Inca core, three peripheral	Concentrated in Inca core and south of Titicaca, widespread but scarce in periphery	Cuzqueño identity?
Lirpu: disc with suspension tab	Two Inca core, two peripheral	Concentrated in Inca core, widespread but scarce in periphery	Cuzqueño identity? See discussion in text
Bola: spheroid and elaborated	Two Inca core, three peripheral	Concentrated in Inca core, widespread and moderately common in periphery	Cuzqueño identity?
Tool: plumb bob	Two Inca core	Rare but concentrated in Inca core, none in periphery	Cuzqueño identity?
Tool: crowbar	Two Inca core	Rare but concentrated in Inca core, widespread but very scarce in periphery	Cuzqueño identity?
Conical "bell"	One Inca core, one peripheral	Possibly concentrated south of Titicaca, widespread but somewhat scarce in periphery	Provincial, spread by empire? See text
Tupu: drooping	Three Inca core, one peripheral	Concentrated south of Titicaca, scarce in Inca core, widespread but scarce in periphery	Provincial, spread by empire?
Sheet strip: headband?	Two Inca core, two peripheral	Concentrated on Peruvian coast, scarce in Inca core, scarce in southern periphery	Provincial, spread by empire?
Tweezers: in general	Two Inca core, three peripheral	Concentrated on Peruvian coast, scarce in Inca core, widespread and moderately common in periphery	Provincial, spread by empire?
Tweezers: triangular	Two Inca core assemblages	Concentrated on south and central Peruvian coast, scarce in Inca core, very scarce in rest of periphery	Provincial, spread by empire?
Tiny spoon	One Inca core: Machu Picchu	Concentrated on central Peruvian coast, scarce in Inca core, scarce in some of periphery	Provincial, spread by empire?
Small disc, one hole	Three Inca core, one peripheral	Concentrated in Inca core, central highlands, central and south Peruvian coast, widespread but scarce in periphery	General central Andean?
Tupu: round	Three Inca core, two peripheral	Concentrated in Inca core and Titicaca regions, widespread and common in periphery	General Andean

[a] "State issue" (Lechtman 2007).   [b] Larrea 1941.   [c] Lechtman 2007.   [d] Guaman Poma 1615.

the Late Horizon, in others it was introduced or popularized by the Inca (Owen 1986; Costin et al. 1989; Lechtman 2007:336–337). These tupus were probably part of that process of technological change under the Inca. Tupus with cast animal heads are uncommon outside the Inca core, and there is only a single example among the eight Late Horizon assemblages discussed earlier. Like the half-round-headed tupus, then, tupus with cast animal heads may have originated in the Inca core, been disseminated through imperial activities, and even been recognizable as Inca in style, but were probably not used systematically to signify Inca affiliation.

Plain round-headed tupus (type 1001), by contrast, are widespread in many regions from Titicaca north, with only a slight concentration in the Inca core (Figure 2.2A). More of them come from the southern Titicaca area. It would be difficult to argue from this map that round-headed tupus were related to Inca expansion or signified Inca identity. Round-headed tupus are known from many Wari contexts, including Conchopata (Isbell 1985; William Isbell, personal communication, 2012), Pikillacta (Lechtman 2005:135-139), Aqo Wayqo (Ochatoma Paravicino and Cabrera Romero 2001:110), and Cerro Amaru (Topic and Topic 1984, undated field notes on Cerro Amaru metals, pp. 21-43). They may have been spread by Wari or Tiwanaku, or both, or simply had more time to diffuse broadly than did types that perhaps developed later.

Many types and features of tupus seem to have originated in the southern Titicaca area (Figures 2.3D through 2.5A). One type with drooping corners (type 1014, Figure 2.3D) was even found in enough of the Late Horizon assemblages to hint that it could have been spread from its southern center by Inca expansion. None of these southern Titicaca types is common in the Inca core, but all do occur there, and occasional examples are found in distant parts of the empire. Lechtman (2007:330) argues that the Inca adopted their imperial tin-bronze alloy from the metalworkers of the altiplano south of Lake Titicaca. The southern Titicaca tradition of tupu forms seems to have traveled the same route to the Inca heartland and from there to the rest of the empire in ever decreasing numbers. Perhaps some were carried by yanacona retainers from the southern altiplano, or made by southern altiplano metalsmiths relocated to Cuzco or beyond. People outside the altiplano might have recognized these types as exotic, perhaps even identifying them as coming from the southern Titicaca area.

Artifacts that seem to be oversized representations of tupus are also limited to the southern Titicaca area (Figure 2.8B). Not only are they very large for tupus, but they also have various styles of thickened or very wide handles in place of the pin shaft of a tupu.

Tupus with round heads and two spiral ornaments or a small rounded tab both seem to be concentrated in the central highlands of Peru, and both types occur occasionally in the Inca core as well (Figure 2.7A, B). These may be additional examples of metal types that reached the Inca capital region with relocated yanaconas or through exchange facilitated by the empire. Two other types, one with a squat oval head and the other with a simple, slightly thickened head like a finishing nail, seem characteristic of the Moquegua region (Figure 2.5B, C), although examples of only the squat ovoid tupu (type 1003) appear in the Inca core.

The region northeast of Titicaca seems almost cut off from Inca metalworking. Four distinctive types of tupus are concentrated there (Figure 2.6A, B, C, D). These types did not reach the Inca core and were only rarely carried even into the southern Titicaca area. The database does not include a single example from any other region. The insularity of this metalworking tradition suggests that the region was much less involved with the rest of the Inca empire in exchanges of people, goods, and ideas than was the southern altiplano. This finding agrees with impressions based on ceramics, architecture, and other lines of evidence (Chapin 1961).

Several types of axially symmetrical tupus (types 1040, 1041, 1042, and 1044; Figure 2.7C, D) are found almost exclusively in northern and central coastal Peru. In this case, however, other objects from the area did reach the Inca core, suggesting that these axially symmetrical tupus might have fallen out of use prior to the Late Horizon.

Possible Lime Dippers

Two categories of artifacts resemble tupus, but probably served some other function, perhaps as dippers to extract powdered lime from a container while chewing coca. One category is a range of what look like miniature tupus with tiny, elaborately cast heads less than 6 mm across and sharp, narrow shafts generally only 1.5 to 2.5 mm in diameter and usually 60 to 90 mm long (Appendix G, Figure G2, types 2410 to 2439). These would probably have been too small to function well as clothing fasteners and would not have been very visible as clothing ornaments. They are found primarily in the southern Titicaca region, but also with less frequency in the Inca core and very rarely elsewhere in the Inca realm (Figure 2.8C). This distribution suggests that they may have been carried around the empire by people from the southern Titicaca region or perhaps were adopted by some Cuzqueños as recognizably exotic items.

The other category also resembles tupus, in that they bear the same heads as do tupus found nearby (Appendix G, Figure G2, types 5221 to 5225). Unlike tupus, though, they have fat, blunt shafts generally 5 to 9 mm in diameter, totaling 100 to 200 mm long. These are not suited to push through a textile, but might serve to pick up powdered lime when wetted. Interestingly, these fat-shafted implements are found primarily in the portion of the southern Titicaca region adjacent to the northeastern Titicaca region, but the tupus with the same styles of heads are primarily found slightly to the north, in that adjacent region (Figures 2.6A, C, D and 2.8D).

Tumis

T-shaped tumis are concentrated in the Inca core and have a wide distribution (Figure 2.9A; see Figures 2.9B through 2.11D), much like that of half-round-headed tupus and cast animal-head tupus (Figures 2.2B through 2.3B), but in far greater numbers. This pattern suggests that T-shaped tumis as a general form could have been spread or popularized by the growth and operation of the Inca state, although their utilitarian nature and their variable presence in the dated assemblages suggest that they were not explicit symbols of the state. Of the 51 T-shaped tumis in the database with known temporal associations, all but two are Late Horizon and the remainder date to either the Late Horizon or the Colonial period. Most variants of T-shaped tumi blade forms and handle treatments are distributed in roughly the same widespread but Cuzco-centric pattern (Figures 2.9B, C, 2.10A, B, C, and 2.11A), rather than being concentrated in different regions. This pattern suggests that the various kinds of T-shaped tumis are not local developments, but rather all spread from the Inca core as part of one process. On the other hand, the backswept type 2846 (Figure 2.9D) seems generally central and southern, and cast figures or scenes on the handle (Figure 2.10D) are characteristic of the central coast and north of Peru, suggesting either regional variation in a type of tool spread by Inca personnel, or perhaps pre-existing local traditions of T-shaped tumis.

Lechtman (2007:336–337) labels fancy cast animal-headed tumis as "standard issue" Inca items. Animal-headed T-shaped tumis (Figure 2.10C), like the scarcer disc-headed T-shaped tumis (Figure 2.11A), are distributed in much the same pattern as the other tumi types and the stylistically similar animal-head tupus, consistent with dissemination from the Inca core, but not reliably present in the dated assemblages. While these tumis were particularly distinctive in technology and appearance, and presumably would have connoted Cuzqueño origins, they might have been just specific aspects of a more general diffusion of T-shaped tumis throughout the empire.

Bola Weights
Finely finished cast bola weights of copper alloys, both spheroidal and in various decorative shapes, also have a fairly broad distribution that is concentrated in the Inca core (Figures 2.24C, D and 2.25C). The spheroidal ones might be ubiquitous enough in the Late Horizon assemblages to be potential Inca objects. All variants of these bola weights have a distinctive attachment hole traversed internally by a bar around which a cord could be threaded. These objects, embodying the same lost-wax casting technique and restrained sculptural style as the animal-headed tupus and tumis, could have been dispersed in the same incidental way through activities of Inca state personnel. Most are found in the highlands, probably because bolas were most useful for hunting in open *puna* grasslands and adjacent environments.

Cruder but functionally analogous bola weights made of lead with attachment holes in a U shape or straight through are found around Jauja, in the central highlands (Figure 2.25A). Three much larger lead bola weights with circumferential grooves for attaching cords were collected by Adolph Bandelier from two sites south of Titicaca (Figure 2.25B). Mayer (1994) illustrates many cast bronze representations of the same form, some with suspension holes with crossbars and a thick cord depicted filling the circumferential groove, from vague proveniences in the same general region. Stone bola weights of similar size and shape are found in the Inca heartland (Salazar and Burger 2004a:165–166) and beyond. Not only bola weights, but also lead objects in general are rare in museum collections and publications, and they are limited largely to the central coast and highlands (Figure 2.47A), suggesting that these two highly localized traditions of lead bolas probably had no direct connection to the Inca.

Discs
Small, thin sheet metal discs under 40 mm in diameter with a single hole near the edge (type 5422) were also common enough in Late Horizon assemblages to perhaps have been spread by the Inca empire. These discs often still have a thread knotted through the hole, suggesting that they were sewn onto textiles (Salazar and Roussakis 2002:282). They are concentrated in the Inca core, but equally concentrated in the central highlands, and relatively less but still significantly so on the south and central coast of Peru (Figure 2.37B). This pattern suggests that while these small discs with a single hole might have been associated with Cuzqueño identity, they were more probably simply in general use in the central Andes. Other regions emphasized variants that differ in size, number and position of holes, or by convex versus flat form (Figures 2.37A, C, D and 2.38A, B).

Axes and Yauris
Metal axe heads of many different forms are widespread throughout the Andes, although they may make up a higher proportion of the metals from highland areas than coastal ones (Figure 2.15C; compare to the entire dataset in Figure 2.1A). Most of the axe data are from Mayer (1986, 1992, 1994, 1998). Their ubiquity and regional variation indicate that axes in general were undoubtedly widespread before the rise of the Inca state, and Mayer identifies or implies many regional styles of axes in his monumental compendia of photographs, not all of which are addressed here. A few specific types and characteristics were evidently linked to the Inca.

The hafting technique based on projecting tangs on either side of the back of the blade is widespread and was evidently popular in the Inca core, as well as in other regions (Figure 2.15D). Variants with rectangular tangs, curved tangs, and tangs combined with a single small hole (Figure 2.16A, B, C) were common in the Inca core and other areas. These broadly dispersed and slightly differing patterns suggest that hafting styles were probably established in regional traditions before the Late Horizon, although they do not rule out dissemination from the Inca heartland. A different hafting style with a single large hole through a thick base with no tangs was clearly an Ecuadorian tradition (Figure 2.16D).

Blade forms also tend to be widespread, with different regions of greatest popularity and no particular concentration in the Inca core. Relatively long blades that narrow towards the cutting edge, ranging from fairly broad to spike-like forms, are found primarily in the southern half of the Inca realm (Figure 2.17A). Long rectangular to very slightly flaring blades have a similar distribution, but are more numerous (Figure 2.17B). Short rectangular blades are more tightly concentrated in two separate, presumably unrelated traditions: some Ecuadorian axes of the thick, large-holed style have short rectangular blades, as do some of the thinner, tanged axes of the southern Titicaca and Cochabamba areas (Figure 2.17C.) Trapezoidal blades are the most uniformly widespread, with no obvious regional concentration other than the many pre-Inca examples from the anomalous metal-rich burials of Vicus in northernmost Peru (Figure 2.17D). Broad crescent blades of various forms are widespread, but especially common in Ecuador (Figure 2.18A), while wide, straight-edged blades ("transverse rectangular") are uncommon but primarily found in the eastern central Andes (Figure 2.18B).

Other features are more regionally specific, such as bars or points on both sides of the axe blade, and a hook on one side of the blade, both clearly features of the tradition of northwest Argentina (Figure 2.19C, D). A few axes with sidebars were used in the Inca core and even farther away in northern Peru, perhaps by people moved from the south by the Inca state. Axes cast with a hafting socket rendered as a sculptural head and face are primarily from Vicus, where they likely predate the Inca (Figure 2.20D), as may other forms with simpler hafting sockets from northern Peru (Figure 2.20C).

Specific combinations of features are the most diagnostic, including two apparently Inca forms. Wide blades combined with small, variant tangs and no mounting hole are found primarily in Ecuador, where they have a particular blade shape that Mayer (1992) called "hoja-hoz," and in a presumably unrelated style east of Lake Titicaca with other wide blade shapes (Figure 2.20A). Tanged spike-form axes with a small mounting hole and a long, narrowing blade are found primarily southeast of Lake Titicaca (Figure 2.20B). What museum visitors might think of as the most typical Andean axe form, a trapezoidal blade with rectangular tangs and no hole (type 4250), is in fact found in precisely the widespread but Cuzco-centric distribution expected of an artifact type disseminated by the activities of the Inca state (Figure 2.18C). Oddly enough, there are only three examples of these "classic" axes among the 740 metal artifacts from dated Inca assemblages (see Table 2.1), two from Machu Picchu and one from Ollantaytambo, suggesting that these axes could have been dispersed according to local needs rather than used everywhere as routine markers of Inca identity or force. Axes with curved tangs, no hole, and a wide crescent blade, Mayer's "forma de ancla" (type 4470), have a similar distribution, although they are scarcer in Peru and Bolivia relative to Ecuador and northwest Argentina (Figure 2.18D). Again, the pattern fits expectations for an artifact spread by the Inca state.

These "ancla" axes tend to be particularly finely shaped and finished. T-shaped axes were generally cast in simple, open, single-valve molds that produced an asymmetrical casting that had twice the desired relief or thickness changes on the mold side, and a flat but differently textured surface on the open side. Mayer (1986, 1992, 1994, 1998) illustrates many of these molds. These castings then had to be fairly heavily forged to their final symmetrical form in the vertical plane and to create a consolidated, matching smooth surface finish on both sides. "Ancla" axes often have a ridge or parting line along both sides, indicating that they were cast in symmetrical, smooth-surfaced two-part molds that joined tightly and were precisely aligned. This more complex technology produced castings that were already symmetrical in the vertical plane and had the same finish on both sides. These castings were closer to their final form and finish, requiring less forging to complete. While more skill and effort would have been required initially to make the two-part molds, this technology would have produced axes with less cost in time and forging labor per piece, and with more predictable, repeatable shapes. Both would have been desirable characteristics for "state issue" equipment (Lechtman 2007).

This more refined and labor-efficient technology might be expected to have been a later stage in the development of Inca metalworking. The spatial distribution of "ancla" axes (Figure 2.18D) independently suggests the same thing. Compared to "classic" T-shaped axes, "ancla" axes are relatively more common in the northern and southern extremities of the empire, which Inca personnel and artifacts reached only late in the state's expansion. "Ancla" axes are relatively less common in Peru and Bolivia, which may have experienced their primary influx of Inca material culture before the two-piece mold technology was in extensive use. That "classic" T-shaped axes were also widespread in the northern and southern extremities of the state suggests that "ancla" axes did not replace, but rather supplemented, them. An alternative interpretation is that the "ancla" axes were more associated with conquest, still ongoing or recent in the northern and southern periphery at the arrival of the Spanish, while "classic" T-shaped axes were more needed for ongoing operations of the state and so were more uniformly distributed throughout its territory.

A modest number of axes have a tubular socket for a wooden handle and a projecting tab opposite the blade (Appendix G, Figure G13, types 4620 to 4690). This hafting technique is a representation in cast metal of a hafted tanged axe with its leather binding stitched together at the back (Ambrosetti 1904:237–242; Nordenskiöld 1921:61–65; Latcham 1938:318–319, 341–342). Axes with this socketed hafting are clearly concentrated in northwest Argentina, but with a number of examples far away in Cuzco (Figure 2.19A). This pattern resembles the distribution of axes with sidebars (Figure 2.19C), down to the scattered examples in northern Peru, at different sites. Both might be traces of the same process of interaction between the Inca core and northwest Argentina, which would have involved moving workers and their tools, or perhaps metalworkers and their stylistic preferences, from northwest Argentina to Cuzco, and from there to northern Peru.

Larrea (1941) identified a subset of this kind of axe with a long, rod-like point and argued on ethnohistorical grounds that it was called a yauri (type 4690) and was an explicit symbol of Inca authority (also see Lechtman 2007:339–340). Many of Guaman Poma's illustrations show Inca rulers and military officials holding weapons that may be yauris (Guaman Poma 1615). Of the seven examples in the database, six are from Cuzco and one from the southern Titicaca area (Figure 2.19B). Two miniatures that may have functioned as tupus or lime dippers are from Cuzco and the Island of the Sun. This geographic distribution, although consistent with Larrea's ethnohistorical argument, does not have the empire-wide dispersal necessary to independently imply a symbolic role for this type.

Star-shaped Mace Heads and Axe-maces
As noted earlier, Guaman Poma illustrates many of the Inca rulers, soldiers, and some nonmilitary Inca officials such as the chief courier (*Hatun Chasqui*) holding maces with star-shaped heads, sometimes in battle and sometimes in administrative, ceremonial, or diplomatic situations (Guaman Poma 1615). One drawing has the captured Inca Tupac Amaru holding a star-shaped mace while being escorted in chains, suggesting that Guaman Poma may have seen the mace more as a symbol than as a dangerous weapon (Guaman Poma 1615:451). Cobo (1983:246) is probably referring to star-shaped maces when he describes a kind of weapon that was also used as an insignia of the Inca ruler.

Metal mace heads in general are widespread in the Andes, although they were perhaps relatively more common in Peru and Bolivia than in the northern and southern reaches of the Inca empire (Figure 2.21A; compare to the entire dataset in Figure 2.1A). Although rounded mace heads, or possibly haft weights or clod breakers, of stone are common in many regions, metal ones are relatively scarce and largely restricted to the central coast and north of Peru (Figure 2.21B). Disc-shaped mace heads are also primarily found in northern Peru, especially in large numbers in the burials at Vicus, plus a few stylistically different examples from the southern parts of the Inca realm (Figure 2.21C). Star-shaped mace heads as a general category are widespread (Figure 2.21D), but some variants are more regionally specific. Forms with a central cylinder are found primarily on the central coast of Peru and northwards (Figure 2.22A). A less common form with points shaped more like vertical fins or blades is entirely restricted to the central and south coast of Peru (Figure 2.22B).

The classic form of star-shaped mace heads, with medium-length, rounded points and no central cylinder, is distributed in just the pattern expected of artifacts disseminated by the Inca state, virtually the same as "classic" T-shaped axes, "ancla" axes, and animal-headed tupus and tumis (Figure 2.22C; compare to Figures 2.3B, 2.10C, and 2.18C, D). Like those other types, though, "classic" star-shaped mace heads are not found consistently in the dated Late Horizon assemblages, with four examples from Sacsawaman, two from a single grave in Ica, and one from Quebrada de la Vaca, but none from Machu Picchu, Ollantaytambo, or other Inca sites. Like "classic" axes, their distribution probably reflects characteristically Inca responses to specific local needs, rather than a uniform suite of Inca items needed anywhere to signify Inca identity or the state. Star-shaped mace heads are another type that Lechtman (2007:336–341) identifies as "standard issue," suggesting that they were probably available primarily to military leaders as insignia. Their meaning might fall somewhere between the apparently explicit, official significance of some headdress frontals and what was likely a customary or ethnic significance of such items as half-round-headed tupus.

Axe-maces are far less common than the "classic" star-shaped mace heads from which they clearly derive. Lechtman (2007) assesses them in much the same way. Their distribution, heavily concentrated around Cuzco with a few examples at distant sites to the south (Figure 2.22D), is consistent with her interpretation of axe-maces as "state issue," but is a bit thin to suggest that in itself. Their relatively greater concentration around Cuzco, together with their much smaller numbers, might suggest that axe-maces signified higher rank or closer connections to the imperial core than did the more common simple star-shaped mace heads.

Lirpus: Discs with Suspension Tabs

Called lirpu (Quechua for "mirror") by Peruvian archaeologists, these flat, sturdy discs with a suspension tab (types 5610 and 5620) are depicted by Guaman Poma as pectoral ornaments worn by warriors like a necklace (Gonzales Holguín [1608] 1952:318, 516; Guaman Poma 1615; Petersen 1970:118–119). They are almost certainly not mirrors for viewing a reflected image, but may have been associated with warfare in general and intended to reflect sunlight for symbolic reasons in that context (Salazar 2001:122; Nielsen 2007). Guaman Poma's only use of the term "lirpu" (1615:117, spelled "lirpo") refers to women's attire, but the object is not illustrated. He shows what we now call lirpus on the chests of high-ranking Inca soldiers, from a high-status *orejon* guard of the captive Inca Huascar, to a well-dressed fighter celebrating Coya Raymi, to several named military leaders, including Challco Chima (Guaman Poma 1615). He also depicts them on pre-Inca *Auca Runa* (war-like people) and Challco Chima's Cañarí opponents, suggesting that the chronicler associated them with ranking soldiers in general, rather than with Inca identity or allegiance (Guaman Poma 1615:63, 163; Salazar 2001:122; Nielsen 2007). Yet all three of the examples from Machu Picchu come from two burials that also contained tupus (Table 2.6), which are usually associated with women (Lechtman 2007:332; see also the same passage in Guaman Poma [1615:117]). (Bingham [1930, fig. 137] illustrates four lirpus from Machu Picchu. However, lirpu "d" is not now in the collection and a lirpu numbered ANT.017849, in the collection but not in Bingham's illustration, was purchased as part of the private Alvistur collection of artifacts that probably come primarily from the general Cuzco region.) Among the Late Horizon assemblages, lirpus are proportionally most common at Sacsawaman. Sacsawaman functioned as a fortress during the conquest, which fits with a military interpretation. Yet Sacsawaman also has a high density of tupus, suggesting that the assemblage includes plenty of items used by women, or buried with them. One lirpu from Sacsawaman came from the burial of a woman with two tupus (Salazar 2001:121). Salazar (2001:121; Salazar and Burger 2004a:186–187) identifies the Machu Picchu examples as mirrors and links them to women as well.

Like the half-round-headed tupus and other items mentioned above, lirpus are concentrated in the Inca core and thinly scattered elsewhere in the empire (Figure 2.32A), suggesting that they were spread by actions of the Inca state. However, they are too scarce both geographically and in Late Horizon assemblages (see Table 2.1) to have been explicit insignia of Inca identity unless they were limited to a very few Inca officials. The burial associations make that interpretation unlikely. Insignia of high rank would not have been buried with multiple yanacona women at Machu Picchu. Why lirpus seem related to both women and warfare, cross-cutting both status and political allegiance, begs for further investigation.

Earspools and Headdress Frontals

Historical sources indicate that wearing earspools was a prerogative of the Inca nobility that was occasionally granted to individuals or ethnic groups (Garcilaso de la Vega 1961:6, 12, 13, 139, 188; Cobo 1983:208, 245). Guaman Poma almost always depicts Inca rulers and nobles with earspools (Guaman Poma 1615). Yet the archaeological distribution of metal earspools (types 1300 to 1311) is limited almost exclusively to the Peruvian south, central, and north coasts (Figure 2.31C). Among the Late Horizon assemblages, they are found only in Ica. As noted earlier, metal earspools were presumably used by too few people, of too high status, to turn up regularly in the quotidian assemblages studied here. The interpretation of earspools as explicit symbols of nobility and imperial office depends primarily on documentary sources. The strong coastal Peruvian pattern remains to be explained.

In Guaman Poma's illustrations, important figures other than the Inca himself often wear headgear with a flat ornament mounted on the forehead. Guaman Poma consistently depicts four shapes that could represent sheet metal cutouts: a disc, a horseshoe shape with squared ends pointing down, a crescent moon shape with pointed ends facing up, and a shape like a vertical trapezoid with concave sides and the wider end down (Guaman Poma 1615). All four shapes are shown with a central dot or small circle, perhaps a mounting hole. Guaman Poma may have understood these shapes to have specific meanings, but that is not clear. All three illustrations of his own father and grandfather show them wearing the horseshoe frontal, suggesting that frontal shapes were related to descent or inherited roles (Guaman Poma 1615). Of the twelve men shown wearing a specific four-armed ornament below the chin, all but two also wear the crescent moon frontal, suggesting that these items had meanings that were related (Guaman Poma 1615). All four forms are worn by a variety of identified and unidentified officials and nobles. Guaman Poma depicts concave-sided frontals almost twice as often as the other types, on identified state officials ranging from the governor of the royal roads (*Governador de los Caminos Reales*), to a provincial administrator (*Corregidor de Provincias*), to the inspector of the realm (*Vecitador y Vedor de Estos Reinos*) (Guaman Poma 1615). At least some frontals may have had meanings independent of the Inca administrative system, since Guaman Poma shows the war-like *Auca Runa* wearing both horseshoe and disc frontals before the Inca existed (Guaman Poma 1615:63).

The horseshoe shape and crescent moon shapes are not clearly identifiable among the metal artifacts in the database. The disc frontals might correspond to the artifacts coded here as type 5428 (large flat disc with a central hole) or as type 5466 (large concave disc with a central hole). Of the four type 5428 flat discs in the database, three are from Ancon, and one is probably from Chan Chan. The one type 5466 concave disc was found at Sacsawaman.

The concave-sided form is clearly equivalent to the sheet metal frontals coded here as type 5311 (see Appendix G, Figure G12). Three of the eight concave-sided frontals in the database seem to be silver, and two seem to be silver-copper alloys, befitting markers of high status. The others might originally have had enriched silver surfaces as well, which are easily lost as a copper-silver alloy corrodes. They tend to be found in places important to Inca ritual practice where high-status people associated with the Inca state might have visited or been buried, including two on the Island of the Sun in Lake Titicaca, one each at Pachacamac, Sacsawaman, and Ollantaytambo, and three from various places around Cuzco (Figure 2.36B). These eight concave-sided frontals might have been explicit symbols of Inca office or of high status on other grounds. They were evidently limited to a few important officials. Guaman Poma's illustrations suggest that this headgear was restricted to fewer people than were large earspools, making the scarcity of metal earspools in the highlands by contrast even more puzzling.

Three other frontal shapes not illustrated by Guaman Poma may have had specific and possibly hierarchical meanings, perhaps related to an altiplano ethnic group or the south-central region of the empire. Type 5316 has a single crescent with the points facing up and a central stem or plume (Appendix G, Figure G12). Mayer (1994) identifies this type as a cutting tool, but it is distinguishable from other flat tumi or knife forms not only by its shape, but also by its two small, thread-sized central mounting holes and the lack of a larger, cord-sized hole at the end of the handle. Type 5320 has a rectangular plaque topped by a trapezoid or wide, flaring plume (Appendix G, Figure G12). Type 5312 combines and multiplies the other two, comprising a stack of two figures resembling the crescent and plume of type 5316, topped by a small version of the rectangle and trapezoid of type 5320 (Appendix G, Figure G12). This combination of elements that are also found separately suggests that the two simpler forms may have had discrete meanings and that the wearer of the combined form might have had a role that combined or oversaw those indicated by the other two. All are found primarily on the Island of the Sun in Lake Titicaca, presumably in relation to pilgrimages there, with a few examples from the Moquegua area and Cochabamba province (Figures 2.35B, C, D). Four additional examples of the crescent and plume type 5316 are known from Bolivia, but have only vague proveniences (Mayer 1994: lamina 23). Other types of headdress frontals, as well as sheet metal headdress structures to support them, are found primarily on the north and central coasts of Peru (Figure 2.36A; Appendix G, Figure G12), although various feather-like or rectilinear forms coded as "long plumes" are found in northern Peru and other styles of long single or double plumes occur on the Island of the Sun (Figure 2.35A; Appendix G, Figure G12).

Other Possibilities

There is no doubt that certain solid and hollow human figurines (types 1512 to 1515 and 1517 to 1532; see Appendix G, Figure G4, type 1514) represent a Cuzqueño style. Because many of these in museum collections have no provenience, and many are among the gold and silver showpieces that were not consistently sought for the database, the distribution of the small sample here is not very meaningful. None were found at Machu Picchu.

The discussion of Late Horizon assemblages highlighted a subset of metal strips (type 3190; Salazar and Burger 2004a:185) as objects that might have been spread through Inca channels. These long, flexible sheet metal strips have one or more holes at the ends and are often curved in diameters appropriate for use as headbands or waistbands. It is frequently difficult to distinguish fragments of these from other metal strips. Nevertheless, most of the examples of type 3190 that have holes probably fall in this category, so a map of this subset roughly approximates the distribution of these putative headbands (Figure 2.39A). They are primarily found along the Peruvian coast and around Moquegua, with two examples at Sillustani. The only two examples from the Inca core are from Sacsawaman and Machu Picchu (ANT.017872). This distribution suggests that these headbands might have been adopted by the Inca from coastal regions.

Sheet metal gauntlets or armlets were showy items, often with enriched gold or silver surfaces, that were probably functional and symbolic armor (Appendix G, Figure G11, type 3057). They are typically catalogued and published as single items, not pairs. Because they tend to be found with the precious metals that were not a focus of this research, they are underrepresented in the database. Nevertheless, this type is found occasionally throughout the Inca empire (Figure 2.36C). They are not particularly concentrated in the Inca core, and the apparent concentration in the Titicaca region reflects a single large collection of precious metals from Sillustani. Virtually identical pieces are known from pre-Inca burials on the north coast of Peru, suggesting that they could be a widespread, general Andean type, not one spread by the Inca.

Mayer (1986) illustrates and discusses many examples of a possibly related artifact type he calls a "brazal." These are roughly cast objects sometimes found as single items in burials, and were apparently worn on the forearm. They are found primarily in northwest Argentina and San Pedro de Atacama, and nowhere else in the Inca realm (Figure 2.36D). They may have gone out of use before the Inca reached the region, or they may have been part of a local military technology or iconography that the Inca would have had no interest in disseminating.

A dozen peculiar heavy cast copper alloy objects in the American Museum of Natural History were found only around Cuzco (Appendix G, Figure G11, type 3153; Figure 2.46A). The function of these objects is obscure and, although they must have related somehow to activities at the imperial capital, they do not seem to have been disseminated around the empire in the way that other types were.

False Leads from Machu Picchu:
Spoons, Tweezers, and Conical "Bells"

Several object types from Machu Picchu, described and illustrated both by Bingham (1930) and Mathewson (1915), might seem to be typical Inca artifacts, but are not. The two tiny spoons depicting long-beaked birds are one example, but the distributions of these tiny spoons in general (Figure 2.26C), and the ones decorated with the figure of a bird in specific (Figure 2.26D), are almost entirely coastal. There is not a single additional spoon of any type among the other Late Horizon assemblages discussed above (see Table 2.1). These objects are coastal, not characteristically Inca at all.

The same is true of the triangular tweezers from Machu Picchu (type 1101; Appendix G, Figure G3). Tweezers in general (Figure 2.27A), and the flat-bladed triangular type in particular (Figure 2.27C), are clearly a coastal, not Inca, type. Bingham's (1930) illustration is a bit misleading, in that it seems to show two triangular tweezers from Machu Picchu (Bingham 1930, fig. 157e, g). In fact, there is only one finished typical triangular tweezer from Machu Picchu, plus a blank that was clearly intended to be made into one. One tweezer in Bingham's illustration (Bingham 1930, fig. 157e) is not mentioned in the caption and is actually a side view of either the completed example (Bingham 1930, fig. 157g) or a hypothesized intended final state of the unfinished blank (Bingham 1930, fig. 157d), not an additional artifact. The two other similar tweezers shown (Bingham 1930, fig. 157a, b) are rounder in shape and have thin, convex blades, as opposed to the thick, flat, tapering ones of the triangular form. These rounded and triangular variants are almost always unambiguously distinguishable, both in the Machu Picchu assemblage and on the coast. The distinctive step in the thickness of the neck of the triangular tweezers is also heavily concentrated on the central and south coasts, with the two examples from Machu Picchu making up half the sample from the Inca core (Figure 2.27B). Tweezers as a whole, regardless of type, are far more common on the coast than in the highlands, from north-central Chile to the Gulf of Guayaquil, in Ecuador (Figure 2.27A). Different types were more common in different regions, but most were concentrated in the south and central coast regions of Peru (Figures 2.27A through 2.31A). Exceptions include pointed tweezers, which are concentrated around Jauja in the central highlands of Peru (Figure 2.30C), compound curved strip tweezers, which are an Ecuadorian type (Figure 2.30D), and notched tweezers, which come from the north-central coast of Chile (Figure 2.31B).

By contrast, it is difficult to interpret the distribution of cast conical "bells" (Figure 2.33A, B, C; see Appendix G, Figure G4, types 1900 to 1903). They are widely distributed, without a single clear center of concentration, although the southern Titicaca area is a plausible guess. Because they sometimes occur in sets of two, three, or more, on the maps they seem to be concentrated in multiple places. Since four examples come from Machu Picchu and three from an unequivocally Inca burial on La Plata Island, Ecuador, they were clearly used by people associated with the Inca state. However, they were not *consistently* used by Inca personnel, since there are no others in the remaining six Late Horizon assemblages discussed earlier. Stylistically, these objects may be related to other objects cast by the lost-wax method, such as the cast bola weights and animal-headed tupus and tumis, which seem to have been spread by Inca state activities. They could also be related (see discussion below) to cast ornaments found in the southern Titicaca region (Figure 2.33D; Appendix G, Figure G4, types 1551 and 1552). This connection suggests that the conical "bells" may have originated in the southern Titicaca area and either been adopted and spread by the Inca themselves, or disseminated widely as the Inca resettled some of their subjects for royal and imperial ends.

Southern Titicaca Metalsmiths among the Inca
The southern Titicaca area was an important center of metallurgical innovation in the Andes (Lechtman 1979:2), and was the source of the tin-bronze technology that became nearly universal across the Inca empire (Lechtman 2007:33). Many types and features of metal artifacts that are common in the Inca core are equally or more concentrated in the southern Titicaca region, including round-headed tupus (Figure 2.2A), thin half-round tupus (Figure 2.2C), drooping tupus (Figure 2.3D), long-taper tupus (Figure 2.4B), tupus with globular cast neck joins or neck steps (Figure 2.4C, D), straight-backed and flaring-backed T-shaped tumis (Figure 2.9B, C), plain-headed and loop-headed tumis (Figure 2.10A, B), tiny pins or lime dippers (Figure 2.8C), possibly conical "bells" (Figure 2.33A, B, C), and possibly bola weights (Figures 2.24C and 2.25C). Clearly, southern Titicaca metalworking strongly influenced not only the material, but also the style and repertoire of Inca metalworking. Ethnohistoric sources tell us that the Inca moved Chimu metalworkers from the north coast to Cuzco and other provincial Inca centers (Cieza de León 1959:328), and that they gathered smiths from Pachacamac, Ica, and Chincha on the central and south coasts (Rostworowski 1999:78; Lechtman 2007:320). The empire evidently also swept up metalworkers from the southern Titicaca region.

One feature of some tupus and tumis shows these processes of movement and stylistic synthesis particularly well. Tumis with a well-defined globular form joining the handle and blade (Appendix G, Figure G8, types 2841 and 2842, and Figure G9, type 2846) are rarer, but have roughly the same distribution (Figure 2.11B) as do other tumis (Figure 2.9A). They are concentrated in the Inca core, relatively common in the southern Titicaca region, and widely dispersed throughout the rest of the empire from Bolivia northward, albeit not farther south, suggesting that this feature was used in the core and disseminated to much of the periphery. Tupus with a very similar style of join at the neck are concentrated on the Island of Titicaca and elsewhere in the southern Titicaca region (Figure 2.4C). They also occur occasionally in the Inca core, but are almost unknown farther away. Twenty-one of the 25 tupus with these globular joins have round heads. Three others have half-round heads, and one is indeterminate. Since round-headed tupus seem to be an ancient form in the Andes, some of these tupus could be pre-Inca. These patterns could be explained if the globular join feature originated on round-headed tupus in the southern Titicaca area, was carried to the Inca heartland by resettled southern Titicaca smiths, and there was incorporated into not only more round-headed tupus, but also some of the characteristically Cuzqueño half-round-headed tupus and T-shaped tumis that were then spread throughout the Inca empire.

Cuzqueño and General Andean Types at Machu Picchu

Machu Picchu was a royal estate or country palace, largely constructed as a single project for the Inca Pachacuti Yupanqui, and staffed with yanacona retainers resettled from various regions that Pachacuti had recently conquered (Salazar 2001, 2004, 2007; Burger 2004; Niles 2004; Salazar and Burger 2004b). Most of the artifacts from the site come from the activities and burials of this multi-ethnic population of support staff, *camayoc* craft producers, and their families (Salazar 2007). The quotidian metal goods they brought with them, acquired, or made were a correspondingly cosmopolitan mix of Cuzqueño, exotic, and blended objects.

Some 29% to 32% of the quotidian metals at Machu Picchu probably referred to Cuzco (Tables 2.1 and 2.4). The 40 small discs with a single hole, mostly a single lot of 38 probably from one textile, make up 22% of the assemblage and would have seemed typical of Cuzco and the central Andean highlands and coast in general (Tables 2.1 and 2.4). Another 8% would have seemed generically Andean, or from broad portions of the Andes (Table 2.4). The roughly 20% that apparently referred to other regions are discussed later in this section (Table 2.5). The remaining 18% to 21% are currently unclassifiable as to geographic reference. Many of these are tools such as chisels and celts, fragmentary, or raw material, some associated with metal production.

The most common metal artifacts at Machu Picchu other than small discs are the 23 half-round-headed tupus of assorted kinds (types 1010 to 1012; Table 2.1; Figures 2.2B, C, D and 2.3A). As the previous discussions showed, these half-round-headed tupus may have been recognized as typical of Cuzco or Inca ethnicity, but they probably were not explicit symbols of imperial affiliation. They constitute a comparable percentage of the metal assemblages at Machu Picchu and at Ollantaytambo, which, as another of Pachacuti's royal country estates, probably had similar functions and staff (see Table 2.1; Rostworowski 1999:188–189; Niles 2004; Salazar 2004). Half-round-headed tupus make up an even higher percentage of the metal assemblage from Sacsawaman (Table 2.1).

Several other tupus from Machu Picchu probably expressed Cuzqueño or Inca ethnicity or tastes. Tupu ANT.017885 is adorned with a pair of cones of the same form, size, and style as two single-cone tupus known from Cuzco (Figure 2.3C; Appendix G, Figure G2, types 1061 and 1062). While this double-cone tupu is unique in the database, it must have seemed closely related. Tupu ANT.017841, with a cast head resembling a star-shaped mace head (Appendix G, Figure G2, type 1083), may also have harkened to the general Inca style of cast metalwork expressed in animal-headed tupus and tumis, as well as the star-shaped mace heads themselves that were apparently disseminated by the Inca state.

Many people at Machu Picchu used plain, round-headed tupus. The percentage of these tupus in the Machu Picchu metal assemblage is comparable to that of other Late Horizon assemblages, but considerably less than at Sacsawaman. As argued earlier, round-headed tupus were probably not linked to Inca identity. Instead, they were likely part of the larger background of Andean material culture (Figure 2.2A). Their display may have indicated some degree of wealth or status, but they probably did not have a more specific connotation.

The round-headed tupu ANT.017836, cast with a relief of the sun on one side and a crescent, possibly the moon, on the other, is unique in the entire database. While the casting technology might be Inca, the style is out of place, possibly reflecting Colonial influence (see Salazar and Burger 2004a:211–212). As a probably Colonial artifact, it is not included in the analysis presented here.

There are two metal needles with pierced eyes at Machu Picchu (ANT.018449 and ANT.018482). Pierced-eye needles are found mostly in the central highlands and farther south, especially in the southern Titicaca area (Figure 2.26B). This distribution spans the Inca heartland, but is not at all concentrated there. Instead, metal needles of any kind seem strangely scarce in the Inca core. Pierced-eye needles probably would not have had any regional significance to Cuzqueños and other people in the southern Andes, since they were so widespread, although they might have connoted the south to people from northern Peru or Ecuador.

T-shaped tumis were common at Machu Picchu, in percentages comparable to those at Ollantaytambo and Sacsawaman. Like the half-round-headed tupus, T-shaped tumis probably expressed Cuzqueño identity without referring explicitly to the empire (Figures 2.9A, B, C, D, 2.10A, B, C, and 2.11B). The similar percentages of T-shaped tumis at Machu Picchu and Ollantaytambo reinforce the likely similarity of the activities and inhabitants at the two sites. Oddly enough, T-shaped tumis also make up a similar percentage of the Late Horizon assemblage from the region northeast of Titicaca, which otherwise shows only limited signs of interaction with the Inca empire. The more distant Late Horizon assemblages from Ica, Jauja, and La Plata Island have lower proportions of T-shaped tumis. The higher proportions of T-shaped tumis in the Late Horizon assemblages from the Inca core might reflect activities conducted at royal estates and at Sacsawaman, or the kinds of personnel who worked and were buried there.

As noted earlier, the meanings of lirpus (types 5610 and 5620) are ambiguous. While their geographic distribution (Figure 2.32A) suggests that they were associated with the Cuzco region, Guaman Poma depicted them on pre-Inca people and even the Inca's Cañarí enemies (Guaman Poma 1615:63, 163). The three examples from Machu Picchu (or four, see Bingham 1930, fig. 137) might have been seen as typically Cuzqueño, or not.

The three cast spheroid copper alloy bola weights (type 1801) from Machu Picchu may have been typically Cuzqueño objects (Figure 2.24C; see discussion

Table 2.4. Metal artifacts from Machu Picchu that would not have appeared exotic there.

Catalog number	Type description	Provenience	Meaning: regional reference
Tupu			
ANT.016679b	Tupu: half-round	Cave 38	Cuzqueño identity?
ANT.017822	Tupu: half-round	Cave 62	Cuzqueño identity?
ANT.017824	Tupu: half-round		Cuzqueño identity?
ANT.017825	Tupu: half-round		Cuzqueño identity?
ANT.017827	Tupu: half-round		Cuzqueño identity?
ANT.017831	Tupu: half-round	Cave 76	Cuzqueño identity?
ANT.017832	Tupu: half-round		Cuzqueño identity?
ANT.017833	Tupu: half-round		Cuzqueño identity?
ANT.017835	Tupu: half-round		Cuzqueño identity?
ANT.017838	Tupu: half-round		Cuzqueño identity?
ANT.017881, 017955, 017959	Tupu: half-round		Cuzqueño identity?
ANT.018431	Tupu: half-round		Cuzqueño identity?
ANT.018451	Tupu: half-round		Cuzqueño identity?
ANT.018477	Tupu: half-round	Grave 26	Cuzqueño identity?
ANT.017823	Tupu: half-round, head thick as shaft		Cuzqueño identity?
ANT.017829	Tupu: half-round, head thick as shaft	Cave 68	Cuzqueño identity?
ANT.018430	Tupu: half-round, head thick as shaft		Cuzqueño identity?
ANT.016679a	Tupu: half-round, > semicircular	Cave 38	Cuzqueño identity?
ANT.016679c	Tupu: half-round, > semicircular	Cave 38	Cuzqueño identity?
ANT.017821	Tupu: half-round, > semicircular		Cuzqueño identity?
ANT.017848	Tupu: half-round, > semicircular		Cuzqueño identity?
ANT.017885	Tupu: cone, double, with loop		Cuzqueño identity?
ANT.017841	Tupu: small star mace head, no hole		Cuzqueño identity?
ANT.016681	Tupu: round	Cave 37	General Andean
ANT.017836	Tupu: round		General Andean
ANT.017840	Tupu: round		General Andean
ANT.017845	Tupu: round		General Andean
ANT.017846	Tupu: round		General Andean
ANT.017847	Tupu: round		General Andean
ANT.017869	Tupu: round		General Andean
ANT.017870	Tupu: round		General Andean
ANT.017968	Tupu: round		General Andean
ANT.018450	Tupu: round		General Andean
T-shaped tumi			
ANT.016685	T-shaped tumi: straight back (globular join)	Cave 38	Cuzqueño identity? Or south Titicaca?
ANT.017852	T-shaped tumi: straight back		Cuzqueño identity?
ANT.017853	T-shaped tumi: straight back		Cuzqueño identity?
ANT.017854	T-shaped tumi: straight back	Section 44A	Cuzqueño identity?
ANT.017855	T-shaped tumi: straight back		Cuzqueño identity?
ANT.017856	T-shaped tumi: straight back		Cuzqueño identity?
ANT.017857	T-shaped tumi: straight back		Cuzqueño identity?
ANT.017858	T-shaped tumi: straight back		Cuzqueño identity?
ANT.017859	T-shaped tumi: straight back		Cuzqueño identity?
ANT.017860	T-shaped tumi: straight back		Cuzqueño identity?

TABLE 2.4 CONTINUED.

Catalog number	Type description	Provenience	Meaning: regional reference
ANT.017861	T-shaped tumi: straight back		Cuzqueño identity?
ANT.017864	T-shaped tumi: straight back		Cuzqueño identity?
ANT.017865	T-shaped tumi: straight back		Cuzqueño identity?
ANT.017868	T-shaped tumi: straight back	Cave 54	Cuzqueño identity?
ANT.017911	T-shaped tumi: straight back		Cuzqueño identity?
ANT.017963	T-shaped tumi: straight back		Cuzqueño identity?
ANT.017971	T-shaped tumi: straight back		Cuzqueño identity?
ANT.017862	T-shaped tumi: slightly flaring back		Cuzqueño identity?
ANT.017863	T-shaped tumi: slightly flaring back	Station 9A	Cuzqueño identity?
ANT.017866	T-shaped tumi: slightly flaring back		Cuzqueño identity?
ANT.017867	T-shaped tumi: slightly flaring back		Cuzqueño identity?
ANT.017962	T-shaped tumi: tiny cast blade	Cave 54	Cuzqueño identity?
Bola			
ANT.017965	Bola: spheroid		Cuzqueño identity?
ANT.018426	Bola: spheroid		Cuzqueño identity?
ANT.018447	Bola: spheroid		Cuzqueño identity?
Tool			
ANT.017909	Tool: plumb bob		Cuzqueño identity?
ANT.018478, 018479	Tool: crowbar	Section 44A	Cuzqueño identity?
Axe			
ANT.017901	Axe: "classic" T-shaped		Cuzqueño identity?
ANT.017967	Axe: "classic" T-shaped	Room 24A	Cuzqueño identity?
ANT.017904	Axe: "ancla" with curved tang, no hole, wide crescent		Cuzqueño identity?
ANT.017969	Axe: indeterminate haft, trapezoidal blade		Unclear; Cuzqueño?
ANT.017899	Axe: rectangular tang, no hole, wide blade, atypical		Unclear; Cuzqueño?
Lirpu: disc with suspension tab			
ANT.017877	Lirpu: disc with suspension tab	Station 9A	Unclear; Cuzqueño?
ANT.018454	Lirpu: disc with suspension tab	Station 9A	Unclear; Cuzqueño?
ANT.018480	Lirpu: disc with suspension tab	Grave 26	Unclear; Cuzqueño?
Disc			
ANT.017871	Disc: plain, flat, 1 hole near edge, <40 mm diameter (38)	Cave 2A	General central Andean?
ANT.017886	Disc: plain, flat, 1 hole near edge, <40 mm diameter		General central Andean?
ANT.017888	Disc: plain, flat, 1 hole near edge, <40 mm diameter		General central Andean?
Needle			
ANT.018449	Needle: pierced-eye, indeterminate		General central and south Andean
ANT.018482	Needle: pierced-eye, indeterminate	Cave 37	General central and south Andean

above). They make up a slightly lower proportion of the metal assemblage at Machu Picchu than at Sacsawaman or Jauja, but more than at Ollantaytambo, where they are absent. It would be unwise to read too much into these proportions, because several bola weights could represent a single weapon.

The plumb bob ANT.017909 (Appendix G, Figure G6, type 2740) embodies the same casting technology and distinctive hole-and-crossbar attachment scheme as do the cast bola weights, and would probably also have been seen as an Inca or Cuzqueño object. The only other example in the database comes from Sacsawaman. Both sites were foci of stone construction activity, although many other sites were, as well. A single heavy crowbar (Appendix G, Figure G6, type 2750, now in two pieces numbered ANT.018478 and ANT.018479) was found at Machu Picchu, and a similar crowbar was found at Sacsawaman. Eleven others come from the Cuzco area, two from the Island of the Sun, two from Tiwanaku, and one from Pikillacta, very roughly paralleling the distribution of Late Horizon, and perhaps earlier, work and rework with monumental stone (Figure 2.45A). The absence of such construction tools from the unfinished site of Ollantaytambo is interesting, but may not be significant given how scarce these items are.

The Machu Picchu metals assemblage has a much higher percentage of small, thin, flat copper alloy discs with one hole near the edge (type 5422, less than 40 mm in diameter) than does any of the other Late Horizon assemblages in the database (Figure 2.10C). Forty of these discs account for almost a fifth of the assemblage. On the other hand, 38 of them come from one burial cave, possibly from a single decorated item. It might be more correct to count just three items decorated with small discs at Machu Picchu, which would make this assemblage similar in this respect to the others from the Inca heartland. The Machu Picchu assemblage is presented here both ways (see Table 2.1), with the discs all tabulated as separate items and with the set of 38 counted as a single artifact. This makes a modest difference in all the other percentages, since it reduces the total count of artifacts from the site significantly. As noted earlier, these discs could have been associated with Inca ethnicity or affiliation, but they were more likely seen as a widespread central Andean type that would not have had strong regional connotations.

Machu Picchu is unique among the Late Horizon assemblages in having many axes (Table 2.1). Six axes of various types constitute more than 3% of the metals collection. There are only two axe fragments in all of the other major Late Horizon assemblages. Two additional axes in the Machu Picchu collection (ANT.017898 and ANT.017900) were acquired at known sites some distance from Machu Picchu. Three others (ANT.017902, ANT.017905, and ANT.017906) were purchased with the Alvistur collection and have no provenience other than probably the general Cuzco area. Another (ANT.017903) is a modern reproduction for metallurgical testing (see Appendix D, Table D.2). As already noted, a variety of axes were used widely in the Late Horizon, with many features dispersed in broad regional patterns that probably predate the Inca state (Figures 2.15C through 2.20D). Variations of trapezoidal and wide crescent blade shapes are represented at Machu Picchu, as are both rectangular and curved hafting tangs. The style and workmanship of the axes varies considerably. Two are the classic T-shaped axes that seem to have been spread by the Inca (Figure 2.18C) and another (ANT.017904) is Mayer's "ancla" type, which also seems to have spread through Inca activities, as discussed earlier (Figure 2.18D). All three would probably have connoted Cuzqueño identity, if not Inca state affiliation. The remaining three axes are harder to place. One is an atypical variant form and two are fragmentary. The many axes at Machu Picchu were clearly not the work of a single smith or shop, nor were they standard issue to a work crew. The axes probably came to Machu Picchu with at least several different people who acquired them independently, such as the yanaconas or mitimaes who were buried there (Salazar 2004:45–46). Alternatively, if the axes were collected by some one person or institution for use at Machu Picchu, they were gathered from disparate sources, although all the types would have been available in Cuzco.

The objects called "celts" in this typology (Appendix G, Figure G13, types 4010 to 4090) may have had a variety of functions, but most were probably blades for foot plows, adzes, or similar implements (see Ambrosetti 1904:199–200; Latcham 1938:320–321, 341; Mayer 1986:34). Although examples of this heterogeneous set of types were used at Machu Picchu and elsewhere in the Inca core, they have an odd distribution that is densest at opposite ends of the Inca realm, in coastal and lowland Ecuador and highland northwest Argentina (Figure 2.15B). Maybe these more recently conquered areas were where agricultural reclamation work was most intense at the end of the Late Horizon, in which case the celts would be more associated with terracing or landscape modification than with cultivation. Such widespread, variable, utilitarian, and simple objects may not have been recognized as characteristic of any particular region. A similar percentage of celts occurs at Sacsawaman, but there are none from Ollantaytambo or several of the other Late Horizon assemblages.

A single heavy-duty chisel was found at Machu Picchu (type 2710, ANT.017907). These grade into celts, but are imprecisely distinguished by being smaller and often showing battering damage (upsetting or mushrooming) on the back end, or nicks and dents rather than abrasive wear on the cutting edge. Heavy chisels are common around Cuzco, and thinly distributed elsewhere, primarily in the northern half of the empire (Figure 2.15A). This pattern suggests that heavy chisels might have been spread by activities of the Inca state, although again, such simple and variable items seem unlikely to have connoted the Inca state or Cuzqueño identity. The only other example among the dated Late Horizon assemblages is from Coquimbo, Chile.

Three light-duty chisels (Appendix G, Figure G6, type 2700) at Machu Picchu were probably hafted and used for fine craft work, most likely in wood. These tools are missing from all the other Late Horizon assemblages except the one from around Jauja. The widespread distribution of these chisels looks somewhat concentrated in northwest Argentina (Figure 2.14B), but as with the celts, their ubiquity, simplicity, and variability probably means that this is an old type or one that developed in various places, not associated with any one regional tradition.

A similar distribution of the even more variable catch-all category for assorted other cutting tools, punches, spatulas, and so on (Figure 2.14D; see Appendix G, Figure G6, type 2715) suggests that fine chisels were probably distributed more in response to the intensity of general small craft work than to regional traditions. Some small tool forms were characteristic of certain regions, such as the modern-looking "formón" chisels found mostly on the central and north coast of Peru (Figure 2.14C).

The unusually high proportions of axes, celts, fine chisels, and the heavy chisel at Machu Picchu, together with the plumb bob and crowbar, might suggest that some suite of potentially related activities was emphasized more at Machu Picchu than at other royal country estates, Sacsawaman, and provincial centers. Interpreting this unusual assemblage as reflecting one or several functions is difficult, though, because there is little agreement on what the metal items were used for. Suggestions range from weaponry through forestry, agriculture, woodwork, stonework, architectural or terrace construction, and still other alternatives (see below; Salazar and Burger 2004a; Gordon, Section One, pages 52–56, 68–69).

Exotics and Cosmopolitanism at Machu Picchu

People at Machu Picchu would have recognized some 20% of the metal artifacts used there as exotic (Tables 2.1 and 2.5). Some of these exotic artifacts probably came to Machu Picchu in the hands of yanacona retainers drawn from regions conquered by Pachacuti (Burger 2004:94–97; Salazar 2007:165–283). Others could have been acquired from the diverse mix of goods circulating in the imperial capital. A few objects combine features from peripheral regions and the Inca core. In a few cases (described below), it is clear that a single individual owned objects that referred to multiple places. Some people from distant regions picked up characteristically Inca metal items. At least one Cuzqueña owned a variety of exotic metal goods. In some contexts, commonplace metals from different regional traditions were used together, or people with goods that referred to different regions were buried together. The quotidian metal assemblage suggests that the Inca practice of moving people around the empire created an eclectic and cosmopolitan atmosphere at Machu Picchu.

Coastal Exotics
The "fisherman" handleless transverse knife, ANT.017973 (Salazar and Burger 2004a:193–194), would have been of obviously foreign origin at Machu Picchu. To those with knowledge of the provinces, it would have referred to the north coast. The stair-step motif and the cast decoration of a man tugging at a fish on a line are north coastal, perhaps Chimu, in both style and content. Even apart from the iconography and casting style, this form of knife is rare, and almost every other example in the database comes from the north or central coast (Figure 2.13B). The map figure and one of the illustrations of type 2830 (Appendix G, Figure G8) are of

a very similar knife from the Vicus area that has the same stair-stepped end, but a different scene depicting a monkey and bird (AMNH 41.2/6734).

A few other items at Machu Picchu might have referred to the north or central coast of Peru. The three split bells (Appendix G, Figure G4, types 2000 to 2002) from Machu Picchu (ANT.017892, ANT.017988, and ANT.018439) might have been recognized as north or central coast types. Split bells in general are concentrated on the north and central coast of Peru, and also in the Inca heartland (Figure 2.34A). Split bells that seem to be forged from thick sheet material, rather than cast, are clearly concentrated on the central and north coast, plus one example at Machu Picchu, two from the Titicaca area, and one from Arica, Chile (Figure 2.34C). Although the cast versions look to be concentrated around Cuzco and Machu Picchu, the eleven examples shown as two large symbols in the Inca core are virtually equaled by the ten more dispersed examples from the north coast of Peru and the three from the central coast (Figure 2.34B; the map symbol for Machu Picchu includes not only the two cast split bells from that site, but also two others from another site a few kilometers away). Given the structure of the Inca state, it seems more likely that this pattern would result from coastal bells being adopted in Cuzco than from Cuzqueño bells being disseminated only to the coast of Peru. There are no close matches for the Machu Picchu split bells in the database, but the two cast bells have a long stalk with a suspension hole at the end, a feature that is also seen on three more elaborately decorated bells from Cuzco.

The ambiguous object ANT.017980 has roughly the form and size of a copper alloy ingot of the type that is strongly concentrated at Chan Chan (Figure 2.45B). Irregular chunks of metal that seem to be the products of refining or remelting operations are also concentrated in and near Chan Chan, but have a wider distribution than the formally consistent ingots (Figure 2.45C). Metallographic analysis by Mathewson (1915:535, 579, 602; object 21) found the Machu Picchu artifact to be homogenous, cold-worked and annealed to a soft state. Both Mathewson and Gordon (see Section One, pages 18 and 26) conclude that it was a piece of stock ready to be worked into some specific form. An ingot, by contrast, might be expected to be in an as-cast state, with obvious coring due to rapid cooling. It is possible, though, that ingots were not circulated in this raw state, but were sometimes or routinely lightly worked and annealed as part of their production process. If so, this Machu Picchu artifact could be an ingot. Alternatively, it might be an ingot that had been worked only slightly, so that it had not yet departed much from its original form. It is tabulated here as an ingot, but more careful formal and metallographic comparison to known ingots would be necessary to confirm or correct its identification.

Chimu metalsmiths worked for the empire in Cuzco and in some provincial capitals (Cieza de León 1959:328), but with only the "fisherman" knife, a few split bells similar to ones from Cuzco, and the possible ingot to suggest specifically north coast origins, it seems more likely that these objects reached Machu Picchu in the hands of their owners or by exchange than through the work of a Chimu smith who worked at Machu Picchu.

TABLE 2.5. Metal artifacts and features of artifacts from Machu Picchu that would have referred to some other region.

Catalog number	Type	Provenience	Meaning: regional reference
ANT.017973	Knife: handleless transverse	Room 24A	North coast of Peru, Chimu
ANT.017980	Possible ingot		North coast of Peru, Chimu?
ANT.017892	Split bell: cast		North and central coast of Peru?
ANT.017988a	Split bell: cast		North and central coast of Peru?
ANT.018439	Split bell: cast	Cave 63	North and central coast of Peru?
ANT.018434	Needle: loop-eye, indeterminate section		Central to northern coast of Peru and highlands
ANT.018626	Needle: loop-eye, rectangular section	Section 41A	Central to northern coast of Peru and highlands
ANT.016684	Tweezer: straight, transitional	Cave 37	Central coast of Peru
ANT.017890	Tiny spoon: bird finial	Grave 26	Central coast of Peru
ANT.017970	Tiny spoon: bird finial	Cave 66	Central coast of Peru
ANT.017912	Plume holder	Section 40A[a]	Central coast of Peru, possibly coast in general
ANT.017875	Ring: edgewise strip applique	Terrace[b]	Central and south coast of Peru
ANT.017891	Tweezer: teardrop	Room 64A	Central and south coast of Peru
ANT.017893	Tweezer: triangular	Grave 26	Central and south coast of Peru
ANT.017972	Tweezer: triangular		Central and south coast of Peru
ANT.017895	Tweezer: teardrop, transitional		Central and south coast of Peru
ANT.017896	Tweezer: teardrop, transitional		Central and south coast of Peru
ANT.017857	T-shaped tumi (neck step on handle)		Central and south coast of Peru
ANT.017874	Ring: plain sheet (lays flat on finger)	Cave 53	North, central, south coast of Peru
ANT.017897	Plate handle from formed sheet		North, central, south coast of Peru
ANT.017864	T-shaped tumi (traced decoration)		North, central, south coast, central highlands
ANT.017873	Strip: possible bracelet (traced decoration)	Room 39A	North, central, south coast, central highlands
ANT.017877	Lirpu: (traced decoration)	Station 9A	North, central, south coast, central highlands
ANT.018442	Tweezer: pointed		Central highlands
ANT.018440	Tweezer: flaring		South coast of Peru
ANT.017872	Strip: headband? (from thin sheet)		Coast of Peru

TABLE 2.5 CONTINUED.

Catalog number	Type	Provenience	Meaning: regional reference
ANT.016683	Tiny tupu or lime dipper: other cast head	Grave 26	Southern Titicaca area
ANT.016685	T-shaped tumi (globular join)	Cave 38	Southern Titicaca area
ANT.018427	Conical "bell": with arms	Cave 57	Southern Titicaca area?
ANT.018428	Conical "bell": with arms	Cave 57	Southern Titicaca area?
ANT.016682	Conical "bell": indeterminate subtype	Cave 37	Southern Titicaca area?
ANT.018437	Conical "bell": indeterminate subtype	Cave 97	Southern Titicaca area?
ANT.017876	Plaque: cast ornamented crescent; knife?		Southern Titicaca area[c]
ANT.016678	Flat tumi: T variant	Cave 14	Southern Titicaca area
ANT.017819	Tupu: drooping (marginal example)	Cave 63	Southern Titicaca area?
ANT.017914	Knife: possible long oval blade		Northwest Argentina?

[a] Section 40A between rooms 24A and caves 4A, 5A, and 6A, just south of the stairway at the east corner of the house on the southeast side of the Sacred Plaza.

[b] Terrace north of the main stairway.

[c] *Contra* Salazar and Burger: "[I]ts source may have been the Cañari ethnic group from the eastern Andean slopes of Ecuador" (Salazar and Burger 2004a:194).

Several types of metal artifacts from Machu Picchu have broader coastal distributions with a more southerly focus. Bangles or pendants (type 3020) vary considerably and are found almost exclusively on the north, central, and south coasts (Figure 2.42A). The bangle (ANT.017891) from Machu Picchu is similar to examples from Ancon, Ica, Chuquitanta, and Pachacamac, all on the central coast. Finger rings are also primarily coastal (Figure 2.32B, C, D). The plain sheet strip ring (ANT.017874) from Machu Picchu is the only Peruvian highland example in the database of a type that is common on the north, central, and south coasts (Figure 2.32C; Appendix G, Figure G4, type 1601), while a ring with traces of applied decoration (ANT.017875) is similar to central coast examples from Chincha, Ancon, "near Lima," and the Island of San Lorenzo, off Lima (Figure 2.32D; Appendix G, Figure G4, type 1603).

Tiny metal spoons (Appendix G, Figure G4, types 1700 to 1702) have been identified variously as dippers for lime used in chewing coca, as snuffing implements, and as ear cleaners (Eaton 1916:26; Antze 1930:41; Cordy-Collins 1996:268; Salazar and Burger 2004a:184). They are almost exclusively coastal, concentrated especially on the central coast (Figure 2.26C). The two examples from Machu Picchu (ANT.017890 and ANT.017970) are decorated with a flying and a standing bird, respectively. Similar birds, which adorn about half of all the tiny spoons in the database, are concentrated on the central coast, just like other varieties of tiny spoons (Figure 2.26D). They would almost certainly have been recognized as exotic at Machu Picchu, and possibly associated specifically with the central coast.

The plate handle fabricated from formed silver sheet stock (ANT.017897) may have connoted the south, central, and north coasts of Peru in two senses. First, metal vessels in general came primarily from those regions (Figure 2.39B). Second, this silver plate was made in a technological style based on fabricating complex objects from formed and repoussé sheet metal parts joined by tabs, hooks, slots, crimps, and similar mechanical joints (Lechtman 1988, 1996b). This fabrication style is found mostly on the north, central, and south coasts (Figure 2.41C). Sheet metal work in general was most elaborated and prevalent on the Peruvian south, central, and north coasts. Discs and other sheet metal objects decorated with the repoussé technique are particularly common there (Figures 2.38C and 2.41B), as are sheet metal mummy masks (Figure 2.39D), pieces and packets of sheet scrap with irregular, unfinished cut edges (Figure 2.45D), and unidentifiable sheet fragments, generally tallied here as representing a single unknown sheet metal item regardless of how many pieces make up a given lot (Figure 2.41D).

Another example of this sheet metal fabrication technology is the squashed conical sheet metal object ANT.017912. Although this artifact has been identified as an "armlet" or ornamental sheathing for a ceremonial staff or tool (Salazar and Burger 2004a:188), it more closely resembles five "plume holders" (Appendix G, Figure G12, type 3110; Baessler 1906:119) from a single Late Horizon grave in Ica (Uhle's site T, grave A). Four other plume holders have long, tubular extensions from the small end, two from Chepen (AMNH B/5182) and two from Pacasmayo (Appendix G, Figure G11, type 3112; Baessler 1906, figs. 506, 507). All share the same general form, size, and fabrication technology using interlocking tabs and slots. Several of the coastal examples retain a layered internal packing of various plant, wool, and textile materials in the conical section that may have supported a conical feather arrangement. Some of the Ica examples have a wood dowel projecting from the narrow end of the cone, whereas the ones from Chepen and Pacasmayo are each joined to a long, tubular metal shaft. In use, these objects would have looked like long-handled feather dusters. They may be the handles of the drooping parasol-like implements depicted by Guaman Poma (1615:120, 134, 138, 140, 142) in scenes with Inca queens (*coyas*). The geographic distributions of both the sheet metal technology (Figure 2.41C) and the plume holder type (Figure 2.39C) suggest that the one at Machu Picchu would have been recognized as an exotic coastal item.

Tweezers are also found primarily on the coast, especially the central and south coasts (Figure 2.27A). Tweezers were certainly known in the Inca core, accounting for about 4% of both the Machu Picchu and the Sacsawaman assemblages, but they were more common in coastal Late Horizon assemblages, at more than 7% of the Ica assemblage and over 20% in Lambayeque. Moreover, no one type was common in the Inca core or concentrated there. Instead, highland tweezers were an eclectic sampling of the wide variety in use on the coast. Any given tweezer in the Inca core, or at Machu Picchu specifically, would have been an unusual or unique object in most people's local experience.

Far from being typical Inca artifacts, the two triangular tweezers from Machu Picchu (ANT.017893 and ANT.017972) would have seemed just as exotic as the tiny spoons. Many of these tweezers come from the central and south coasts, and very few from the Inca core (Figure 2.27C). The straight-transitional tweezers (ANT.016684; type 1109; Figure 2.29B) and the flaring tweezers (ANT.018440; type 1111; Figure 2.29C) at Machu Picchu would also have seemed foreign, harking to the central and south coasts. The distinctive step or notch in the thickness of the neck of the two triangular tweezers at Machu Picchu is recognizable on 42 other tweezers in the database, most having the same triangular shape, some with the teardrop shape (Appendix G, Figure G3, type 1103), and a few others. This feature, too, is strongly concentrated on the central and south coasts (Figure 2.27B), with only four examples in the database from the Inca core. The only tweezers at Machu Picchu that are not definitely out of place in the Inca core are one that falls in a catchall category and two (ANT.017895 and ANT.017896) that are classified as an uncommon transitional type (Appendix G, Figure G3, type 1104) that also comes from the south and central coasts (Figure 2.28A).

A long, flexible strip of copper alloy with an enriched silver surface (ANT.017872) may have been a headband or belt for someone at Machu Picchu (Salazar and Burger 2004a:185). As discussed earlier, this type is most commonly found on the Peruvian coast and around Moquegua (Figure 2.39A). Fairly generic in design, it might not have seemed foreign in a society that regularly marked status with elaborate headgear. Nevertheless, both the type of artifact and the silver-surfaced sheet material are much more common on the coast, so this example might have connoted coastal traditions.

Two objects from Machu Picchu have traced decoration that would probably have been seen as exotic. Traced decoration is made by driving a tool, such as a chisel or punch, into a metal surface, leaving a linear or point impression with slightly raised edges. Series of these impressions can form lines, hatching, stippling, or other patterns. Tracing is distinct from engraving, in which grooves are cut out by a sharp tool that removes some metal, and from repoussé, in which a tool is pressed or driven against the back of a thin sheet metal object to raise areas on the front for a bas-relief effect. Traced decoration is most common on the north, central, and south coasts (Figure 2.40A). Most examples from the southern Titicaca area are different in style, typically with floral motifs that suggest European influence, probably making them irrelevant to pre-Columbian traditions. Traced decoration varies widely, and certain patterns and styles were characteristic of certain regions, or perhaps even certain sites. No thorough analysis was attempted here, but, for example, single punctate dots as filler elements are found primarily on the central coast of Peru (Figure 2.41A). Crosshatching in areas not delimited by lines, and areas of punctate dots that are delimited by lines, occur mostly on the south and central Peruvian coast and to some extent in the central highlands (Figure 2.40B, C). Crosshatching in areas delimited by lines was a style primarily of the north coast of Peru (Figure 2.40D). The style of traced decoration on the two Machu Picchu objects, in which areas that are filled with punctate stippling are delimited by mostly straight lines from areas that are smooth, is strongly concentrated in the central coast, south coast, and central highlands (Figure 2.40B; Owen 2001:269). The two Machu Picchu examples are the only ones in the database from the Inca core. ANT.017873 is a thick, stiff copper alloy strip with an enriched silver surface and may have been a bracelet (Salazar and Burger 2004a:180). It is remarkably similar to several fragments of decorated strips from around Jauja (Owen 2001:269, item 45). ANT.017877 is a lirpu with traced decoration on the suspension tab and is very similar to one from the southern Titicaca area, although this piece seems out of place there (Appendix G, Figure G14, type 5610; AMNH 41.1/4200; Salazar and Burger 2004a:187). A third object from Machu Picchu, a T-shaped tumi (ANT.017864) has some less diagnostic traced decoration that might belong to the same tradition. The decorated Machu Picchu items might have reminded people of the central highlands, but given the conspicuous presence of central and south coast tweezers and tiny spoons, the traced designs are more likely to have referred to the central and south coasts.

Altiplano Exotics

Several items at Machu Picchu probably reminded people of the southern Titicaca region. The drooping tupu, ANT.017819 (Appendix G, Figure G1, type 1014), and the tiny cast pin or lime dipper, ANT.016683 (Appendix G, Figure G2, type 2439, third from the left, with oblate spheroid head; Eaton 1916, pl. I:8), are both types that are concentrated in the southern Titicaca area and rare in the Inca core (Figures 2.3D and 2.8C). A T-shaped tumi (ANT.016685) has the distinctive globular join between the blade and the handle that may have originated as a feature of southern Titicaca tupus (Figure 2.11B; see discussion above). As noted earlier, the four conical "bells" or hair ornaments from Machu Picchu are part of an ambiguous distribution that suggests dispersal through Inca networks from an origin in the southern Titicaca area (Figure 2.33A, B, C), possibly related to solid ornaments that are more clearly concentrated at the south of Lake Titicaca (Figure 2.33D). A flat tumi (ANT.016678; type 5115) has a flat handle with a cutout hole, similar to the flat tumis concentrated in the southern Titicaca area and farther south (Figure 2.12A, C). The crescent-shaped, blunt-edged ornament with spirals along the top (ANT.017876) is very similar to an object from Tiwanaku (Appendix G, Figure G10, type 3364; AMNH 41.1/4204), in which the central two spirals on each side of the Machu Picchu example are replaced by a quadrupedal animal in profile. It more distantly resembles the one example of type 3362 (Appendix G, Figure G10), from Mutquin in northwest Argentina. Salazar and Burger (2004a:194–195) identify ANT.017876 as a knife and relate it to the Cañari of Ecuador (Idrovo 2000: 253–259). Spiral motifs in general are widespread in the Andes, with an apparent concentration on the central and south coast (Figure 2.42B). They are expressed in such different ways on so many kinds of artifacts that they probably do not represent a single concept or origin.

Other Exotics

The unusual pointed tweezer ANT.018442 (type 1115; Figure 2.30C) would have seemed exotic at Machu Picchu. Unlike other types of tweezers, which are concentrated on the coast, most examples of this type come from the central highlands around Jauja.

A small, flat, elongated oval artifact (ANT.017914) may be a simple, unhafted knife blade (type 2839) related to the tradition of flat knives of various shapes that are typical of northwest Argentina (Figures 2.13C and 2.14A). The long oval form, similar to the blade of a straight-backed T-shaped tumi without a handle, is unusual in that it always lacks the central hole near the back edge found on the other shapes of knives. This form is so plain that identification and interpretation cannot be very certain, but this artifact may be the one exotic from northwest Argentina at Machu Picchu.

Finally, the needles at Machu Picchu represent an unusual mix of types (see Appendix G, Figure G4, loop-eye type 1201, pierced-eye type 1204, and simple flapless bent loop-eye type 1207). Needles are relatively scarce at Machu Picchu, as in all but one of the other Late Horizon assemblages in the database, constituting from zero to 3.5% of seven of the major assemblages (see Table 2.1). The exception is around Jauja, where needles make up almost 18% of the assemblage. Despite having few needles overall, Machu Picchu is the southeasternmost site in the database where loop-eye needles are found (Figure 2.26A). The two Machu Picchu loop-eye needles, ANT.018626 and ANT.018434, are the only ones in the database from the Inca core. (ANT.018434 is broken at the eye, so its identification is less obvious.) All the other loop-eye needles come from the central coast, central highlands, and farther north. The loop-eye needles at Machu Picchu suggest the presence of one or more people, possibly women, from the northern half of the empire.

As noted above, there are also two pierced-eye needles at Machu Picchu (ANT.018449 and ANT.018482). Both are broken at the eye. While the identification of ANT.018482 is fairly clear, ANT.018449 is an ambiguous, battered silver-colored bar or shaft with what is probably, but not unequivocally, the base of a broken pierced eye at one end. Most pierced-eye needles are found in the central highlands and farther south (Figure 2.26B), so these may imply textile workers of either Cuzqueño or southern origins. Finally, there is one more ambiguous artifact (ANT.018433) that may be a simple needle made by bending the end of the shaft over on itself (type 1207), without the additional features of the securing flaps of loop-eye needles or the piercing and narrowing of the head in pierced-eye needles. These two more specialized needle forms result in smooth, narrow eyes that would not catch on fibers in use, while a simple bent loop such as ANT.018433 would tend to catch and pull fibers in the weaving or sewing process. The only other two examples in the database of this form are differently proportioned and somewhat more carefully made; both are from Huando, near Lima.

Technological and Stylistic Syntheses

Some of the quotidian metals at Machu Picchu suggest the fusion of regional concepts and styles in single pieces. For example, the silver plate handle ANT.017897

(Salazar and Burger 2004a:191) is a rendition of an obviously Inca ceramic item in a foreign metalworking style. The plate handle was made in the coastal technological style of sheet metal fabrication with mechanical joins (Figures 2.39B and 2.41C; Lechtman 1996b). The object itself, however, was a metal version of a characteristically Inca handled ceramic plate. Metal dishes, reserved for Inca nobility, are rarely found in Inca archaeological contexts (Salazar and Burger 2004a:191). This plate was not a quotidian item, but people who saw it would probably have recognized both the Cuzqueño or imperial Inca nature of the plate and the exotic coastal metalwork applied to imperial ends.

One T-shaped tumi from Machu Picchu (ANT.016685) suggests a synthesis of ideas from different regional metalworking styles. As a T-shaped tumi, it is a type of object that was common in the Inca core and was probably spread by Inca expansion (Figure 2.9A; see discussion above). This tumi has the distinctive globular join between the handle and the blade that, as discussed above, may have originated as a feature of round-headed tupus from the southern Titicaca area (Figures 2.4C and 2.11B). The globular join might have been recognized as a new or exotic feature incorporated into an essentially Inca artifact, whether or not it was known to have come from the area around Tiwanaku.

Another T-shaped tumi from Machu Picchu (ANT.017857) incorporates a different regionally specific feature. This tumi is the only one in the database with the distinctive neck step that is otherwise found almost exclusively on tweezers from the central and south coasts (Figure 2.27B). The neck step is located at the base of the loop on the tumi's handle, opposite the side toward which the end is doubled over. This arrangement makes the neck step clearly visible, with the same appearance as it has on tweezers. Neck steps could be either decorative or the result of a technique used to thin an area to be bent in a tight arc. In either case, this tumi is an otherwise Inca type that incorporates an exotic feature associated with a specific distant province.

Finally, two tiny spoons, ANT.017890 and ANT.017970 (Salazar and Burger 2004a:184), are nicely cast objects that embody the technology of lost-wax casting and the tin-bronze alloy that both became widespread in the Late Horizon (Mathewson 1915; Nordenskiöld 1921; Lechtman 1976, 1979, 2007; Owen 1986). The objects themselves, though, were typical not of the Inca core, but of the central coast (Figures 2.26C, D). They represent a fusion of the technological style associated with the Inca and the types of metal objects used on the central and adjacent coasts. Given that these tiny spoons are so rare in the highlands, this fusion may have occurred in the coastal provinces, as coastal metalsmiths adopted tin bronze. The principal Inca contribution could have been access to tin, and then the political unity that facilitated the wider dissemination of objects in this hybrid style, and perhaps smiths familiar with it.

Types Notable by their Absence

Some types of metal artifacts—such as earspools, metal dishes, and insignia of office like certain headdress ornaments—are presumably not found at Machu Picchu because, being rare and precious, they would have traveled back to Cuzco with their noble owners (Salazar 2004:45–45). The absence of some other kinds of metal artifacts is more telling. For example, there are no axe-monies or comparable items such as stacks of "feathers" (types 3104 to 3107; Figure 2.43A; Hosler, Lechtman, and Holm 1990), no "North Coast" tumis (types 5000 to 5080; Figure 2.43B), and no heavy socketed points (types 5130 to 5145; Figure 2.43C; Lechtman 1979) at Machu Picchu, or for that matter anywhere in the Inca core, with the exception of two wide-bladed socketed points (type 5144) from Cuzco (Figure 2.43C). All of these are northern Peruvian or Ecuadorian types. All are often found as caches of many similar items, in some cases stacked or bundled, suggesting that they were stores of wealth and more or less formal media of exchange (Lechtman 1979; Hosler, Lechtman, and Holm 1990). Either the economic system in which they functioned was no longer operating in the Late Horizon, or the Inca apparently had little interest in it.

Cast metal spindle whorls are also common on the north and central coasts, but completely absent from Machu Picchu (Figure 2.43D). While the loop-eye needles at Machu Picchu hint at the presence of textile workers, perhaps women, from the northern half of the empire, the absence of metal spindle whorls that those same people could easily have brought with them argues against it.

Nose ornaments of various types were used occasionally on the central coast and northern regions of Peru, and in parts of Ecuador, and would also have suggested the presence of people from the northern part of the empire had any been found (Figure 2.31D), as would the distinctive Guayas tumi form from central lowland Ecuador (Figure 2.13A) or axes in the thick, large-hole style without tangs (Figure 2.16D). None of these items occur at Machu Picchu.

In the same way, any of a variety of metal artifacts would have indicated the presence of people from the Chilean coast or northwest Argentina, including notched tweezers (Figure 2.31B), "Atacama earrings" (Figure 2.44A), "manoplas" (Figure 2.44B), elaborate cast representations of axes, or *tokis* (Figure 2.44C; Ambrosetti 1904), and "brazales" (Figure 2.36D). All but the tweezers may have been features of a local technology and iconography of violence and authority, so it is not clear that these items would have been welcome in Inca contexts, even if people and goods from the southern reaches of the empire had been traveling towards Cuzco or peripheral parts of the empire.

The same reasoning might explain the dramatic absence of metal projectile points from not only Machu Picchu, or even the Inca heartland, but from virtually all of the central Andes, Bolivia, and northernmost Chile (Figure 2.24A). Flat metal projectile points in generally triangular shapes, analogous to lithic points, were rare everywhere in the Andes except at Cerro Junin, Manabi, Ecuador, where many socketed points are so anomalous that they may suggest European influence (Figure 2.23A). Long spike points with a hollow chamber and hole possibly intended to whistle in flight were strongly concentrated in highland Ecuador, although Mayer (1998) catalogs many examples with vague proveniences that are said to come from northern Peru (Figure 2.23C). Long barbed points come primarily from Vicus in the far north of Peru, so they may pre-date the Inca, and may pertain to fishing, rather than combat (Figure 2.23D). The most common form of metal projectile point has a square or circular sectioned straight bar from about 6 to 30 cm in length with a tapered point at each end. Some of these might be tools for other purposes, and a few tools catalogued in the catchall "other tool" category (type 2715) might actually be projectile points. Mayer (1986) considered the Chilean and Argentine examples to be awls or punches ("punzones"), but classified virtually identical artifacts from Ecuador as projectile points (Mayer 1992). Their identification in many cases is clearly debatable. Interestingly, there are relatively few objects of this form from Peru south of the far north coast, Bolivia, or Chile, so their absence in the central part of the Inca empire is generally correct, whatever their function was. If they are primarily projectile points, their odd distribution at the northern and southern forested extremes of the empire would correspond well to ethnohistorical accounts in which bows and arrows were used primarily by the Inca's forest-dwelling opponents.

Spearthrowers, or atlatls, on the other hand, were used along much of the coast and had been since long before the Inca, although many did not involve metal parts (Figure 2.24B; Owen 1998). Metal spearthrower hooks and grips are known primarily from the south, central, and north coast of Peru, while not a single example in the database comes from the Inca core. While the presence of metal projectile points or atlatl parts at a site such as Machu Picchu might suggest soldiers brought in from the Peruvian coast or more distant reaches of the empire, the metals suggest that the Inca did not move such foreign fighters, or their weapons, into the interior of the empire in significant numbers.

An Eclectic Cuzqueña and Other Cases
When Inca policy threw together personnel from multiple regions at Machu Picchu, it could have created a fragmented society of closed and opposed ethnic groups. Instead, the quotidian metals at Machu Picchu suggest a more cosmopolitan scene, in which people from different regions mixed in both life and death, and at least some developed eclectic tastes that combined styles from Cuzco and one of the provinces, or even referred to multiple regions of the empire.

For example, Salazar (2001:119–123, 2007:171) describes grave 26 at Machu Picchu (Eaton 1916:22–29), which contained the remains of a 45-year-old woman who was buried with goods that included several fine Cuzco–Inca ceramic vessels, two large half-round-headed tupus, a tweezer, a lirpu, and a bird-headed lime spoon (Eaton 1916:22–29, pl. I, VI). Eaton also illustrates a tiny pin or lime dipper (ANT.016683) among these grave goods (see Table 2.6). The burial was in a privileged location within the fill of a stone-faced terrace with two short stairways at the foot of a towering rock outcrop, quite different from the interments of most yanacona retainers in caves and crevices around the flanks of Machu Picchu. Salazar (2001:117–127) suggests that several individuals buried nearby might have been sacrificed for her funeral, and that the woman may have participated in rituals involving the moon and Pachamama. This was evidently a Cuzqueña of some status, albeit presumably not nobility.

Yet the metals she was buried with are not typical of those found at Cuzco (Table 2.6). Instead, her triangular neck-step tweezers, for example, would have been unusual in Cuzco, but typical of the central or south coast (Figure 2.27B, C). The lime spoon is common to the central coast (Figure 2.26C, D). The tiny cast pin or lime dipper is typical of the southern Titicaca area (Figure 2.8C). Only the two half-round-headed tupus and the lirpu are particularly Cuzqueño types (Figures 2.2B and 2.32A). This privileged woman was buried with ceramics that clearly labeled her as a Cuzqueña (Salazar 2007:171) and with metals that not only reiterated her origins in Cuzco, but also referred to two or even three other, distant provinces of the empire. The metal objects could have been acquired in the cosmopolitan center of Cuzco, or perhaps even from the multi-ethnic population of Machu Picchu, and would have made a recognizably eclectic mix of exotic items. Did these references to distant places play a role in her possible ritual activities, or do they suggest a taste for the exotic fruits of empire among well-to-do people from the capital?

Cave 63 is arguably another case of an individual buried with multiple geographic references, including Cuzqueño pottery and metals from the coast and the southern Titicaca area (Table 2.6). This cave contained the remains of a single adult male, but the goods included a tupu and a conical "bell," both typically associated with women (Eaton 1916:61–62). The ceramics included a *"pelike-shaped jug"* (Bingham 1915b:264), a two-handled, wide-mouthed tall jug form that is typically Inca (Eaton 1916:61, pl. IX:3, 4, XII:4, XIII:1, 2). Both the tupu and the conical "bell" may refer to the southern Titicaca area, but the tupu is a borderline case that could also be classified as a half-round-headed Cuzco type, and the reference of conical "bells" is only tentatively identified (Figures 2.3D and 2.33A, B, C). The split bell might refer to the north and central coast, but this attribution is also tentative (Figure 2.34A, B). The tweezers and pendant are of unknown subtypes, but the tweezers are probably coastal (Figure 2.27A).

Three adults were buried in cave 37 with another eclectic mix of goods (Table 2.6; Eaton 1916:26–38). The many ceramics include several Cuzco–Inca vessels and a pair of provincial deep plates that were probably from the Titicaca basin (Eaton 1916, pl. X, XI, XII; Salazar and Burger 2004a:138, 140, 142–143). A pierced-eye needle and a round-headed tupu would have been generic Andean items for people at Machu Picchu (Figures 2.2A and 2.26B). A pair of tweezers referred to the central coast (Figure 2.29B). A conical "bell" probably referred to the same southern Titicaca area as the deep plates, although examples are also known from the central coast (see Figure 2.33A and discussion above). Unfortunately, it is impossible to tell which goods were buried with which individuals. This cave might have contained one relatively wealthy individual from Cuzco, a less wealthy individual from the southern Titicaca region, and a relatively poor person from the central coast, interred together in the same small space to which their survivors returned for peri-

TABLE 2.6. Machu Picchu contexts that contained multiple metal objects. Some artifacts mentioned in the field report by Eaton cannot be securely matched to objects in the museum collection.

Catalog number	Type	Meaning: regional reference
Grave 26		
ANT.018477	Tupu: half-round	Cuzqueño identity?
?	Tupu: half-round [a]	Cuzqueño identity?
ANT.018480	Lirpu: disc with suspension tab	Unclear; Cuzqueño?
ANT.017890	Tiny spoon: bird finial	Central coast of Peru
ANT.017893	Tweezer: triangular	Central and south coast of Peru
ANT.016683	Tiny tupu or lime dipper: other cast head	Southern Titicaca area
Cave 37		
ANT.018482	Needle: pierced-eye, indeterminate	General central and south Andean
ANT.016681	Tupu: round	General Andean
ANT.016684	Tweezer: straight transitional	Central coast of Peru
ANT.016682	Conical "bell": indeterminate subtype	Southern Titicaca area
Cave 38		
ANT.016679b	Tupu: half-round	Cuzqueño identity?
ANT.016679a	Tupu: half-round, > semicircular	Cuzqueño identity?
ANT.016679c	Tupu: half-round, > semicircular	Cuzqueño identity?
ANT.016685	T-shaped tumi: straight back (globular join)	Cuzqueño identity? Globular join: Southern Titicaca area?
Cave 63		
ANT.018439	Split bell: cast	North and central coast of Peru?
ANT.017819	Tupu: drooping	Southern Titicaca area?
? Conical "bell" [b]	Southern Titicaca area?	
? Tweezers [b]	Coast of Peru?	
? Pendant [b]	Unknown	
Station 9A		
ANT.017863	Tumi	Cuzqueño identity?
? Tumi [c]	Cuzqueño identity?	
? Tumi fragment [c]	Cuzqueño identity?	
? Tupu [c]	Unknown	
ANT.018454	Lirpu: disc with suspension tab	Unclear; possibly Cuzqueño identity?
ANT.017877	Lirpu: (traced decoration)	Unclear; possibly Cuzqueño identity? Traced decoration: North, central, south coast of Peru, or central highlands
Room 24A		
ANT.017967	Axe: classic T-shaped	Cuzqueño identity?
ANT.017973	Knife: handleless transverse	North coast of Peru, Chimu

[a] Eaton 1916, pl. 1.
[b] Eaton 1916:61–62.
[c] Eaton 1916:84.

odic rituals. That would suggest a degree of tolerance and mixing by both ethnicity and economic standing. It is also possible that the goods were not so unequally distributed, in which case one or more of these individuals was buried with a combination of Cuzco–Inca ceramics, provincial Inca ceramics, or provincial metals from the southern Titicaca area or the central coast.

Two cases suggest that other Cuzqueños were not so interested in exotic styles, or perhaps that some people from the provinces adopted primarily Cuzco references. The one female in cave 38 was buried with four metal items that all referred to Cuzco, but no ceramics at all (Table 2.6; Figures 2.2C, 2.3A, and 2.9B; Eaton 1916:39). The only potentially provincial reference is the globular join on a T-shaped tumi, a possibly southern Titicaca feature on an otherwise Cuzqueño type (Figures 2.9A, B and 2.11B). A small cave labeled station 9A contained the very fragmentary remains of a single adult together with so many grave goods that Eaton (1916:84) suggested that it had probably been a multiple burial (Table 2.6). Of the six metal items, the only arguably provincial reference might be the traced decoration on the suspension tab of a lirpu, an object that was otherwise probably Cuzqueño (Figure 2.32A). Traced decoration in general is concentrated on the north to south coast (Figure 2.40A) and the particular style of angular lines, stippled areas, and smooth areas occurs mostly from the central to south coast and central highlands (Figure 2.40B). However, the one good match to this Machu Picchu lirpu in the database is from the southern Titicaca area (AMNH 41.1/4200), so the regional reference is not certain.

All of the previous examples are from burials. Clearing in room 24A uncovered both a classic T-shaped axe, a possibly Cuzqueño type (Figure 2.18C), and the definitely north coastal "fisherman" knife (Figure 2.13B; Table 2.6). These two items with different geographic references may have been used in the same living context.

Life Histories of Quotidian Metal Artifacts

Considering the regional and Andean context can also shed light on the "life histories" of commonplace metal objects, from manufacture through transportation over long distances, use, damage, loss, intentional destruction, and burial (see Hoffman 1999:119).

Where Did the Metalsmiths at Machu Picchu Come From?
A modest amount of metal production debris at Machu Picchu suggests that one or more metalsmiths worked there. Salazar reports that additional evidence has been found since Bingham's excavations (Mathewson 1915; Salazar 2007:177; Gordon, Section One, pages 9–13, 22, 26, 32, 46). Five pieces seem to be spills or residue from melting, casting, or perhaps refining operations. Three pieces of scored, folded, and irregularly cut sheet material suggest scrap or material intended for remelting. As discussed above, ANT.017980 might be a copper alloy ingot of the style most common at Chan Chan (Figure 2.45B). One object (ANT.017927) is a clearly unfinished triangular neck-step tweezer that had been worked to shape but

not yet perforated or doubled over (Mathewson 1915:534, 592, 593, 601, object 13; Bingham 1930, fig. 157d; Gordon, Section One, Figure 1.5).

Where did the metalsmith, or smiths, at Machu Picchu come from? The paucity of explicitly north coastal references among the quotidian metals has already suggested that they were not from the north coast of Peru. Other evidence points to a smith from the Titicaca basin. Machu Picchu is the only place in the database where metallic tin as a raw material is found. Bingham (1930:193) confirms this identification, citing a chemical analysis of 99.79% tin and a trace of antimony (also see Gordon, Section One, pages 12, 22, 26). The only other examples of metallic tin in the database are two finished artifacts, an axe and a gold celt wrapped with three tin bands, both from San Pedro de Atacama (Le Paige 1961, as cited in Mayer 1994:54–55; Figure 2.47B). Two of the tin pieces from Machu Picchu seem to be very irregular raw smelting or refining products that solidified on a surface of straw-like plant material, while the other two are scored, cut, and crumpled wads of 1.1 to 1.6 mm thick, irregular sheet material from which pieces were evidently cut to add to melting charges of copper or bronze (see Gordon, Section One, pages 12, 22, 26). Tin was almost never used by itself to make finished artifacts. Instead, tin was a component of the copper-tin bronze that became widespread during the Late Horizon. The metallic tin at Machu Picchu was destined to be added to melted copper or bronze to adjust its color, work-hardening properties, and various properties that facilitate casting (Mathewson 1915; Nordenskiöld 1921:109–121; Lechtman 1976, 1979, 1996b, 2007; Gordon, Section One, page 12). Since tin-bronze technology originated in the southern Titicaca area (Lechtman 2007:332–337), and the tin itself must have come from far to the south in Bolivia or northwest Argentina (Nordenskiöld 1921:130–139; Petersen 1970; Lechtman 1976, 2007), the tin at Machu Picchu could indicate the presence of a metalsmith from the southern Titicaca area who brought material along. This smith might have made or brought some of the nine metal items that refer to the southern Titicaca area (see Table 2.5). On the other hand, the spread of tin bronze under the Inca implies that metallic tin probably circulated throughout the Inca empire, so its presence at Machu Picchu might have nothing to do with the origins of a particular smith.

The strongest, albeit still only suggestive, evidence points to at least one metalsmith from the central or south coast of Peru. The one indisputably unfinished metal artifact in the assemblage is the partially completed triangular neck-step tweezer (ANT.017927; type 1101). Because there would have been little value in owning or transporting an unfinished object, this item was most likely made at Machu Picchu, although it is possible that an unfinished blank was brought there for some reason. Both the shape and the neck-step feature of this tweezer are unknown in the southern Titicaca region and rare in the Inca core, but are common on the central and south coasts (Figure 2.27B, C). A central or south coastal smith working at Machu Picchu could also explain the presence of the coastal neck-step feature on another triangular tweezer (ANT.017893) and on a T-shaped tumi (ANT.017857) found there (Figure 2.27B). A central or south coastal smith also could have brought or made some of the many other metal artifacts that refer to the coast (see Table 2.5).

Use of Tupus

Cobo describes tupus as pins that women use to fasten their dresses, "with the edges so thin and so sharp, that they cut many things with them" (quoted in Bandelier 1910:75). Eighty-seven of the 846 tupus in the database, or about 10%, show at least one fairly unambiguous indicator of having been used as cutting tools. Nineteen tupus (2%) have visible evidence of sharpening in the form of extensive scratches perpendicular or parallel to the edge, or both, or distinct bevels on both sides of the edge. Fifteen (2%) show one form or another of nicks, gouges, polishing, or other edge damage that suggests cutting or scraping use. Seventy-eight (9%) have had enough of the top edge of the head worn away by use or sharpening to markedly alter its shape. This last indicator of cutting use is detectable only on tupus for which the original shape is clearly implied by the curvature remaining on the sides. Inferring the original shape is feasible only on round-headed or half-round-headed forms. Many additional tupus of other shapes may be similarly worn, but they generally cannot be identified with confidence because the original head shapes were more variable and are not as clearly implied by the remaining unworn portions. Tupus with signs of cutting wear are concentrated in the southern Titicaca region, with fewer examples in the region north of Titicaca and in the Inca core (Figure 2.8A). For some women, especially in the altiplano, a tupu was an Andean pocketknife.

Four tupus of the 39 from Machu Picchu (10%) have clear evidence of use for cutting and another three are borderline cases not counted in the totals above (Tables 2.1 and 2.7). The custom of using tupus in this way probably did not seem exotic to people at Machu Picchu, since it was well known in Cuzco. Nevertheless, Cuzqueños may have originally picked this practice up from people in the southern Titicaca region, and people at Machu Picchu might have recognized the practice as provincial.

Use of Tumis

T-shaped tumis were functional tools for cutting, chopping, and possibly scraping. Guaman Poma's drawing of the evisceration of Rumiñavi suggests that they may have been used for butchery (Guaman Poma 1615:165). As with tupus, in most cases use-wear cannot be inferred for published examples unless the shape of the blade is sufficiently altered. Nevertheless, in the entire database, 23 of the 423 T-shaped tumis (5%) are probably or definitely sharpened, 32 (8%) show possible or definite signs of cutting wear, and 5 (1%) have possible or definite upset or mushrooming damage from heavy pounding or chopping. A total of 49 T-shaped tumis (11%) show at least one of these signs of use. These percentages would probably be much higher if more of the tumis had been inspected first-hand. As with tupus, tumis with obvious signs of use are almost exclusively found in the Inca heartland and the Titicaca region (Figure 2.11C). Perhaps there were more old and worn-out tupus and tumis in the regions where they originated and had been longest in use, or perhaps tupus and tumis were too precious in the periphery to use as heavily as people did closer to where they were common and more easily replaced.

TABLE 2.7. Evidence of use of tupus at Machu Picchu.

Catalog number	Profile shape	Sharpening	Edge damage
Tupu: round (type 1001)			
ANT.017869	Very flattened top center	None visible	None visible
ANT.017968	Flattened top center	Possibly sharpened	None visible
ANT.017845	Uniform	None	Minor nicks at top of head
Remaining 5	Uniform or not observable	None or not observable	None or not observable
Tupu: half-round (type 1010)			
ANT.017831	Flattened top center	Possibly sharpened perpendicular to edge	Possibly worn with scratches perpendicular to edge
ANT.017835	Flattened top center	Possibly sharpened, with 45° bevel on both sides	Possibly worn, with 45° bevel on both sides
Remaining 12	Uniform or not observable	None or not observable	None or not observable
Tupu: thin head, indeterminate shape (type 1037)			
ANT.017880	Possibly flattened top edge, off center, at angle	None visible	Not clear
ANT.018452	Possibly flattened top edge, center	None visible	None visible
Remaining 2	Not observable	Not observable	Not observable
All other tupu types			
Remaining 13	Uniform or not observable	None or not observable	None or not observable

The T-shaped tumis at Machu Picchu were clearly utilitarian, and they apparently saw heavier use than was typical elsewhere (Table 2.8). The form of T-shaped tumi blades makes it harder to be certain about profile changes due to wear or sharpening. For the sake of comparability to the rest of the database, the following judgments about sharpening and use wear include only my own hand-lens observations made before the objects were cleaned. Among the 22 tumis at Machu Picchu, 3 (14%) are definitely concave in the center of the blade, suggesting considerable use. Another 11 (50%) might be flattened or concave in the center of the blade, for a total of 64% with shape changes that suggest significant use. Seven (32%) of the tumis were probably or definitely sharpened, and 2 (9%) seemed to have signs of edge damage when I examined them. Rutledge (1984) and Gordon (Appendix C, pages 213, 221, 223) report four additional examples of sharpening and another five of use wear (Table 2.8). The difference may be due to better visibility after cleaning, different interpretive criteria, and the addition of one tumi that was not available for examination before cleaning. Combining the observations, 50% of the tumis at Machu Picchu show probable or definite signs of sharpening and 32% have edge damage that may indicate use.

TABLE 2.8. Evidence of use of T-shaped tumis at Machu Picchu. Owen's observations were made with 10× and 20× hand lenses on original corroded surfaces. Some of Gordon's observations (Appendix C) were made on cleaned surfaces and with different equipment. Where Gordon's observations differ, they are given in parentheses.

Catalog number	Profile shape	Sharpening	Edge damage
T-shaped tumi: straight back (type 2840)			
ANT.017852	Possibly flat center of blade	None visible	None
ANT.017853	Possibly slightly flat in center	None visible (suggested[a])	None visible (nicks[a])
ANT.017854	Possibly concave angled center of blade	None visible	None visible
ANT.017855	Possibly concave center of blade	Parallel to edge	None visible
ANT.017856	Possibly flat center of blade	None visible	None (abrasion[a])
ANT.017857	Possibly flat center of blade	None visible (sharpened[a])	None
ANT.017858	Possibly angled center of blade	None visible	None
ANT.017861	Possibly angled flat center of blade	None visible	Not clear
ANT.017864	Concave center of blade	Probably	Possible; post-deposition?
ANT.017865	Possibly flat center of blade	Sharpened	None (striations[a])
ANT.017911	Concave center of blade	None visible	Very upset, nicked, bent
ANT.017971	Possibly flat center of blade, not clear	None visible	None visible
ANT.017868[b]	Probably none	(Sharpened[a, c])	(Use abrasion[b])
ANT.017860	Unclear	Sawtooth notches	Sawtooth notches
ANT.017963	Unclear	Parallel and perpendicular	None visible
ANT.016685	Uniform	None visible	None visible
ANT.017859	Uniform	None visible	None visible
T-shaped tumi: slightly flaring back (type 2841)			
ANT.017866	Possibly concave center of blade	None visible	None visible
ANT.017863	Uniform	Probably parallel to edge	Not clear
ANT.017862[b]	Uniform	Not evaluated	Not evaluated
ANT.017867	Uniform	None visible (sharpened[a])	None
T-shaped tumi: tiny cast blade (type 2849)			
ANT.017962	Uniform	None visible	None
Flat tumi: "T" variant (type 5115)			
ANT.016678	Concave center of blade	Probably	None visible (striations[a])

[a] Observation by Gordon that differs from Owen. See Appendix C, pages 213, 221, 223.
[b] Recorded by Rutledge 1984, not examined by Owen.
[c] Observation by Rutledge 1984.

Use of Axes

The functions of axes, chisels, and related items might seem obvious, but they are not. The names given to these objects are analytical categories created by modern observers, not the ethnocategories of the people who made and used these items.

TABLE 2.9. Evidence of use of axes, celts, and chisels in the entire database. Counts are incomplete, because evidence of use cannot be evaluated for many published examples.

Type	Total n	Sharpening		Edge damage		Mushroomed/Upset		Any use	
		Definite	Possible	Definite	Possible	Definite	Possible	#	%
Axe									
"Classic" T-shaped (4250)	70		1	5		7		9	13
All tanged trapezoidal	99		1	5	1	8		10	10
All tanged wide crescent	82	4	2	5	1	6		7	9
All, including fragments	714	5	10	12	5	19		30	4
Celt									
Straight-sided (4010)	221	2	1	2	2	6	2	9	4
Flaring end (4020)	62	1	1	1	1	4		5	8
Chisel									
Fine (2700)	595	4	1	5	3	22	3	32	5
Heavy (2710)	20		1	2	1	10	1	11	55
Long, flaring (2705)	11							0	0
Tanged flaring "formón" (2716)	23							0	0

A single modern term such as "axe" can lump together types of objects that had different uses. For example, this discussion separates rectangular or flaring "celts" from the "axe" categories used by Mayer (1986, 1992, 1994, 1998) and Gordon (Section One), on the suspicion that they were hafted differently and served different functions. Even identical objects may have been used in multiple ways. Mayer (1986:32–40) suggests that some axes were used for forestry and woodwork, others as functional weapons, and still others as ceremonial weapons or insignia (also see Lechtman 2007:336–341). Guaman Poma illustrates capitán Rumiñavi with an axe, suggesting that axes could be weapons, either real or symbolic (Guaman Poma 1615:165). Gordon (Section One, pages 55–56, 68–69) argues that some axes at Machu Picchu were used for woodwork, others for splitting stone, and others for dressing stone in recesses and interior angles. Some axes and related objects were hafted (Mayer 1986:35–40, pl. 5–10, 18), whereas Gordon suggests that others were handheld and driven by hammer blows like a splitting maul or sculptor's chisel (Section One, page 54).

Of the examples in the whole database (Table 2.9) of sharpening, edge damage, and mushrooming or upsetting from hammer blows to the backs or tangs of axes, 9% to 13% of axes in some categories show at least possible signs of such utilitarian use. Among all axes in the database, only 4% are recorded as showing signs of use. These proportions in the database are certainly much lower than they are in reality, because most axes were recorded from publications, especially Mayer (1986, 1992, 1994, 1998), in which it is rarely possible to identify evidence of use.

Even among the axes that were directly inspected, signs of use are surprisingly rare for what seem to be heavy-duty tools. While some axes were definitely sharpened, and others may have been, many were evidently never intended to have a sharp

TABLE 2.10. Evidence of use of axes, celts, and chisels at Machu Picchu. Owen's observations were made with 10× and 20× hand lenses on original corroded surfaces. Some of Gordon's observations (Section One, page 68, and Appendix C) were made on cleaned surfaces and with different equipment. Where Gordon's observations differ, they are given in parentheses.

Catalog number	Profile shape	Sharpening	Edge damage	Mushroomed/upset on back or end	Face damage[a]	Broken or bent
Axe: rectangular tangs, no hole, trapezoidal blade ("classic") (type 4250)						
ANT.017901	Possible flat portion	Possibly beveled	Slight upset on edge corner	Back: slight to moderate		None
ANT.017967	Uniform	Too corroded	Too corroded to observe	None (hammer marks[a])		Corner of blade broken off
Axe: rectangular tangs, no hole, wide crescent blade (type 4270)						
ANT.017899	Uniform	Possible light sharpening	Minimal nicks	Back: moderate		None
Axe: curved tangs, no hole, wide crescent blade (type 4470)						
ANT.017904	Not observable	Possible light sharpening	Breakage only (indented[a])	None		Edge broken and bent
Axe: indeterminate haft, trapezoidal blade (type 4750)						
ANT.017969	Uniform	Possibly parallel to edge	None (blunt, deformation bands[a])	Not observable	Deep striations	Blade broken off
Axe: indeterminate haft, indeterminate blade shape (type 4701)						
ANT.017974	Uniform	Possible; post-corrosion?	None	Not observable		Blade broken off
Celt: straight or slightly flared sides (type 4010)						
ANT.017966	Uniform	None	None	Not observable	Deep gouges	10° twist, broken off
Celt: straight or slightly flared sides, flared end (type 4020)						
ANT.017975	Uniform	Sharpened	None visible	Not observable	Fine striations	5° twist, broken off
ANT.017964	Not observable	Much of edge is missing	Heavy impact damage	End: slight (none[a])	Striations	None
Celt? Lenticular section, rounded, flared (anomalous unalloyed copper) (type 4030)						
ANT.017908	Uniform	Probably sharpened	Several deep nicks	None		None
Chisel: heavy (type 2710)						
ANT.017907	Flat portion	Possibly, not clear	Flattened, squared off	End: moderate (heavy[a])		None
Chisel: fine (type 2700)						
ANT.017851	Not observable	Not observable	Thin edge battered and bent over	None		None
ANT.017879	Uniform	Too corroded	Too corroded to observe	None		Tip of haft is bent
ANT.018453	Uniform	None visible	None visible	None		None

[a] Observation by Gordon that differs from Owen. See Section One, page 68, and Appendix C, page 229.

cutting edge. With or without a sharp edge, many are virtually pristine, with little sign of ever being used. Gordon (Section One, pages 28–31, 39, 44, 46, 55) finds that all but one of the axes he examined were left in a soft, annealed state, making the scarcity of significant edge damage all the more surprising. The single exception with a hardened edge was purchased far from Machu Picchu and seems to have been sharpened after the formation of a heavy corrosion layer. Given its uncertain recent history, this one piece is equivocal evidence of intentional work-hardening in the Late Horizon. (The direct evidence of use of axes from Machu Picchu is summarized in Table 2.10.)

Gordon's observations (Section One, pages 68–69, Appendix C, pages 213, 221, 223) generally agree with mine, except that he tends to describe the damage as more severe. Although some axes from other sites were apparently never meant to have cutting edges, all the examples from Machu Picchu could once have been sharp. Five of the six axes from Machu Picchu show signs of sharpening, although one was probably sharpened or resharpened after the surface had formed a heavy corrosion layer. Axes used for forestry or woodwork would be exposed to the wear and accidents of fieldwork. They would presumably accumulate nicks on the cutting edge, dents and scratches on their faces, and shape changes from repeated sharpening (for examples, see Mayer 1986:38, pl. 14:271, 274, 276), especially given their soft, annealed state. Most of the Machu Picchu axes do not show this sort of damage. One shows a few minor nicks (ANT.017899). Four are broken (ANT.017974, ANT.017969, ANT.017904, and ANT.017967), yet three of these show little or no other damage to the cutting edge. At the other extreme, two axes in Bingham's collections from other sites, ANT.017902 and ANT.017900, are heavily upset from hammer blows to the back edge and the working edge is severely battered and mashed square, as if it had been pounded on rocks. The minimal edge damage on most of the other axes does not seem consistent with forestry or other repetitive, hard use. The squared edges of ANT.017902 and ANT.017900 would have precluded cutting uses entirely, although they might have been used for detailing stonework, as Gordon suggests (Section One, pages 53–56, 68–69). Alternatively, the blunted edges might be due to intentional destruction in stereotypical ways, as discussed below and as suggested over a century ago by Ambrosetti (1904:188–189).

Observing the same axes, celts, and chisels, Gordon (Section One, pages 53–56, 60–66, 68–69)argues that their damage is so severe that many of them must have been used for dressing or splitting stone, and the remainder for chopping or splitting wood. This dramatic difference in assumptions about the nature and degrees of damage to be expected under different conditions of use calls out for an experimental use-wear study.

Many of the axes from Machu Picchu may have been real or symbolic weapons. The damage that they do show is mostly from blows to the back edge and gross fractures that broke pieces out of the blade. The hammer marks on the back edges are enigmatic unless the axes were handheld and hammered like chisels, as Gordon (Section One, page 54) suggests, but that use should have left evidence on the working edges. The broken blades suggest blows to the broad surface of the axe, as might happen when a hafted axe accidentally falls flat against a rock, or in an intentional act of destruction. The "ancla" axe with curved tangs and a wide, crescent blade (ANT.017904) is a form that Mayer identifies as a weapon (1986:38, pl. 16:306–309). Axes are much more prevalent at Machu Picchu than at Sacsawaman or Ollantaytambo (see Table 2.1), where there should have been comparable needs for tools used in stoneworking, if not forestry. What was different about Machu Picchu? While Sacsawaman has aspects of a fortress, and Ollantaytambo has enclosing walls, Salazar (2004:46–47) points out that Machu Picchu was in a particularly remote and vulnerable setting and, she argues, laid out with unusual attention to defense. The many axes may suggest that Machu Picchu was staffed with more ostentatiously equipped soldiers than were other royal estates.

Use of Celts
The items labeled here as "celts," equivalent to Mayer's flat axes (1986, 1992, 1994, 1998), were probably blades for foot plows, hoes, adzes, or similar implements (see Ambrosetti 1904:199–200; Latcham 1938:320–321, 341). They are widely distributed throughout the Andes (Figure 2.15B) and have roughly the same frequency of signs of use as do axes and fine chisels (see Table 2.9).

The three typical celts (types 4010 and 4020) from Machu Picchu show consistent kinds of use damage (Table 2.10). Two of the three may be sharpened, two of the three were twisted along the long axis and broken off, and all three have different degrees of damage to the flat faces. The damage to two (ANT.017966 and ANT.017975) of the three seems far too light to suggest stonework. The third (ANT.017964) has severe edge damage in the portion of the edge that has not been cut away for metallographic work. The damage and twisting breaks seem consistent with expectations for blades hafted on foot plows or hoes that were used, and occasionally stuck, in heavy soil with rocks.

If so, these celts would be among the few clues about agriculture at Machu Picchu. Salazar (2004:45) notes that there are few indications of farming in the Machu Picchu burials. Both of the twisted and broken celts come from a nonmortuary context, section 40A (Gordon, Section One, page 17, Appendix C, pages 232, 234). The third typical celt has no known provenience within Machu Picchu.

A fourth celt (ANT.017908) has an unusual thick, rounded, lenticular form (Appendix G, Figure G13, type 4030; Salazar and Burger 2004a:190). It is also unusual in being relatively pure copper (Gordon, Section One, pages 13, 18, 20, 56). While it was probably sharpened and has a few deep nicks on the edge, it does not seem to have been used heavily.

Use of Chisels
Fine chisels seem appropriate for woodworking, and Mayer (1986:32–33) includes them in a proposed "culture of woodworking" in northern Chile and northeastern Argentina. They show signs of use in roughly the same proportions as do axes and celts in the whole database (Table 2.9). The three examples from Machu Picchu have similarly modest evidence of use (Table 2.10).

Heavy chisels, on the other hand, tend to show signs of use, often with heavy upsetting or mushrooming damage from being driven with a hard hammer (Table 2.9). The one example from Machu Picchu is no exception, with hammer marks on the end and its working edge squared off but not nicked or gouged, suggesting that it was used against a hard, smooth surface such as a polished stone anvil (Table 2.10).

Upsetting or mushrooming damage on heavy chisels, light chisels, celts, axes, and occasionally other tools is concentrated in the Inca core and southern Titicaca regions, although examples also occur in most regions other than Chile (Figure 2.42C; Table 2.9).

Use of Conical "Bells"

The four conical "bells" from Machu Picchu are examples of a widespread type (Figure 2.33A, B, C) that has been interpreted as earrings (Bingham 1930), rattles (Bandelier 1910, pl. LXVI), little bells (*campanillas*) and personal adornments (Latcham 1938:323–234), and bells worn on the ankles during dances (Salazar and Burger 2004a:186). Three of these "bells" were excavated from a late, intrusive offering on Cerro Baúl in Moquegua, together with a fourth that was slightly larger and had a flat-topped form like a tall cowbell (Donna Nash, personal communication, 2005, 2012). They were worked into a braided or plaited structure made of human hair, suggesting that they were worn in sets as hair ornaments. At Machu Picchu, two were found together in burial cave 57, and in many cases multiples of two to five are reported from a single geographic location. One from La Plata Island (FMNH 308-1-4/4360) still has a mass of unidentified fibers inside, possibly human hair.

These conical "bells" may be related to cast metal anthropomorphic ornaments that Chipayas of the southern Titicaca area wore in their hair in the early twentieth century (Figure 2.33D; Appendix G, Figure G4, types 1551 and 1552). These ornaments are similar in size, shape, and proportions to most conical "bells," but they are solid and flat, rather than conical and hollow. Like the conical "bells," they have a crosswise hole at the top, are long and narrow, and often flare out at the bottom. The solid ornaments typically depict a person with face, hair, and body details in relief, breasts sometimes indicated, and arms with elbows bent and hands over the lower torso. Two conical "bells" have similar details. One from the southern Titicaca area (AMNH 41.1/4195) has a simple face in relief near the apex. Another from "Tiahuanaco" (AMNH B/2801) has a face at the apex, and modeled arms and hands in the same position as on the solid ornaments (Appendix G, Figure G4, type 1903). This example also has a narrow appendage descending from the apex on each side of the face, suggesting two braids of hair. Similar but longer paired appendages that may represent braids are found on many otherwise plain "bells," including the two from cave 57 at Machu Picchu (Appendix G, Figure G4, type 1902; Salazar and Burger 2004a:186).

Three of the solid ornaments in the American Museum of Natural History are labeled "Laurake Pendants tied to the hair Chipaya Indian Bolivia, A. Metraux Expedition (Voss fund) 1939–49." These are so worn that the sculptural details, very clear on other examples, are smoothed away entirely, suggesting perhaps generations of curation and use. At least some of these ornaments are prehistoric; Helsley-Marchbanks (2004; Figures 2.7A, D, 2.8A, 2.10B, 2.11A, B, 2.13D, 2.20D, 2.21A–D,

2.22C, 2.23B, D, and 2.31B, C, D) excavated molds for them from the Late Horizon site of Muyuntasita, Bolivia. If the Chipayas were using these objects for their original purpose, the conical "bells" may also have been used as hair ornaments.

Intentional Destruction

There are 335 metal artifacts in the database, including many different types, that seem to have been intentionally destroyed. Many of these objects are damaged in similar ways, which are difficult to reconcile with accidents or use. Many tupus have the top of the head broken off along a horizontal fold, and both of the remaining projecting sides folded in over the center on the same side. Less often, the shaft of the tupu is sharply bent double, bringing the point up toward the top of the head. Needles are usually simply doubled over sharply. T-shaped tumis typically have both tips of the blade folded in toward the center on the same side, or one or both tips are broken off along the resulting folds. North Coast tumis are folded once or several times, most often with the handle doubled down over the blade, often at an angle rather than straight across the axis of the shape. Discs are typically folded several times, usually starting by folding two opposite edges in toward the center on the same side. Ambrosetti noted apparently intentional destruction of bronze axes in the Calchaqui region (1904:188–189). Among the less massive artifact types, the metal is often cracked or broken along sharp bends, leaving a characteristic straight, sharply upturned fracture. Intentional destruction is common, affecting 81 of the 883 tupus (9% of the sample in the database), 35 of the 416 discs (8%), 32 of the 259 North Coast tumis (12%), 56 of the 423 T-shaped tumis (13%), and many other types, including ones that the process left too fragmentary to identify. These figures probably underestimate the prevalence of intentional destruction, because they count only treatment that can be distinguished from accidental or post-depositional damage, and because the evidence is not clear in many items recorded from publications or other records.

The practice of intentionally destroying metal objects was widespread in the Andes (Figures 2.11C and 2.42D). Like Ambrosetti (1904:188–189), Mayer (1986:38) suggests that axes in the southern region with one tang broken off were intentionally destroyed. The tallies presented here do not make that assumption, erring on the conservative side, since at least some cases could be accidental damage. Axes throughout the Andes may have been intentionally destroyed in other ways as well. The heavy upsetting on the back edges of some axes could not occur if the axe were hafted; it implies direct blows by a hard hammer. In some cases, this upsetting might be due not to unhafted use, as Gordon suggests (Section One, page 54), but rather to the intentional destruction of the axe by using blows against the back edge to flatten the working edge against a rock after removing the haft. Hoffman (1999:116–119) describes a bronze axe from Mallorca that was intentionally destroyed in several ways, including similarly blunting the edge. Some of the Andean axes have upset damage far out on the hafting tangs, or on the ends of the tangs. The blows that caused this damage might have been attempts at destruction, since it is not evident how they would have contributed to either the manufacture or the use of these axes. As noted above, the gross breakage of many Andean axes such as ANT.017904 (Salazar and Burger 2004a:190) may suggest intentionally destructive blows to the broad surface of the blade, especially in the absence of heavy use damage to the working edge.

Aside from its possibly greater frequency in the Peruvian Andes and the altiplano, this practice has no clear geographic focus and probably had no regional or ethnic implications (Figure 2.42D). It affects both T-shaped tumis (Figure 2.11D), which may have been spread by the Inca empire, and North Coast tumis, which certainly were not. The broad distribution of intentional destruction and its application to Inca and non-Inca objects alike suggest that intentional destruction of metal artifacts was an old practice that was already widespread before the Late Horizon.

There is evidence of intentional destruction of tupus, tumis, and a large disc at Machu Picchu (Table 2.11). Some of the damage to axes (Table 2.10) might also have been intentional. Overall, three cases are unequivocal, five probable, and twelve possible but not particularly indicated, plus four possible cases of intentionally broken or blunted axes. From 4% to 13% of the Machu Picchu assemblage was probably or possibly intentionally destroyed.

Salazar (2001:119) suggests that metal objects at Machu Picchu were intentionally destroyed at the death of the owner. If this were so, we might expect to find intentionally destroyed metals predominantly in burials. Unfortunately, only two definite or probable cases of intentional destruction at Machu Picchu come from known contexts. One is a small tupu (ANT.017880), the probably round head of which was apparently bent and broken in the standard way. It was found in mortuary cave 103. The other is the large silver alloy disc ANT.017850 (Gordon, Section One, pages 17, 52, Appendix C, page 220; Salazar and Burger 2004a:186), which was folded in the standard way, folded several additional times, and apparently unfolded again. This disc was found in section 41A, a nonmortuary context, along with an oversized loop-eye needle (ANT.018626) and a wad of crumpled and cut sheet tin (ANT.017978). Since bits of the tin were destined to be added to batches of liquid metal, the destroyed disc may also have been intended for the melting pot.

Clearer answers about the contexts of intentional destruction come from the 26 intentionally destroyed quotidian metal artifacts excavated from sites near Jauja by the Upper Mantaro Archaeological Research Project (UMARP) (Owen 1986, 2001; Norconk 1987; Owen and Norconk 1987; Costin et al. 1989). Around Jauja, intentionally destroyed metal artifacts are no more common in burials than in other contexts (Table 2.12). About 16% of the metals from burials were intentionally destroyed, compared to a nearly identical 17% from nonmortuary contexts. Twenty-three out of 26, or 88%, of the intentionally destroyed metal artifacts were found in nonmortuary contexts such as occupation layers, midden, and fill.

The practice of intentional destruction was clearly established around Jauja before the Late Horizon, since nine of the intentionally destroyed artifacts date to Wanka II, the local period corresponding to the later portion of the Late Interme-

TABLE 2.11. Evidence of intentional destruction and repair at Machu Picchu. See Table 2.10 for axes that could be intentionally destroyed. Only "definitely" or "probably" intentionally destroyed items are counted for regional comparisons.

Catalog number	Breaking or bending damage	Attempted repair	Intentionally destroyed?	Context
T-shaped tumi (types 2840, 2841)				
ANT.017853	One end of blade sharply bent	End flattened back	Probably	
ANT.017858	Both ends of blade sharply bent	Ends flattened back	Probably	
ANT.017864	Both ends of blade sharply bent, one broken off	Ends flattened back	Probably	
ANT.017911	Both ends of blade bent, not sharply (edge upset, nicked, bent)	None	Probably	
ANT.017867	Handle sharply bent	Handle flattened back	Probably	
ANT.017854	End of handle probably broken off	Broken end bent into loop	Possibly	General: section 44A
ANT.017971	End of handle probably broken off	Broken end bent into loop	Possibly	
ANT.017863	End of handle broken off	Failed attempt to unbend?	Possibly	Burial: station 9A
ANT.017861	Half of one side of blade broken off	Failed attempt to unbend?	Possibly	
ANT.017865	Half of one side of blade broken off	Failed attempt to unbend?	Possibly	
ANT.017860	Most of handle and one side of blade broken off	Failed attempt to unbend?	Possibly	
ANT.017868 [a]	Handle and blade slightly bent in several places	None	Possibly	Burial: cave 54
ANT.017963	Not observable	Not observable	Not observable	
Remaining 8	None	None	No	
T-shaped tumi: tiny cast blade (type 2849)				
ANT.017962	Incomplete blade, cause unclear	None	Possibly	Burial: cave 54
Flat tumi: "T" variant (type 5115)				
ANT.016678	Both ends of blade possibly broken off	Ends possibly smoothed	Possibly	Burial: cave 14
Tupu: round-headed and indeterminate probably round-headed (types 1001, 1037)				
ANT.017880	Both sides of head folded in toward center on same side	Possibly partially flattened	Definitely	Burial: cave 103
ANT.017830	Top and both sides broken off, possibly in attempted folding	Failed attempt to unbend?	Possibly	Burial: cave 13
Tupu: half-round-headed variants (types 1007, 1012, 1015)				
ANT.018448	Top folded down, broken off, one side folded in, other gone; wrinkled	Side bent back	Definitely	
ANT.016680	One side broken off, possibly in attempted folding	Failed attempt to unbend?	Possibly	Burial: cave 29
ANT.017848	One side bent 10°, other 30° toward same side, neither sharply	None	Possibly	
Tupu: all types				
Remaining 34	None visible	None	No	
Disc: plain, flat, 1 hole near edge, 40–100 mm diameter (type 5423)				
ANT.017850	Sides folded in; folded vertically; corner folded; top, bottom folded in	Unfolded	Definitely	General: section 41A

[a] Recorded by Rutledge (1984) and Gordon (see Section One, pages 16, 34, 49, Appendix C, page 223).

TABLE 2.12. Contexts of intentional destruction in Upper Mantaro Archaeological Research Project excavations, from 69 separable burials containing 123 or 124 individuals, and extensive nonmortuary excavations. All three of the discs from mortuary contexts date to the Wanka II phase of the Late Intermediate period. Two come from a single burial. Figures do not match the tables in Norconk (1987), because a tupu and a tweezer fragment listed there are more conservatively identified here as an "indeterminate object" and "sheet scrap," and because the table in Norconk (1987) incorrectly lists a needle from a burial in J54=9 twice.

Type	Nonmortuary contexts			Mortuary contexts		
	n	Destroyed	Percentage	n	Destroyed	Percentage
Tupu	28	5	18	1	0	0
Needle	23	2	9	6	0	0
Small disc	33	8	24	10	3	30
Lirpu: disc with suspension tab	1	1	100	0	0	0
Sheet scrap	10	6	60	2	0	0
Indeterminate shaft	30	1	3	0	0	0
Totals	135	23	17%	19	3	16%

diate period. Twelve are from Late Horizon contexts, three are early Colonial, and the chronological position of two is uncertain. Both of the burials that contained intentionally destroyed metal artifacts date to Wanka II.

If intentional destruction was not usually part of a mortuary ritual, then what was its purpose? Some destroyed objects might have been prepared for melting down to make something new. This is especially plausible in cases in which irregular fragments of sheet metal are folded together into packets. However, small items such as discs could have been remelted easily without folding them first, while the standardized forms of destruction of larger items often did not make them particularly compact, as in the case of many tupus with the heads folded up but the shafts still straight. If the primary purpose was to salvage material, a surprising number of objects were destroyed but never actually recycled. Instead, a ritual explanation is still likely in most cases, but in contexts not directly connected to burials.

Repair
Intentional destruction was often not the end of an object's life history. Although little could be done with a broken axe, people routinely tried to salvage destroyed tumis, tupus, and discs (see Table 2.11 for examples from Machu Picchu). Some breakage may have been part of the destruction process, but bending parts back to shape must also have frequently ended in breaking the part off. In these cases, it is difficult to distinguish between intentional breakage and a failed attempt at repair. Some repairs may be modern. The unfolded large silver-colored disc from Machu Picchu, for example, might have been irresistible if found in its folded state. The evidence of repair is so prevalent, though, that it must have been common prehistorically. Of the 20 definitely, probably, or possibly intentionally destroyed items

other than axes from Machu Picchu, 8 (40%) were definitely repaired, and 17 (85%) were at least possibly repaired.

Most repairs were done by unskilled amateurs, not metalworkers. Parts were apparently bent back without annealing them first, causing new bends adjacent to the strain-hardened original ones, cracks, and breakage. Creased or wavy surfaces were not hammered or burnished flat. Even a successful repair usually left the artifact disfigured, cracked, and fragile. Repaired objects would have been obviously recovered from a ritually destroyed state. Even so, such recovered artifacts may have been suitable for daily use or mortuary ritual. Five possible examples of repaired, formerly destroyed metal artifacts were included in burials at Machu Picchu (see Table 2.11), but none is definitive.

Discard, Loss, and Burial
The ways in which quotidian metal artifacts were lost, discarded, or interred at Machu Picchu initially seem to paint a simple picture (Table 2.13). Context information is available for only a fraction of the artifacts and is more complete for the burials than for the rest of the excavations. Among the metal artifacts with known provenience, about two-thirds were interred with the dead. Every tupu, conical "bell," lirpu, tweezer, and tiny spoon of known context at Machu Picchu was found in a mortuary context. Four of the five T-shaped tumis with provenience information were found in burials. More utilitarian and less personal items such as axes, celts, a crowbar, a plume holder, and most of the tin were found in nonmortuary contexts. The Machu Picchu evidence suggests that personal adornments and tumis were carefully held and disposed of only in burials, but more utilitarian metal artifacts were apparently sometimes discarded or lost during use.

The more completely documented metals from the UMARP excavations near Jauja tell a very different story (Table 2.14). The dead in the Upper Mantaro region during the Late Intermediate period, Late Horizon, and early Colonial times were buried in abandoned or still occupied residential compounds within their settlements. This means that UMARP should have recovered roughly the number of burials that corresponded to the residential areas excavated. In this balanced sample, most of the quotidian metal artifacts, about 88%, were found in nonmortuary contexts. Turning the Machu Picchu pattern on its head, in the Upper Mantaro, only 3% of the tupus came from burials. Most or all of the tweezers, discs, and needles, and the one lirpu were found in nonmortuary contexts. The more utilitarian items, as at Machu Picchu, were also not buried with the dead. Eight of the 12 bola weights (many of which were crudely made from lead), both of the chisels, and most of the metalworking materials were discarded or lost in nonmortuary contexts. Unless the Machu Picchu sample with provenience is even more biased toward burials than it appears, the people at the royal country estate were far more careful than the people around Jauja about keeping their metal goods and burying them with the dead. While the artifacts themselves are superficially similar, it seems that when it came to death, the meanings of metal tupus, tweezers, discs, and other

TABLE 2.13. Contexts of quotidian metal artifacts at Machu Picchu. Proveniences from Gordon (see Appendix C; figures shown here may not match Appendix C because of minor differences in the objects examined and in counting broken or multiple items).

Type	Nonmortuary contexts		Mortuary contexts		Unknown contexts
	Objects	Percentage	Objects	Percentage	Objects
Tupu	0	0	11	100	28
Conical "bell"[a]	0	0	4	100	0
Lirpu: disc with suspension tab	0	0	3	100	0
Tiny spoon	0	0	2	100	0
Flat tumi	0	0	1	100	0
Tiny tupu or lime dipper	0	0	1	100	1
Split bell	0	0	1	100	2
T-shaped tumi	1	20	4	80	17
Tweezer	1	33	2	67	6
Needle	1	33	2	67	2
Finger ring	1	50	1	50	0
Plain disc[b]	1	50	1	50	2
Crowbar	1	100	0	0	0
Knife: handleless transverse	1	100	0	0	0
Bola weight	0	—	0	—	3
Plumb bob	0	—	0	—	1
Chisel	0	—	0	—	4
Bangle, sheet ornament, and others	0	—	0	—	2
Ingot (possible)	0	—	0	—	1
Sheet scrap: lead	0	—	0	—	0
Sheet scrap: copper alloy	0	—	0	—	1
Sheet scrap: tin	2	100	0	0	0
Smelting, refining, melting: lead	0	—	0	—	0
Smelting, refining, melting: copper	0	0	1	100	2
Smelting, refining, melting: tin	2	100	0	0	0
Strip (may be headband, bracelet, etc.)	2	100	0	0	1
Celt	2	100	0	0	2
Axe	2	100	0	0	4
Plume holder cone	1	100	0	0	0
Bar fragment	1	100	0	0	1
Indeterminate shaft fragment	0	—	0	—	2
Indeterminate sheet fragment	0	—	0	—	2
Indeterminate, others	0	0	1	100	5
Total	19	35%	35	65%	89

[a] Two of the conical "bells" come from a single mortuary context, cave 57.

[b] Thirty-eight discs from cave 2A are counted here as one item.

TABLE 2.14. Contexts of quotidian metal artifacts in Late Intermediate Period and Late Horizon contexts excavated by the Upper Mantaro Archaeological Research Project near Jauja, in the central highlands of Peru.

Type	Nonmortuary contexts		Mortuary contexts	
	Object	Percentage	Object	Percentage
Tupu	27	96	1	4
Conical "bell"	—	—	—	—
Lirpu: disc with suspension tab	1	100	0	0
Tiny spoon	—	—	—	—
Flat tumi	—	—	—	—
Tiny tupu or lime dipper	1	100	0	0
Split bell	—	—	—	—
T-shaped tumi	0	0	2	100
Tweezer	4	100	0	0
Needle	23	79	6	21
Finger ring	—	—	—	—
Plain disc[a]	41	85	7	15
Crowbar	—	—	—	—
Knife: handleless transverse	—	—	—	—
Bola weight	8	67	4	33
Plumb bob	—	—	—	—
Chisel	2	100	0	0
Bangle, sheet ornament, and others	—	—	—	—
Ingot	1	100	0	0
Sheet scrap: lead	0	0	2	100
Sheet scrap: copper alloy	9	100	0	0
Sheet scrap: tin	—	—	—	—
Smelting, refining, melting: lead	6	100	0	0
Smelting, refining, melting: copper	8	100	0	0
Smelting, refining, melting: tin	—	—	—	—
Strip (may be headband, bracelet, etc.)	6	100	0	0
Celt	—	—	—	—
Axe	0	0	1	100
Plume holder	—	—	—	—
Bar fragment	—	—	—	—
Indeterminate shaft fragment	30	100	0	0
Indeterminate sheet fragment	15	88	2	12
Indeterminate, others	11	92	1	8
Total	193	88%	26	12%

[a] Seven discs from burial J41=8 are counted here as one item.

items were different for the farmers of Jauja and the staff of a royal estate who died far from their homelands.

Summary and Conclusions

Metalworking traditions are geographically distributed in much the same way as ceramic traditions are. The distribution maps (Figures 2.1 through 2.47) describe some of this patterning, which should help with interpreting other metal assemblages. The Inca spread a material, tin bronze, and their technological style of casting it throughout their empire, but their influence on the kinds of quotidian metal objects that people used was surprisingly slight (Lechtman 2007:327–343). There is no consistent Inca metal assemblage or object type analogous to the ubiquitous, uniformly decorated ceramics in Inca corporate style. Inca quotidian metal assemblages differ substantially from site to site, even within the Inca core. Metal assemblages may have been more responsive to functional and other differences between sites than were the obligatory ceramic markers of Inca affiliation such as aryballoids and handled plates. Some metal artifact types and features were prevalent in the Inca core region, but none is present in all or even most Inca contexts. Instead, they form a Cuzqueño repertoire from which different, limited subsets and proportions of types were selected at any given place. Lechtman (2007:336–337) identifies several items of this kind, including fancy T-shaped tumis, T-shaped axes, star-shaped mace heads, and axe-maces, calling them "semi-standardized" and "essentially 'state issue.'" Additional possibilities include half-round-headed tupus, tumis in general, "ancla" axes, cast spherical bola weights, and others (see Table 2.3). Because there is no consistent imperial pattern, Late Horizon metal assemblages are best compared to other assemblages from specific sites and regions. This variability complicates the interpretation of any given assemblage, but it also promises that metals may encode information about the unique activities and networks of interaction at the places where they are found.

Although some metal artifacts were almost certainly recognized as typical of the Inca core, the pattern of variable subsets of the Cuzqueño quotidian metal repertoire suggests that even Cuzqueño metal artifacts were probably selected and used in a personal or situational manner. On a continuum of meanings from "non-Inca" through "associated with Cuzqueños" to "explicitly imperial corporate style," only a very few metal objects, such as concave-sided headdress frontals or yauri pikes, could be categorized near the extreme of explicit symbols of Inca affiliation or office (see Table 2.3). These rare and precious items are not expected to turn up often in archaeological contexts. Other types, such as tumis and tupus with Inca-style cast decorations, half-round-headed tupus, "classic" and "ancla" axes, and star-shaped mace heads, probably connoted Cuzqueño or Inca identity and elevated status, but only on a variable, optional, individual, and situational basis, without the support of sumptuary laws or imperial control of production and distribution.

Some metal objects were part of a broadly shared, probably ancient set of pan-Andean concepts, as in the case of round-headed tupus and some features of axes.

Others would have referred to one of many broad to tightly concentrated regional traditions. People outside each region might have recognized these objects as simply foreign, or might have understood the reference to a known other place. The maps show that some metal objects that some archaeologists may have considered typically Inca in style, including triangular tweezers and tiny spoons decorated with cast birds, are clearly products of peripheral regions. They only occasionally reached the Inca core, and would have signified distant provinces there.

Nevertheless, some kinds of metal objects do seem to have been spread by Inca expansion and the movement of people and goods through imperial channels. Half-round-headed tupus, T-shaped tumis, "classic" and "ancla" axes, cast bola weights, and possibly lirpus all seem to have spread from the Inca core throughout the empire. The variable, inconsistent patterns in which they did so suggest that their dispersal was probably an incidental by-product of other activities, rather than part of any broad economic or political strategy analogous to the uses of decorated ceramics and textiles, or the imposition of Quechua.

Other object types and features with wide distributions seem to have spread not from the Inca core, but from peripheral regions. Various kinds of metal goods from the southern Titicaca region, including several types of tupus and possibly conical "bell" hair ornaments, may have been disseminated by movement and exchange within the empire, even though they were not particularly characteristic of the capital. In one example, the distributions of a characteristic globular feature on the neck of some tupus and T-shaped tumis hint that Inca metalsmiths may have been influenced by smiths in the southern Titicaca region. The Inca may have moved metalsmiths from the southern Titicaca area to Cuzco in much the same way that they commandeered smiths from the coast of Peru. These or other smiths applied the southern feature to Cuzco-style objects, and it spread to the far corners of the empire. Such technological or stylistic syntheses support the ethnohistorical evidence that Inca practices brought smiths from different regions into contact with traditions from other parts of the empire. The geographic distribution of "ancla" axes suggests that Cuzqueño or Inca metalworking technology was advancing in complexity, labor efficiency, and repeatability as the empire grew.

The distributions of some metal artifacts suggest functional explanations. Metal bola weights are most common in the open highlands regions, where they would have served best for hunting. Fishhooks are prevalent along the coast (Figure 2.25D). Other patterns may be more arbitrary matters of cultural style, such as the practice of using tupus as cutting tools in the Titicaca and Inca core regions, or may be long-standing, generalized Andean practices, such as the intentional destruction of metal artifacts.

The staff at Machu Picchu, largely resettled from multiple regions conquered by Pachacuti, used their own distinctive subset of the metal assemblage associated with Cuzco (see Table 2.4) (Burger 2004; Salazar 2004, 2007). Their half-round-headed tupus and a few other tupu types, T-shaped tumis, cast bola weights, and lirpus would all have expressed Cuzqueño identity. The plumb bob and crowbar would have been parts of an Inca technological style of construction. The "classic" T-shaped axes and the "ancla" axe might have been somewhat more formal emblems of imperial military authority or even rank. Like people in Cuzco and throughout the Andes, some residents of Machu Picchu used round-headed tupus, although they probably did not attribute regional or ethnic significance to them.

The quotidian metal artifacts at Machu Picchu are comparable to those at Ollantaytambo, which was another of Pachacuti's royal estates, and probably had similar functions (see Table 2.1) (Niles 2004:50). One key difference is the unusually high proportion of axes at Machu Picchu, compared to their complete absence from Ollantaytambo and many other Inca facilities. Machu Picchu, with its remote and isolated location, may have needed a more ostentatiously armed garrison than did a royal estate in the more accessible portion of the Urubamba valley. Another difference is the prevalence, modest as it is, of metalworking materials at Machu Picchu. There is no hint of metalworking in the Ollantaytambo collection. On the other hand, the quotidian metal assemblages from the royal estates at Machu Picchu and Ollantaytambo are both dissimilar, in different ways, to that of the fortress–sanctuary of Sacsawaman. A different combination of activities evidently occurred there.

Some 29% to 32% of the commonplace metals from Machu Picchu might have signified Cuzqueño identity or affiliation (see Table 2.4). Many of the relocated staff of the royal estate were evidently trying, or being encouraged, to align themselves with the empire. About half of the metal goods probably seemed broadly Andean or so generic that they had no regional or ethnic connotations. People probably recognized another 20% as exotic (see Table 2.5). Many of these were likely brought along by their owners when they moved from distant provinces to serve at Machu Picchu. Among the resettled staff were one or a few metalworkers, probably not from the north coast of Peru, but possibly from the southern Titicaca region or more probably from the central or south coast of Peru. About two-thirds of the likely exotics (see Table 2.5) referred to the north, central, or south coast of Peru, if people could identify where they came from. Most of the remaining objects would have reminded people of the southern Titicaca region. A mix of goods in which markers of the ethnic and political elite are only half again more common than tokens of the exotic suggests a multi-ethnic, eclectic, cosmopolitan society with a considerable acceptance of foreign items and ideas.

The Machu Picchu material even affords a few glimpses of individuals' responses to this cosmopolitan atmosphere. One well-off Cuzqueña was buried with not only fine ceramics and metal goods that proclaimed her ethnic identity, but also metal objects that referred to several distinct regions of the empire. Another person was buried with goods that referred to Cuzco, the southern Titicaca region, and the coast. Three people whose survivors did not mind burying and probably revisiting them together in a single small cave may have been from Cuzco, the central coast, and the altiplano. One or two of them may have been buried with ceramics and metal items from two or even three of those regions. Two other people were buried with exclusively Cuzqueño goods, either maintaining their ethnic identity or thoroughly adopting the style of their masters. Metalsmiths combined technologies, styles, and artifact types from different parts of the empire.

Quotidian metal goods passed from those creative smiths into the hands of their owners, who used them not only to signal identity, origin, and affiliation, but also to pin their shawls, to ornament their hair, or to cut, dig, or threaten. Eventually, perhaps at the owner's death, many metal artifacts were intentionally destroyed in prescribed ways. Many of those were repaired, not well by skilled metalworkers, but expediently by others. These objects apparently returned for a time, defaced and salvaged, to use in life or burial with the dead. Beliefs about the final destination of everyday metal artifacts were not universal. In the central highlands, most ordinary metal goods were eventually lost or simply discarded. At Machu Picchu, the resettled staff in their remote, multi-ethnic, cosmopolitan enclave clung carefully to their modest metal possessions, imbued with meanings, and took them along when they died there, far from the homes of their youth.

Acknowledgments

This section expands portions of my master's thesis (Owen 1986), written under the guidance of Timothy Earle, Christopher Donnan, and James Hill. The original database of Andean metals would not have been possible without the help of Timothy Earle and the many members of the Upper Mantaro Archaeological Research Project; Ellen Howe of the Objects Conservation Department at the Metropolitan Museum of Art; Peter Kvietok and the staff of the American Museum of Natural History; Lawrence Dawson, John Rowe, and Lisa Valkenier at the Phoebe A. Hearst (then Lowie) Museum at the University of California, Berkeley; Richard Burger and Leopold Pospisil of the Yale Peabody Museum of Natural History; Bruce Smith of the Smithsonian Institution; Robert Welsh at the Field Museum of Natural History; John and Theresa Topic; Heather Lechtman; Glenn Russell; and the Anthropology Department of the University of California, Los Angeles, which provided a research grant. Many people have helped me to expand the database more recently, including Peter Bürgi, Niki Clark, Geoffrey Conrad, and Don Rice of the Programa Contisuyo; Patricia Palacios and Yamilex Tejada of the Museo Contisuyo; Pablo de la Vera Cruz and Mario Vera of the Museo Arqueológico of the Universidad Nacional de San Agustín in Arequipa; Patrick Ryan Williams of the Field Museum of Natural History; and Donna Nash of the Cerro Baúl project. Eugen Friedrich Mayer's four large catalogs of photographs and provenience data contributed crucially to the discussion of many artifact types and provided base images for several of the artifact type illustrations. Lucy Salazar provided invaluable information concerning artifacts in the Bingham collection at Yale that had been incorrectly attributed to Machu Picchu, as well as important discussions about the identification of some artifacts. Finally, I thank Heather Lechtman and an anonymous reviewer for their exceptionally helpful comments on an earlier version of this section.

Distribution Map Abbreviations

Region abbreviations for distribution maps, Figures 2.2 through 2.47, on the following pages. MP marks the location of Machu Picchu. The sizes of the circles are proportional to the number of objects at each location. Locations within 10 km of each other are lumped for better visibility.

CCP	Central Coastal Peru
CE	Coastal Ecuador
CHP	Central Highland Peru
Co	Cochabamba region
FSCP	Far South Coastal Peru
HE	Highland Ecuador
IC	Inca Core
Mo	Moquegua region
NCCh	North Central Chile
NCh	Northern Chile
NET	Northeastern Titicaca region
NP	Northern Peru
NWA	Northwestern Argentina
SCP	South Coastal Peru
SLE	South Lowland Ecuador
SPA	San Pedro de Atacama region
ST	Southern Titicaca region

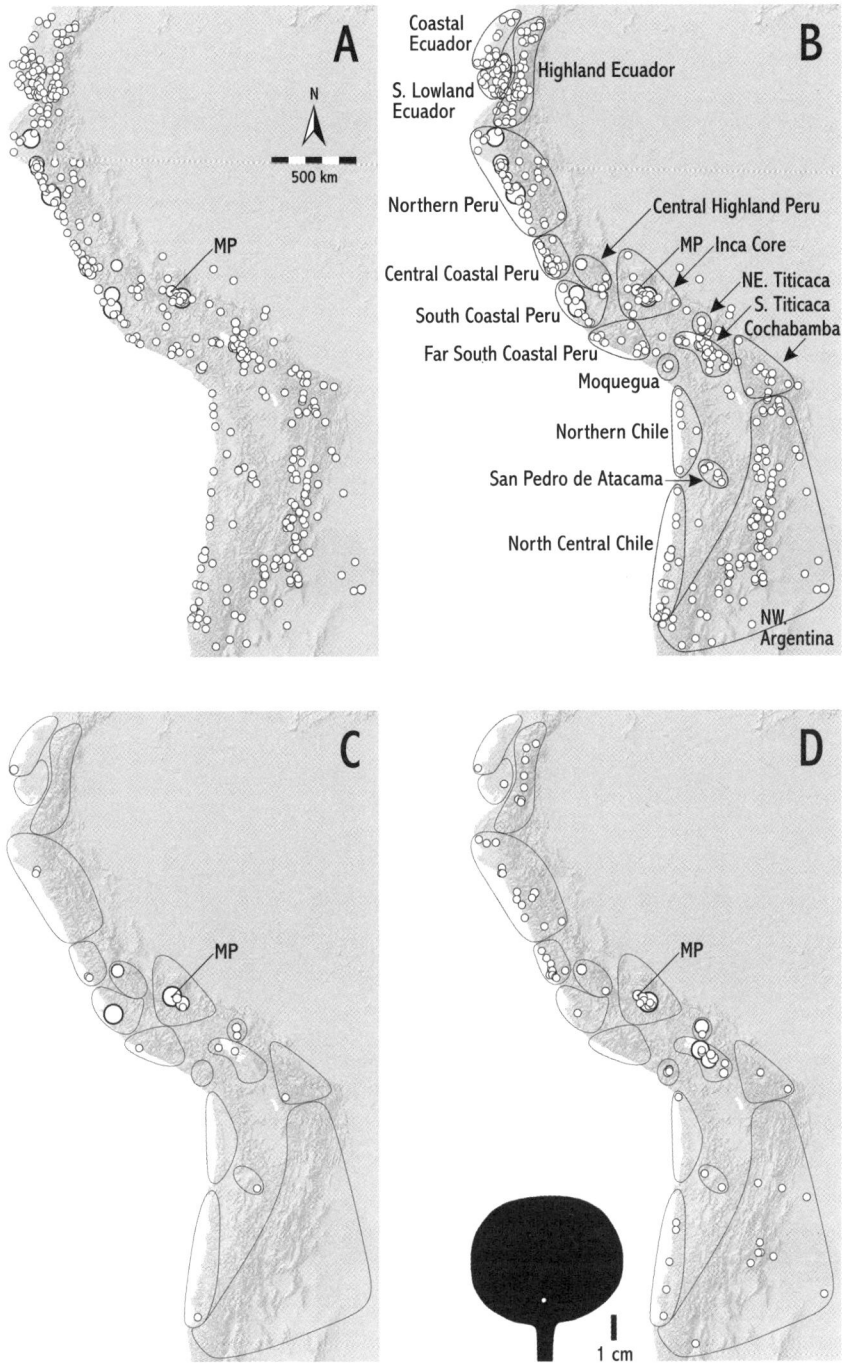

FIGURE 2.1. Distribution maps of the entire metals database, regional metalworking traditions, Late Horizon assemblages, and tupus. **A**, Geographic coverage of the entire dataset; n=10,077 (an additional 43 are outside of the mapped area). **B**, Regional metalworking traditions. **C**, Late Horizon assemblages; n=740. **D**, Tupu: all types; n=846.

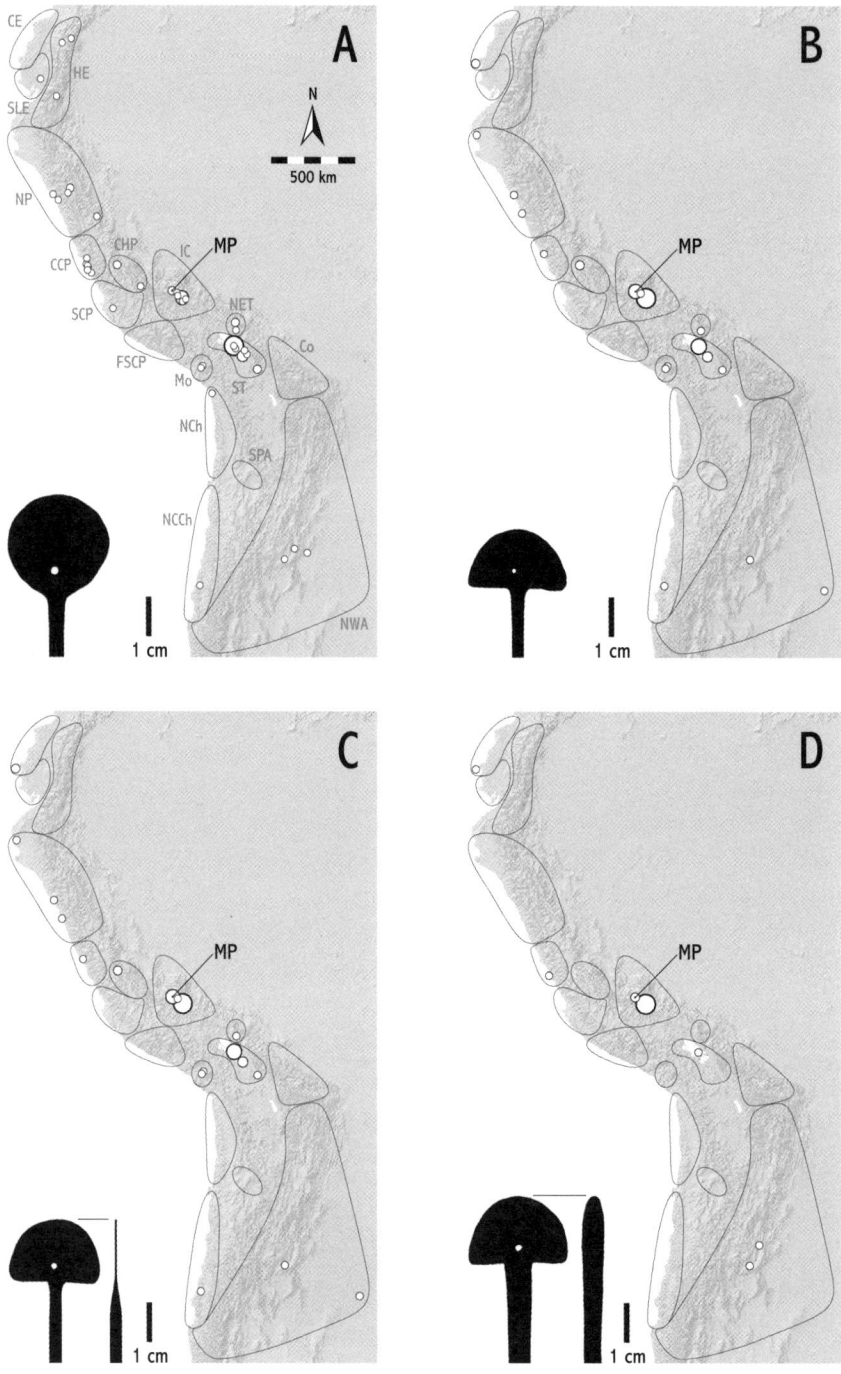

FIGURE 2.2. Distribution maps of tupus. **A**, Tupu: round-headed (type 1001); n=243. **B**, Tupu: half-round-headed, all types (types 1010–1012); n=141. **C**, Tupu: half-round-headed, plain thin head (type 1010); n=89. **D**, Tupu: half-round-headed, head as thick as shaft (type 1011); n=22.

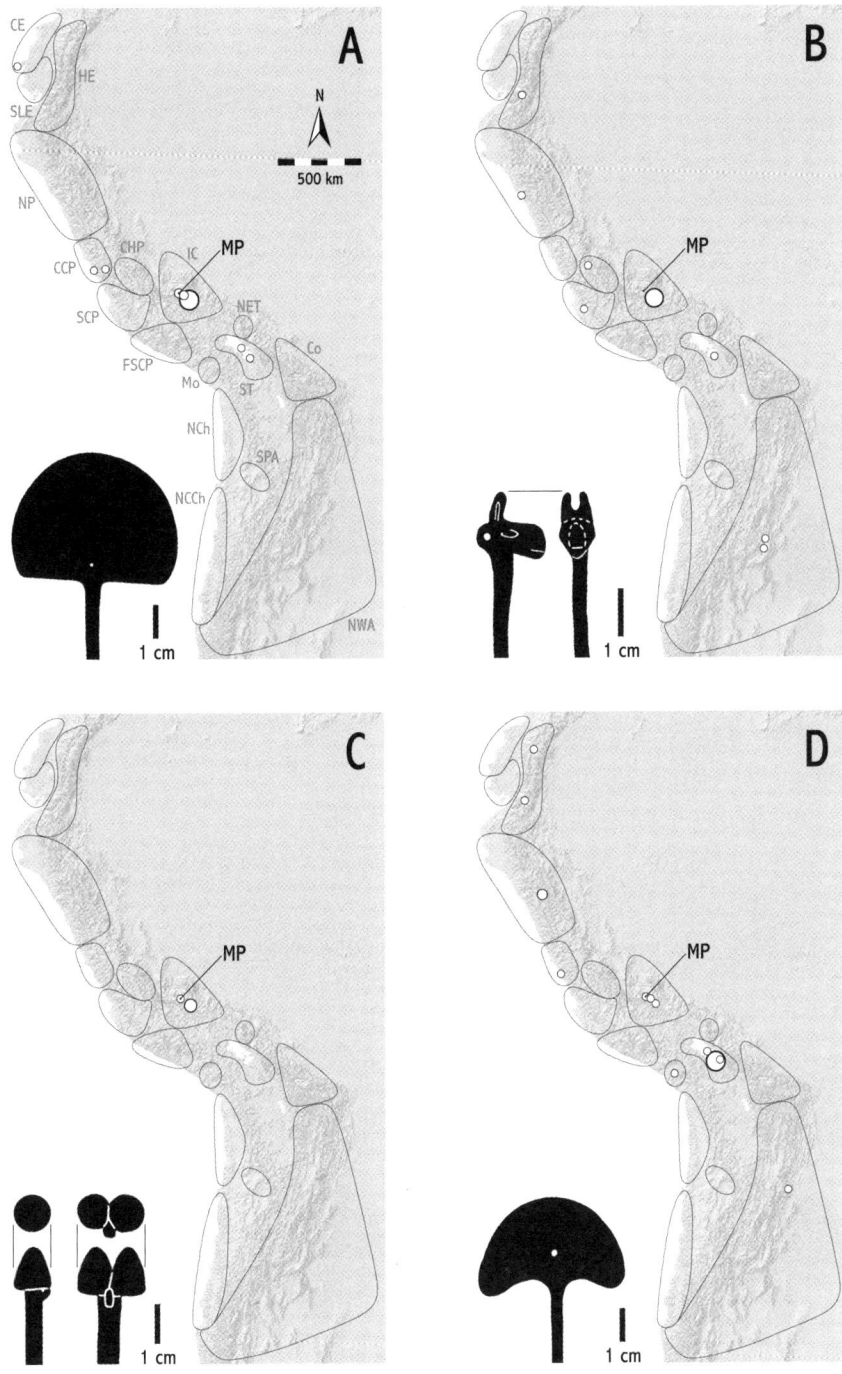

FIGURE 2.3. Distribution maps of tupus. **A**, Tupu: half-round-headed, greater than half circle (type 1012); n=30. **B**, Tupu: cast animal head (types 1055–1058); n=11. **C**, Tupu: single or double cone with loop (types 1061 and 1062); n=3. **D**, Tupu: drooping (type 1014); n=25.

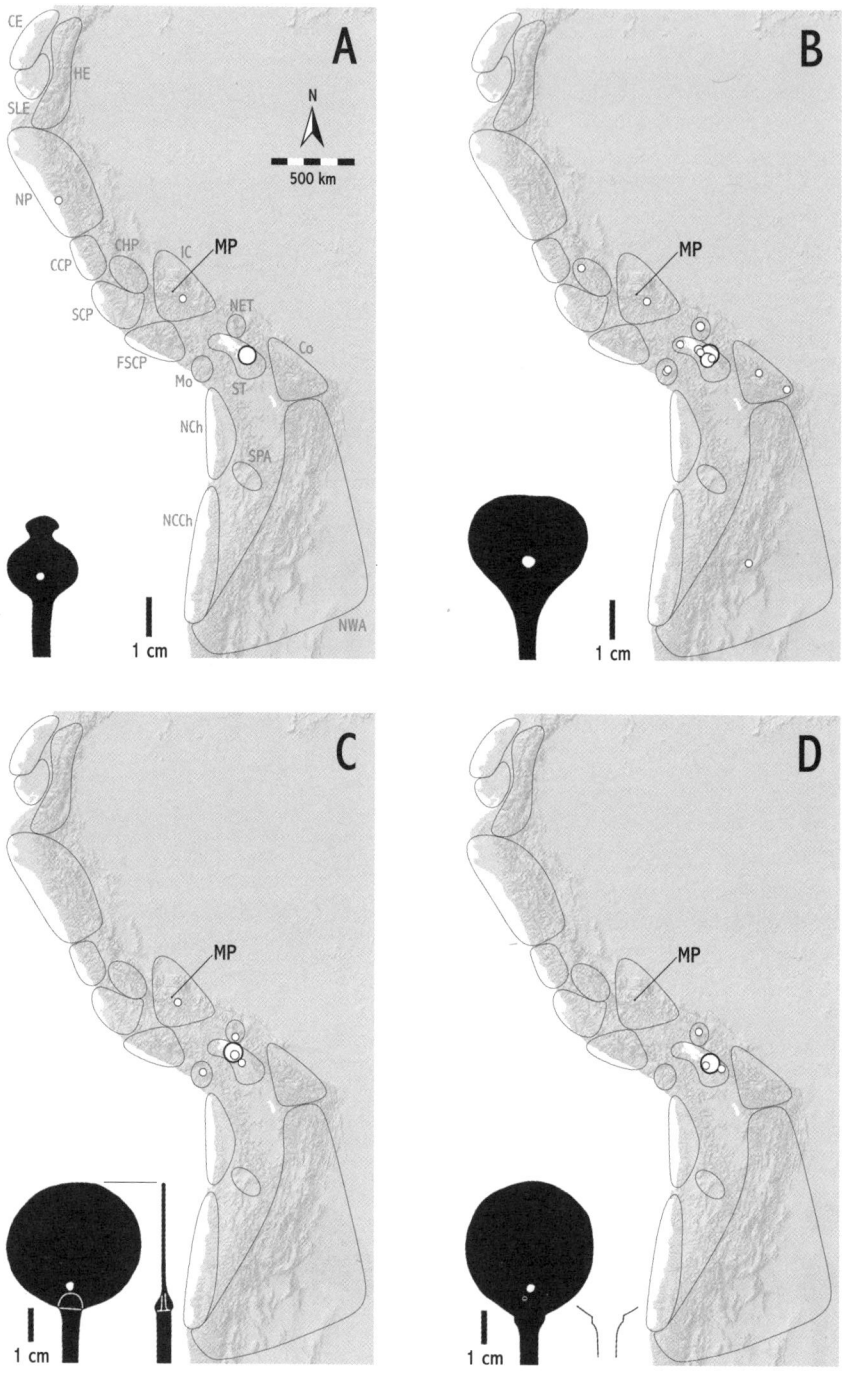

FIGURE 2.4. Distribution maps of tupus. **A**, Tupu: round with flaring bump (type 1023); n=6. **B**, Tupu: long taper (type 1006); n=52. **C**, Tupu: globular neck join, round or indeterminate head; n=21. **D**, Tupu: neck step, round plain or round with two spirals (types 1002 and 1025); n=13.

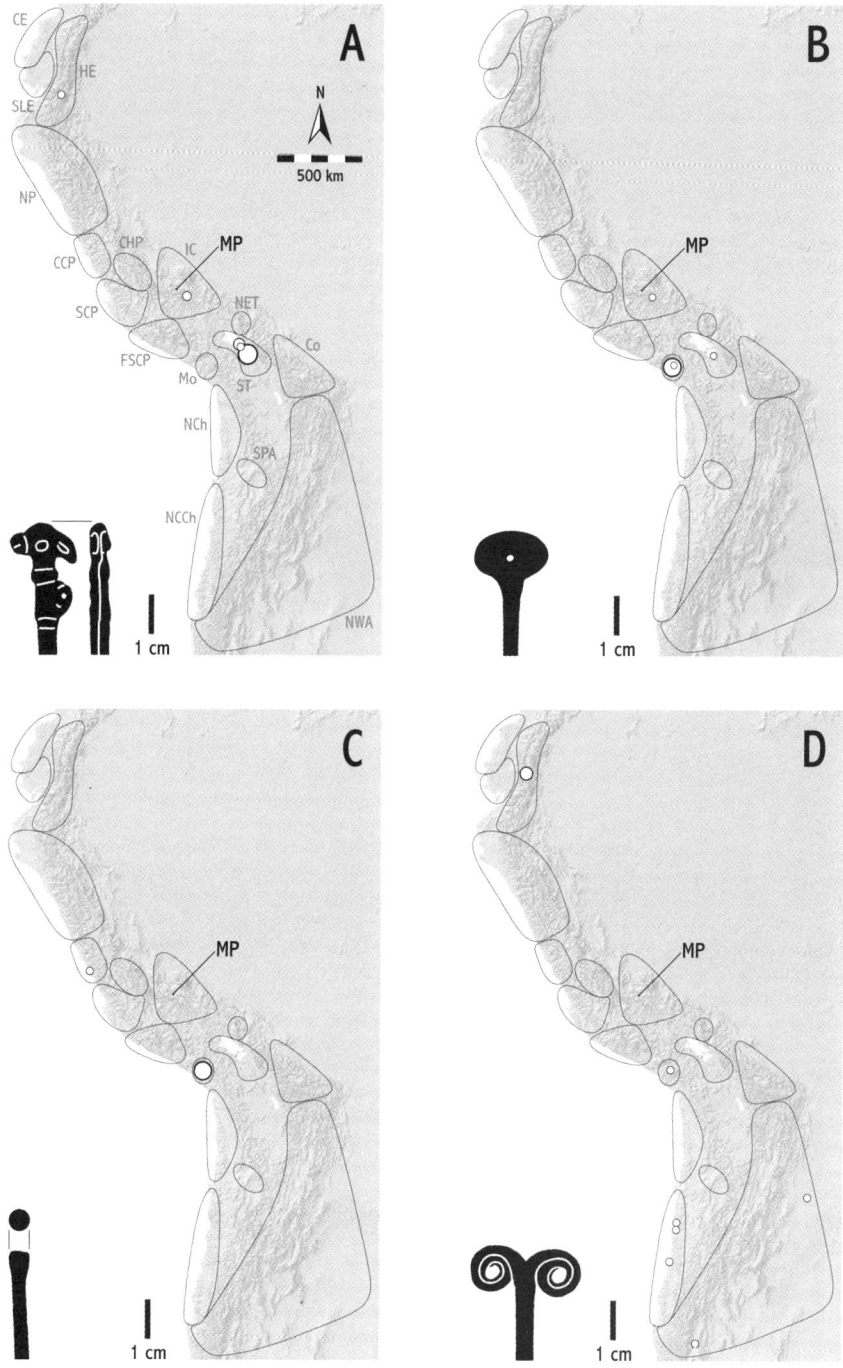

FIGURE 2.5. Distribution maps of tupus. **A**, Tupu: two-piece flat mold (types 1050 and 1051); n=22. **B**, Tupu: squat ovoid head, tapered neck (type 1003); n=9. **C**, Tupu: axial solid, plain, no cross-hole (type 1043); n=6. **D**, Tupu: two spirals (type 1027); n=8.

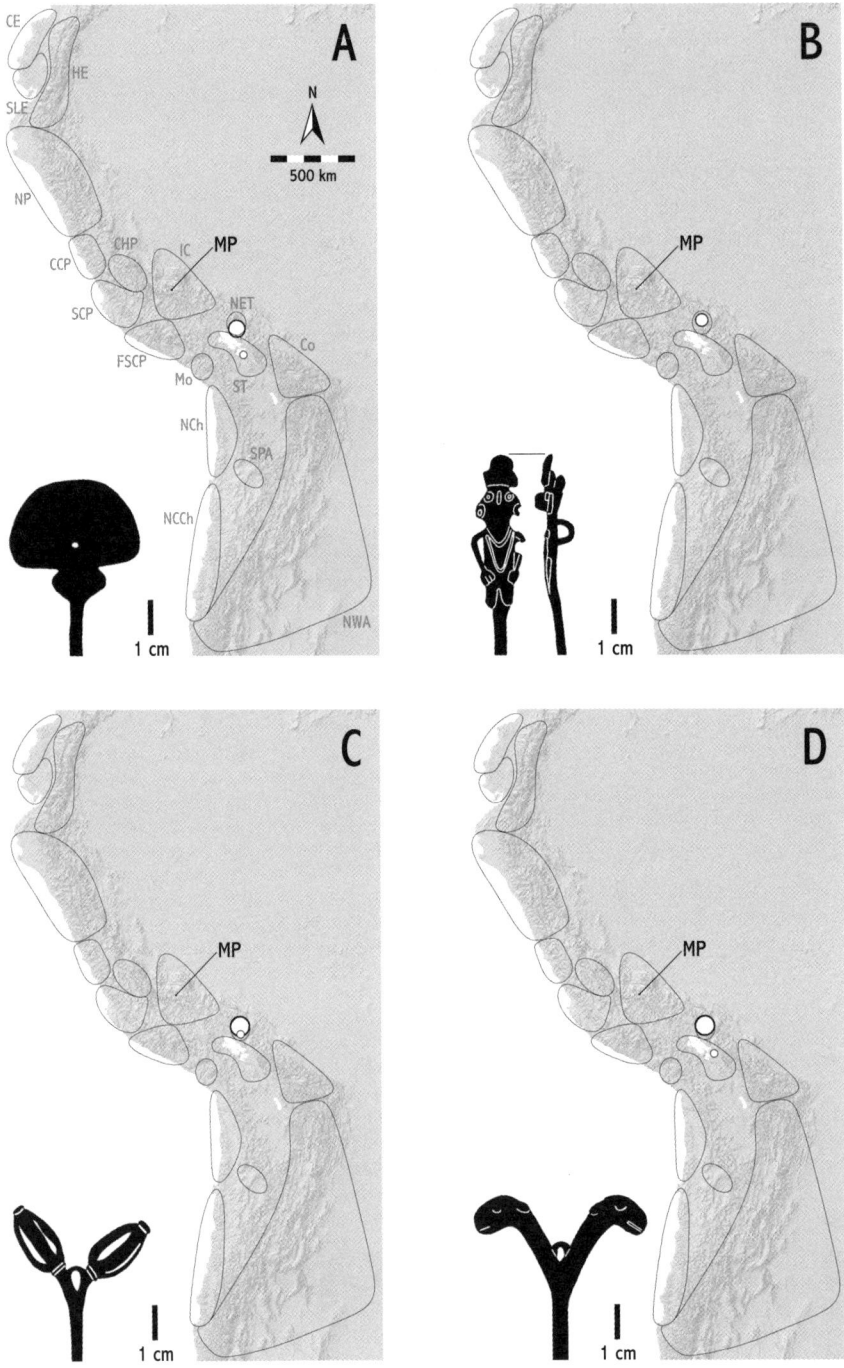

FIGURE 2.6. Distribution maps of tupus. **A**, Tupu: neck lobe (type 1020); n=4. **B**, Tupu: flat figural wire-relief (type 1090); n=3. **C**, Tupu: one, two, or three openwork "rattles" (type 1086); n=35. **D**, Tupu: bifurcated solid cast forms (type 1087); n=9.

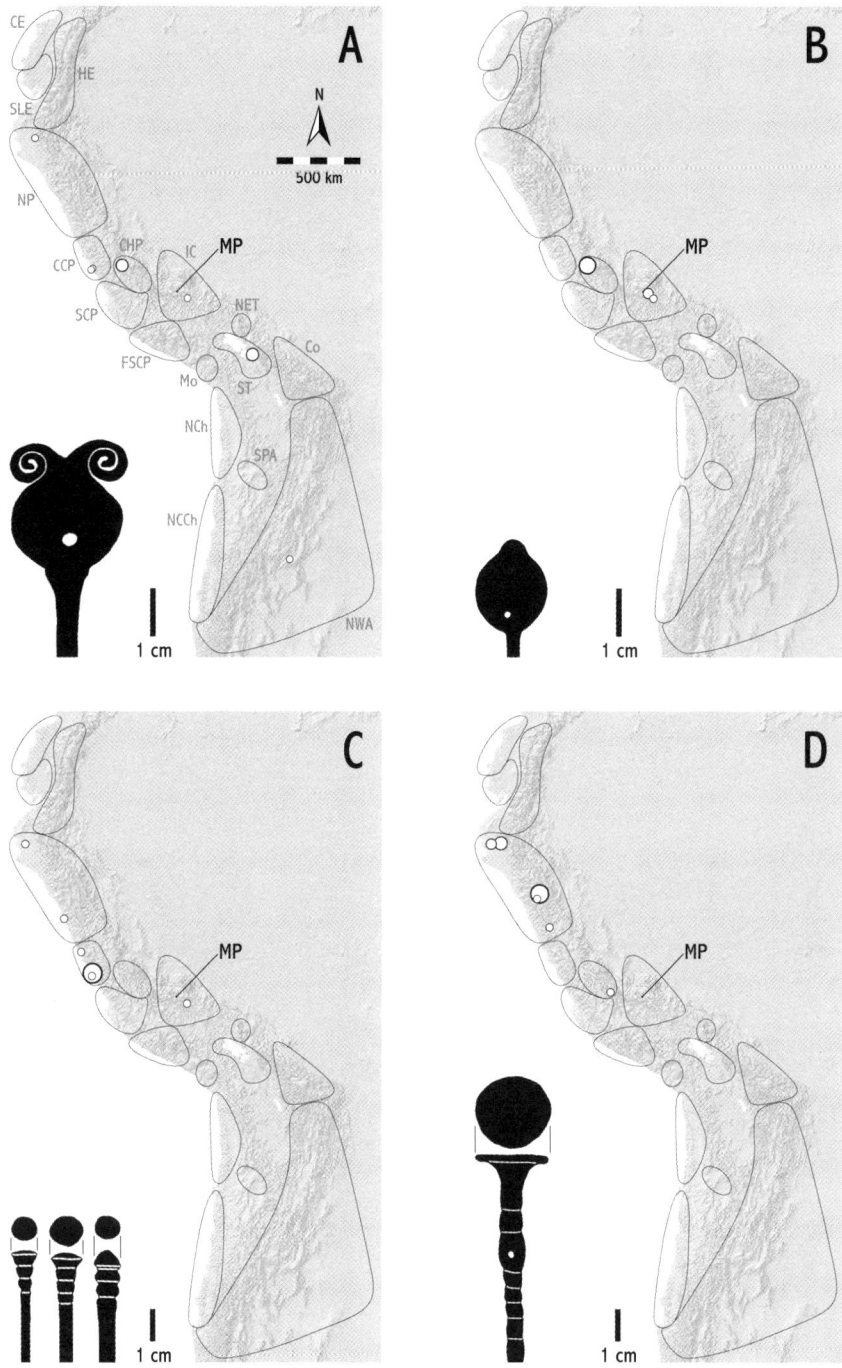

FIGURE 2.7. Distribution maps of tupus. **A**, Tupu: round head with two spirals (types 1024 and 1025); n=9. **B**, Tupu: round head with small bump (type 1022); n=6. **C**, Tupu: axial solid, raised rings, no cross-hole (type 1042); n=14. **D**, Tupu: axial solid, slight to pronounced nail head, with cross-hole (types 1040, 1041, and 1044); n=17.

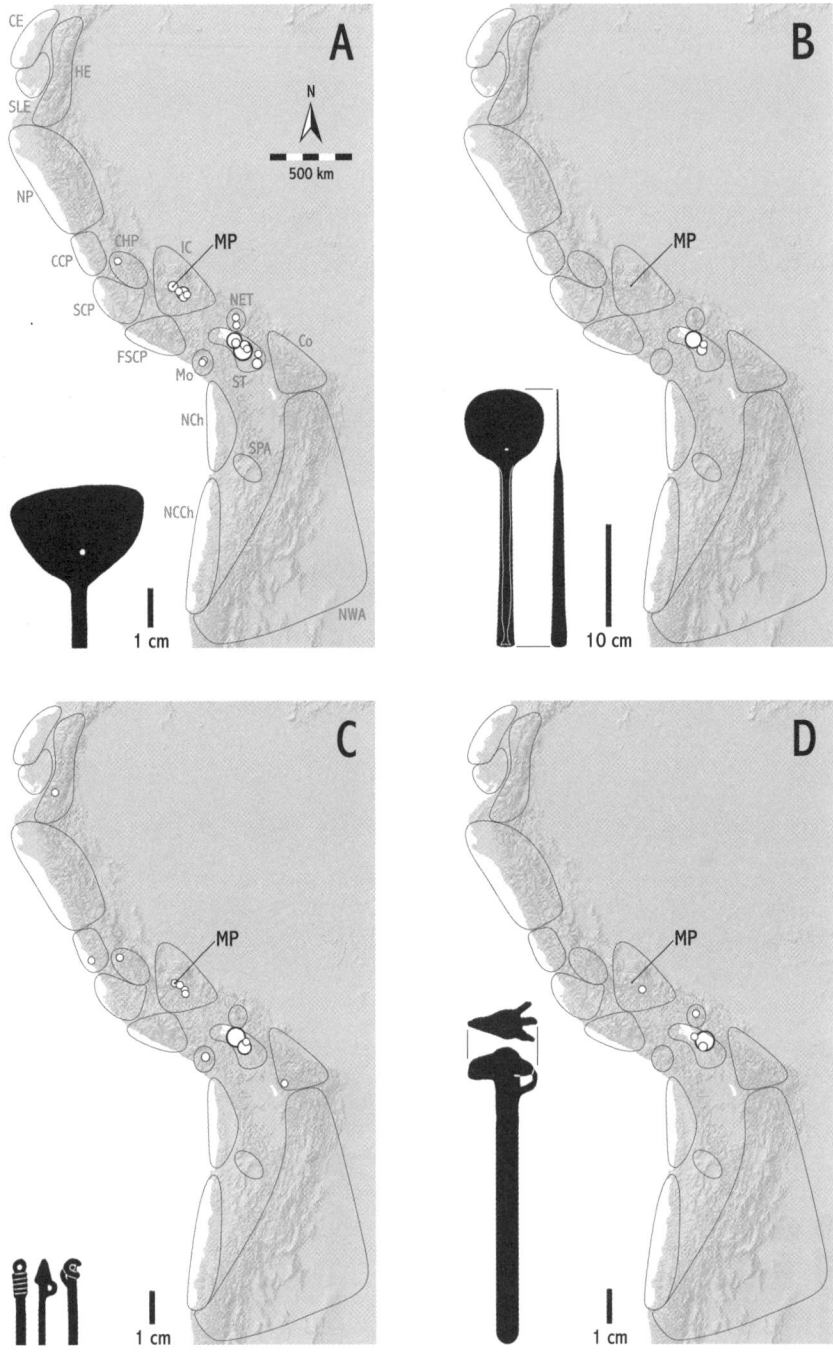

FIGURE 2.8. Distribution maps of worn tupus, oversize tupu-like objects, and possible lime dippers. **A**, Tupu: any type with evidence of sharpening, edge wear, upset (mushrooming), or shape changes on the top edge suggesting cutting use; n=86. **B**, Miscellaneous: oversize round-headed tupu-like object with broad or thick handle (type 3162); n=6. **C**, Tiny tupu or lime dipper: various cast heads (types 2410–2439); n=34. **D**, Fat-shafted, blunt instrument, possibly a lime dipper, with various tupu-like heads (types 2501–2529); n=21.

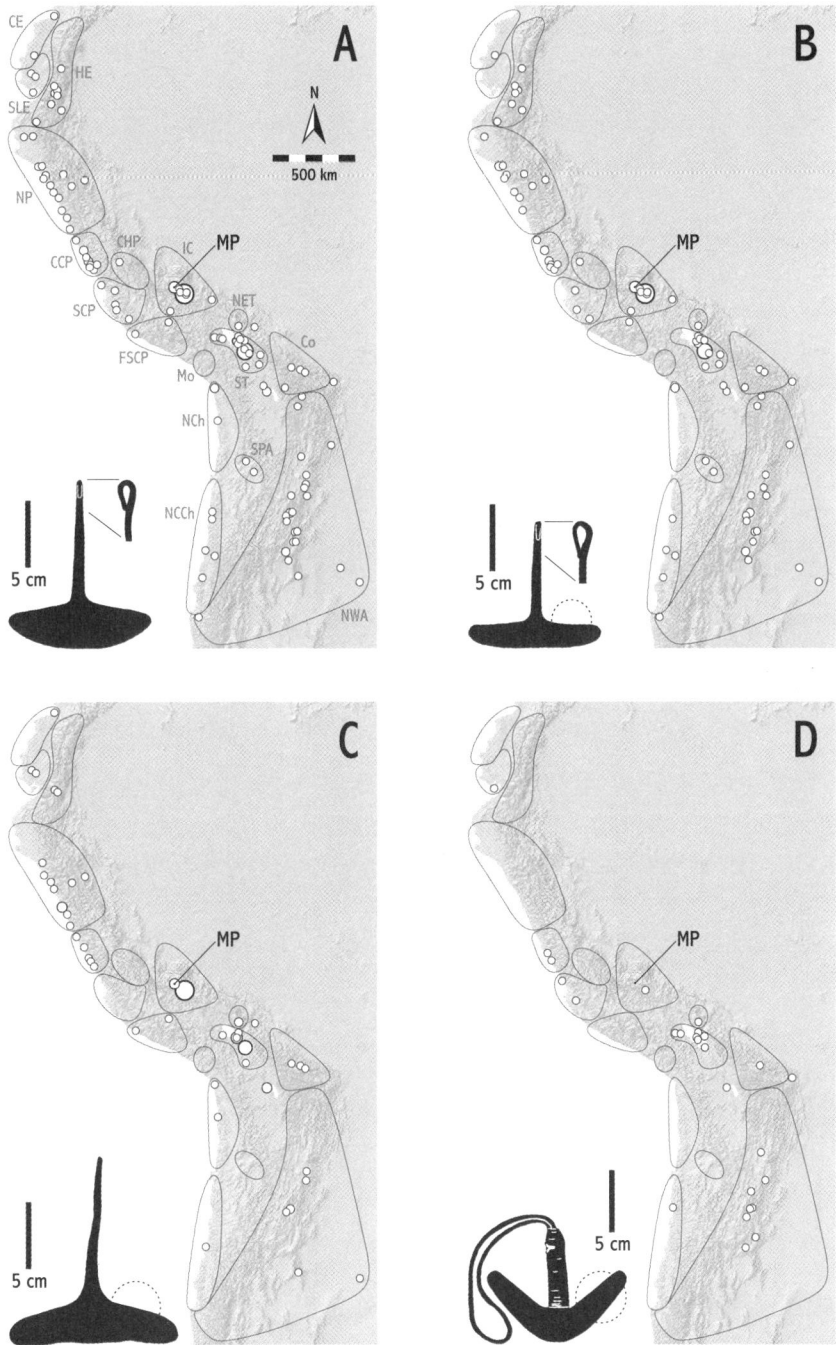

FIGURE 2.9. Distribution maps of T-shaped tumis. **A**, T-shaped tumi: all types (types 2840–2849); n=421. **B**, T-shaped tumi: straight back edge (type 2840); n=272. **C**, T-shaped tumi: flaring back edge (type 2841); n=87. **D**, T-shaped tumi: backswept blade, most less extreme than the illustrated example (type 2846); n=41.

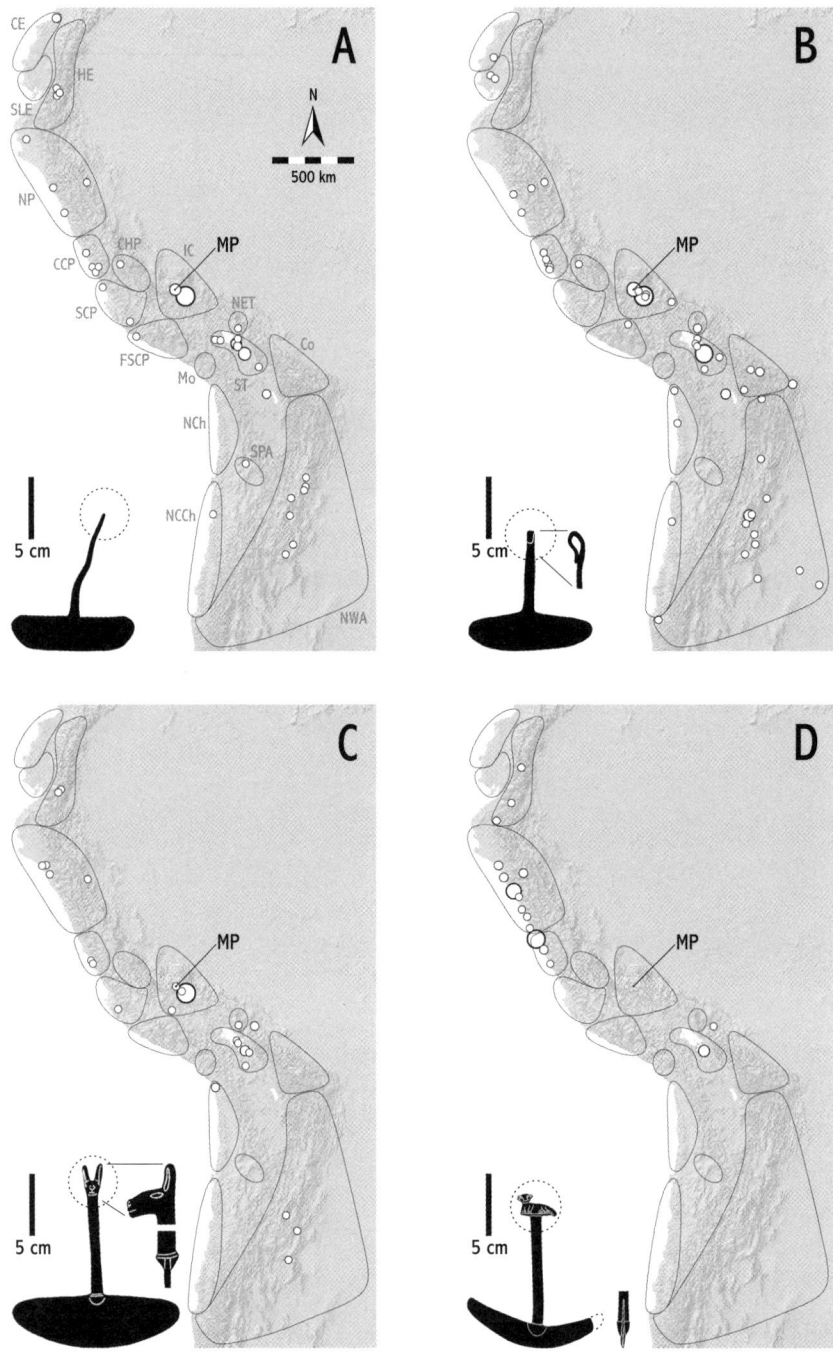

FIGURE 2.10. Distribution maps of T-shaped tumis. **A**, T-shaped tumi: any type with plain head (usually a narrow chisel point, only noted where clearly finished, not broken); n=78. **B**, T-shaped tumi: any type with loop head; n=137. **C**, T-shaped tumi: any type with cast animal head, usually a camelid; n=49. **D**, T-shaped tumi: any type with cast full body figure or scene; n=29.

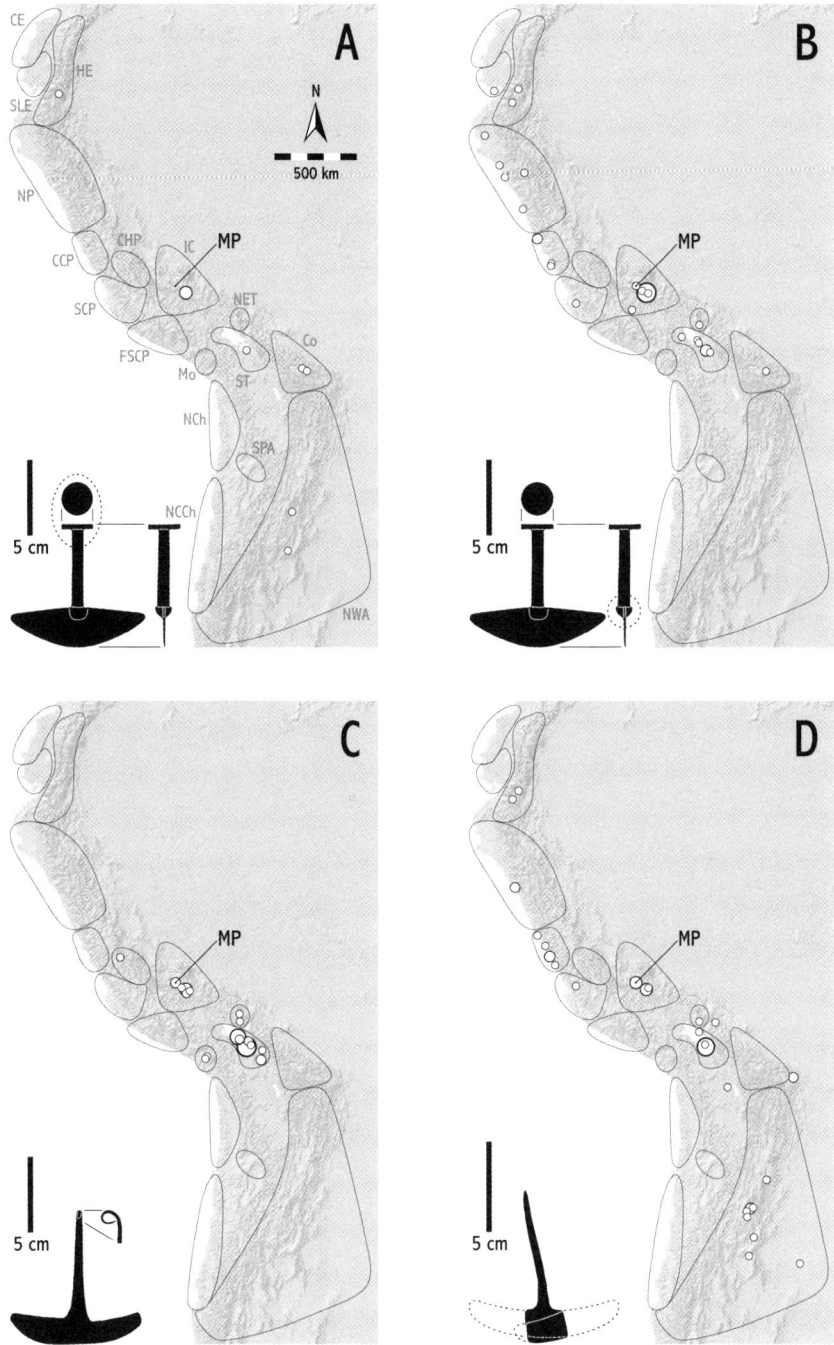

Figure 2.11. Distribution maps of T-shaped tumis. **A**, T-shaped tumi: any type with disc head; n=8. **B**, T-shaped tumi: any type with globular join treatment; n=37. **C**, T-shaped tumis with visible evidence of use, including sharpening, edge wear, upset (mushrooming from pounding), or flattened or concave blade profile in the center; n=48. **D**, T-shaped tumis with evidence of intentional destruction, usually both blade tips bent sharply inward, broken off, or both; n=56.

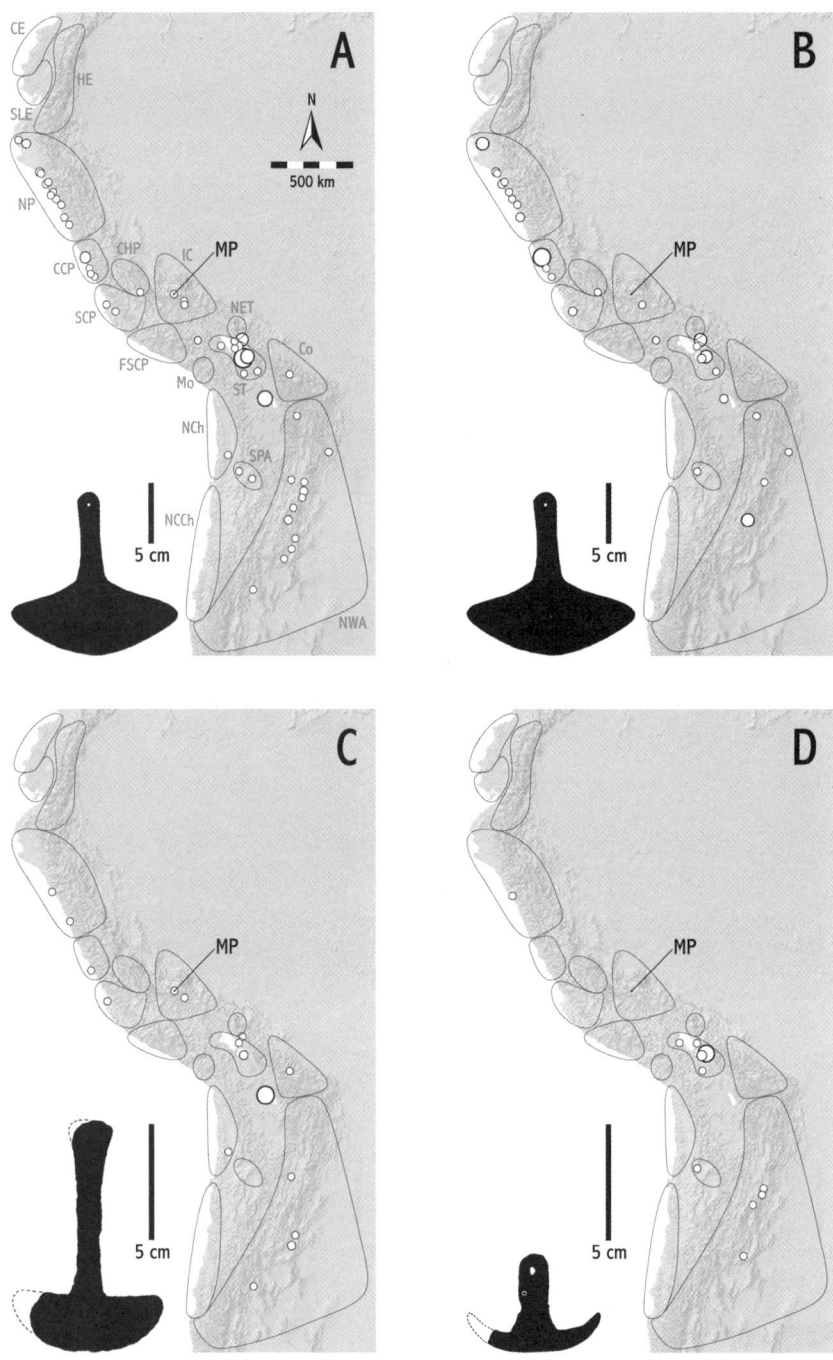

FIGURE 2.12. Distribution maps of flat tumis. **A**, Flat tumi, all types (types 5100–5119); n=94. **B**, Flat tumi: flaring back and crescent edge (types 5100 and 5105); n=44. **C**, Flat tumi: "T" variant, shaped like a T-shaped tumi (type 5115); n=21. **D**, Flat tumi: small backswept blade (type 5116); n=14.

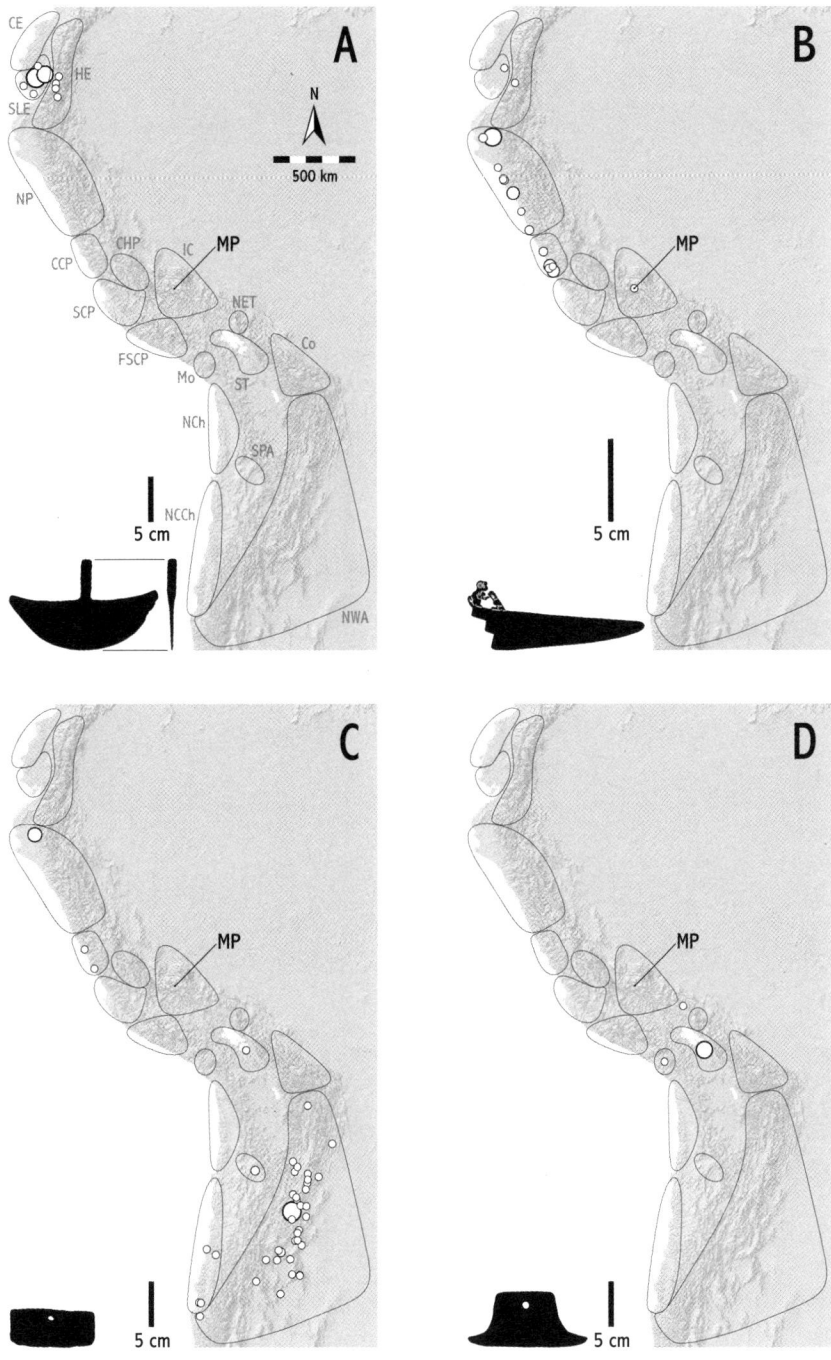

FIGURE 2.13. Distribution of Guayas tumis, handleless transverse knives, and rectangular knives with hole(s) near the back. **A**, Guayas tumi: Mayer 1992 (type 5120); n=39. **B**, Knife: handleless transverse (type 2830); n=31. **C**, Knife: crescent to rectangular to trapezoidal with hole(s) near the back edge (type 2835); n=114. **D**, Knife: rectangular with flaring corners with hole(s) near the back edge (type 2837); n=8.

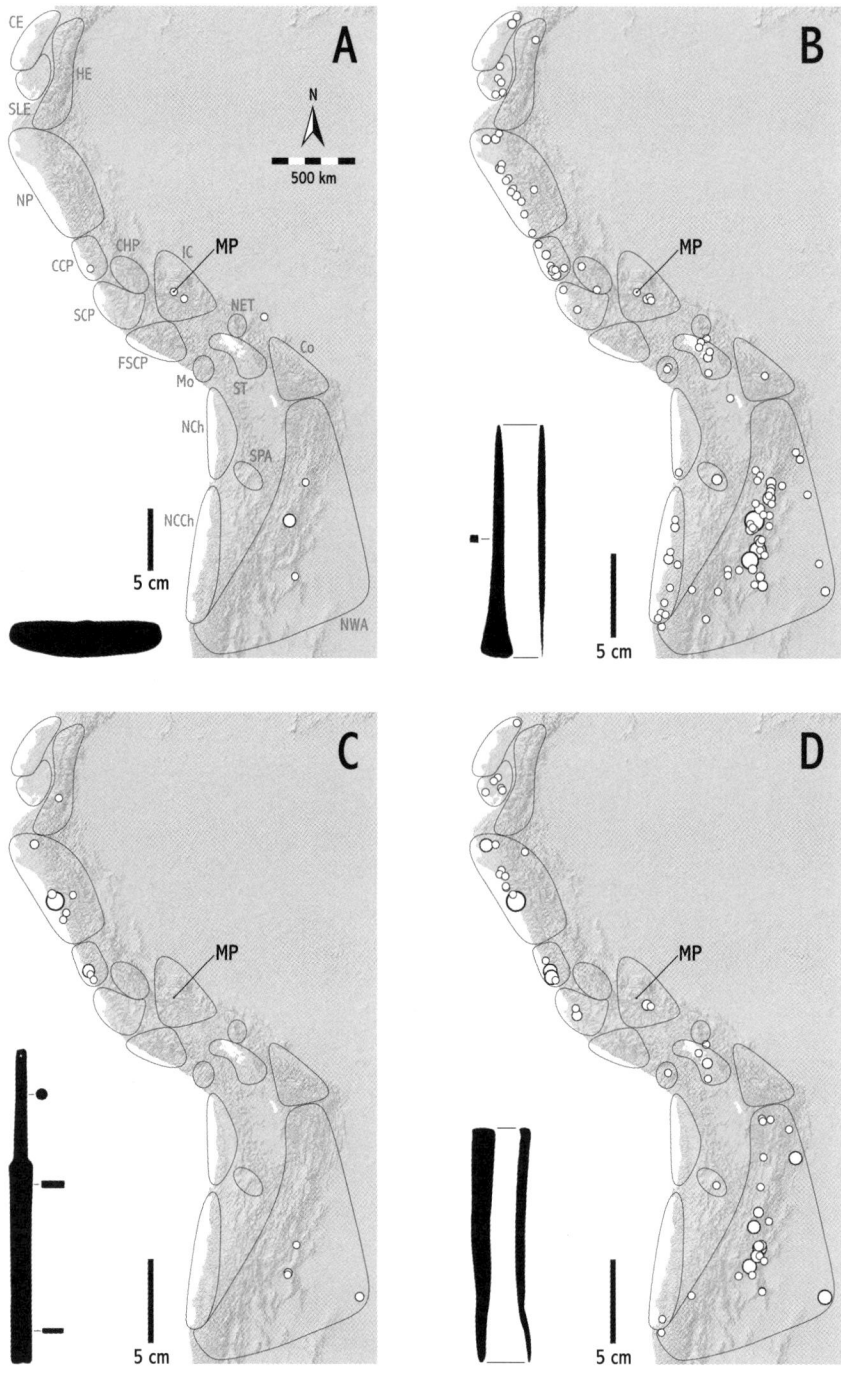

FIGURE 2.14. Distribution maps of long oval knives, chisels, and other tools. **A**, Knife: long oval possible knife blade (type 2839); n=8. **B**, Chisel: fine (type 2700); n=521. **C**, Chisel, "formón" with flat blade and abruptly narrowed hafting tang (type 2830); n=31. **D**, Other tool: cutting tool, punch, spatula, etc. (type 2715); n=115.

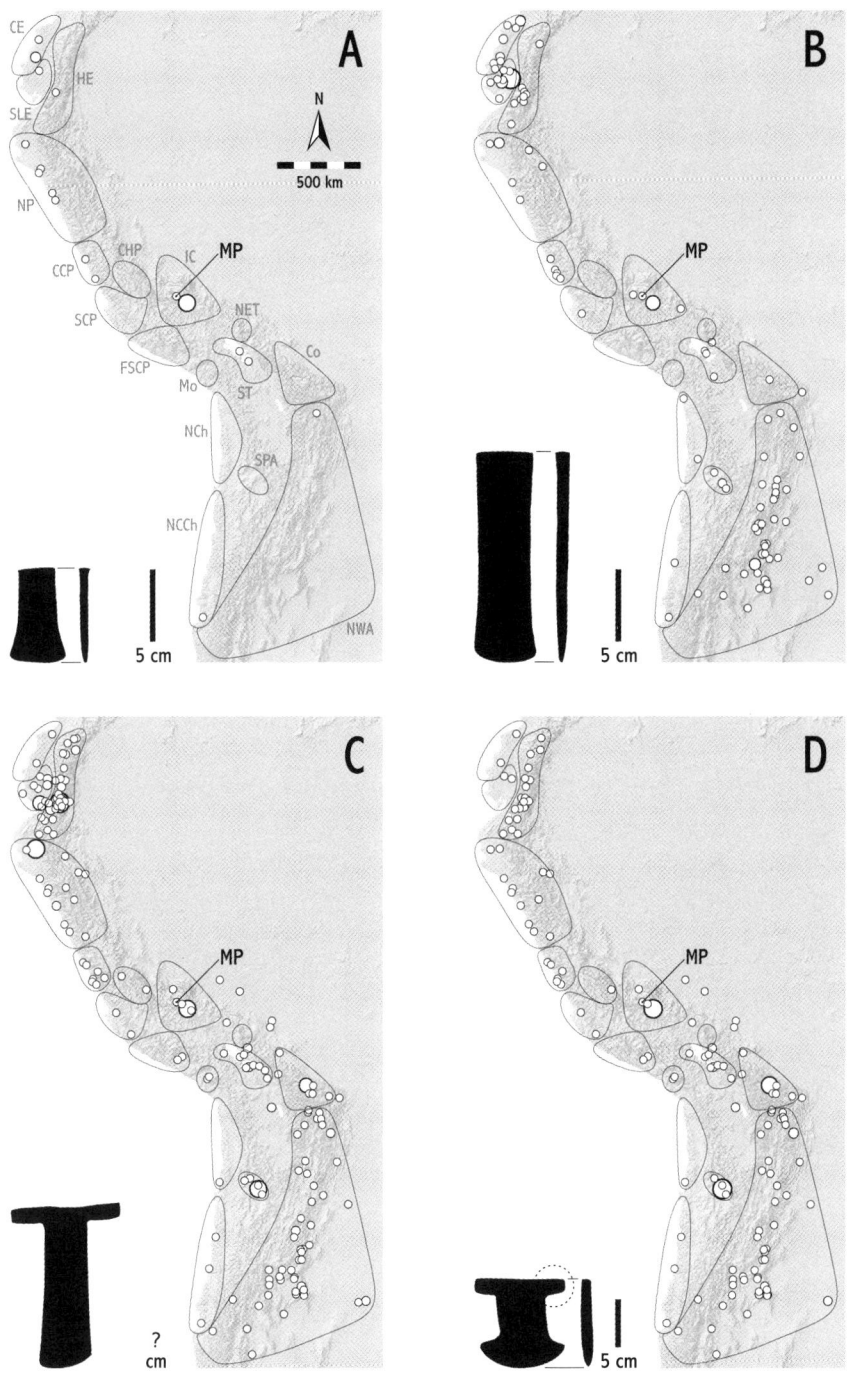

FIGURE 2.15. Distribution maps of heavy chisels, celts, and axes. **A**, Chisel: heavy (type 2710); n=20. **B**, Celt: straight or slightly flared sides, with or without flaring end, probably agricultural tool tip (types 4010 and 4020); n=279. **C**, Axe: all types (types 4140–4996); n=685. **D**, Axe: any type with tangs; n=375.

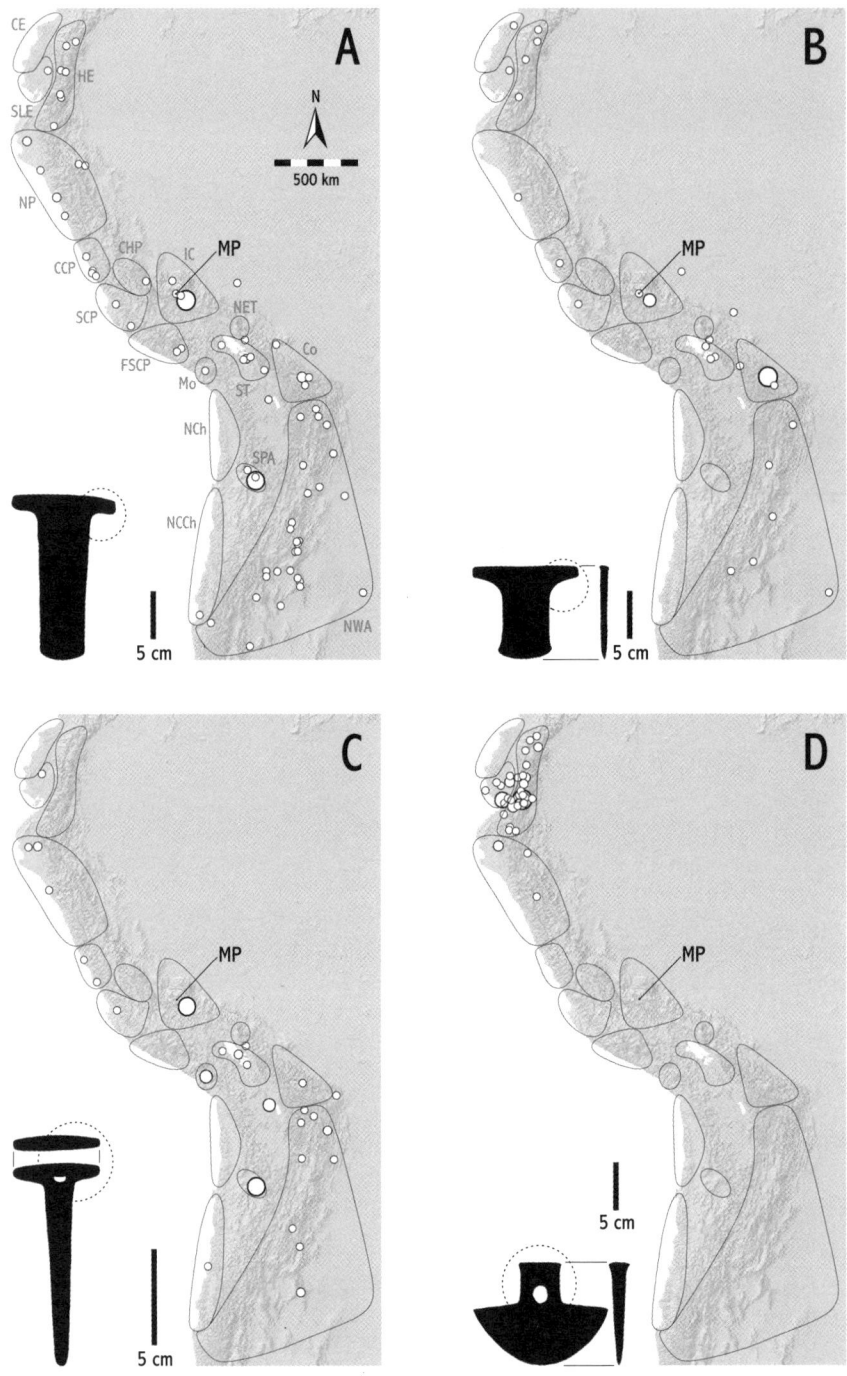

FIGURE 2.16. Distribution maps of axe hafting features. **A**, Axe: any type with rectangular tangs; n=152. **B**, Axe: any type with curved tangs; n=47. **C**, Axe: any type with tangs and one small hole; n=41. **D**, Axe: any type with no tangs and one large hole; n=23.

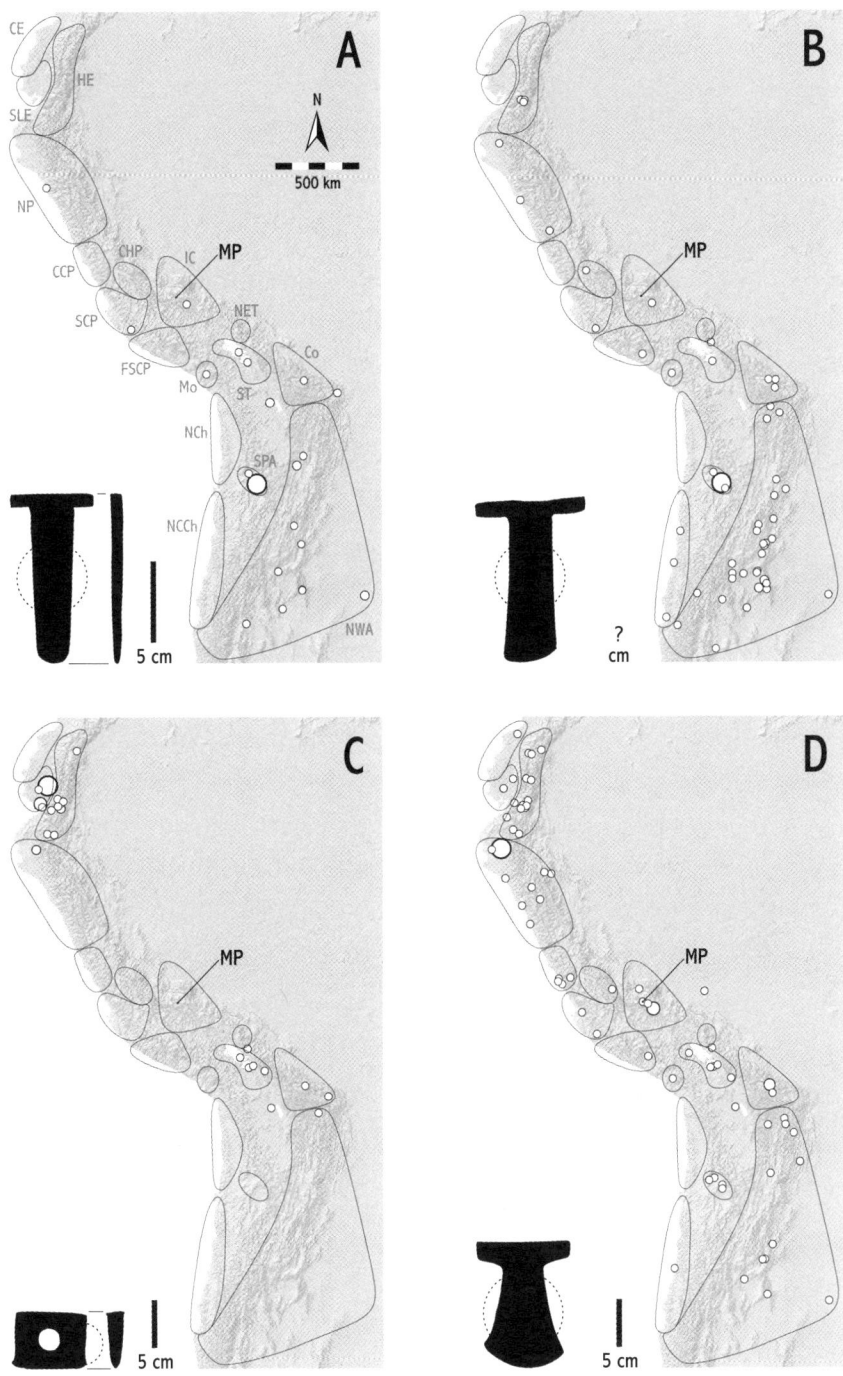

FIGURE 2.17. Distribution maps of axe blade shapes. **A**, Axe: any type with long narrowing blade; n=40. **B**, Axe: any type with long rectangular blade; n=118. **C**, Axe: any type with short rectangular blade (northern cluster are thick with one large mounting hole; southern cluster are thinner with tangs); n=44. **D**, Axe: any type with trapezoidal "hatchet" blade; n=165.

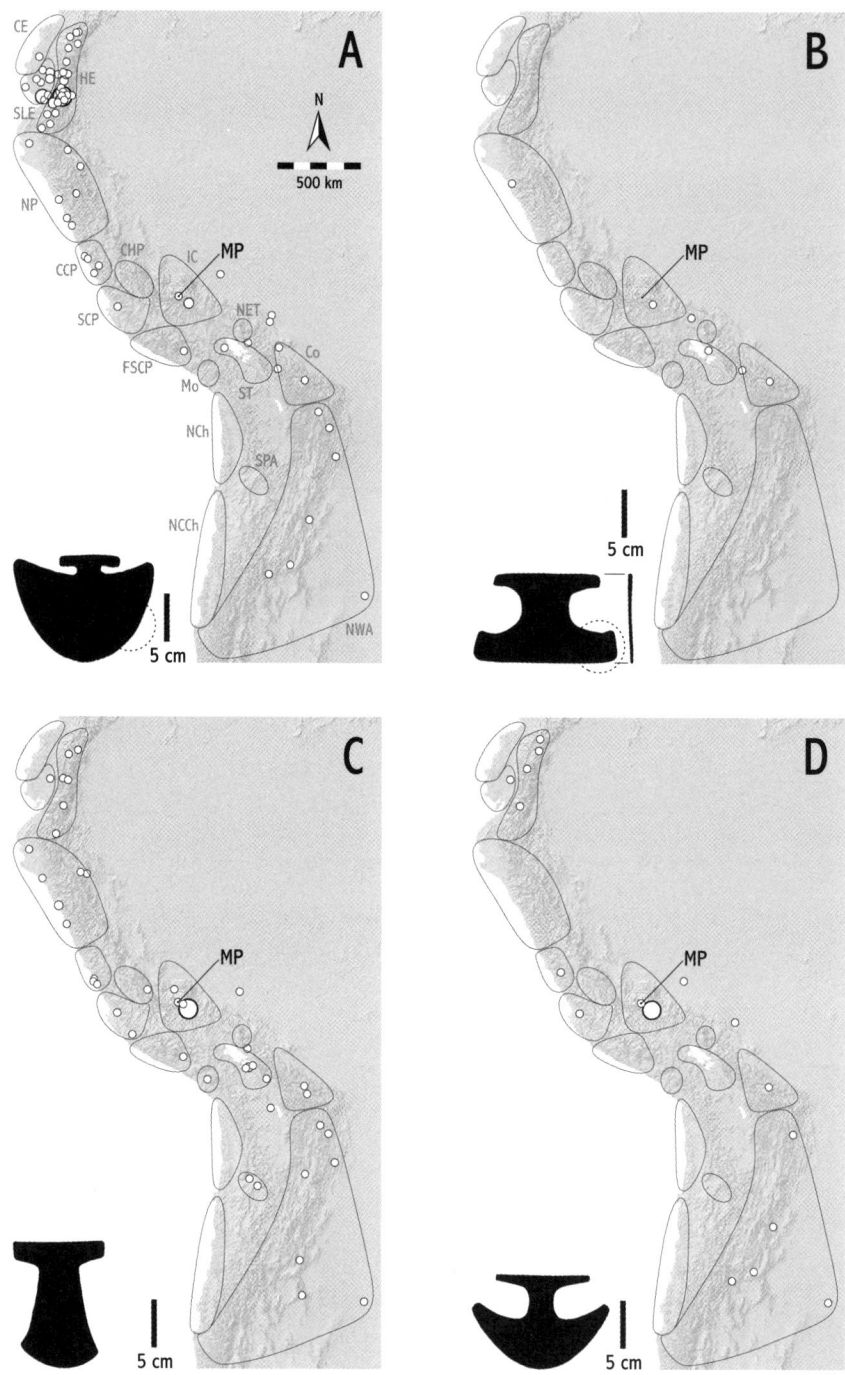

FIGURE 2.18. Distribution maps of axe blade shapes, "classic" axes, and "ancla" axes. **A**, Axe: any type with wide crescent blade; n=261. **B**, Axe: any type with transverse rectangular blade; n=6. **C**, Axe: "classic" form with rectangular tangs and trapezoidal blade (type 4250); n=69. **D**, Axe: "ancla" form with curved tangs and wide crescent blade (Mayer 1986, 1992, 1994, 1998) (type 4470); n=23.

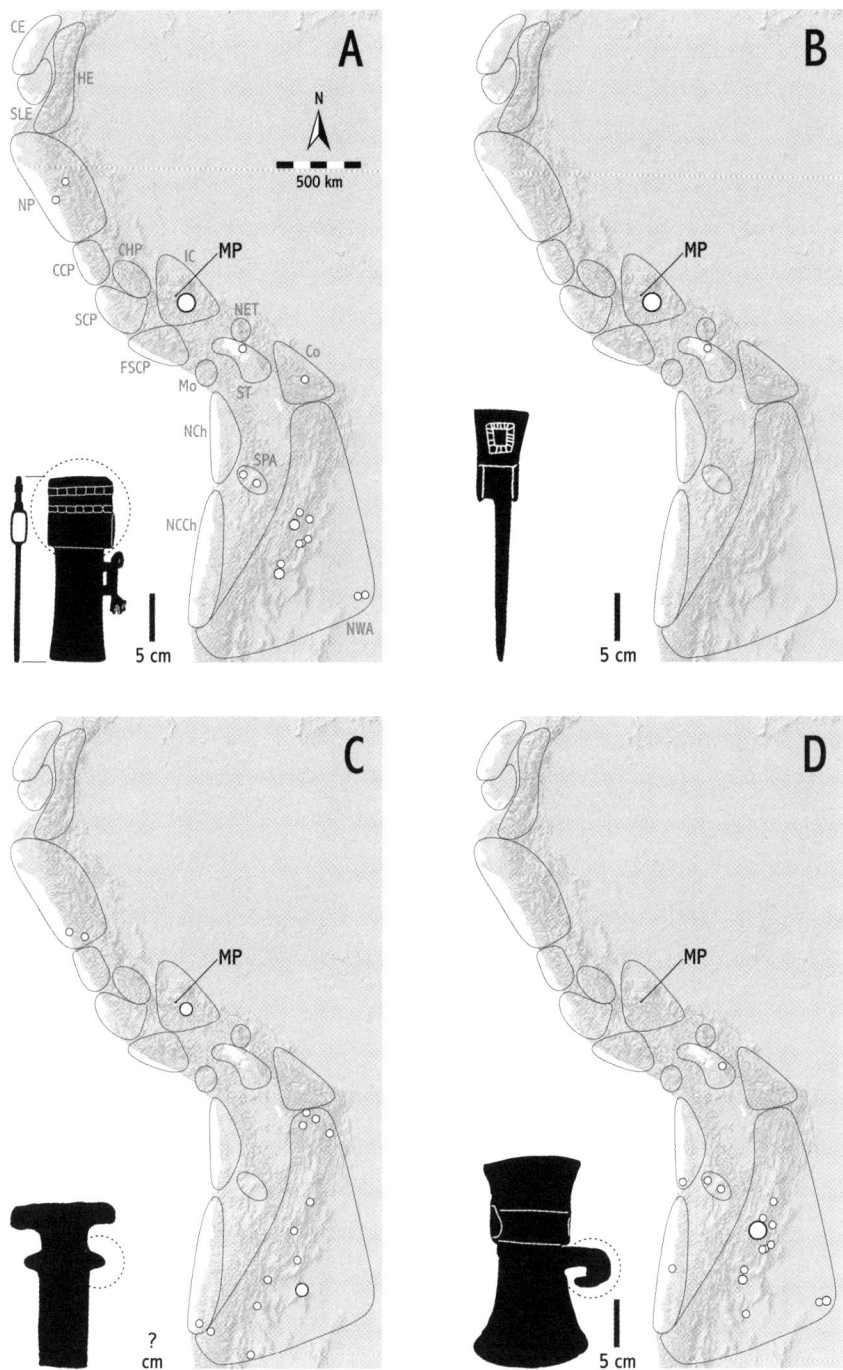

FIGURE 2.19. Distribution maps of socketed axes with tail flap, "yauri" forms, axes with side bars, and axes with hooks. **A**, Axe: any type with socket and tail flap; n=26. **B**, Axe: "yauri" form, with socket, tail flap, and rod-like "blade" (type 4690); n=7. **C**, Axe: any type with side bars; n=18. **D**, Axe: any type with hook; n=22.

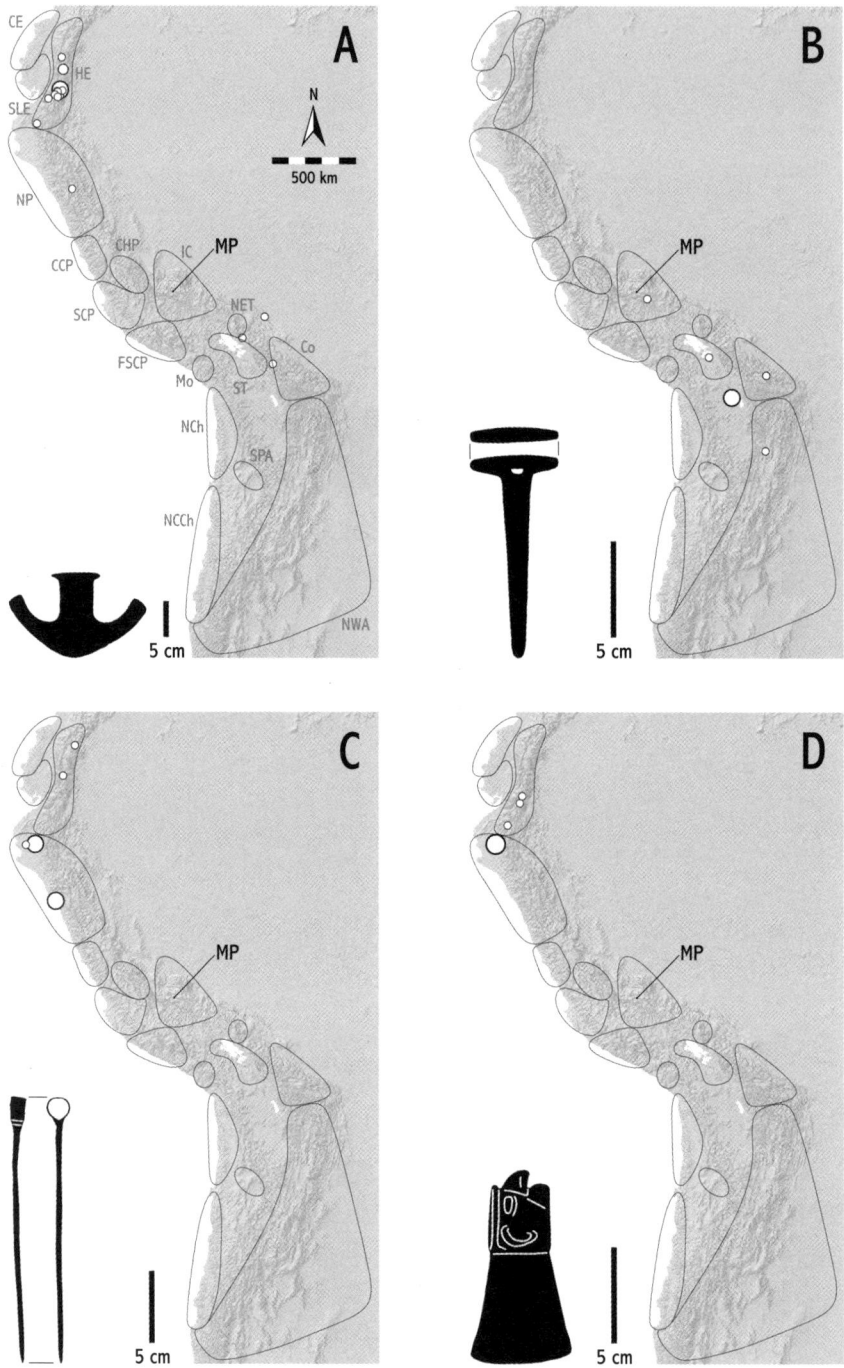

FIGURE 2.20. Distribution maps of regional axe types. **A**, Axe: variant tangs, no hole, wide crescent blade, mostly a subset of Mayer's "acha con hoja-hoz" (type 4570); n=19. **B**, Axe: any tangs, one hole, long narrowing blade (types 4490 and 4591); n=7. **C**, Axe: any type with socket but no tail or face on back of socket; n=9. **D**, Axe: socketed, no tail, trapezoidal blade, face on back of socket (type 4952); n=26.

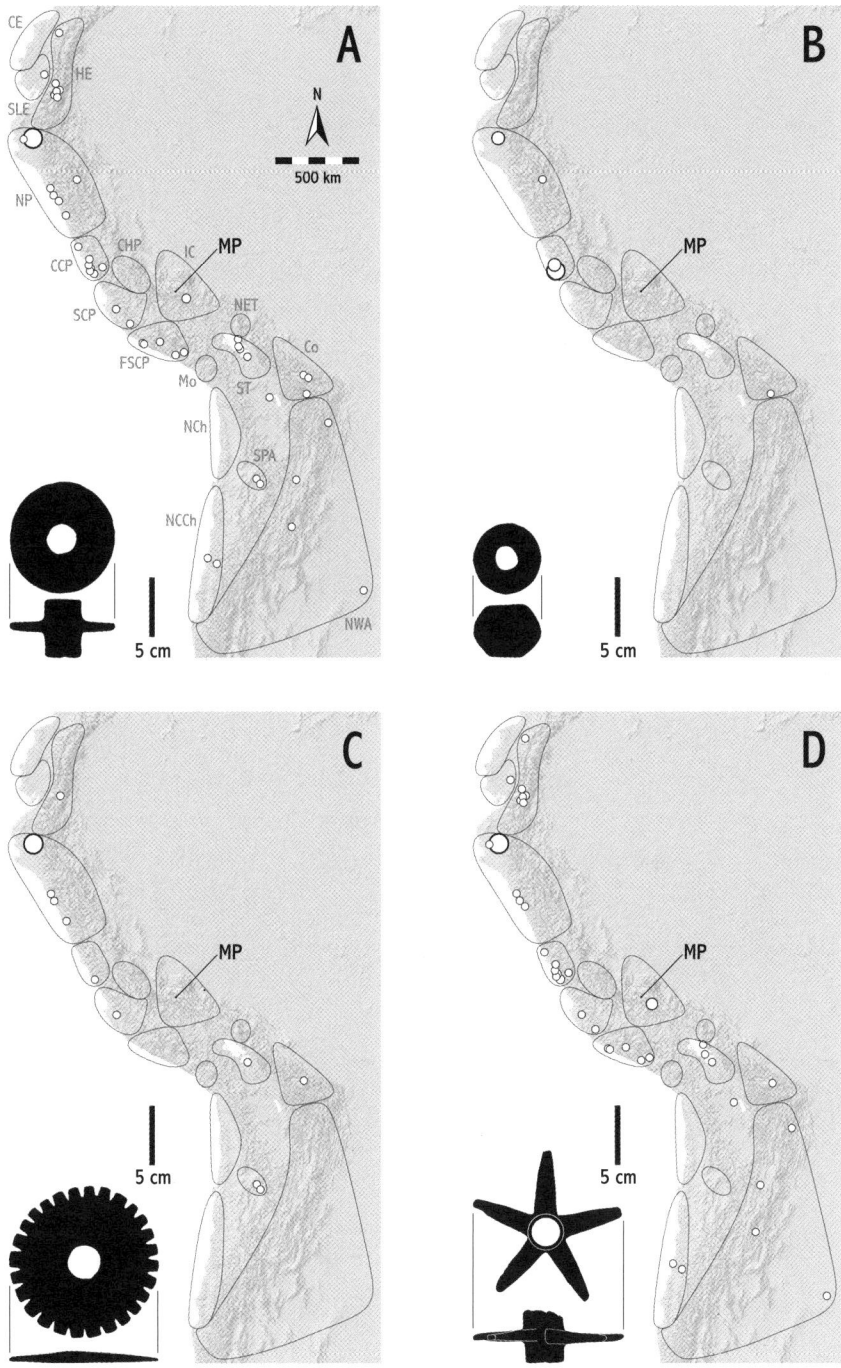

FIGURE 2.21. Distribution maps of mace heads. **A**, Weapon: all mace heads (types 2760–2775); n=370. **B**, Weapon: spherical to cylindrical mace head (type 2770); n=12. **C**, Weapon: disc-shaped mace head (type 2775); n=181. **D**, Weapon: star-shaped mace head, all types except axe-maces (types 2760–2768); n=168.

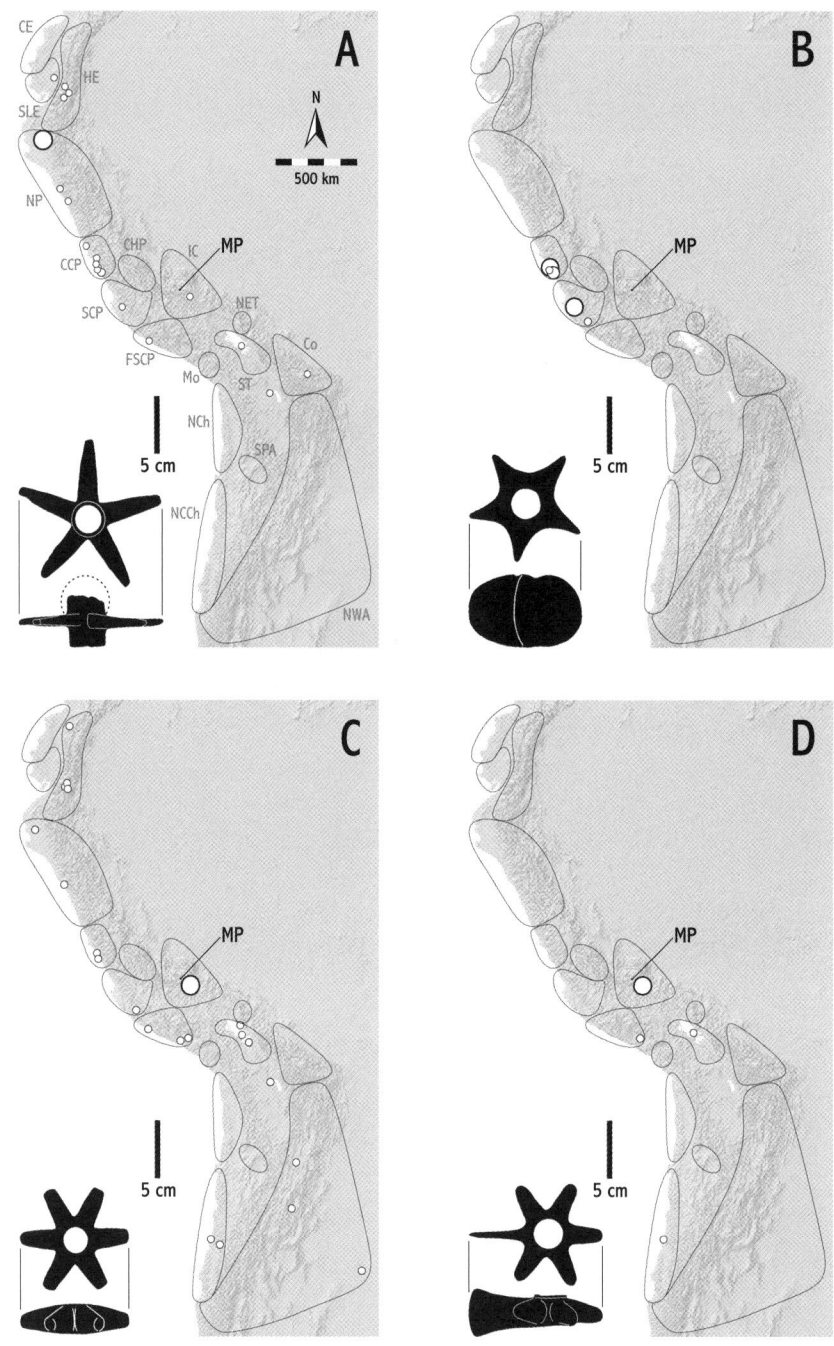

FIGURE 2.22. Distribution maps of star-shaped mace heads. **A**, Weapon: star-shaped mace head with central cylinder (types 2765–2768); n=92. **B**, Weapon: star-shaped mace head with vertical fin points (types 2762 and 2767); n=13. **C**, Weapon: "classic" star-shaped mace head, no central cylinder, medium, rounded points (type 2760); n=44. **D**, Weapon: "axe-mace" (type 2769); n=9.

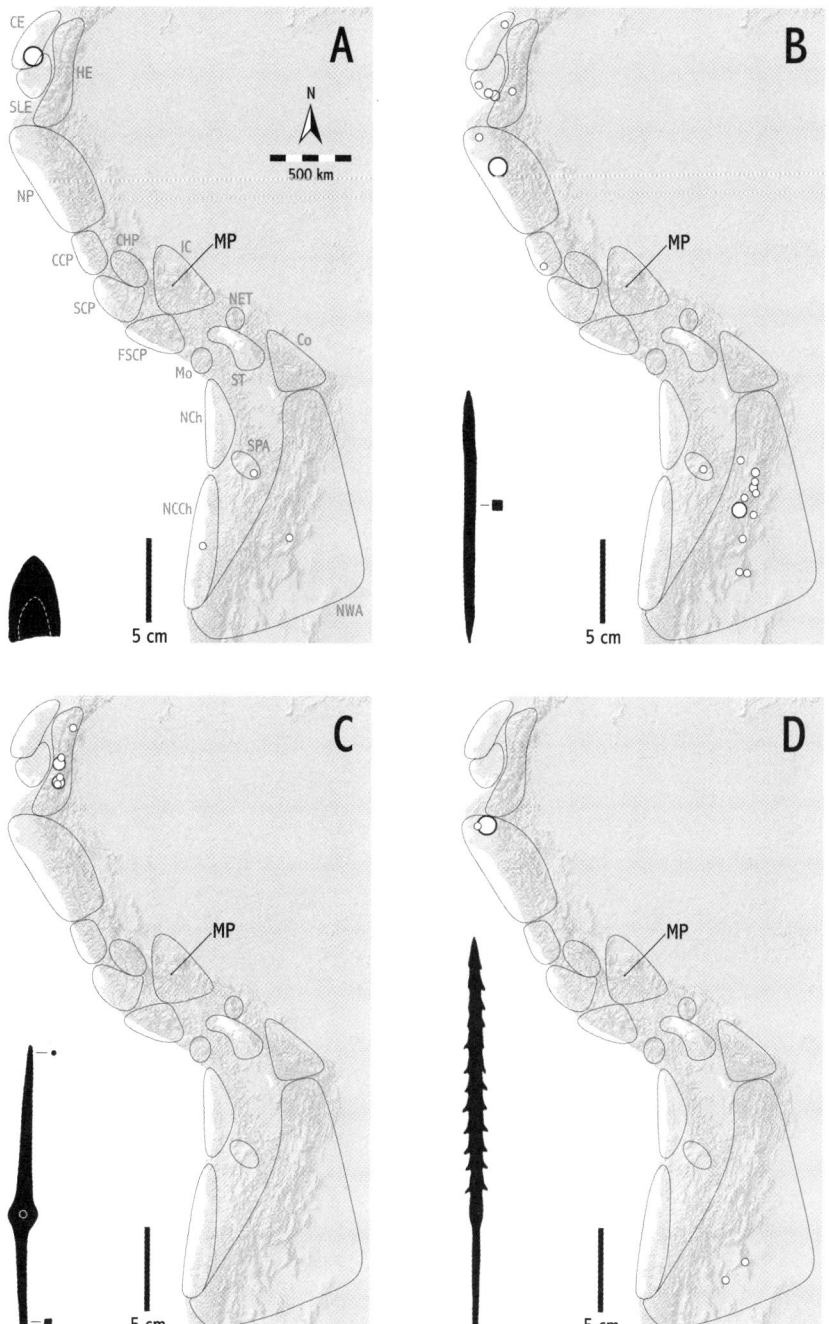

FIGURE 2.23. Distribution maps of metal projectile points. **A**, Projectile point: analogous to lithic points, including flat triangular, flat concave based, and triangular socketed (types 2814–2816); n=13. **B**, Projectile point: long narrow bar, pointed at both ends, often square in section, identification is debatable (type 2817); n=106. **C**, Projectile point: long and narrow with "whistle" hole and chamber (type 2818); n=8, but many additional examples in Mayer (1998) are said to come from the north coast of Peru. **D**, Projectile point: long and barbed (type 2819); n=36.

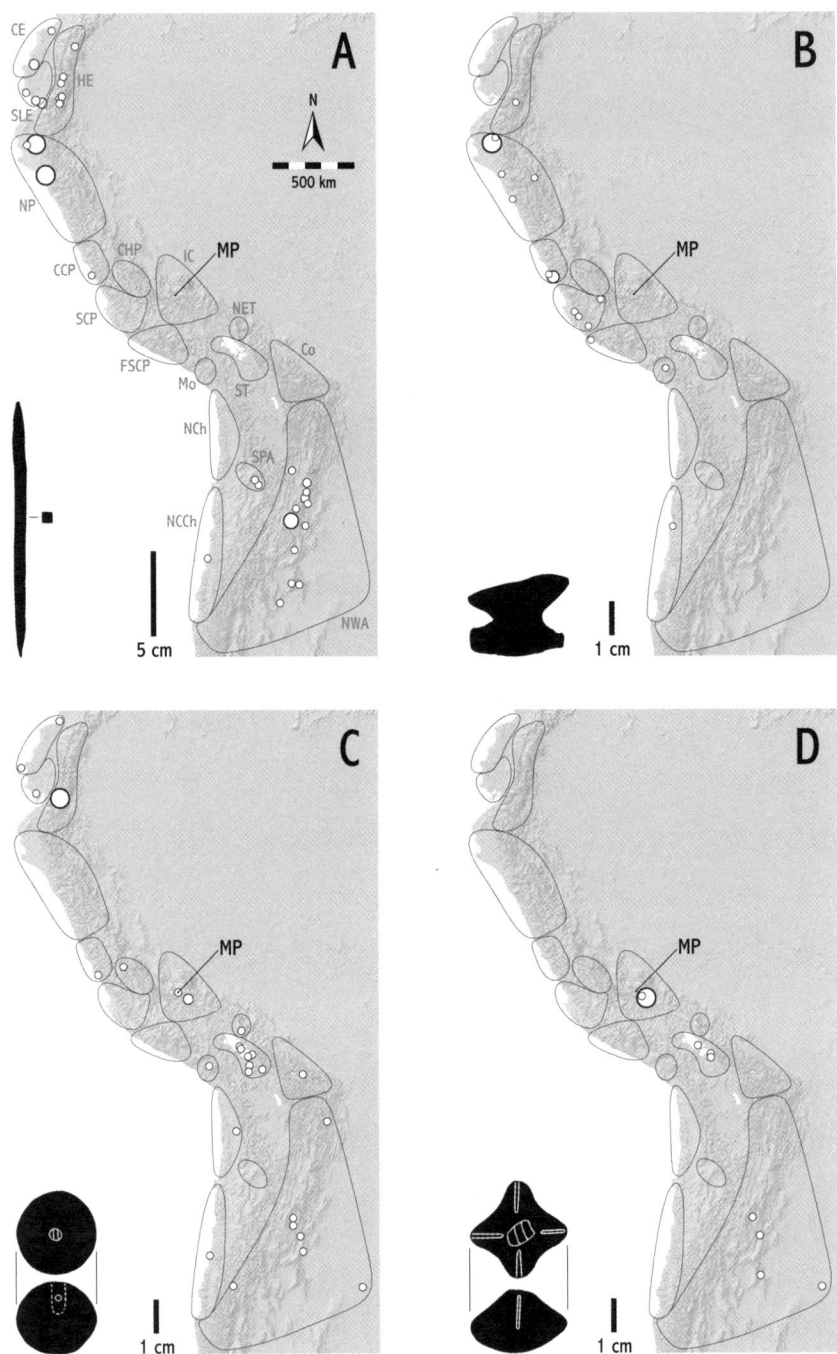

FIGURE 2.24. Distribution maps of all metal projectile points, atlatl parts, and bola weights. **A**, Projectile point: all identifiable metal projectile points (types 2814–2819); n=163. **B**, Weapon: atlatl hook, grip, or both (types 2790, 2800, and 2805); n=43. **C**, Bola weight: spheroid with suspension hole and crossbar (type 1801); n=128. **D**, Bola weight: elaborated shape with suspension hole and crossbar (type 1802); n=60.

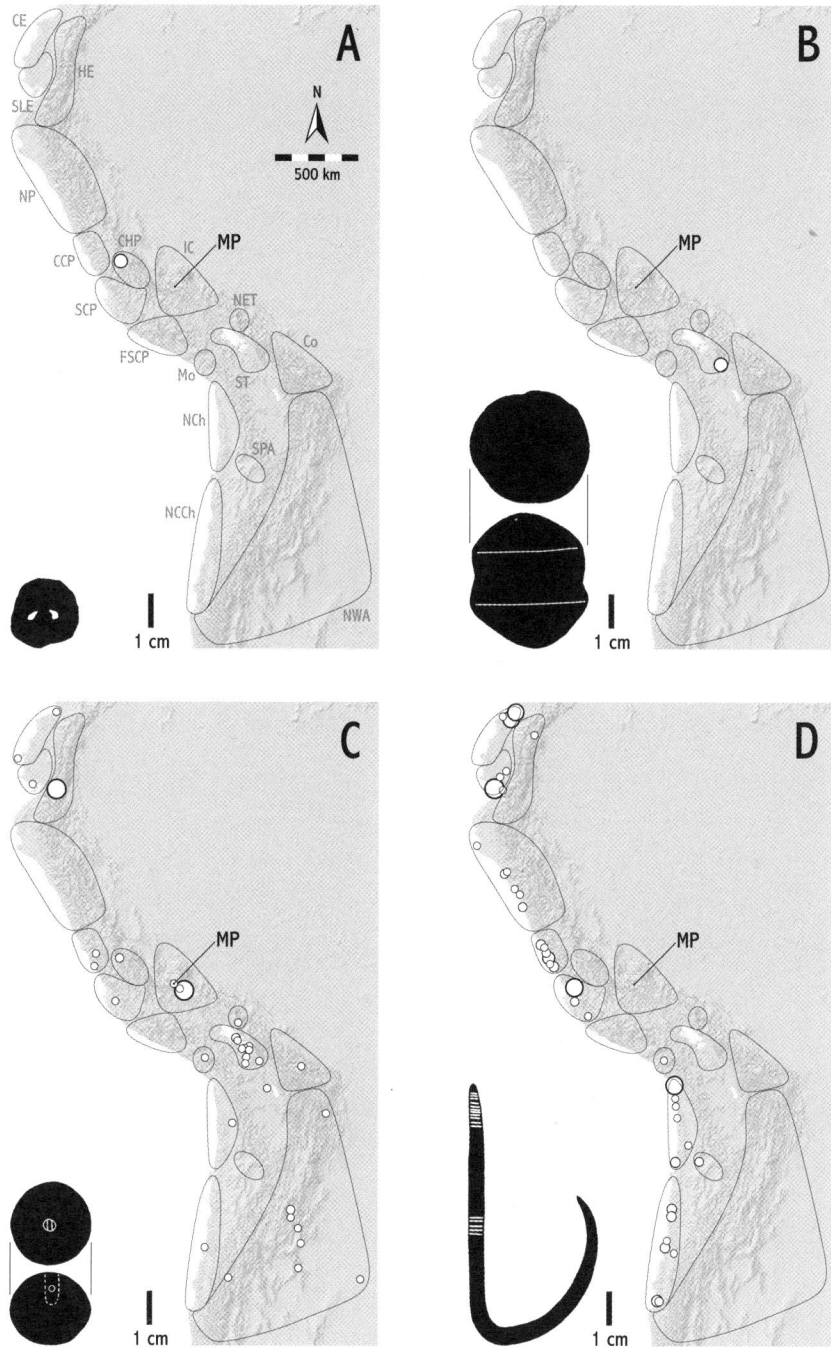

FIGURE 2.25. Distribution maps of bola weights, suspension holes with crossbars, and fishhooks. **A**, Bola weight: Lead (Pb), spheroid with simple or U-shaped hole (type 1804); n=10. **B**, Bola weight: Lead (Pb), circumferential groove, no hole (type 1803); n=3. **C**, Bola weight, all types (types 1800–1809, 1831); n=215. **D**, Fishing implement: fishhook (type 2820); n=212.

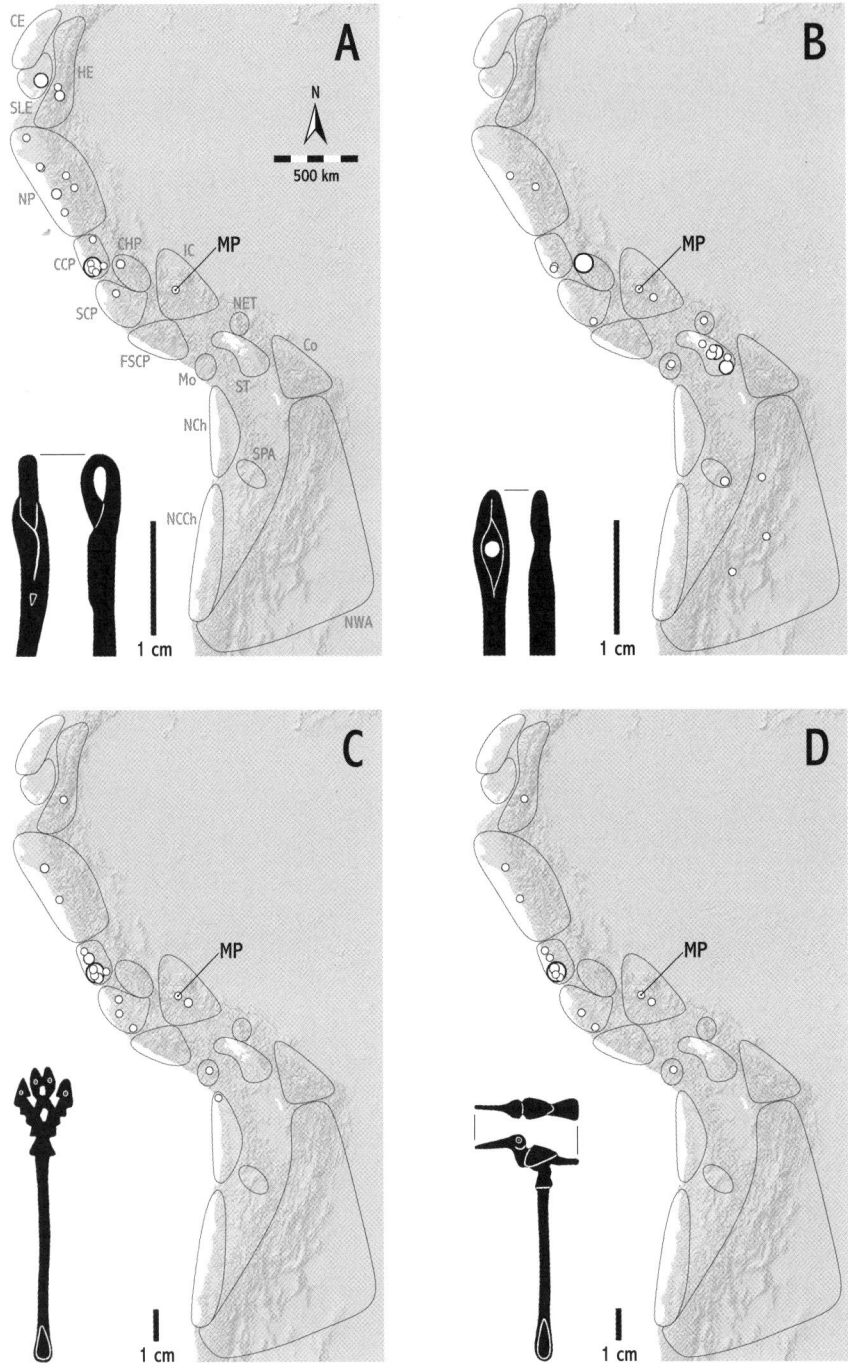

FIGURE 2.26. Distribution maps of needles and tiny spoons. **A**, Needle: loop-eye (types 1201–1203, 1208); n=84. **B**, Needle: pierced-eye (types 1204–1206); n=83. **C**, Tiny spoon: all types (types 1700–1702); n=54. **D**, Tiny spoon: bird finial (type 1701); n=27.

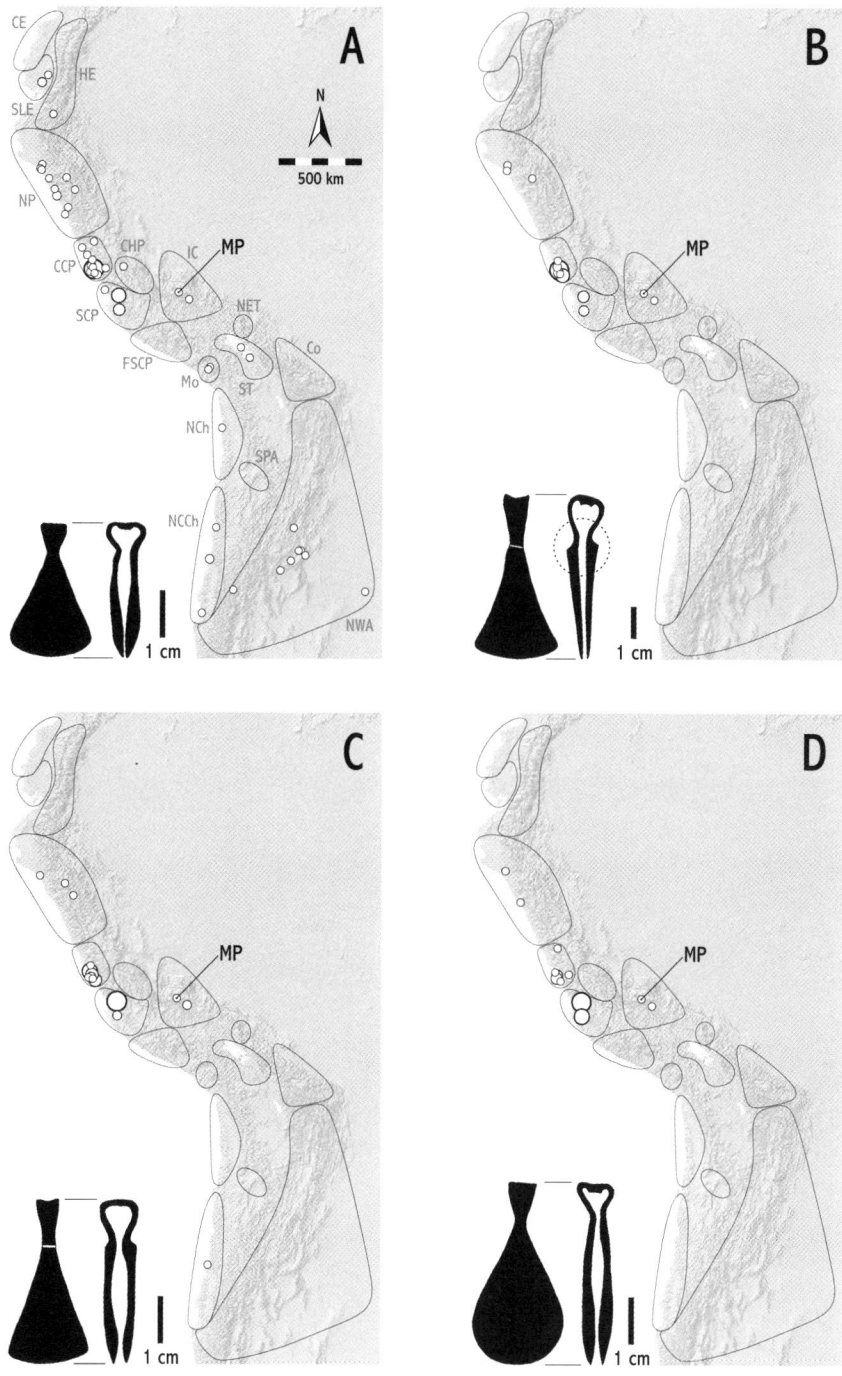

FIGURE 2.27. Distribution maps of tweezers. **A**, Tweezer: all types (types 1100–1128); n=428. **B**, Tweezer: any type with step in thickness of neck; n=44. **C**, Tweezer: triangular, with or without step in thickness of neck (type 1101); n=54. **D**, Tweezer: teardrop (type 1103); n=33.

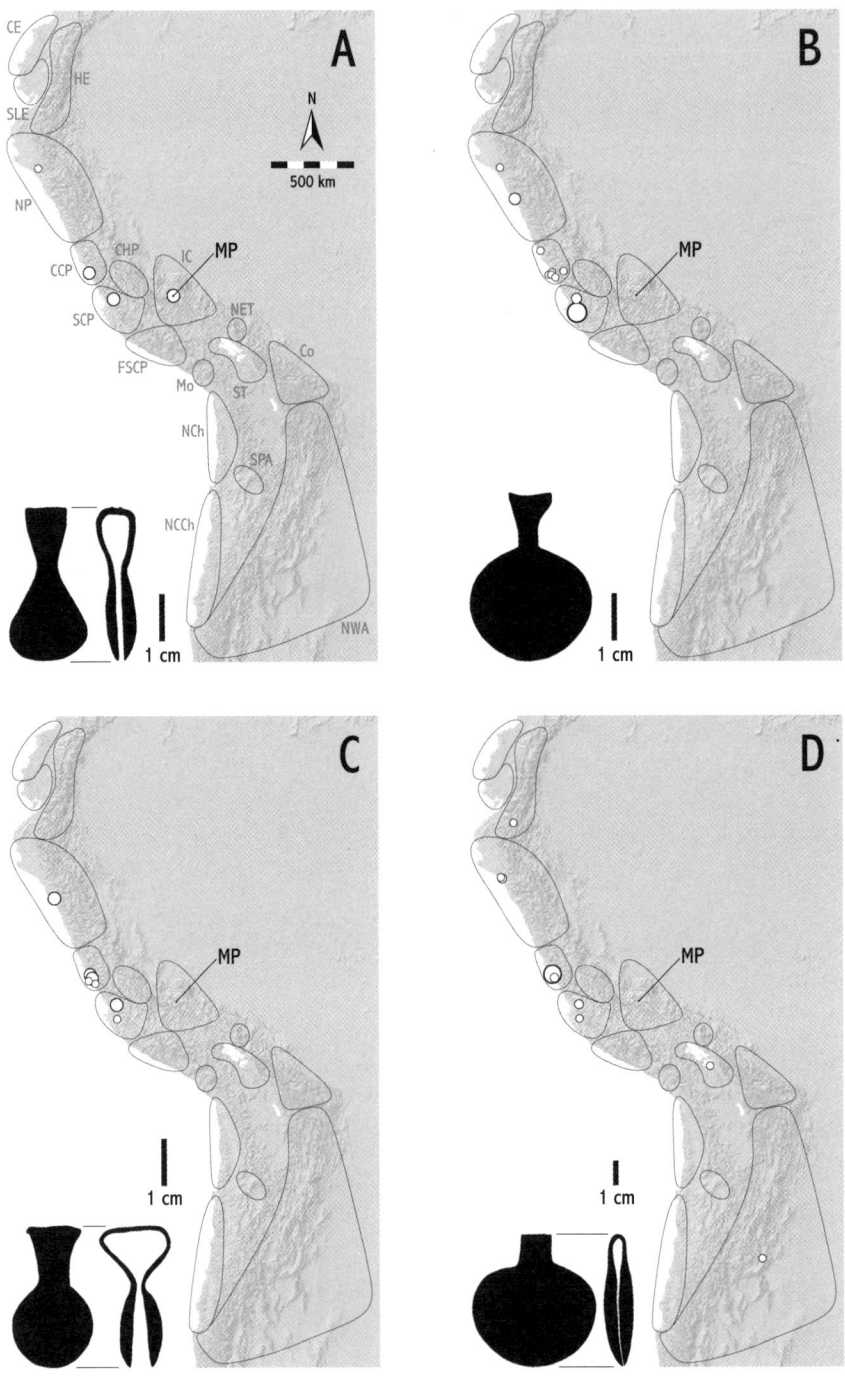

FIGURE 2.28. Distribution maps of tweezers. **A**, Tweezer: teardrop transitional (type 1104); n=7. **B**, Tweezer: circular with flaring neck (type 1105); n=28. **C**, Tweezer: circular transitional (type 1107); n=11. **D**, Tweezer: circular with straight neck (type 1106); n=16.

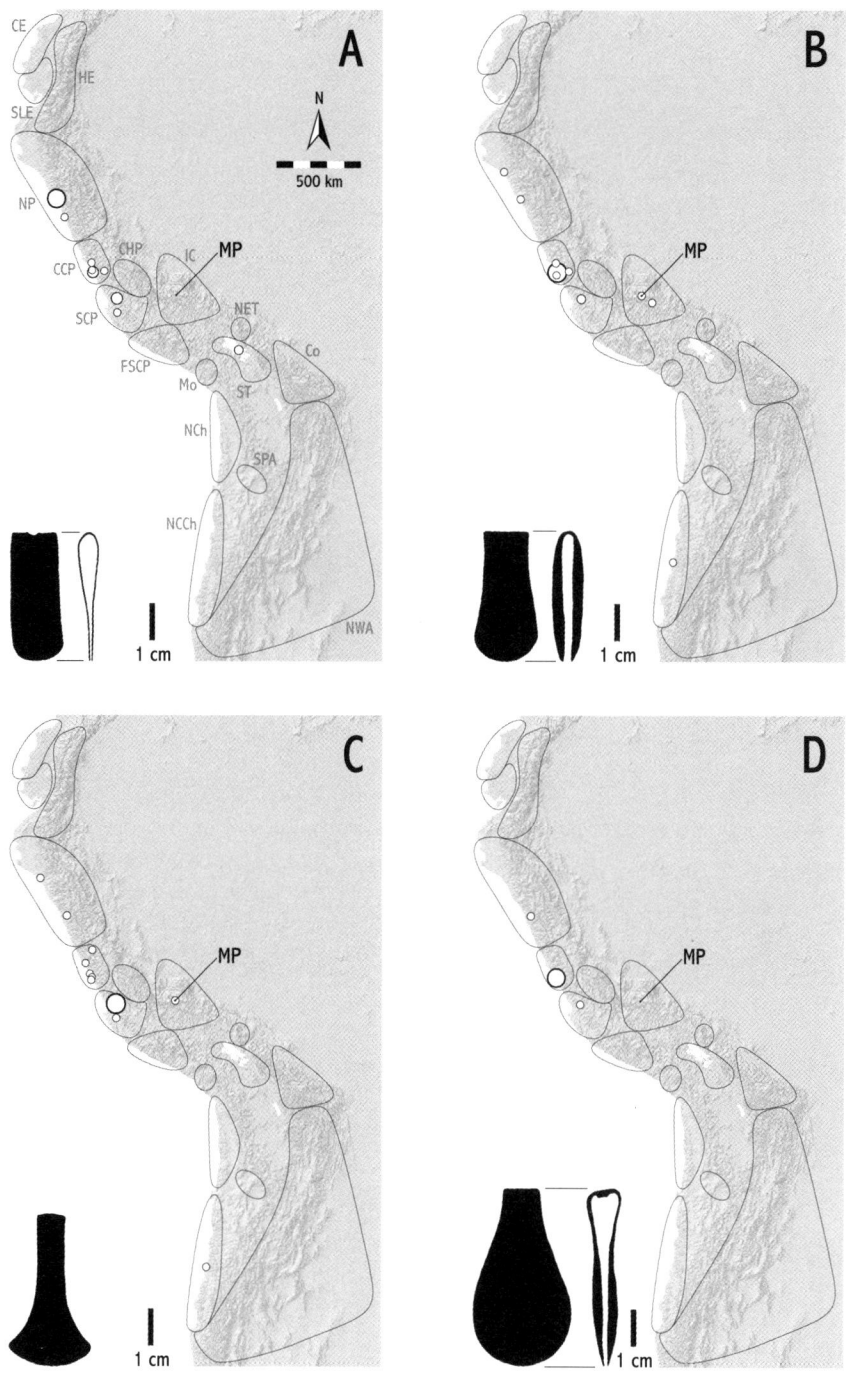

FIGURE 2.29. Distribution maps of tweezers. **A**, Tweezer: straight (type 1108); n=18. **B**, Tweezer: straight transitional (type 1109); n=44. **C**, Tweezer: flaring (type 1111); n=24. **D**, Tweezer: oyster shaped (type 1114); n=6.

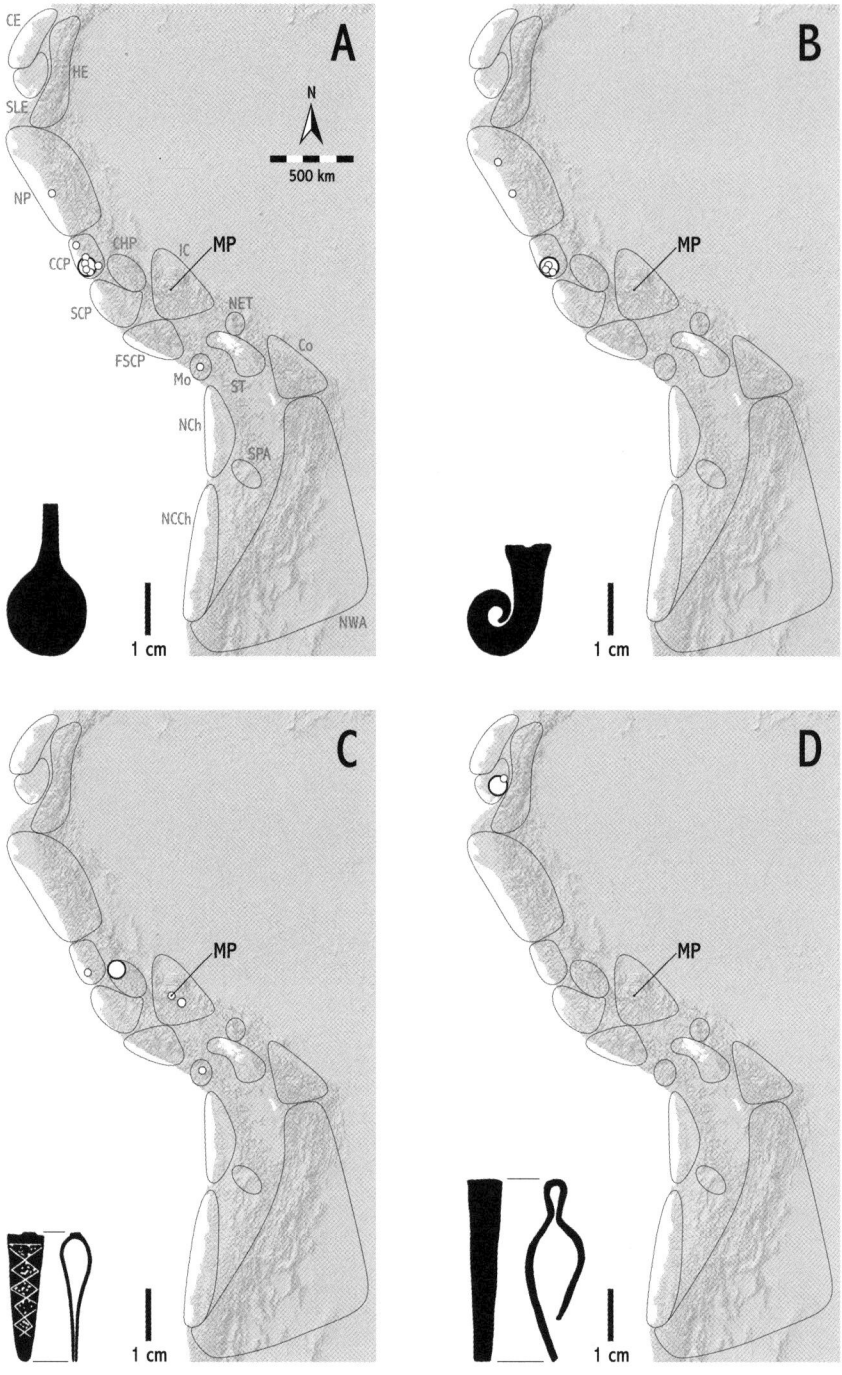

FIGURE 2.30. Distribution maps of tweezers. **A**, Tweezer: narrow necked (type 1113); n=39. **B**, Tweezer: decorative asymmetrical shapes such as figural, spiral, or others (types 1123–1126); n=28. **C**, Tweezer: pointed (type 1115); n=9. **D**, Tweezer: compound curved strip (type 1116); n=19.

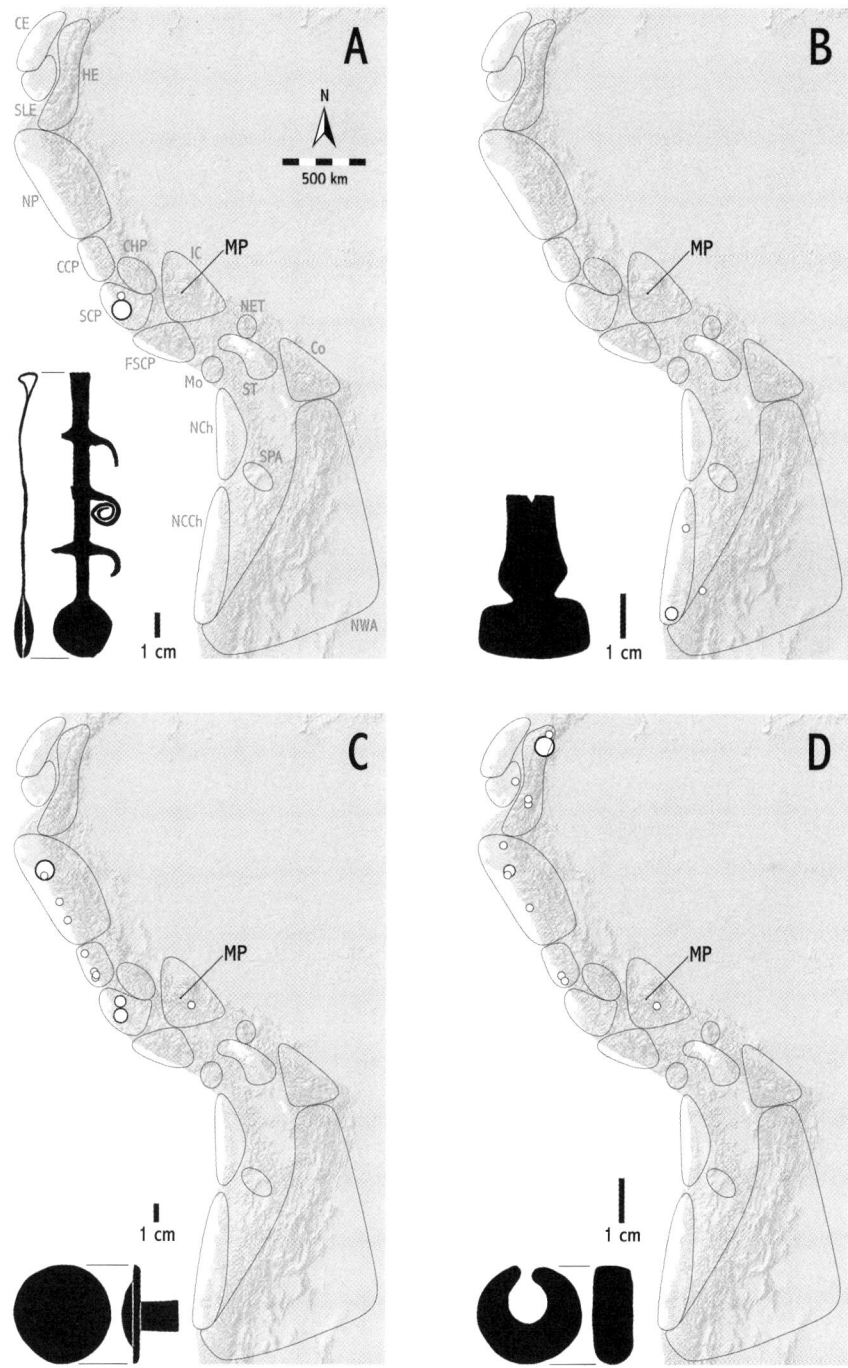

FIGURE 2.31. Distribution maps of tweezers, earspools, and nose ornaments. **A**, Tweezer: applied spiral arms (type 1122); n=12. **B**, Tweezer: notched (type 1120); n=4. **C**, Earspool: all types (types 1300–1311); n=148. **D**, Nose ornament: cast and sheet types (types 2201–2202); n=25.

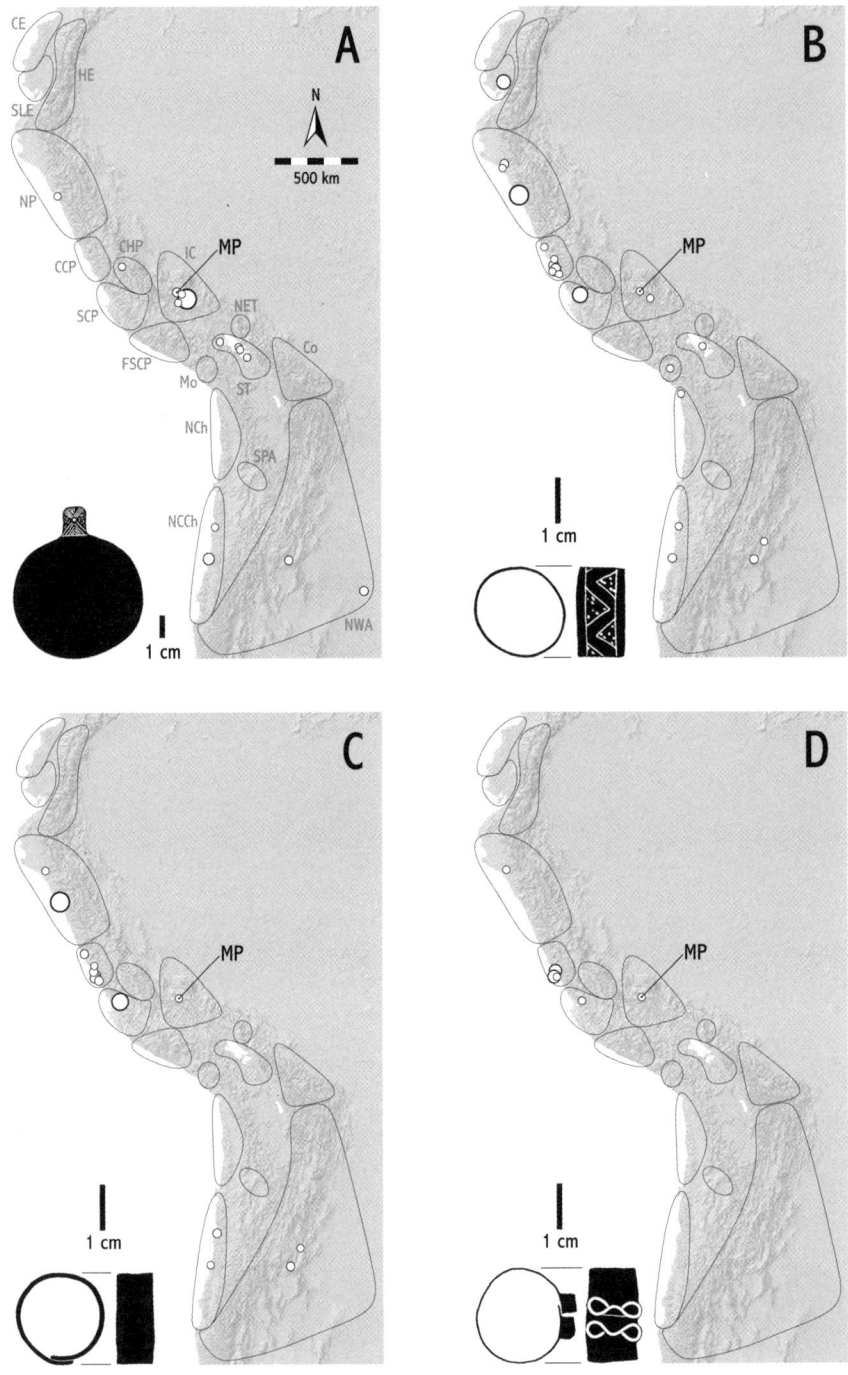

FIGURE 2.32. Distribution maps of lirpus and finger rings. **A**, Lirpu: disc with suspension tab or stem (types 5610 and 5620); n=40. **B**, Finger ring: all types (types 1600–1609); n=144. **C**, Finger ring: plain flat (type 1601); n=88. **D**, Finger ring: narrow strip appliqué (type 1603); n=8.

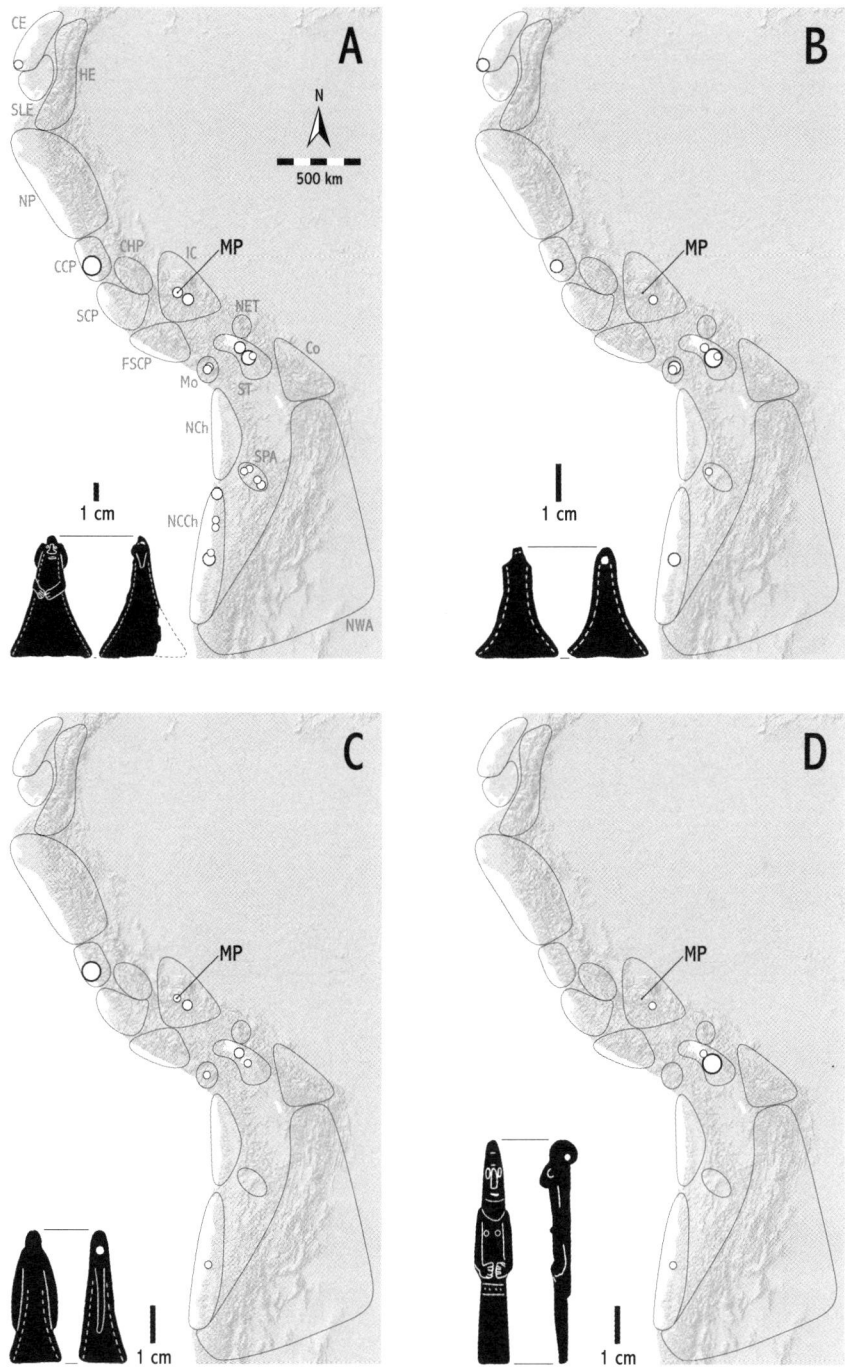

FIGURE 2.33. Distribution maps of conical "bells" and Titicaca figurine hair pendants. **A**, Conical "bell": all types, probably hair ornaments (types 1900–1903); n=64. **B**, Conical "bell": plain, probably hair ornaments (type 1901); n=24. **C**, Conical "bell": with "arms," probably hair ornaments (type 1902); n=19. **D**, Figurine: Titicaca anthropomorphic hair pendant (types 1551 and 1552); n=19.

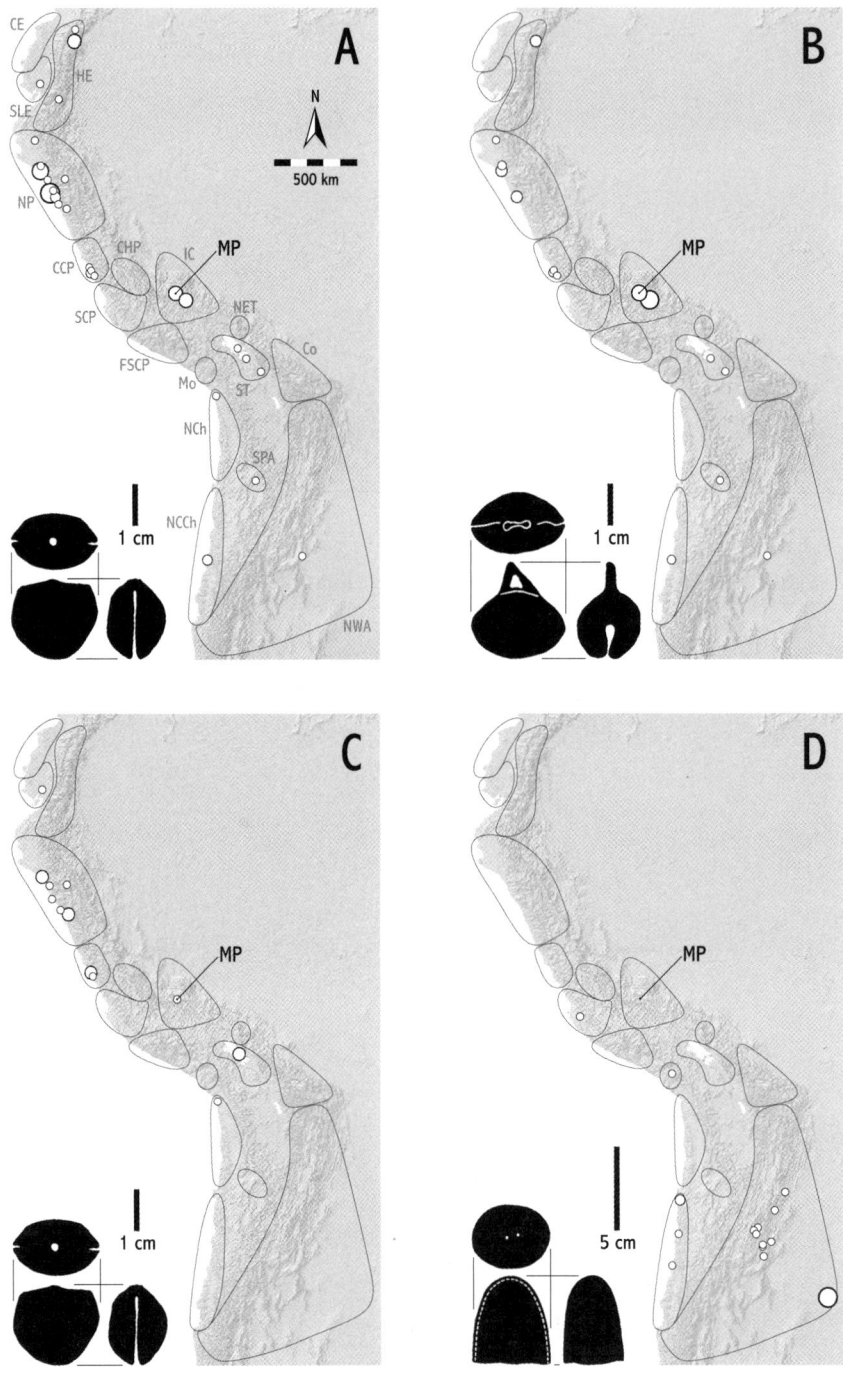

FIGURE 2.34. Distribution maps of split bells and cup bells. **A**, Split bell: all types (types 2000–2002); n=61. **B**, Split bell: cast (type 2001); n=31. **C**, Split bell: forged (type 2002); n=16. **D**, Unsplit bell: all types without split sides, including flat-topped "cowbell" forms (types 2900–2908); n=25.

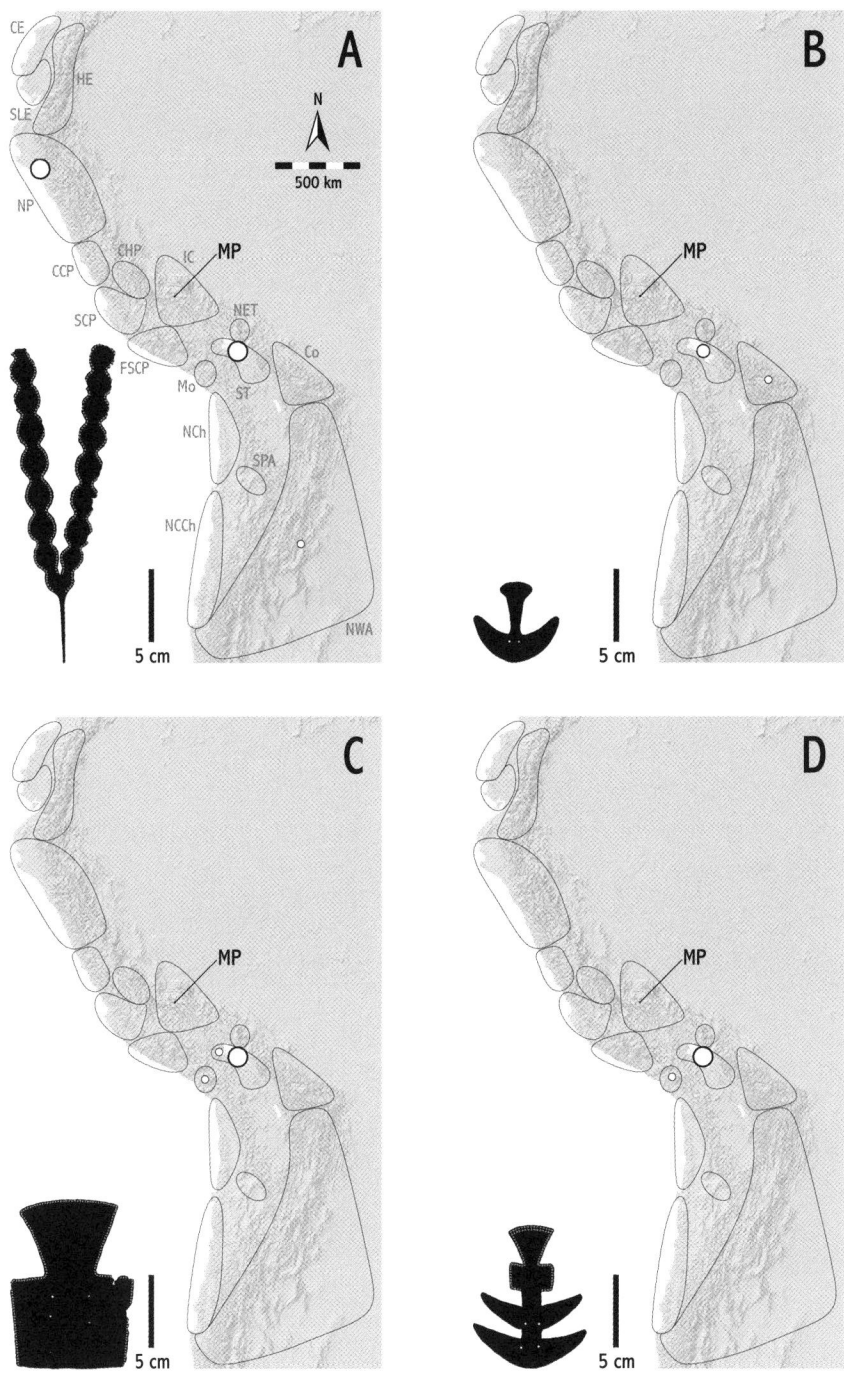

FIGURE 2.35. Distribution maps of headdress frontals. **A**, Headdress: frontal, single or double long plume(s), various forms (type 5310); n=17. **B**, Headdress: frontal, crescent and plume (type 5316); n=3. **C**, Headdress: frontal, trapezoid on rectangle (type 5320); n=11. **D**, Headdress: frontal, stacked crescents (type 5312); n=10.

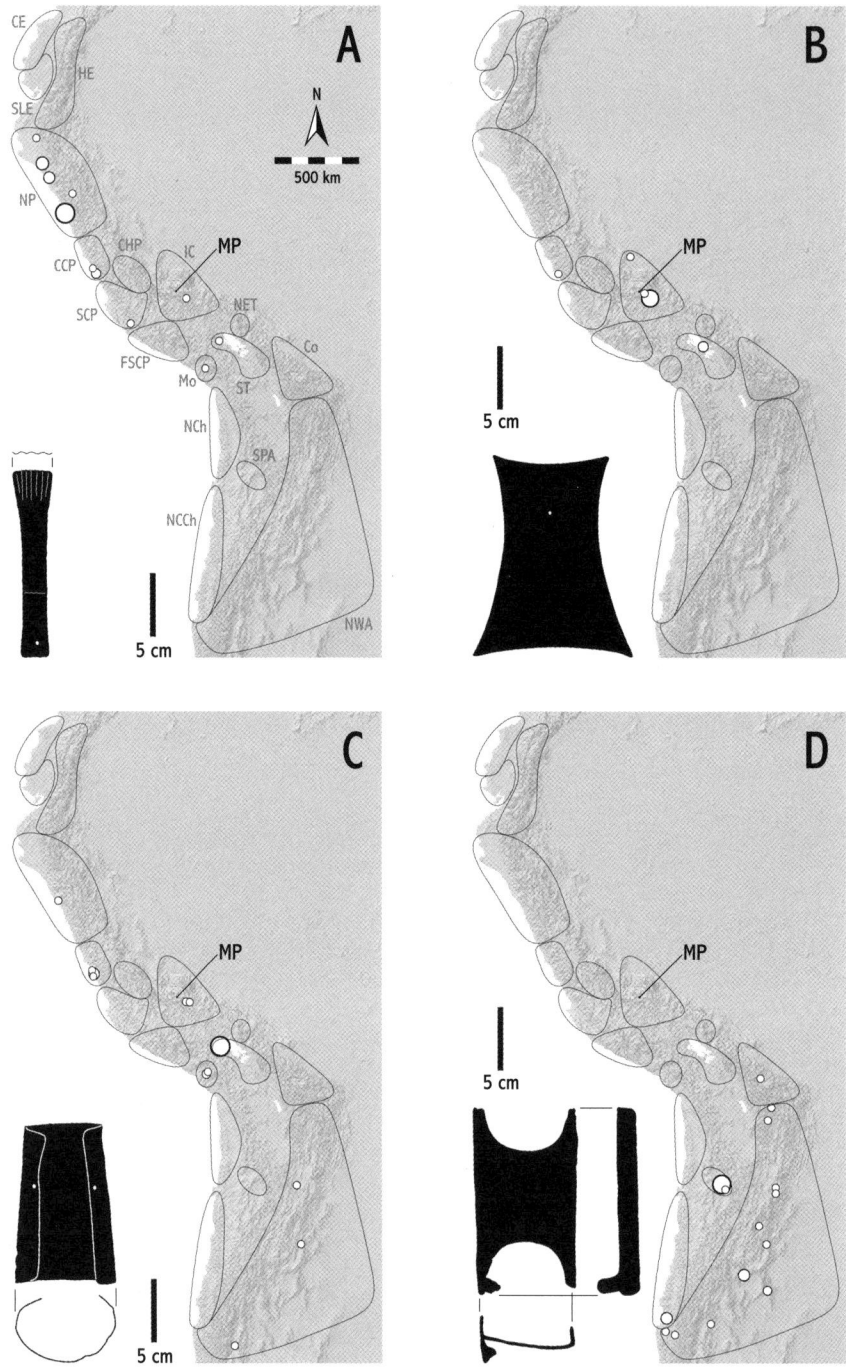

FIGURE 2.36. Distribution maps of headdress frontals and structures, gauntlets, and "brazales." **A**, Headdress: frontal, short plume and wide elaborated, and cylindrical or conical headdress structures (types 5315, 5317, and 5325); n=28. **B**, Headdress: frontal, concave sided (type 5311); n=8. **C**, Ornament: sheet metal gauntlet (type 2057); n=28. **D**, Miscellaneous: "brazal" arm ornament or protector (Mayer 1986) (type 3145); n=24.

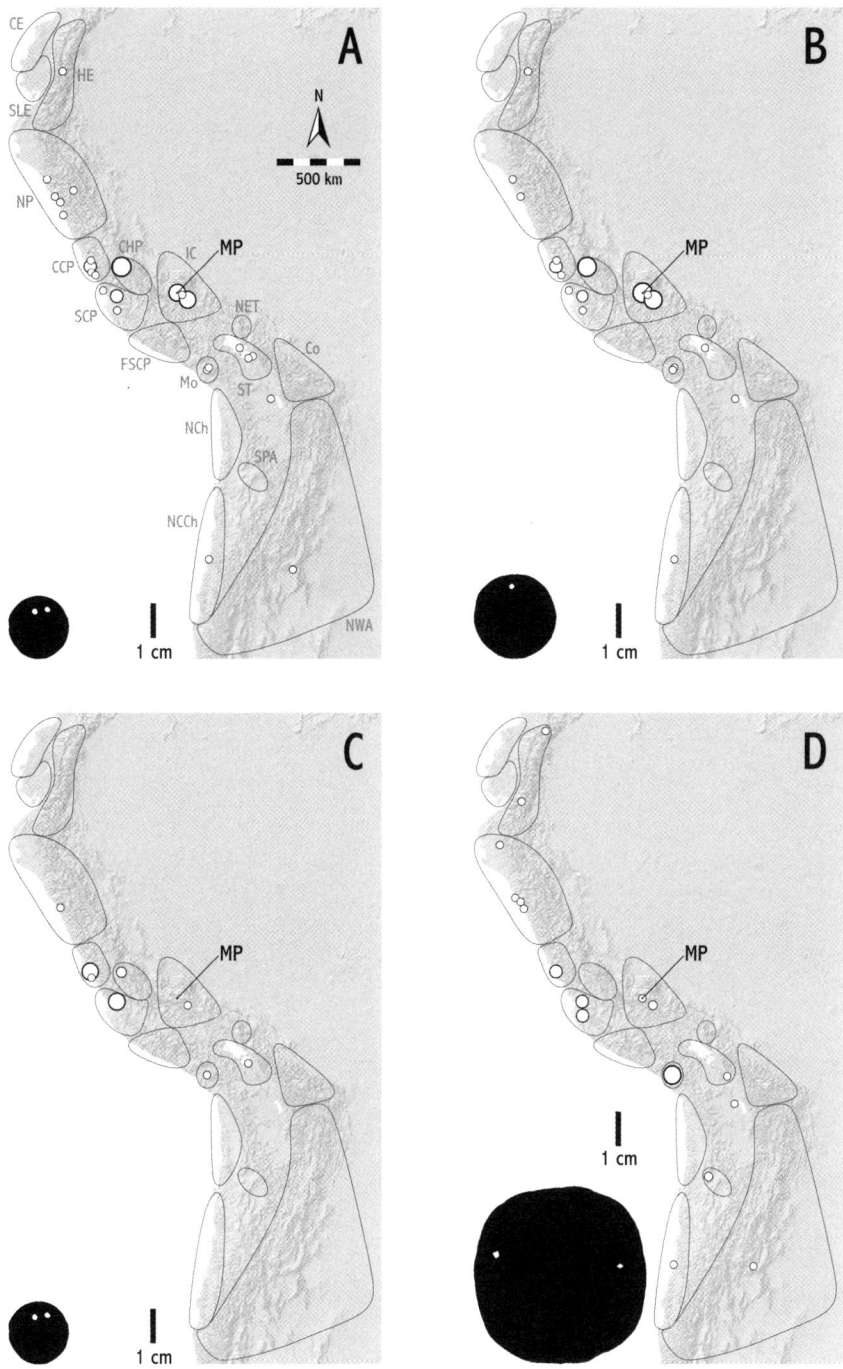

FIGURE 2.37. Distribution maps of plain, flat, thin sheet metal discs. **A**, Disc: small (up to 40 mm), plain, flat, any hole number or location; n=216. **B**, Disc: small (up to 40 mm) plain, flat, one hole close to edge (type 5422); n=171. **C**, Disc: small (up to 40 mm), plain, flat, two holes close together near edge (type 5432); n=13. **D**, Disc: medium (40 to 100 mm), plain, flat, any hole number or location; n=28.

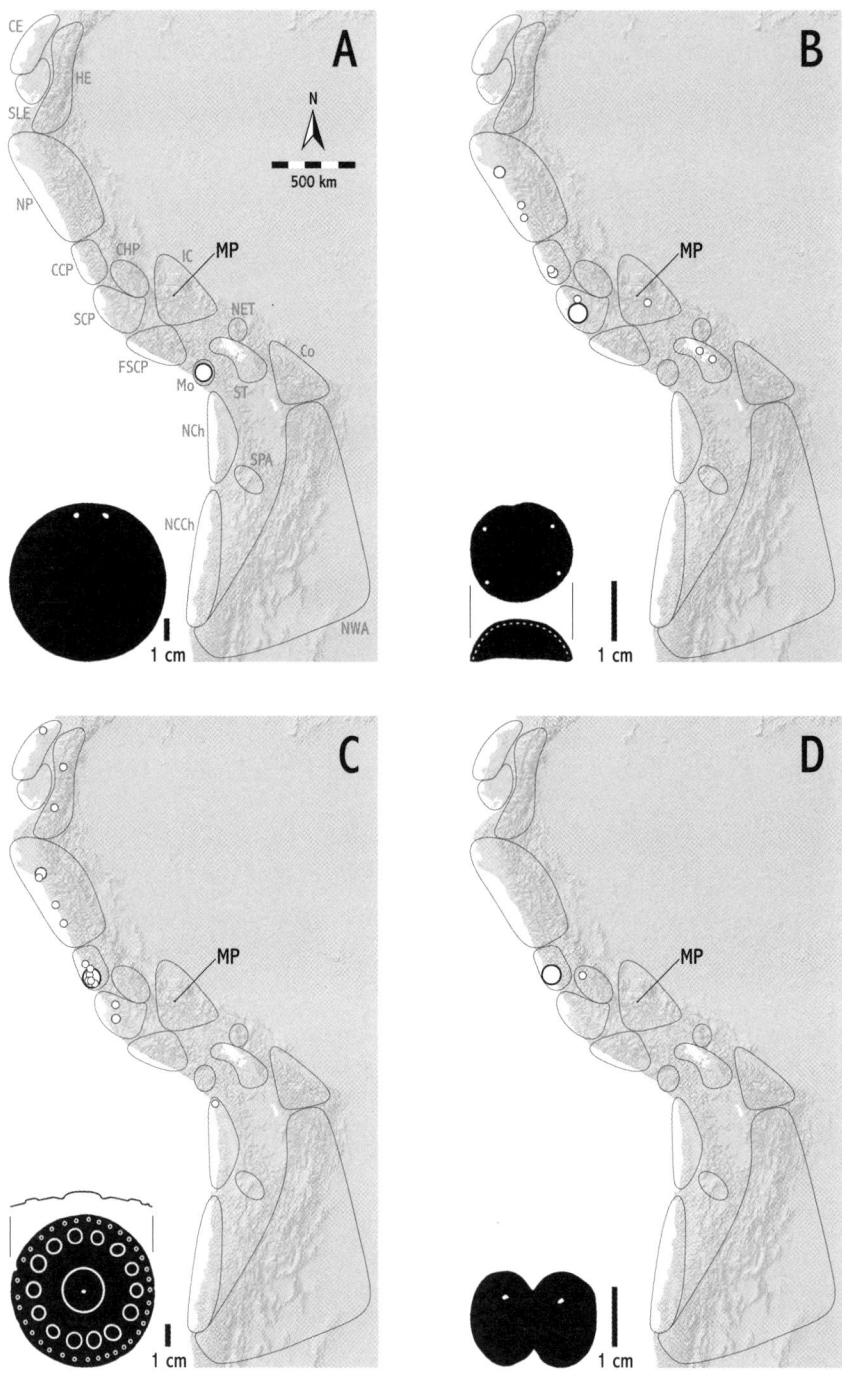

FIGURE 2.38. Distribution maps of thin sheet metal discs. **A**, Disc: medium (40 to 100 mm), plain, flat, two holes close together near edge (type 5433); n=10. **B**, Disc: convex, plain, any size, any hole number or location; n=109. **C**, Disc: repoussé or pierced decoration (types 5512–5514); n=41. **D**, Disc: two or three joined discs (type 5670); n=10.

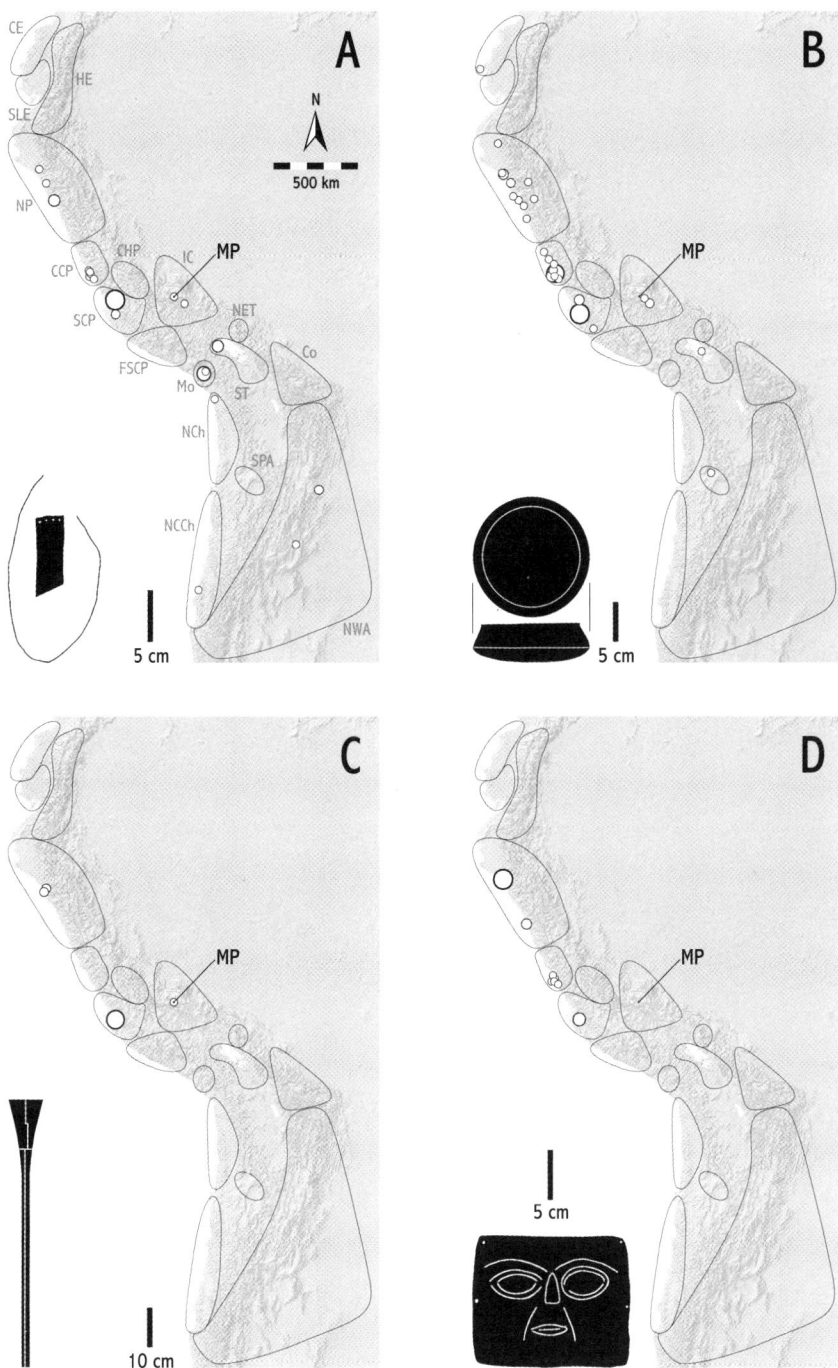

FIGURE 2.39. Distribution maps of strips, metal vessels, plume holders, and mummy masks. **A**, Miscellaneous: strip with one or more holes, mostly flexible, possibly headbands, belts, or similar (type 3190 with holes); n=61. **B**, Vessel: all types (types 1400–1411); n=188. **C**, Miscellaneous: plume holder (types 3110–3112); n=10. **D**, Miscellaneous: mummy mask (type 3130); n=21.

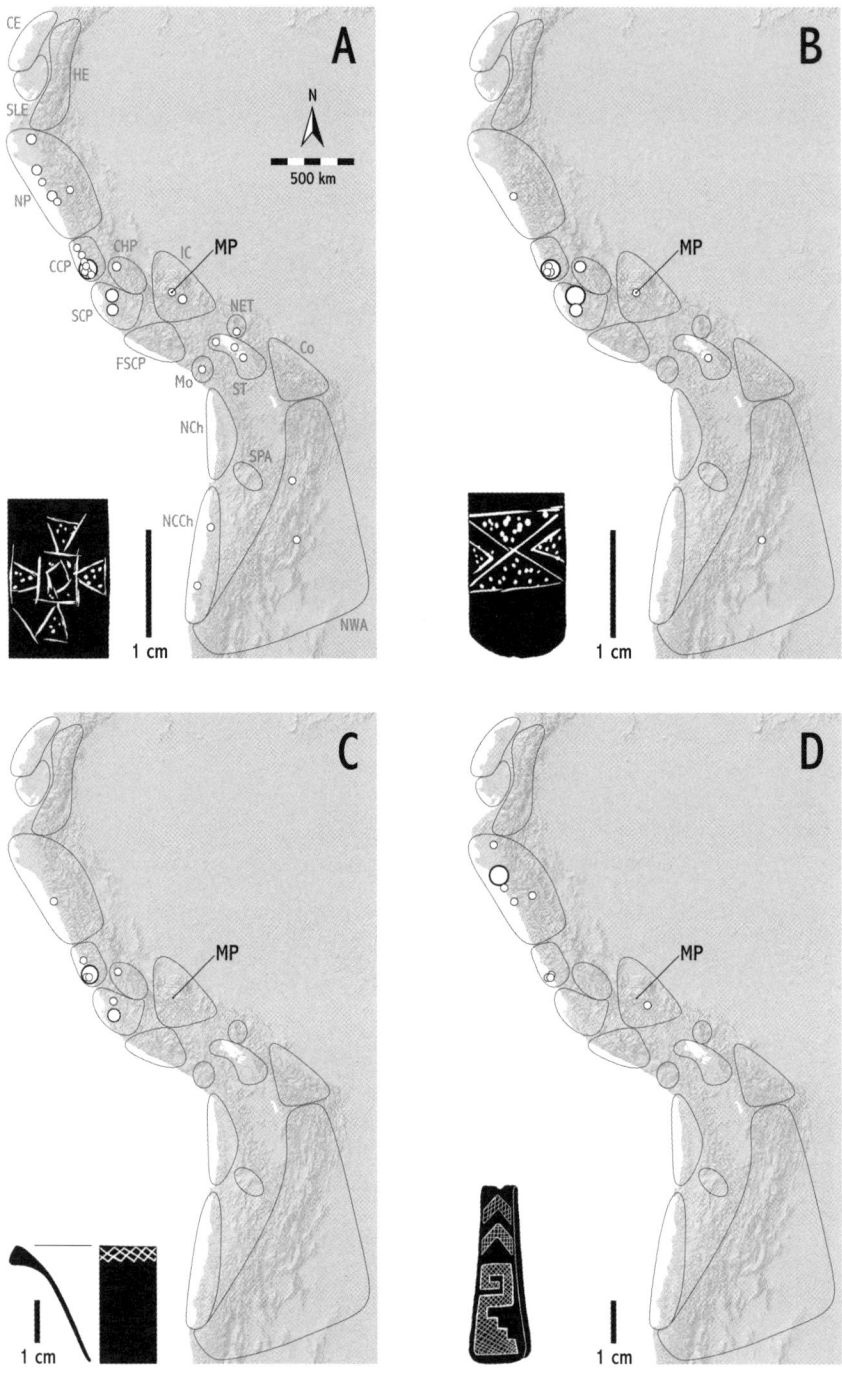

FIGURE 2.40. Distribution maps of traced decoration. **A**, Any type with traced decoration: any design except clearly historical; n=131. **B**, Any type with traced decoration: punctate fill delimited by lines; n=42. **C**, Any type with traced decoration: crosshatching not delimited by lines (mostly vessel rims); n=17. **D**, Any type with traced decoration: crosshatching delimited by lines; n=17.

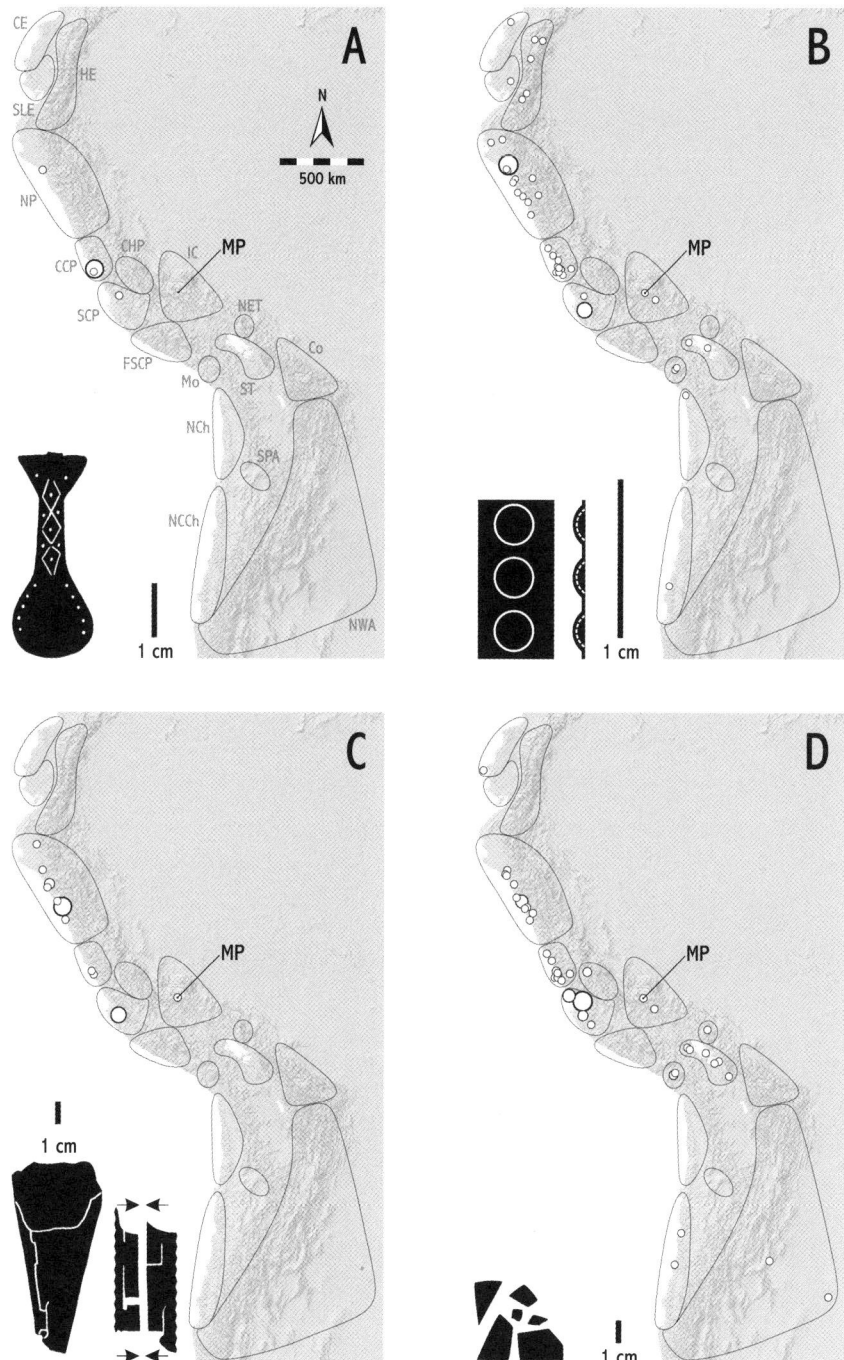

Figure 2.41. Distribution maps of traced decoration, repoussé, sheet metal fabricated with tabs, slots, and so on, and sheet metal fragments. **A**, Any type with traced decoration: single dots as filler elements; n=8. **B**, Any type with repoussé decoration; n=703. **C**, Any type made from sheet metal assembled with tabs, slots, straps, crimps, and so on (underrepresented in this dataset); n=27. **D**, Indeterminate: sheet fragments of unidentifiable object types, many lots counted as one item (type 3210); n=377.

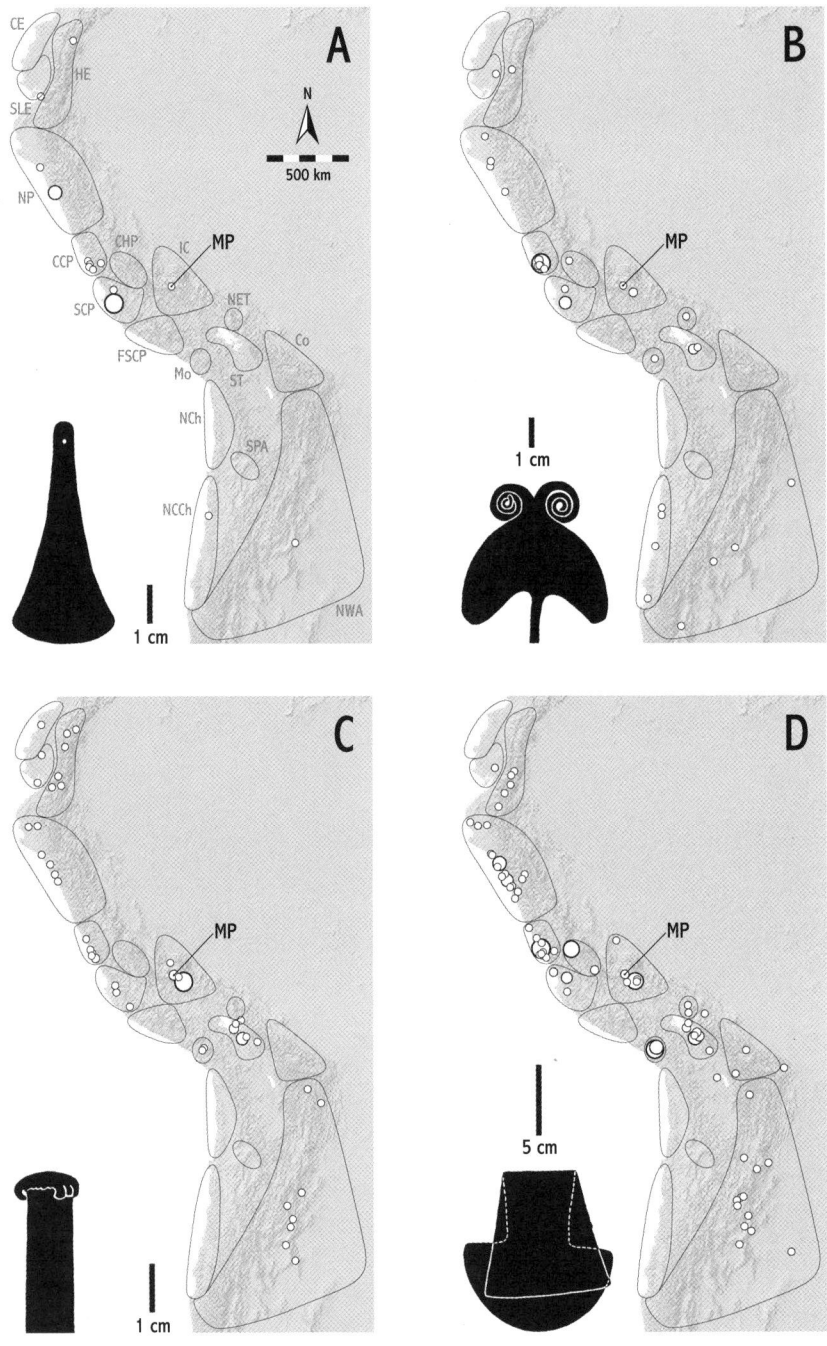

FIGURE 2.42. Distribution maps of bangles, spiral motifs, upset (mushrooming), and intentional destruction. **A**, Ornament: bangle or pendant, many forms, some possibly used as cutting tools (type 3020); n=173. **B**, Any type with spiral motifs; n=81. **C**, Any type with upset (mushrooming) use damage; n=91. **D**, Any type, intentionally destroyed; n=335.

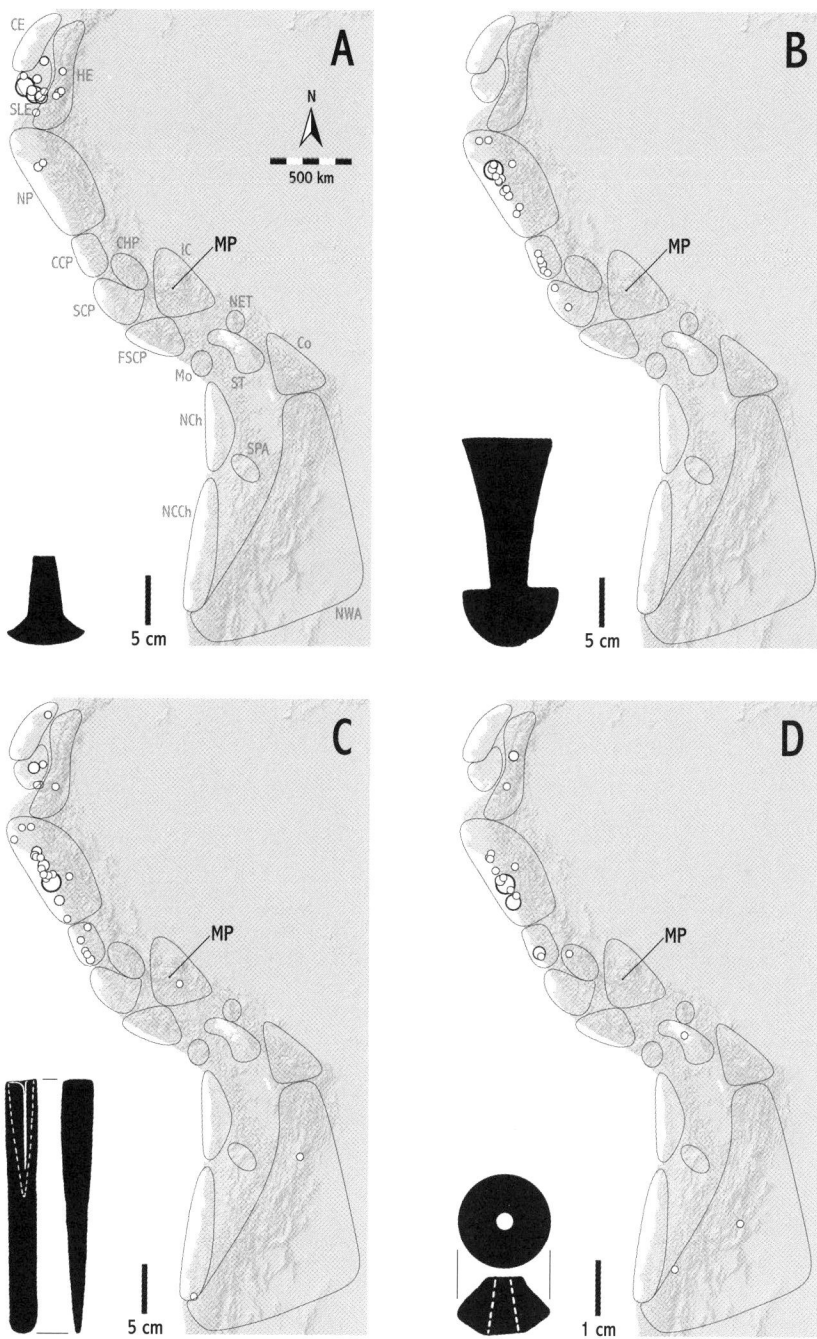

FIGURE 2.43. Distribution maps of axe-monies, North Coast tumis, socketed points, and metal spindle whorls. **A**, Axe-monies and related types (see Hosler, Lechtman, and Holm 1990) (types 3103–3108); n=106, but hundreds more are shown in Mayer (1992, 1998) with vague proveniences. **B**, North coast tumi (types 5000–5080); n=259, but hundreds more are shown in Mayer (1998) with vague proveniences. **C**, Socketed point (types 5130–5145); n=214, but hundreds more are shown in Mayer (1998) with vague proveniences. **D**, Other tool: spindle whorl (type 2720); n=189.

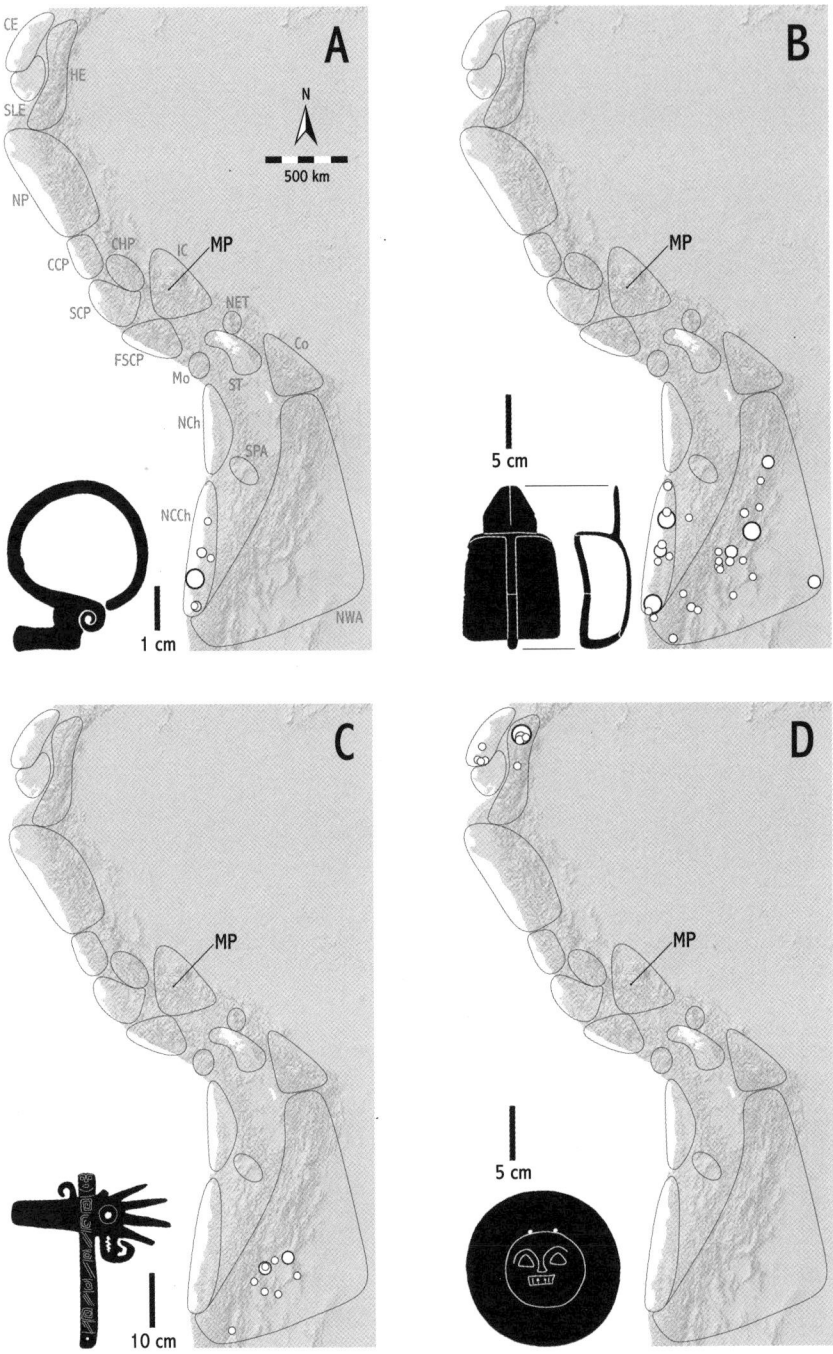

FIGURE 2.44. Distribution maps of Atacama "earrings," "manoplas," "tokis," and "tincullpas." **A**, Ornament (?): "Atacama earring," possibly atlatl finger loop (type 3055); n=22. **B**, Miscellaneous: "manopla" or "knuckle duster" (type 3150); n=55. **C**, Miscellaneous: elaborated representation of an axe with metal handle ("toki"), or just the head (type 3159 and 3160); n=11. **D**, Other disc variant: large disc with central raised face, "tincullpa" (type 5650); n=64.

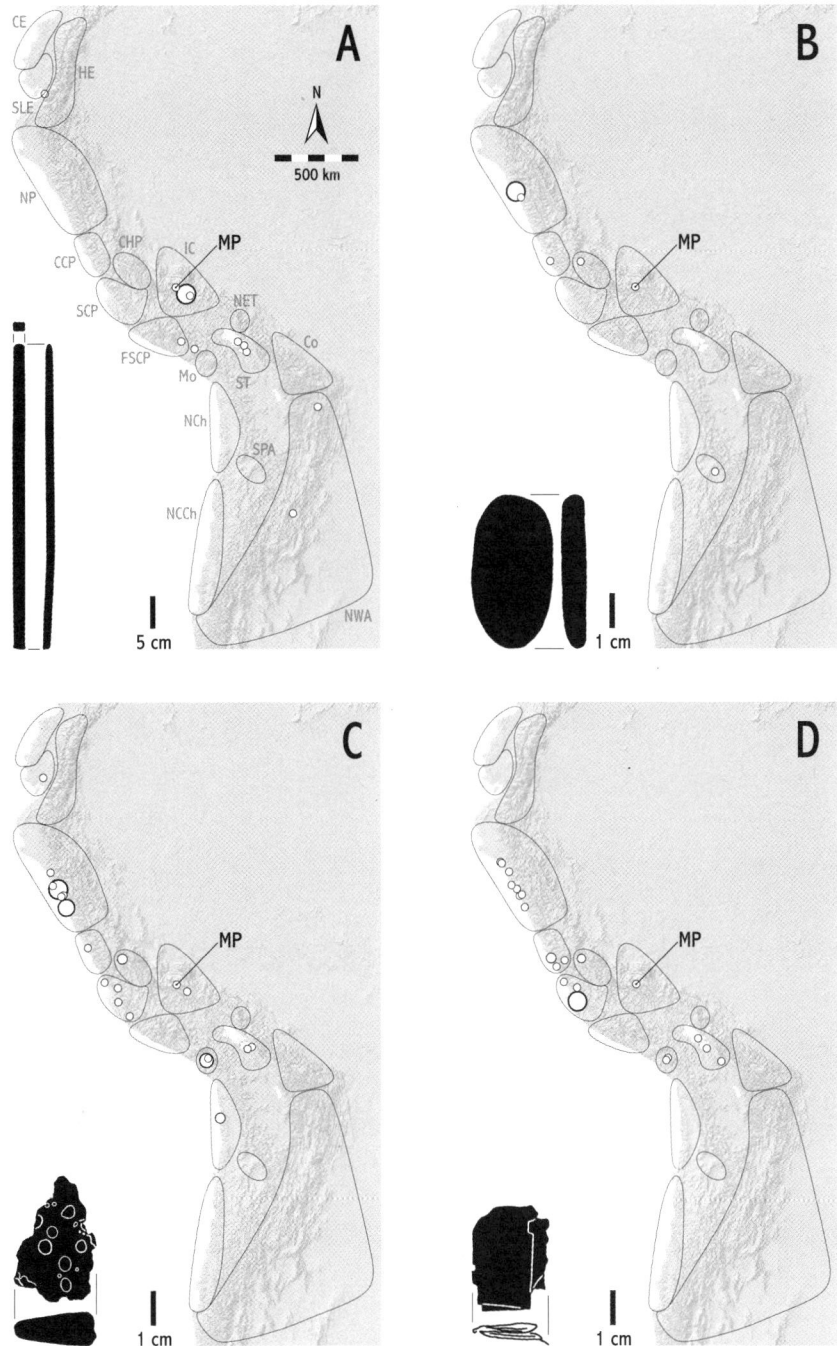

FIGURE 2.45. Distribution maps of crowbars and production materials. **A**, Other tool: crowbar (type 2750); n=25. **B**, Production: ingot (type 2930); n=20. **C**, Production: smelting or refining products, melting surplus, or prill (types 2920–2922); n=178. **D**, Production: sheet scrap identified by being cutmarked, jagged-shaped, folded, and/or stacked (type 2933); n=143.

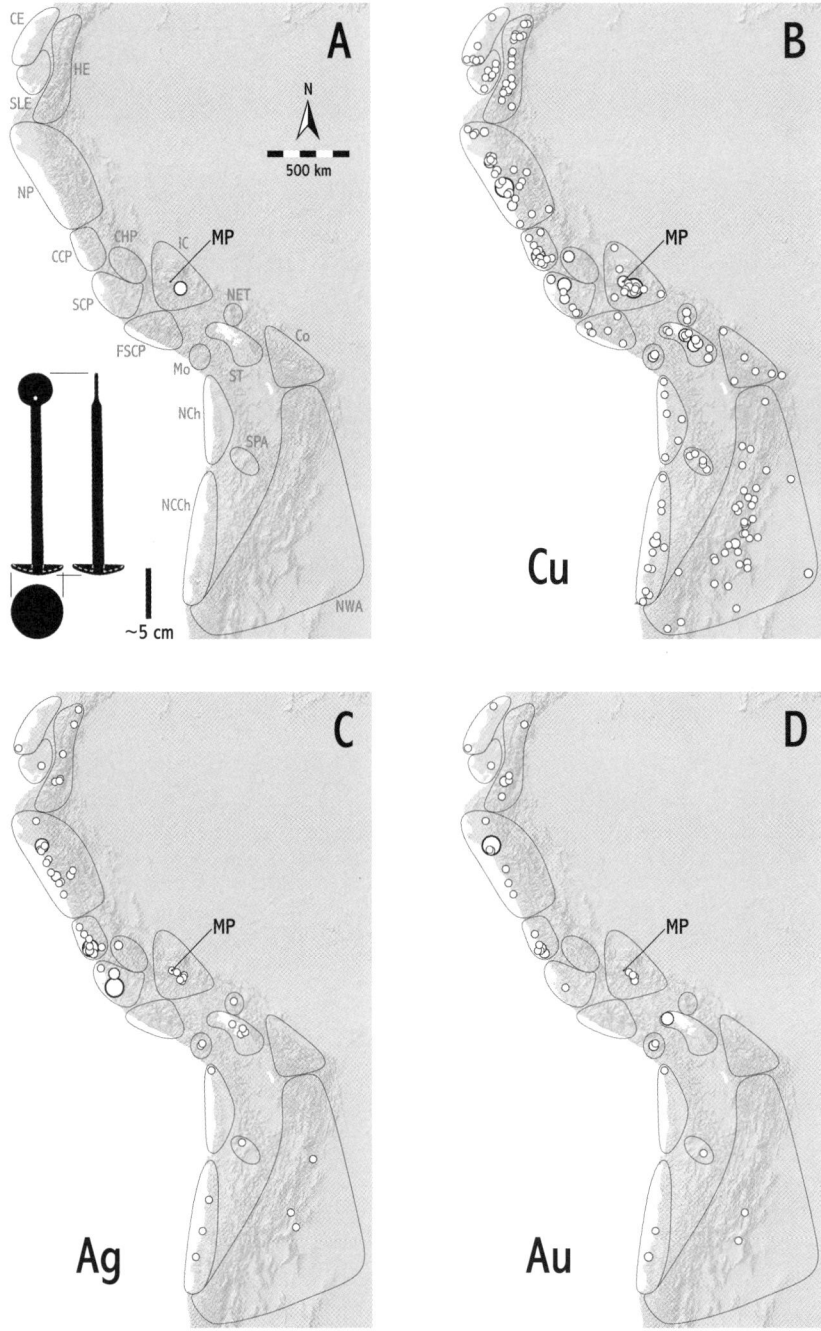

FIGURE 2.46. Distribution maps of "sea anchors," copper (Cu), silver (Ag), and gold (Au). Apparent composition was not coded for objects from Mayer (1986, 1992, 1994, 1998). **A**, Miscellaneous: heavy cast object vaguely resembling a miniature sea anchor (type 3153); n=12. **B**, Any type that seems to be of copper or copper alloy, without visible gold, silver, or silver corrosion products; n=4673. **C**, Any type with any visible silver surface or evident silver corrosion products; n=1602. **D**, Any type with any visible gold surface; n=218.

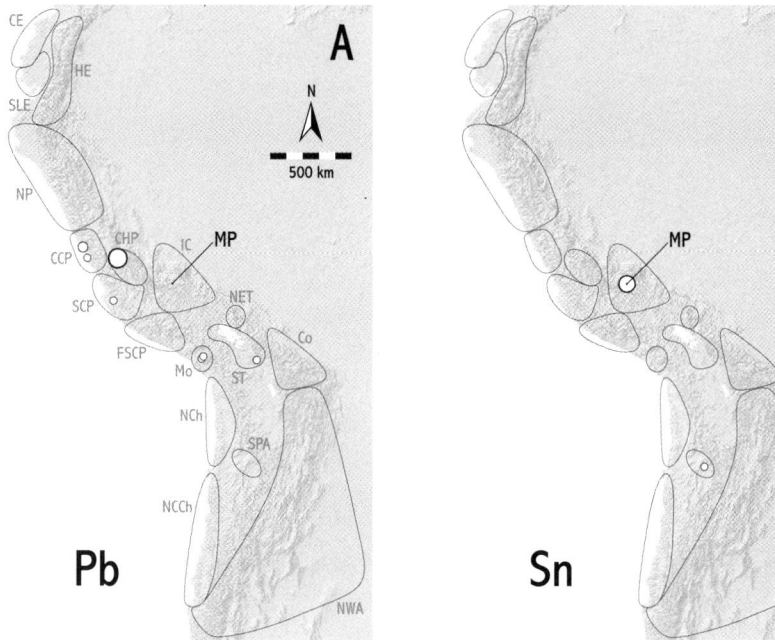

FIGURE 2.47. Distribution maps of lead (Pb) and tin (Sn). Apparent composition was not coded for objects from Mayer (1986, 1992, 1994, 1998) except for two objects apparently of tin from San Pedro de Atacama (see Le Paige 1961). **A**, Any type made from lead; n=36. **B**, Any type made from tin; n=6.

APPENDIX A

Technical Descriptions of Selected Artifacts

See Section One, "Metal Artifacts from the 1911–1912 Yale Expeditions to Peru"

ANT.017898 "T" Axe with Asymmetrical Crossbar
This axe was purchased by H. Bingham at Espiritu Pampa on the Conservidayoc River in 1911, and was examined by Foote and Buell (1912), who machined three recesses on one side to reach metal free of corrosion for study. Their chemical analysis showed the axe is made of bronze containing 87.6% copper (Cu), 12.0% tin (Sn), 0.35% sulfur (S), and 0.08% iron (Fe).

Indentations on the top of the crossbar indicate that the axe was pounded on in use. The faces are relatively free of markings, but there is a bright band about 5 mm wide along the cutting edge, perhaps the result of cleaning in 1912. The sharp blade profile (see Figure 1.34) and the absence of wear marking on the blade are consistent with the use of this axe for cutting wood.

Metallographic sections at the end of the crossbar and the side of the blade at the cutting edge show that the copper-tin α solid solution is fully recrystallized but with composition gradients remaining from the cored, as-cast microstructure. Inclusions of copper sulfide (Cu_2S) are abundant (see Figure 1.19). The microstructure is free of the α – δ constituent that would ordinarily be present in this alloy due to coring. This constituent, if initially present, may have been dissolved during the annealing that recrystallized the bronze.

The elongation of the sulfide inclusions shows that the tip of the axe was hammered to attain its relatively slender profile (see Figure 1.20). After the annealing that recrystallized the bronze, additional forging deformed the recrystallized grains to a distance of about 20 mm back from the tip, and left the tip slightly work-hardened (see Table 1.17). The elongated sulfide inclusions are intersected by, rather than parallel to, the blade surface. This shows that the edge was further sharpened by grinding after the blade was forged. Either this end of the casting was free of porosity or the forging closed up any porosity that was present in the as-cast metal. The metal in the crossbar was forged enough to cause it to recrystallize, but not enough to eliminate the gross porosity in this part of the casting (Figure A1).

This axe was cast to shape, and was hammered all over to produce the approximately 5% deformation needed to induce recrystallization when annealed. The tip

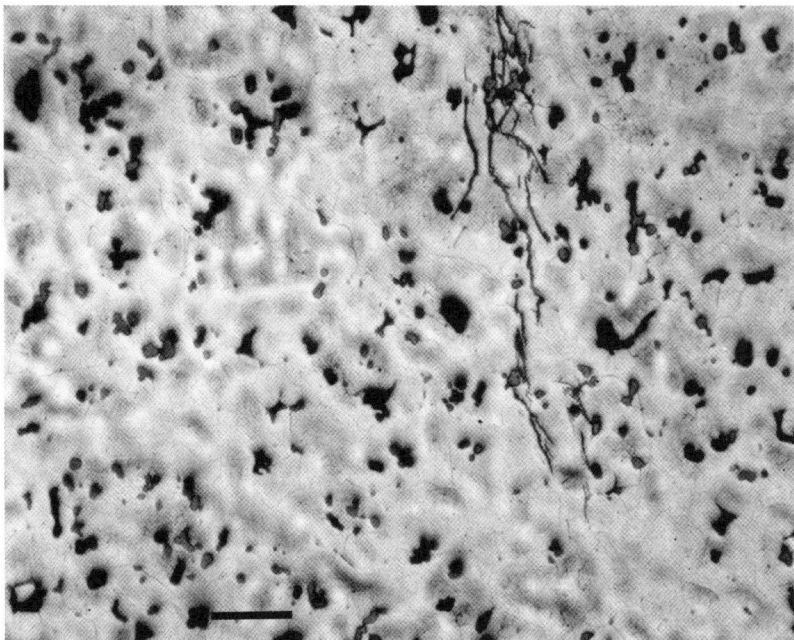

Figure A1. Section through the end of the crossbar of axe ANT.017898 showing the gross porosity and shrinkage cracks present in the bronze. Shading is due to residual gradients in tin concentration from the coring in the as-cast structure. Hydrogen peroxide etch; original magnification 100×. Length of scale bar 0.1 mm.

was forged to a profile slim enough to make this a useful tool for cutting wood, and was left in the slightly work-hardened condition. Its hardness was further enhanced by the high tin content of the alloy. This seems to be a purpose-designed tool that could be hafted for use as an axe and, as the indentations on the top of the crossbar show, was pounded on when used as a handheld tool.

ANT.017899 "T" Axe

This axe (Figure A2) is unusual in its large width in comparison to its length, the low tin content of the bronze (0.6%), and its somewhat misshapen appearance. The bottom edge is nicked and seems to have been sharpened by rubbing on a rough stone surface. The top of the crossbar was indented after the anneal that recrystallized the bronze, as is shown by the strain-line markings in the metal near the top of the axe (Figure A3). Examination of the section of the end of the crossbar shows extensive porosity in the center part of the casting.

This axe was cast to shape, then forged all over to attain at least 5% deformation, and annealed to recrystallize the bronze. The crossbar was pounded on in subsequent use. The appearance of the working edge suggests that this axe may have been used in food preparation rather than in work on wood or stone.

APPENDIX A   193

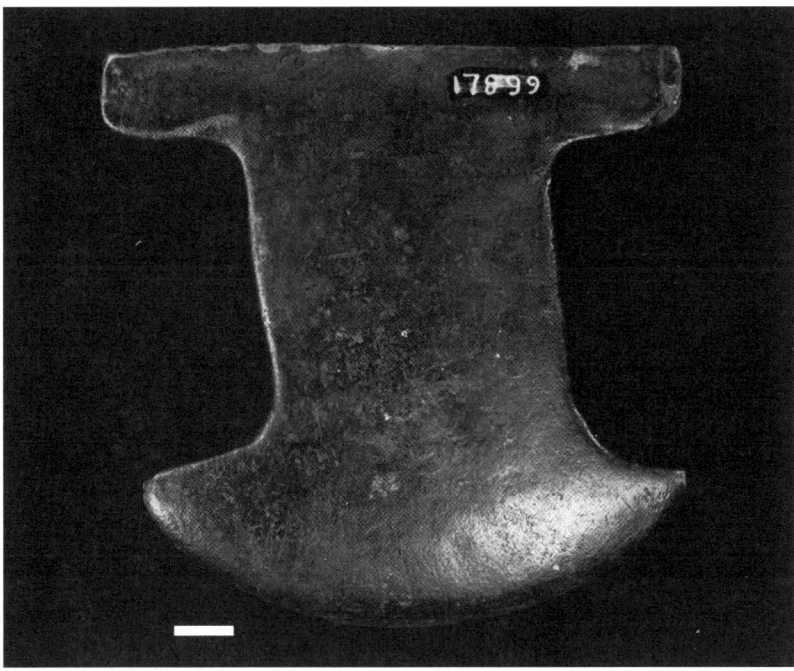

FIGURE A2. Axe, ANT.017899, 95 × 91 mm. Photographed in 1982. Length of scale bar 1 cm.

FIGURE A3. Strain lines and distortion of the annealing twins near the top of the crossbar of axe ANT.017899 show that the axe was hammered on. Original magnification 200×. Length of scale bar 0.1 mm.

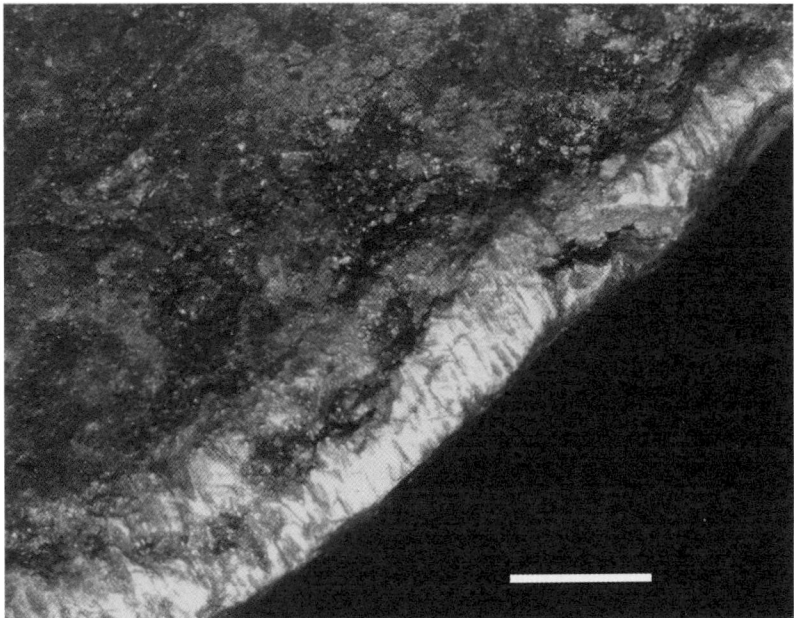

FIGURE A4. Hard use has formed a striated lip and broken loose fragments of bronze from the edge of axe ANT.017900. Original magnification 15×. Length of scale bar 1 mm.

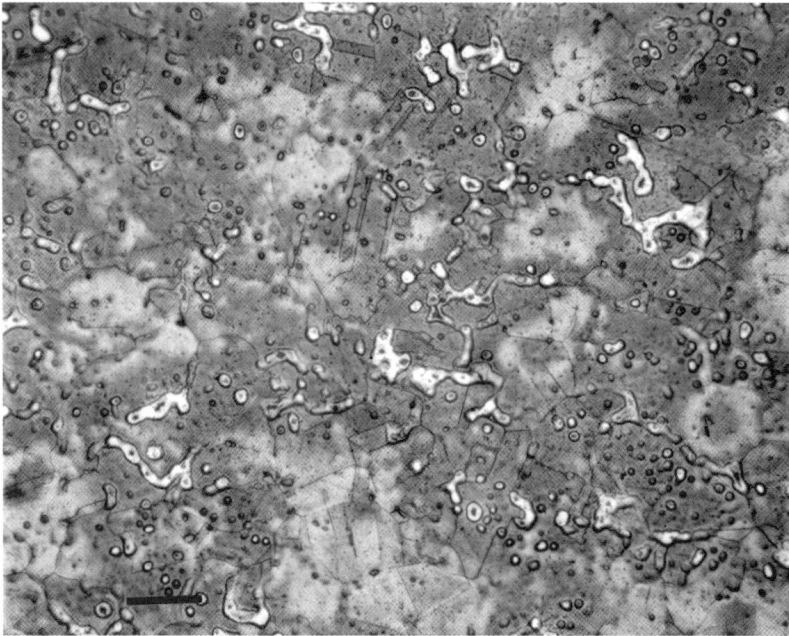

FIGURE A5. Microstructure of metal 15 mm back from the edge of axe ANT.017900. Coring in the as-cast structure has formed solute concentration gradients revealed by shading developed by the hydrogen peroxide etch. Original magnification 100×. Length of scale bar 0.1 mm. See also Plates 2 through 6.

ANT.017900 "T" Axe

Hiram Bingham purchased this axe in 1911 near Rosalina on the Urubamba River, about 100 km from Machu Picchu. Foote and Buell (1912) drilled metal from the top of the axe for analysis, ground the metal adjacent to the drill hole, milled three recesses on one side for hardness measurements, and polished one of these recesses to examine the microstructure. Their analysis showed that the bronze is composed of 93.7% copper (Cu), 5.6% tin (Sn), 0.6% silver (Ag), and 0.11% sulfur (S). Results of a microprobe analysis are given in Table 1.7. The silver content is unusual among the bronzes in the collection.

Pounding on the top of the crossbar, probably with hammerstones, left the surface heavily indented. The edge of the blade is blunt (see Figure 1.40) with a lip turned over at the edge (Figure A4). Striations cut into the lip show sliding contact with a rough stone surface. Additional long striations made by chip formation are present on the axe face. The corner of the blade has been broken off by a brittle fracture.

Evidence that this axe has seen hard use is found in the micrographs of the edge of the blade and the end of the crossbar. The lower part of the blade has started to split by the formation of cracks running up the section (see Figure 1.40 and Plate 5). Strain lines are present in the metal 10 mm back from the blade tip, but are no longer evident 15 mm back from the tip.

The bronze is fully recrystallized (see Plate 3). Particles of copper sulfide (Cu_2S) and shrinkage porosity are present throughout the structure (see Plate 6). Lack of elongation of these inclusions shows that the tip of the blade was not forged to shape. The steep hardness gradient behind the tip (see Table 1.17) resulted from use of the tool rather than from work-hardening the blade before use. All of this evidence shows that this axe was lightly forged and annealed before use.

Hydrogen peroxide and ferric chloride etches as well as Klemm's tint reveal strong concentration gradients retained from the coring in the as-cast microstructure (Figure A5 and Plates 2, 3, and 4) The constituents present in the cored zones were determined with a series of microprobe measurements across one of the darkened areas:

	As	S	Ag	Sn	Cu
Average composition	1.1%	0.2%	1.1%	6.2%	91.0%
Edge of cored zone	0.85	0.0	1.14	4.77	93.2
Middle of dark zone	1.86	0.0	2.60	8.92	86.3
Bright core	2.25	0.0	4.44	11.49	81.8

The bright core visible in Plate 4 is a separate microstructural constituent, since the concentration of silver and tin at the center of the cored zones exceeded the solubility of these elements in copper. Other silver- and tin-rich particles present in the structure have the following compositions:

	Cu	Sn	Ag	As
Silver-rich	6.8%	9.4%	82.3%	1.1%
Tin-rich	64.9	31.5	3.0	0.5

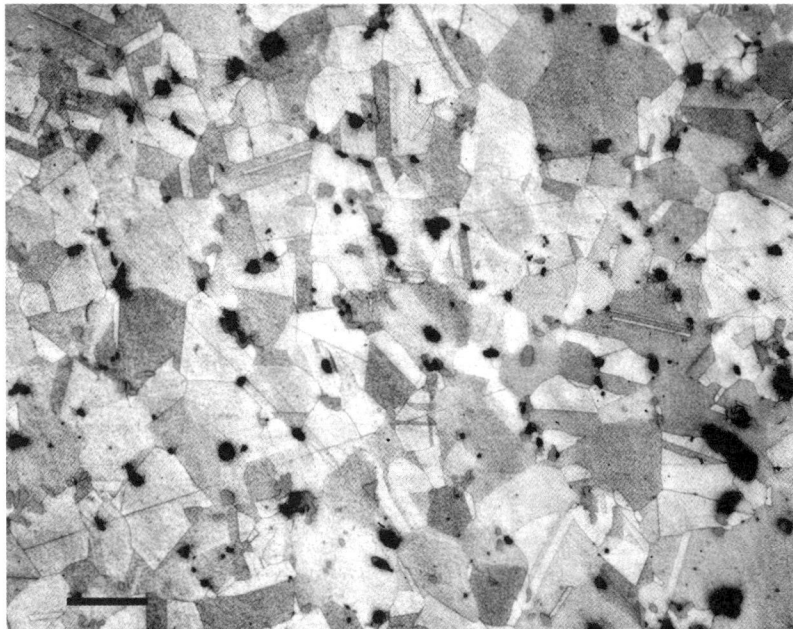

FIGURE A6. Microstructure of a section near the center of the end of the crossbar of axe ANT.017902 showing that the bronze is recrystallized and contains much porosity. Original magnification of 100×. Length of scale bar 0.1 mm.

FIGURE A7. Microstructure at the top surface of the crossbar of axe ANT.017902 showing the deformation of the metal at this surface. Original magnification 100×. Length of scale bar 0.1 mm.

We interpret this axe as a tool used in stone masonry. The silver content, which is not large enough to influence the mechanical properties, is probably an accidental impurity. Its presence in this one axe is consistent with the evidence that Inca artisans used metal from many different sources.

ANT.017902 "T" Axe

This axe (see Figure 1.3) had the typical 5% tin bronze composition. The top surface is heavily indented by hammer blows that have turned over a lip at the edge. The ends of the crossbar are also indented, perhaps from being used to hammer with. The edge of the blade is blunt and deeply indented (see Figure 1.35) with part of its edge turned over from impact with a rough rock surface. An incipient crack has started to form at one end of the blade. Continued use of the tool would have resulted in a breakage of the blade similar to that in axe ANT.017900.

A metallographic section at one end of the crossbar showed that the bronze is fully recrystallized and has a high level of porosity in the interior of the section (Figure A6). Grains within a millimeter of the top surface contain strain lines that resulted from the hammering that indented the top of the bar (Figure A7).

This axe was cast to shape and finished by light forging, followed by annealing that recrystallized the bronze. It was probably used in stone masonry.

ANT.017907 Chisel

This chisel (see Figure 1.4) has the typical bronze composition of 6% tin. The top has been heavily indented by hammer impacts that have caused some lateral flow of the metal. A crack near the top shows that the metal had been strained to near its limit of ductility. The edge is blunt and apparently flattened from use.

A metallographic section at the top corner shows fully recrystallized metal with abundant sulfide inclusions and sparse porosity. The porosity may be lower than in the "T" axes because of the smaller size of the chisel. The sulfide inclusions are undistorted, which indicates that the chisel was not shaped by forging. Hammering on the chisel while in use has heavily deformed the metal near the top surface (see Figure 1.38).

This chisel was cast to near its final shape, lightly forged, and then annealed to recrystallize the bronze. It was probably used in stone masonry work.

ANT.017908 Axe Head

The shape of this tool (Figure A8) and its nearly pure copper content, are unusual characteristics among the items found at Machu Picchu. It is free of significant surface markings, other than some striations parallel to the cutting edge (which suggest sharpening), and some small indentations in the edge. Small notches have been cut into the side near the top.

A metallographic section near the top shows recrystallized copper metal and the $Cu–Cu_2O$ eutectic structure. The larger inclusions contain a dark constituent identified as a copper-tin oxide by microprobe analysis (Figure A9).

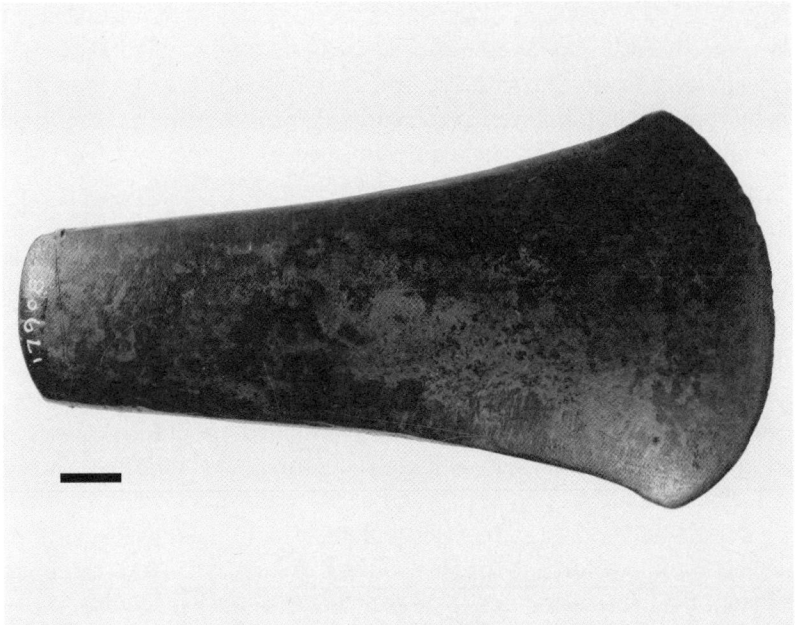

FIGURE A8. Axe head (ANT.017908), 120 × 61 mm. Photographed in 1982. Length of scale bar 10 mm.

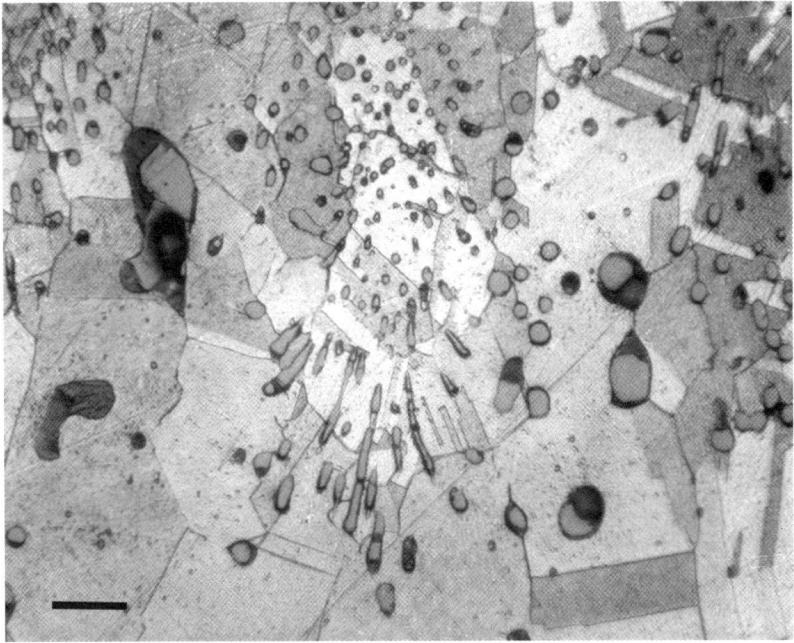

FIGURE A9. Microstructure at the top of axe ANT.017908 showing the Cu–Cu_2O eutectic structure. Original magnification 500×. Length of scale bar 0.02 mm.

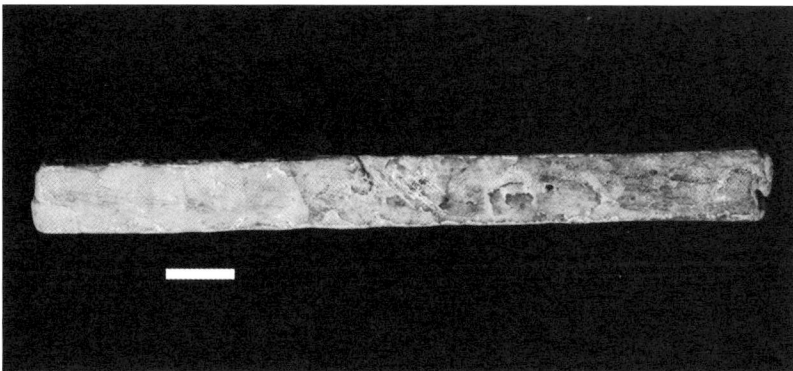

FIGURE A10. Bronze bar (ANT.017913), 197 × 10 mm. Photographed in 1982. Length of scale bar 1 cm.

After casting, this tool was lightly forged and then annealed to fully recrystallize the copper. Any use of the tool must have been for light work, since it left few traces on the metal surface and there are no slip lines in the metal near the top, where a chisel or axe would have been hammered on in heavy work.

ANT.017913 Hammered Bronze Bar

Indentations on the surface of this bar reproduce the shape of the hammerstone used in forging (Figure A10; see also Figure 1.26). The microstructure shows that the bronze has been annealed at least once during forging. The approximately 8:1 aspect ratio of the sulfide inclusions indicates substantial elongation of the bar in the forging operations. The annealing has eliminated the concentration gradients that would have been present in the as-cast stock. There are only faint traces of additional forging after the last anneal. Bands of inclusions have provided paths for corrosion to enter deeply into the metal.

This item is unusual in showing evidence of heavy forging and the abandonment of a work in progress. Most of the bronze artifacts, other than a few small pieces of sheet metal, received only light forging by the Machu Picchu metalsmiths.

ANT.017962 Llama Head Knife

This knife (see Figure 1.13) has a bronze blade and stem surmounted by a cast-on head made of a copper-bismuth-tin alloy. Mathewson took drillings from the stem for chemical analysis, finding that the bronze contains 3% tin with a trace of silver and sulfur. The sections that he cut through the top of the stem and the head were available for reexamination. The microstructure of the stem shows the bronze is recrystallized and retains composition gradients inherited from the coring in the as-cast structure (see Figure 1.23).

The microstructure of the head consists of two constituents (Figure A11). The dendrites have a composition of 90% copper and 10% tin. The interdendritic spaces

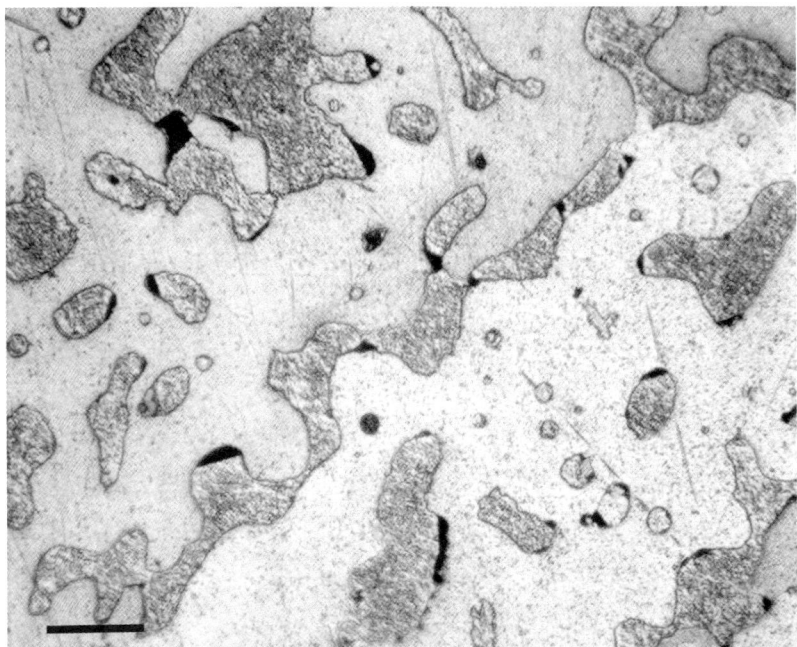

Figure A11. Microstructure of the head of knife ANT.017962. The knife head has an as-cast structure consisting of grains of copper-tin solid solution having a dendritic structure. The filling in the interdendritic spaces is a bismuth-copper alloy. Ferric chloride etch; original magnification 500×. Length of scale bar 0.02 mm.

are filled with an alloy composed of 93% bismuth and 7% copper. Since copper is not soluble in bismuth the copper appears as a separate constituent within the bismuth matrix (Figure A12).

The stem of the knife was cast, lightly forged, and annealed. It was placed in a clay mold and the head cast onto the stem. As the copper-tin-bismuth used for the head cooled, copper-tin dendrites formed at high temperature with the liquid bismuth becoming trapped between the dendrite arms. The pouring operation sufficiently intermixed the two immiscible liquids so that there was no gravity segregation. Because the interdendritic spaces were not interconnected, the bismuth could not drain away. The solid alloy has a distinctive color, lighter than that of bronze. Attaining this color may have been the reason for the selection of this unusual alloy.

ANT.017964 Chisel

Mathewson's chemical analysis showed that this chisel is made of bronze containing 3.7% tin. The cutting edge is heavily indented, upset, and in places turned over from hard use. Striations on the sides indicate that the chisel was inserted deeply into a stone work piece. However, there are no indentations on the top of the chisel such as would be left by pounding on it.

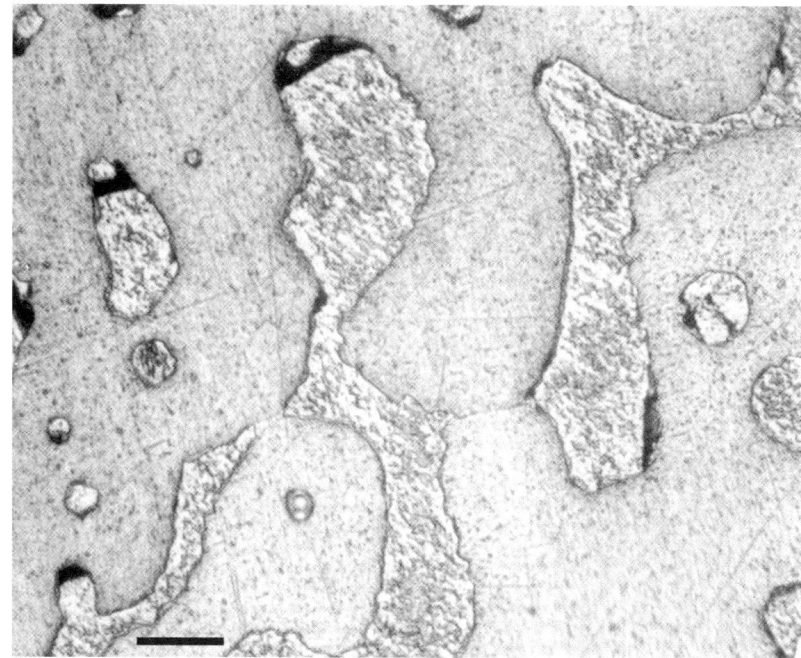

FIGURE A12. Microstructure of the head of knife ANT.017962 at higher magnification showing the two constituents of the copper-bismuth alloy. Ferric chloride etch; original magnification 1000×. Length of scale bar 0.01 mm.

Mathewson found an unusual microstructure in this chisel. Small grains with strain lines are intermixed with large, undeformed grains (see Figure 1.22). He interpreted this as evidence that the tip of the chisel was hot-forged to shape. To test this hypothesis he did a laboratory study of hot-forging using metal taken from the side of the chisel, and was able to duplicate the structure shown in Figure 1.22. The maker of the chisel hot-forged a zone extending less than 10 mm back from the tip. Elsewhere the maker hammered the metal enough so that it would recrystallize when heated to annealing temperature, but not enough to distort the sulfide inclusions in the metal.

ANT.017966 Chisel

This chisel (Figure A13) is made of bronze containing 5.5% tin. Its top was broken off sometime before it was found. This left a rough fracture surface with no evidence of plastic flow. The faces of the chisel are deeply gouged in the longitudinal direction. Finer, transverse striations at the tip show that the tool was sharpened by rubbing it on a rough stone surface. The center plane of the chisel is twisted to an angle of about 12° from top to bottom.

Reexamination of the side of the chisel that Mathewson had smoothed and polished showed abundant sulfide inclusions and porosity. The inclusions are un-

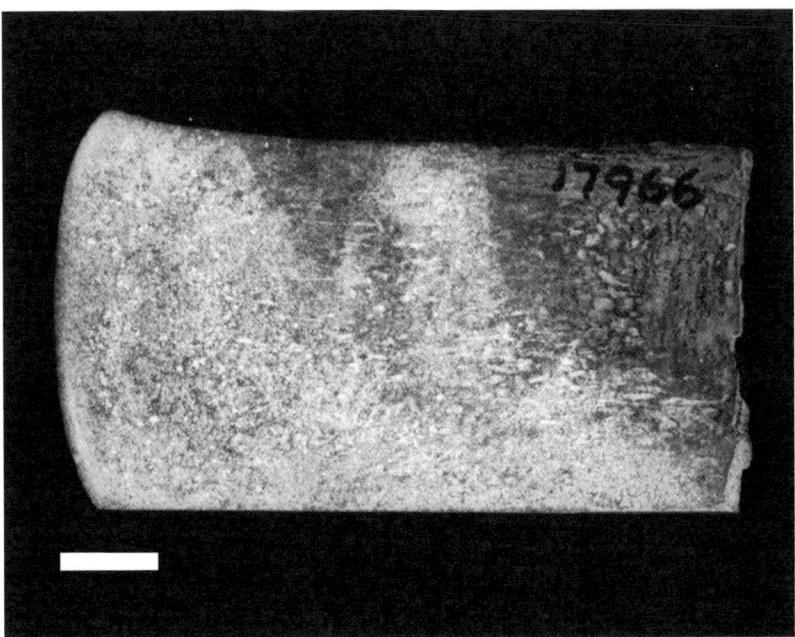

Figure A13. Chisel (ANT.017966), 69 × 40 mm. Photographed in 1982. Length of scale bar 1 cm.

deformed except in a band about 1 mm thick at the tip; here they are elongated in a direction perpendicular to the edge. This shows that the tip of the chisel was forged to shape.

It appears that this chisel was used for splitting rock. At some time it was twisted, as in an attempt to force open a fracture in the work piece, and then broken.

ANT.017967 "T" Axe

The copper and 4% tin alloy used to make this axe (Figure A14) contains about 0.4% each of silver and sulfur. As found, one corner of the blade had been broken off. The fracture was brittle.

The section that Mathewson cut from one end of the crossbar was repolished and etched (Figure A15). The bronze is recrystallized, and a few of the grains contain strain lines. Traces of the coring present in the original casting are visible in the micrograph. There are many shrinkage cracks as well as sulfide inclusions in the metal. Cracks like these are probably responsible for the brittle fracture of the bronze at the corner of the blade tip.

ANT.017969 Broken Axe Blade

This is interpreted as the blade of a "T" axe broken off just below the crossbar (Figure A16). It is made of 5% tin bronze. Surface markings left by abrasion that cut chips from the bronze show that the edge was sharpened by rubbing against rough

PLATE 1

Microstructure of the interior of the copper-silver alloy headband ANT.017872 showing the elongation of the original copper-rich dendrites resulting from the heavy forging used to convert a cast blank plate into a thin strip. No etch; original magnification 700×. Length of scale bar 0.05 mm. (Compare Figure 1.25.)

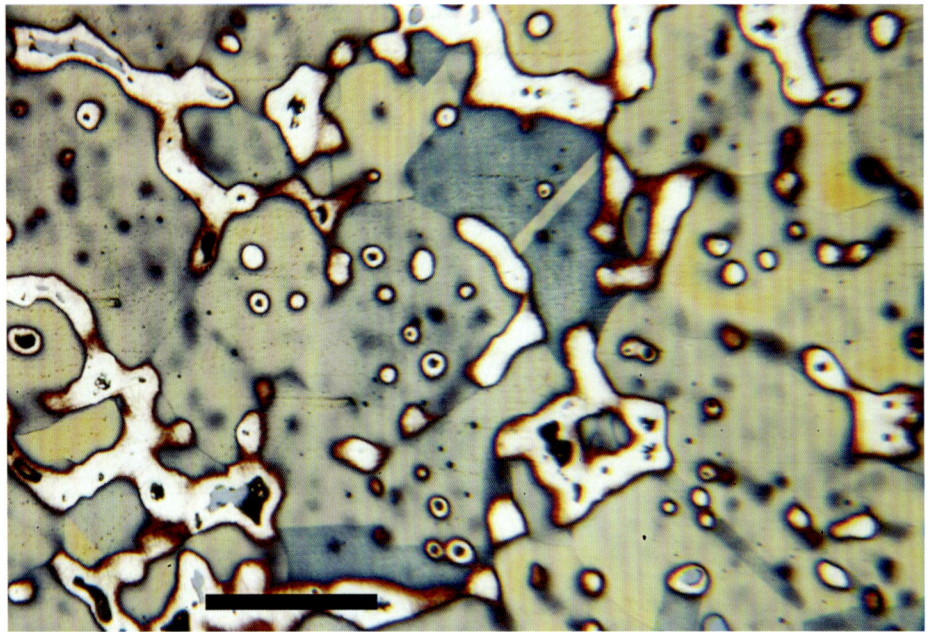

Plate 2

Microstructure of metal 15 mm back from the edge of "T" axe ANT.017900. The specimen was treated with Klemm's stain to better reveal the composition gradients within the alloy. Original magnification 337×. Length of scale bar 0.05 mm. (Compare Figure A5.)

Plate 1

Microstructure of the interior of the copper-silver alloy headband ANT.017872 showing the elongation of the original copper-rich dendrites resulting from the heavy forging used to convert a cast blank plate into a thin strip. No etch; original magnification 700×. Length of scale bar 0.05 mm. (Compare Figure 1.25.)

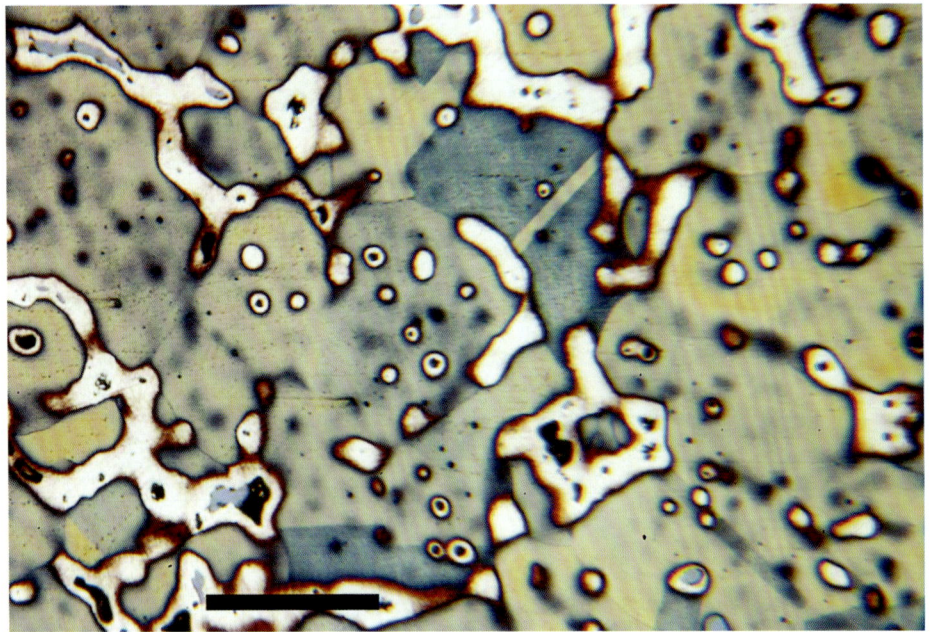

Plate 2

Microstructure of metal 15 mm back from the edge of "T" axe ANT.017900. The specimen was treated with Klemm's stain to better reveal the composition gradients within the alloy. Original magnification 337×. Length of scale bar 0.05 mm. (Compare Figure A5.)

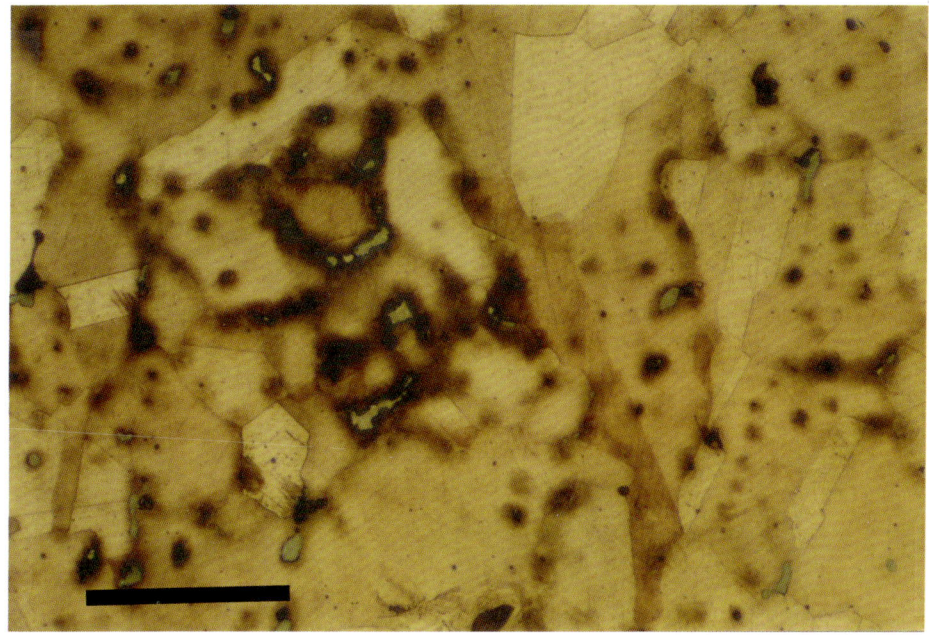

Plate 3

Microstructure of metal 15 mm back from the edge of "T" axe ANT.017900. Composition gradients resulting from coring as the bronze solidified from the melt are shown as color gradients. Light gray spots are sulfide inclusions. Ferric chloride etch; original magnification 300×. Length of scale bar 0.1 mm.

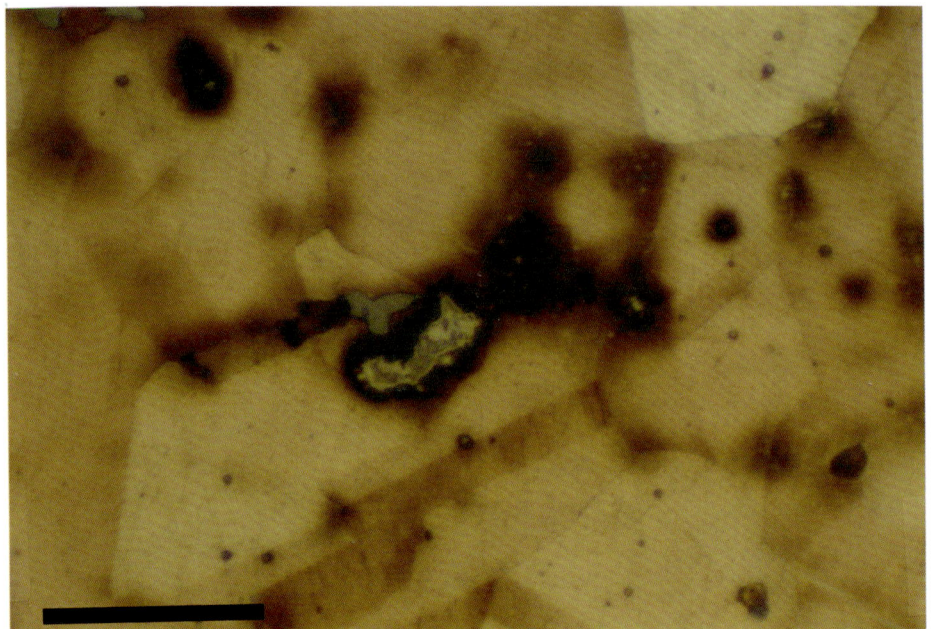

Plate 4

Microstructure of metal 15 mm back from the edge of "T" axe ANT.017900. The gray area is a sulfide inclusion. The bright area in the center of the dark staining is a separate constituent enriched in arsenic, silver, and tin. Ferric chloride etch; original magnification 700×. Length of scale bar 0.05 mm.

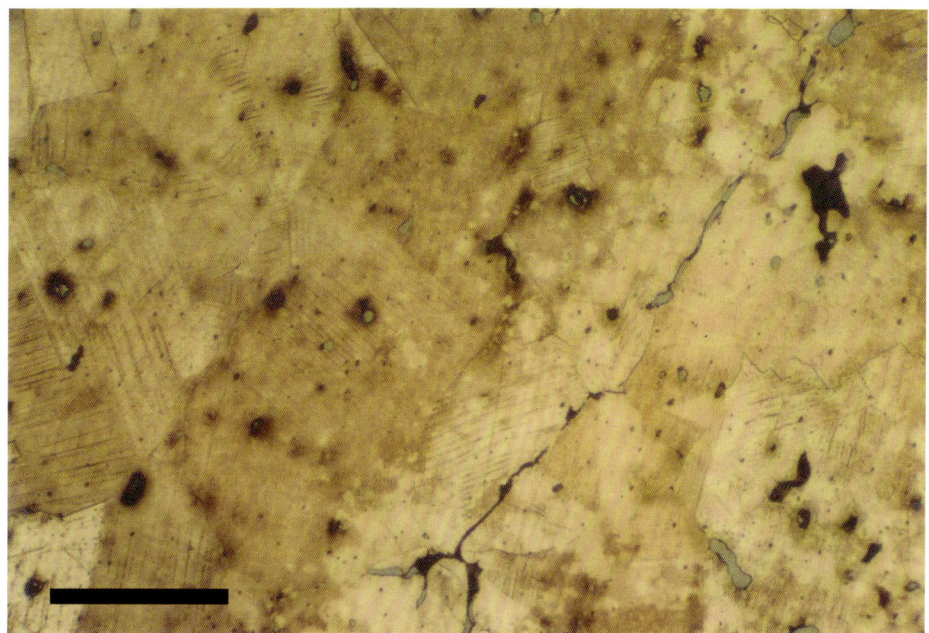

PLATE 5

Microstructure of metal 15 mm back from the edge of "T" axe ANT.017900. A crack following a line of sulfide inclusions and voids weakens the bronze. Ferric chloride etch; original magnification 300×. Length of scale bar 0.1 mm.

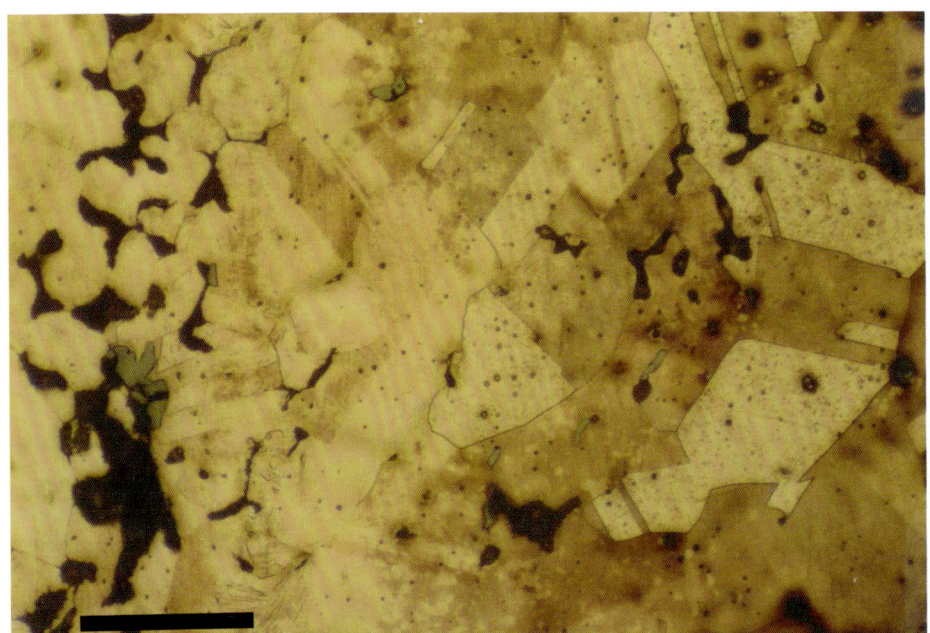

PLATE 6

Microstructure of metal 20 mm back from the edge of "T" axe ANT.017900. Shrinkage porosity is present. Ferric chloride etch; original magnification 300×. Length of scale bar 0.1 mm.

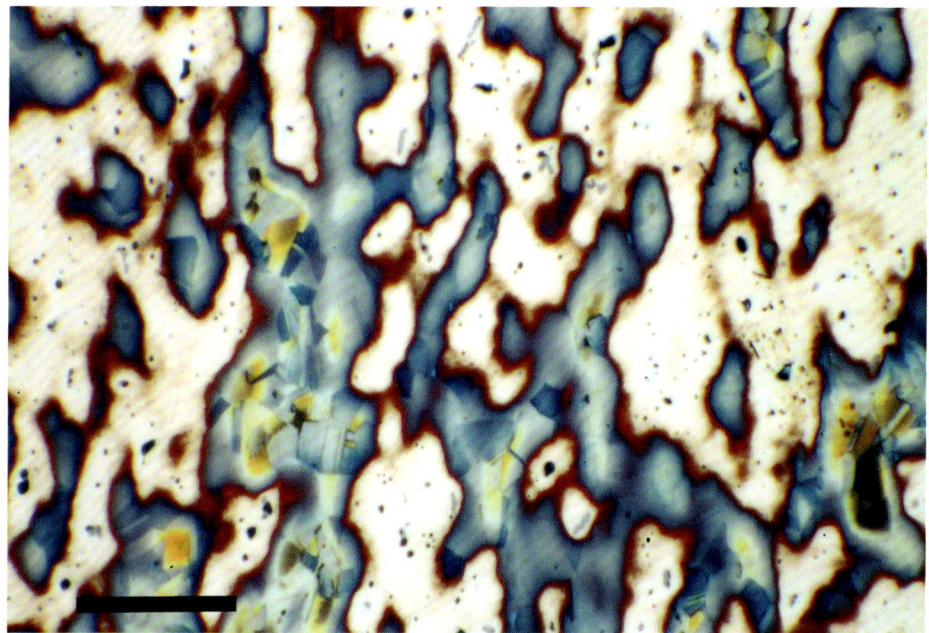

PLATE 7

Microstructure of bronze 5 mm back from the tip of chisel ANT.017975. The specimen was treated with Klemm's stain to better reveal the composition gradients within the alloy. Original magnification 210×. Length of scale bar 0.1 mm.

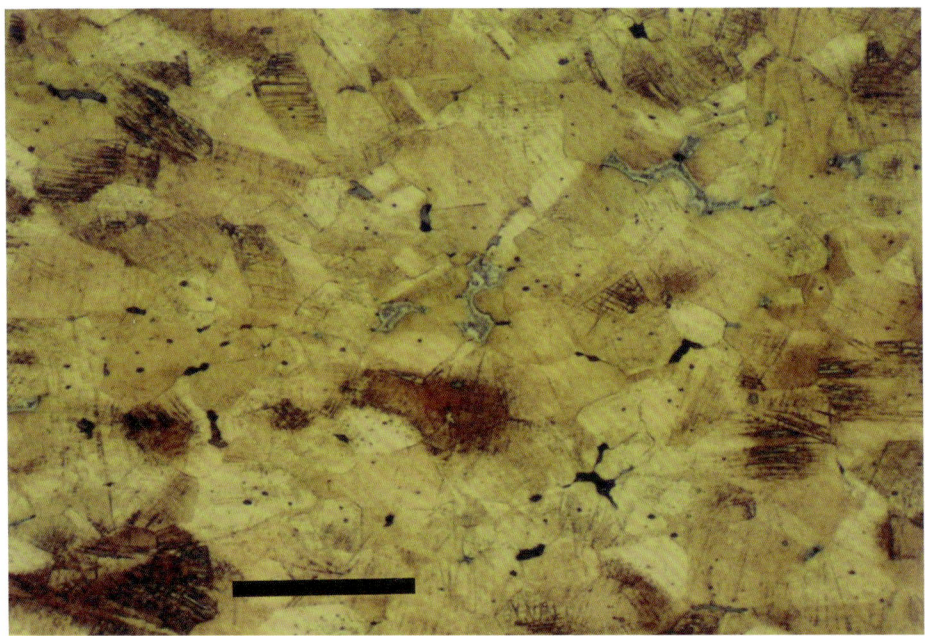

PLATE 8

Microstructure of bronze near the top of chisel ANT.017975 showing coring, small areas of the α–δ eutectoid, concentration gradients caused by coring, and small shrinkage porosity. Ferric chloride etch; original magnification 300×. Length of scale bar 0.1 mm. (Compare Figure A26.)

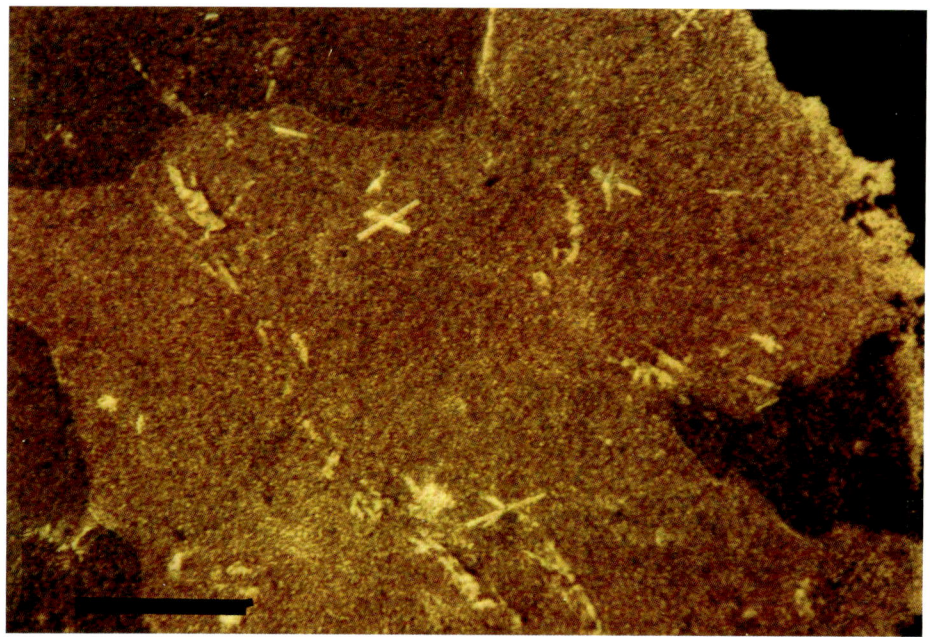

PLATE 9

Microstructure of tin sheet ANT.017982. The grain size is large. Bright features, often rectangular, are particles of hardhead. Original magnification 539×. Length of scale bar 0.05 mm.

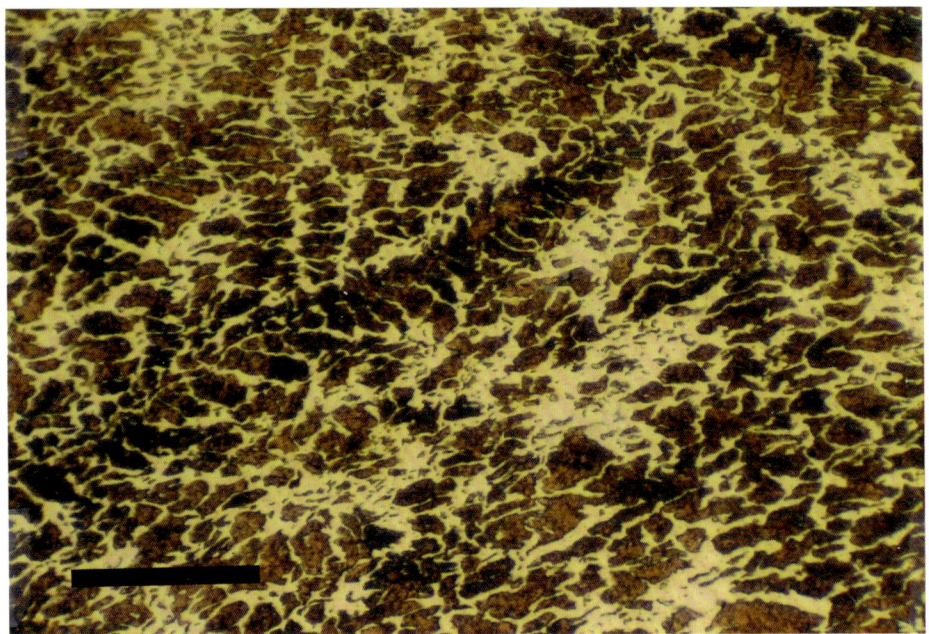

PLATE 10

Microstructure of copper-silver alloy forged bar ANT.018449 showing the silver-rich (bright) and copper-rich (dark) solid solutions. Traces of the original dendritic structure of the copper-rich phase remain in the structure. Ferric chloride etch; original magnification 300×. Length of scale bar 0.1 mm. (Compare Figure 1.24.)

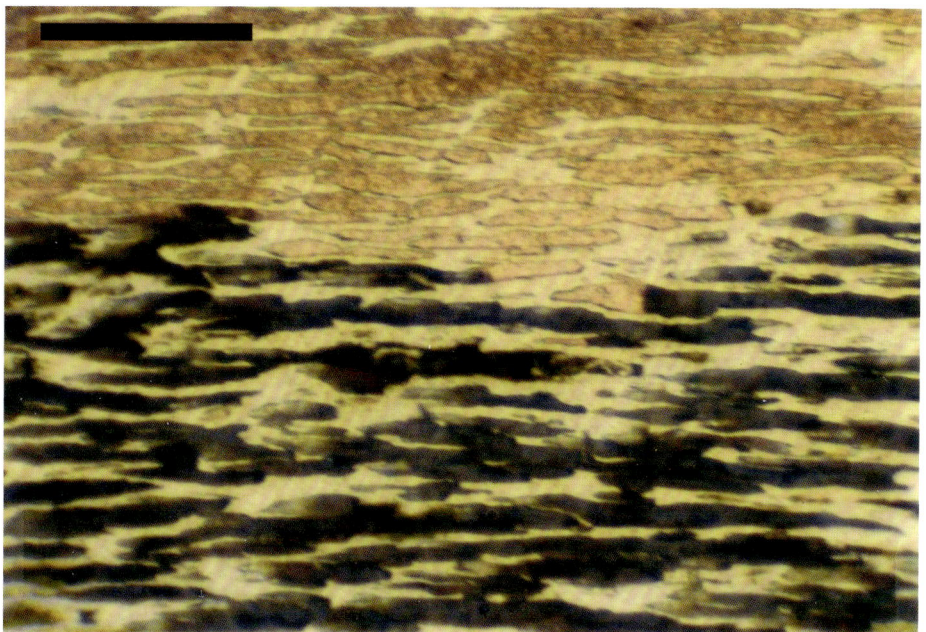

Plate 11

Microstructure of a section at the surface of copper-silver alloy forged bar ANT.018449. Forging has elongated the structure at the surface of the bar. Subsequent treatment has preferentially removed the copper-rich phase near the surface. No etch; original magnification 700×. Length of scale bar 0.05 mm. (Compare Figure 1.32.)

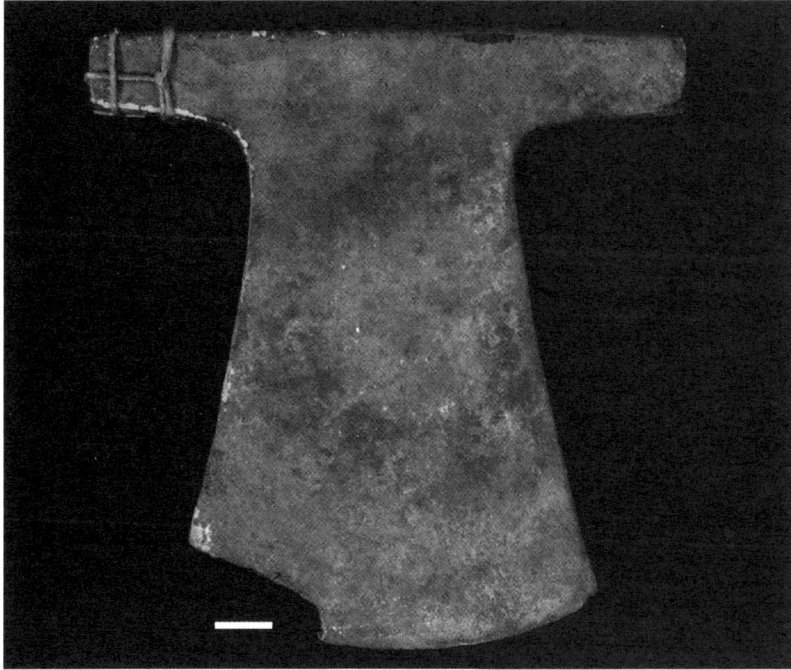

FIGURE A14. Axe (ANT.017967), 103 × 100 mm. Photographed in 1982. Length of scale bar 1 cm.

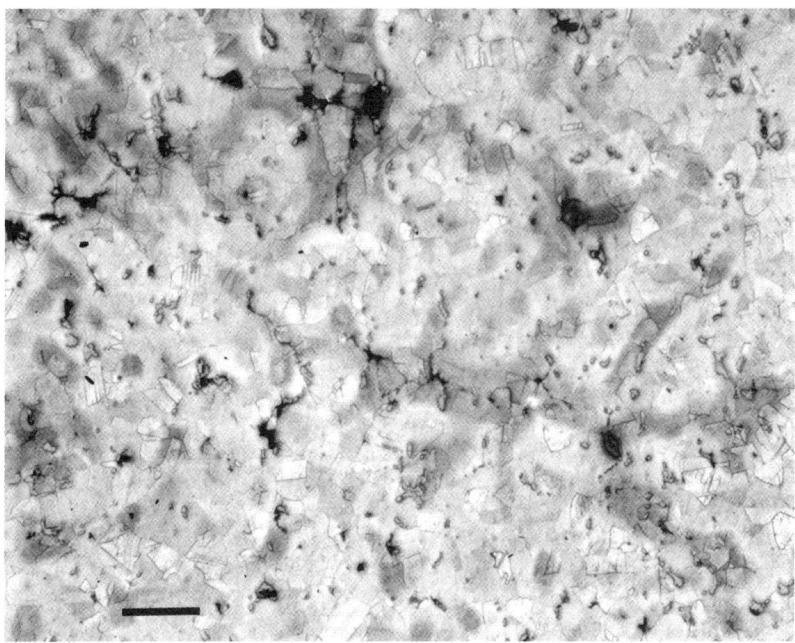

FIGURE A15. Microstructure at the end of the crossbar of axe ANT.017967 showing voids caused by shrinkage and solute concentration gradients due to coring that formed during solidification of the casting. Ferric chloride etch; original magnification 100×. Length of scale bar 0.1 mm.

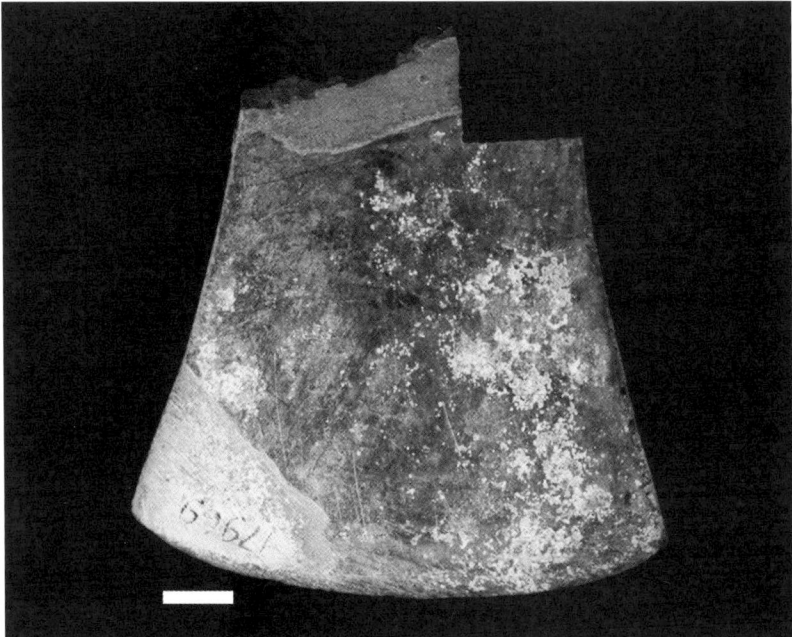

FIGURE A16. Broken axe blade (ANT.017969), 75 × 73 mm. Photographed in 1982. Length of scale bar 1 cm.

FIGURE A17. Photograph of 5 mm back from the edge of broken axe blade ANT.017969 showing striations caused by sharpening the blade. Original magnification 15×. Length of scale bar 1 mm.

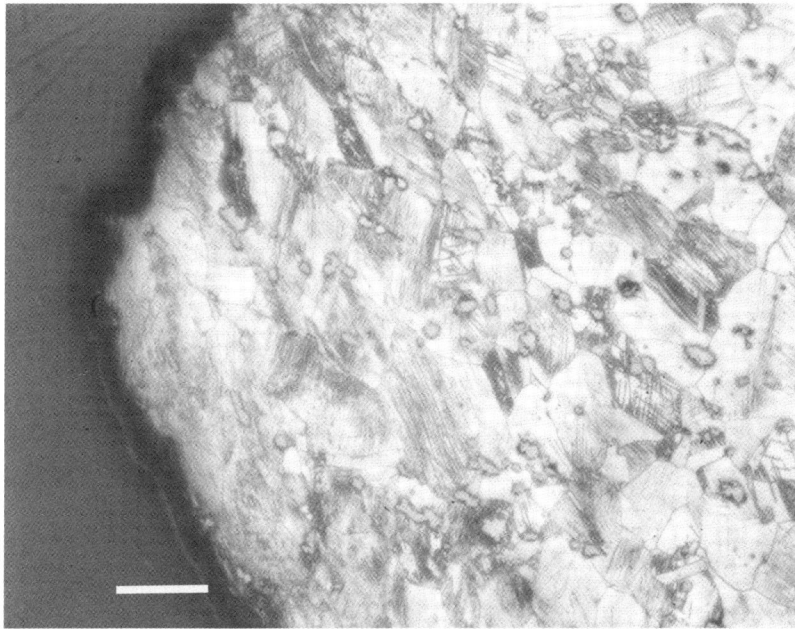

FIGURE A18. Microstructure of the tip of axe blade ANT.017969 showing sulfide inclusions and strain lines concentrated near the edge. Hydrogen peroxide etch; original magnification 100×. Length of scale bar 0.1 mm.

stone (Figure A17). However, the tip of the blade remained blunt and unhardened (Figure A18). It would not have been suitable for cutting wood.

Mathewson removed a piece, 7 × 9 mm, from the broken end at the top of the axe blade to use in his laboratory experiment. He found that this metal could be rolled to a rod 4 mm in diameter before the bronze began to crack as it passed through the rolls. The metallographic section at the tip of the blade (Figure A18) shows the presence of abundant sulfide inclusions. The magnified view (Figure 1.39) shows heavy strain lines throughout the metal near the edge of the blade. This tool was used in work, such as chipping stone, that deformed a zone of metal along its edge. Concentrated gross porosity in the upper part of the blade contributed to fracture, probably caused by an oblique blow while the blade was inserted in a recess in rock that an artisan was shaping.

ANT.017970 Lime Spoon
Mathewson cut sections through the head and the stem for study. He found that the head retained an as-cast structure, while the stem had been forged and annealed. His chemical analysis showed that the bronze has a relatively high 13% tin content. Bronze with more than 10% tin is considered difficult to forge. However, Mathewson was able to successfully hammer out a sample of metal taken from the stem of this lime spoon.

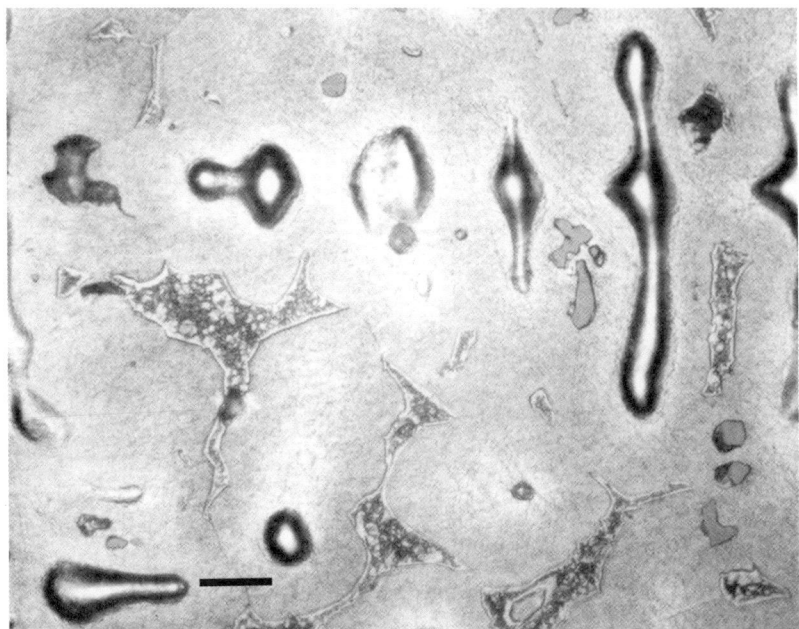

FIGURE A19. Microstructure of the head of lime spoon ANT.017970 showing sulfide inclusions and regions of α–δ eutectoid structure. Ferric chloride etch; original magnification 500×. Length of scale bar 0.02 mm.

FIGURE A20. Microstructure of the head of lime spoon ANT.017970 near its outer edge showing preferential corrosion of the α–δ eutectoid constituent. Hydrogen peroxide etch; original magnification 500×. Length of scale bar 0.02 mm.

FIGURE A21. Blade fragment (ANT.017974), 56 × 26 mm. Photographed in 1982. Length of scale bar 1 cm.

FIGURE A22. Microstructure showing the profile of broken axe blade ANT.017974. Ferric chloride etch; original magnification 15×. Length of scale bar 1 mm.

FIGURE A23. Enlarged view of the tip of the blade section of axe blade ANT.017974 (shown in Figure A22). Original magnification 50×. Length of scale bar 0.2 mm.

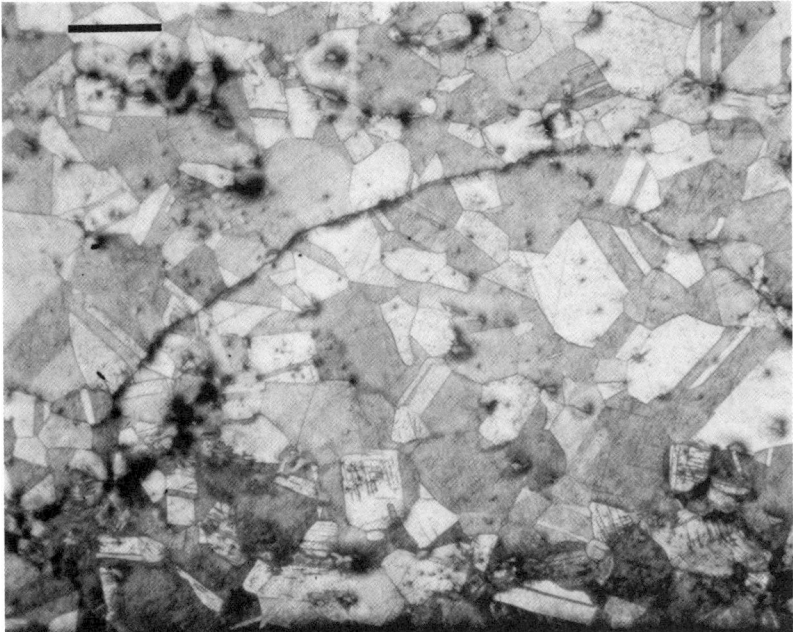

FIGURE A24. Microstructure of a section of broken axe blade ANT.017974 at 8 mm from the tip of the blade. Ferric chloride etch; original magnification 100×. Length of scale bar 0.1 mm.

FIGURE A25. Broken chisel (ANT.017975), 60 × 40 mm. Photographed in 1982. Length of scale bar 1 cm.

Repolishing and etching of the section that Mathewson took from the head shows that the cast structure consists of large grains with dendritic structure and coring. The most porosity is found in the thickest part of the casting. Because of the high tin content of the alloy, coring has resulted in formation of the brittle α–δ eutectoid constituent in the interdendritic spaces (Figure A19). Since this is not a continuous constituent in the microstructure, it does not embrittle the metal, as Mathewson demonstrated. Corrosion preferentially attacks the α–δ eutectoid constituent. The resulting cavities can then nucleate cracks that provide channels for further penetration of the corrosion reactions (Figure A20).

ANT.017974 Axe Blade Fragment

This blade (Figure A21) fragment carries surface markings showing that there had been some sharpening of its tip by rubbing it on rock. The tip is moderately sharp, and the edge does not appear to have been indented by use. The fracture is brittle, with multiple crack paths on the tensile side.

A section parallel to that cut by Mathewson shows the rounded shape of the blade tip (Figure A22) and that the tip profile was shaped in part by grinding, since the metal surface cuts across lines of inclusions. The lack of strain lines (Figure A23), coupled with the lack of any increase in hardness near the tip, suggests that

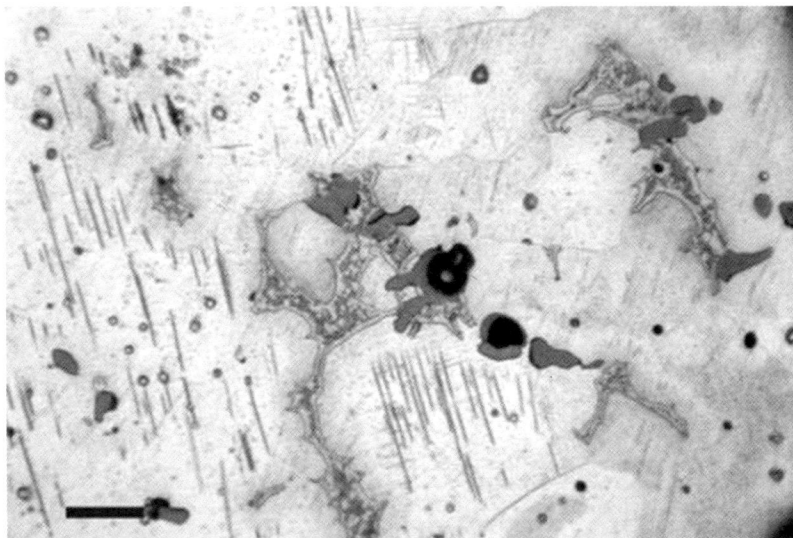

Figure A26. Section near the top of chisel ANT.017975 showing high porosity and the presence of islands of α–δ eutectoid resulting from coring in this bronze with a relatively high tin content. Original magnification 700×. Length of scale bar 0.02 mm. See also Plates 7 and 8.

the axe broke on the first attempt to use it. The failure was due to gross casting defects, such as the one shown in Figure A24.

ANT.017975 Broken Chisel

Although this chisel (Figure A25) seems to have been sampled by Mathewson, it cannot be identified with any of the artifacts described in his paper. The bronze has a slightly higher tin content, 7%, more than that found in most of the chisels and axes at Machu Picchu.

The edge of this chisel was sharpened by rubbing it on a rough stone surface, as shown in Figures 1.36 and 1.37, to produce a profile that could be used for splitting wood. The absence of indentations on the blade edge shows that this tool was not used for work on stone. Parts of the chisel faces, which have suffered little corrosion damage, reveal that the as-cast surface finish of the original casting is much smoother than would be the case if a sand mold rather than one made of clay had been used for the casting.

A metallographic section of the tip shows strain lines present in only a few of the grains. This finding indicates that, while the chisel was used as a tool, it was not used in heavy work, such as stone masonry. The chisel retains the tin concentration gradients that developed as a result of coring during solidification of the original casting (see Plate 7). Enough tin was concentrated in some interdendritic spaces to form patches of the α–δ eutectoid constituent (Figure A26; see also Plate 8). There is more porosity in this part of the chisel than there is near the tip. This may account for the failure of the chisel near its top rather than at the blade.

APPENDIX B

MICROGRAPH LOCATIONS

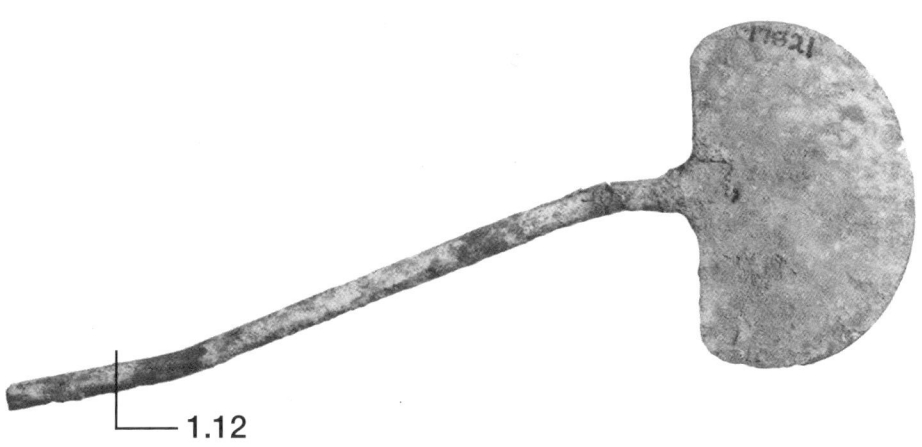

FIGURE B1. Shawl pin, ANT.017821; see Figure 1.12.

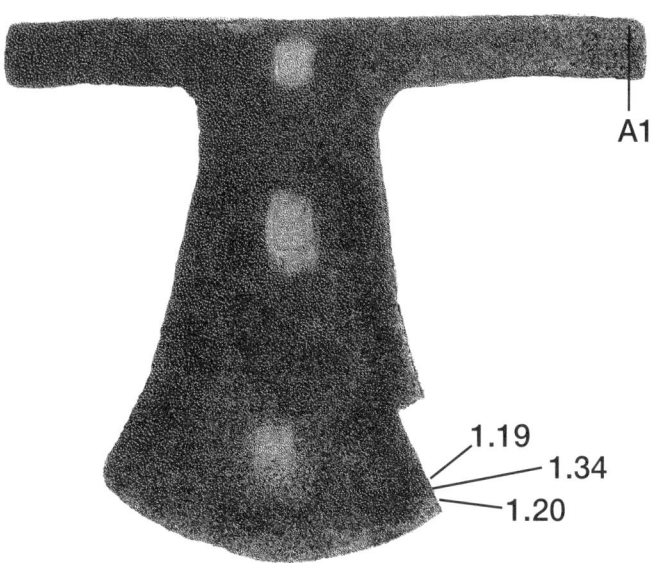

FIGURE B2. "T" axe, ANT.017898; see Figures 1.19, 1.20, 1.34, A1.

Figure B3. Axe, ANT.017899; see Figure A3.

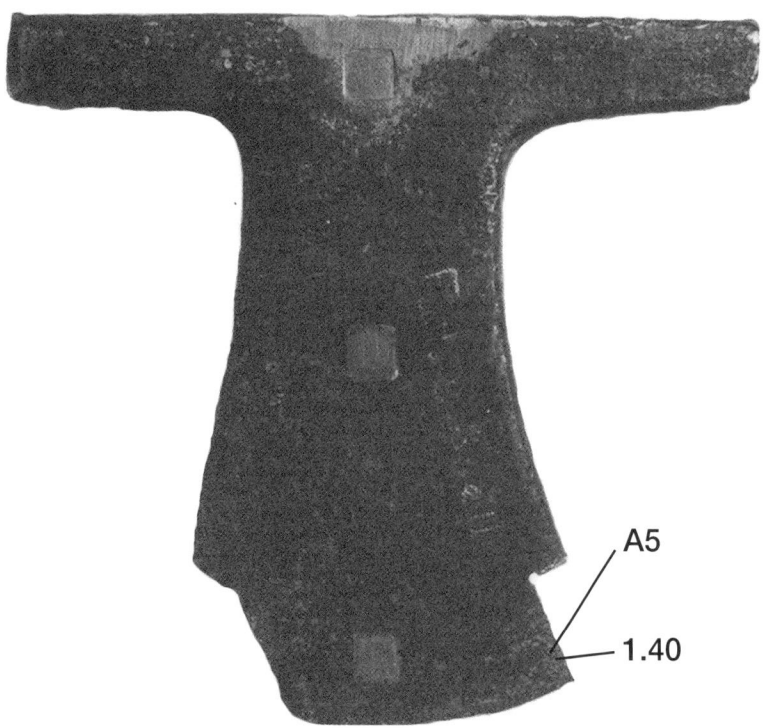

Figure B4. Axe, ANT.017900; see Figures 1.40, A5.

APPENDIX B 213

FIGURE B5. Axe, ANT.017902; see Figures 1.35, A6, A7.

FIGURE B6. Chisel, ANT.017907; see Figure 1.38.

Figure B7. Axe, ANT.017908; see Figures 1.10, A9.

Figure B8. Llama-head knife, ANT.017962; see Figures 1.23, A11, A12.

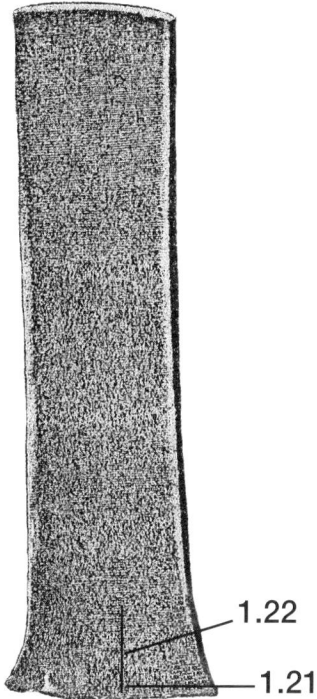

FIGURE B9. Chisel, ANT.017964; see Figures 1.21, 1.22.

FIGURE B10. "T" axe, ANT.017967; see Figure A15.

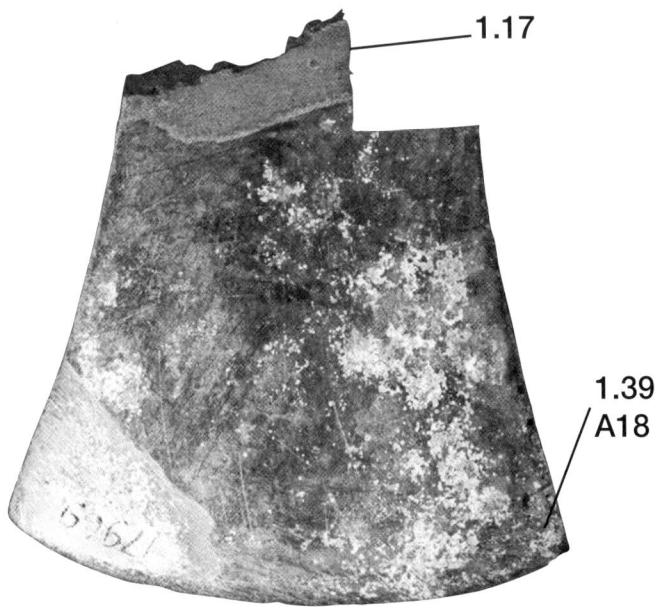

FIGURE B11. Axe blade, ANT.017969; see Figures 1.17, 1.39, A18.

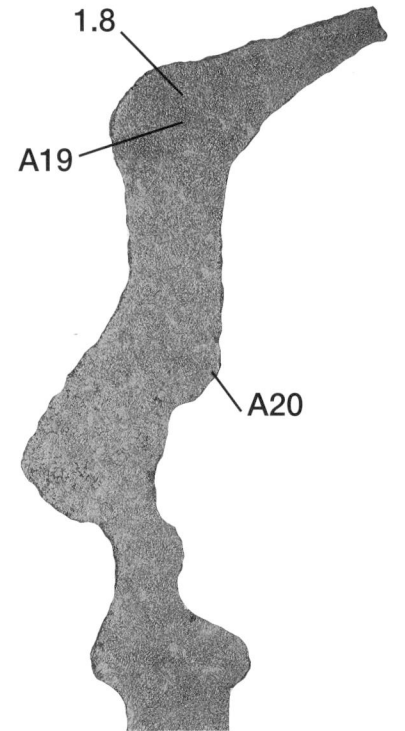

FIGURE B12. Bird-head lime spoon, ANT.017970; see Figures 1.8, A19, A20.

APPENDIX B 217

FIGURE B13. Broken axe blade, ANT.017974; see Figures 1.16, A22, A24.

FIGURE B14. Chisel, ANT.017975; see Figures 1.36, 1.37, A26.

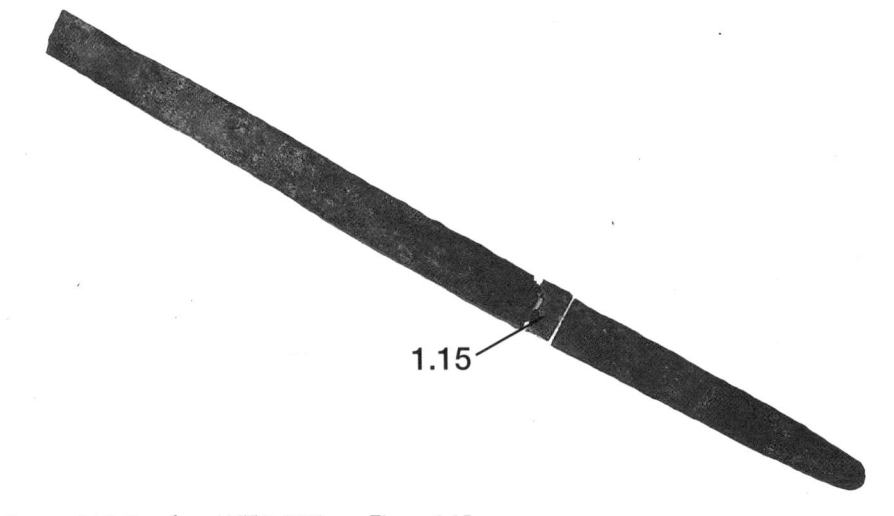

Figure B15. Crowbar, ANT.018478; see Figure 1.15.

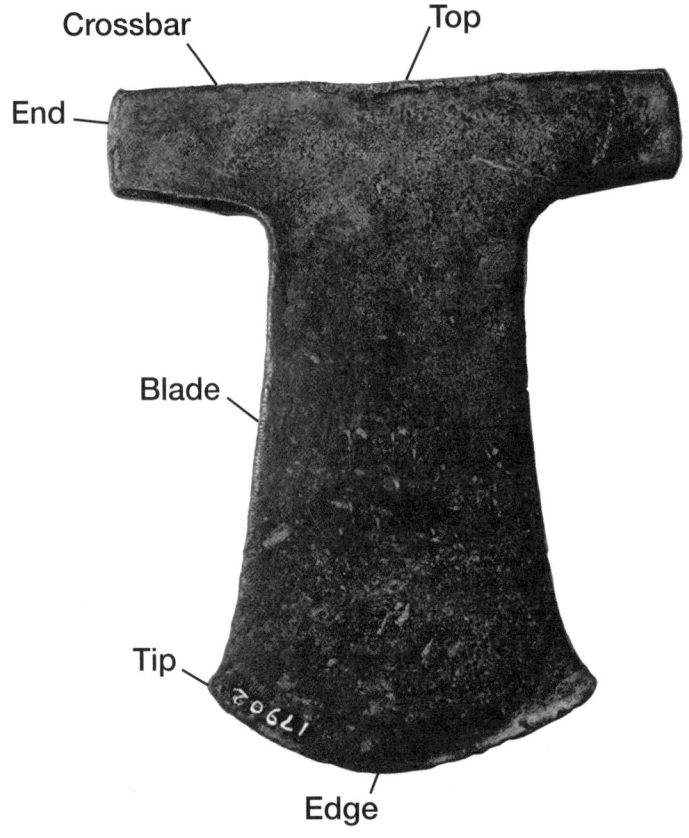

Figure B16. Description of the parts of an axe (ANT.017902).

CATALOG OF METAL ARTIFACTS IN THE COLLECTION OF THE 1911–1912 YALE PERUVIAN SCIENTIFIC EXPEDITIONS

See Section One, "Metal Artifacts from the 1911–1912 Yale Expeditions to Peru"

YPM Catalog Number ANT.016677; *Exhibit Catalog* 130
Description Tweezers
Dimensions 48 × 47 mm; *Weight* 3.4 g
Material Silver alloy
Source Grave 45

Rutledge (1984) reports this misclassified as a knife in the YPM catalog. Joined with ANT.017956 and ANT.018435, this makes a complete tweezers. Illustration: Eaton (1916, pl. II, item 11).

YPM Catalog Number ANT.016678
Description Tumi knife
Dimensions 64 × 41 mm; *Weight* 8 g
Material Bronze
Source Cave 14 (Eaton 1916, pl. II, item 1)

This is probably No. 22 in Mathewson's (1915) Table I. The knife appears to be unfinished, but striations at the cutting edge indicate both sharpening and use.

YPM Catalog Number ANT.016679a; *Exhibit Catalog Number* 135
Description Shawl pin
Dimensions 170 × 32 mm; *Weight* 9 g
Material Silver-copper alloy
Source Cave 38

ANT.016679b and ANT.016679c are similar in dimensions and shape suggesting a standardized product. Marks left from forging are abundant on the shaft.

YPM Catalog Number ANT.016679b; *Exhibit Catalog Number* 135
Description Shawl pin
Dimensions 145 × 36 mm; *Weight* 7 g
Material Silver-copper alloy
Source Cave 38 (Eaton 1916)

Illustration from Eaton (1916, pl. II, item 8)

YPM Catalog Number ANT.016679c
Description Shawl pin
Dimensions 167 × 31 mm; *Weight* 9 g
Material Silver-copper alloy
Source Cave 38 (Eaton 1916, pl. II, item 10)

YPM Catalog Number ANT.016680
Description Shawl pin
Dimensions 161 × 43 mm; *Weight* 15.1 g
Material Silver-copper alloy
Source Cave 29 (Eaton 1916)

Traces of the shaping of the originally rectangular section of the shaft to rounded form are well preserved.

YPM Catalog Number ANT.016681
Description Small pin
Dimensions 70 × 13 mm; *Weight* 2 g
Material Silver-copper alloy
Source Cave 37 (Eaton 1916)

Illustration from Eaton (1916, pl. II, item 5)

YPM Catalog Number ANT.016682
Description Earspool or pendant
Dimensions 22 × 15 mm; *Weight* 1.5 g
Material Bronze
Source Cave 37 (Eaton 1916)

This fragment may be from a pendant/bell like ANT.018427 and ANT.018428. Illustration: Eaton (1916, pl. II, item 3)

YPM Catalog Number ANT.016683
Description Lime spoon
Dimensions 73 × 7 mm; *Weight* 7 g
Material Bronze
Source Grave 26 (Eaton 1916)

This pin has a flat head and a semicircular loop at one end. Illustration: Eaton (1916, pl. I, item 8)

YPM Catalog Number ANT.016684
Description Tweezers
Dimensions 17 × 12 mm; *Weight* Approximately 1 g
Material Bronze
Source Cave 37 (Eaton 1916)

This tweezers is in poor condition. The arms have a shallower dish shape than other examples of tweezers in the collection. Illustration: Eaton (1916, pl. II, item 6)

YPM Catalog Number ANT.016685
Description Small knife
Dimensions 68 × 65 mm; *Weight* 28 g
Material Bronze
Source Cave 38 (Eaton 1916)

Described by Mathewson (1915) as No. 1 in his Table I; for analysis, see Table 1.5. Mathewson sectioned this knife through its center plane, and later reattached the halves with a copper insert and pins. He found that the thick sections retain their as-cast structure while the thinner parts had been lightly forged and the entire piece annealed. The absence of deformation makings in the metal around the hole shows that it was part of the original casting. This knife is of much more substantial construction than most in the collection, but does not seem to have been used for heavy work. Illustration: Eaton (1916, pl. II, item 7)

YPM Catalog Number ANT.017819
Description Shawl pin
Dimensions 231 × 60 mm; *Weight* 19.3 g
Material Bronze
Source Grave 63 (Eaton 1916:61)

This pin was relatively free of corrosion. The lower 66 mm of the shaft is broken. The head is about 0.5 mm thick. Marks of forging are present at the join of the stem and head; facets show how the stem was forged to a round cross section.

YPM Catalog Number ANT.017820; *Exhibit Catalog Number* 135
Description Shawl pin
Dimensions 235 × 59 mm; *Weight* 25.6 g
Material Silver alloy
Source No data

This pin is very similar to ANT.017838. The hole has a flat edge on one side and is beveled on the other, indicating that it was punched rather than drilled.

YPM Catalog Number ANT.017821
Description Shawl pin
Dimensions 197 × 70 mm; *Weight* 51.5 g
Material Silver alloy
Source No data

This pin was heavily encrusted with corrosion, and the end had been broken off the stem. Metallographic analysis was done on a small section taken from the stem. Analysis shows that the alloy falls on the silver-rich side of the eutectic composition.

YPM Catalog Number ANT.017822
Description Shawl pin
Dimensions 204 × 51 mm; *Weight* 15.1 g
Material Silver alloy
Source Cave 62 (Eaton 1916)

Part of the head, which is less than 0.5 mm thick, is missing; the shaft is faceted from forging.

YPM Catalog Number ANT.017823
Description Shawl pin
Dimensions 270 × 25 mm; *Weight* 37 g
Material Bronze
Source No data

This is No. 11 in Mathewson's Table I; see Table 1.5 for his analysis. He took samples from both the head and shaft. The shaft was subsequently reassembled with a threaded joint. He measured scleroscope hardness of 14 to 18 (HV 72 to 80), indicating lack of work-hardening.

His micrograph from the flattened end has recrystallized grains with some strain lines showing that there was further hammering after the last anneal. Since the sulfide particles are not elongated, the overall forging deformation was less than about 25%. The pin was cast to shape and finished by cold-forging with an anneal. The hole in the head is partially closed on one side by forging. Mathewson demonstrated that this is the side away from the anvil. This pin, along with ANT.017892 and ANT.017837, is one of a matched set of three.

YPM Catalog Number ANT.017824
Description Shawl pin, broken
Dimensions 55 × 37 mm; *Weight* 6.3 g
Material Silver alloy
Source No data

Part of the head of this pin had been broken off. A break in the stem revealed porosity at the center of the stem, which is marked with hammer indentations from forging.

YPM Catalog Number ANT.017825
Description Shawl pin
Dimensions 210 × 3.5 mm; *Weight* 17.6 g
Material Silver alloy
Source No data

Forging indentations are visible on the shaft. Much of the head is missing.

YPM Catalog Number ANT.017826
Description Shawl pin
Dimensions 112 × 27 mm; *Weight* 10.5 g
Material Silver alloy
Source No data

Forging marks and facets are present on the shaft.

YPM Catalog Number ANT.017827
Description Shawl pin
Dimensions 136 × 45 mm; *Weight* 26 g
Material Silver alloy
Source No data

An attached tuft of fiber is probably the remains of a string used to fasten the pin to a shawl.

YPM Catalog Number ANT.017828
Description Knob-head shawl pin
Dimensions 130 × 18 mm; *Weight* 15.5 g
Material Bronze
Source No data

Although heavily corroded, the remains of a knob rather than flat head survive.

YPM Catalog Number ANT.017829
Description Shawl pin
Dimensions 278 × 24 mm; *Weight* 39.6 g

Material Bronze
Source Eaton (1916) reported discovery of this pin in "Cave 68…it yielded a woman's bronze pin 27.7 cm in length"

This pin is a close match to ANT.017823 and ANT.017837. Hammer facets indicate that it was cast and given a final forging to shape.

YPM Catalog Number ANT.017830
Description Shawl pin
Dimensions 109 × 30 mm; *Weight* 8.4 g
Material Bronze
Source "Cave 13—a heavy bronze pin about eleven centimeters long had been interred with remains" (Eaton 1916)

Pieces have been broken from the top of the pin.

YPM Catalog Number ANT.017831; *Exhibit Catalog Number* 135
Description Shawl pin
Dimensions 100 × 28 mm; *Weight* 4.2
Material Silver alloy
Source Cave 76 (Eaton 1916:67)

Surface evidence shows that the shaft was hammered to shape and the hole in the head was punched.

YPM Catalog Number ANT.017832
Description Shawl pin
Dimensions 184 × 42 mm; *Weight* 14 g
Material Bronze
Source No data

This pin is heavily corroded, leaving little metal to study.

YPM Catalog Number ANT.017833; *Exhibit Catalog Number* 139
Description Shawl pin
Dimensions 156 × 19.5 mm; *Weight* 7.6 g
Material Bronze
Source No data

Limited corrosion makes forging facets at the join of the stem and head easily seen. Cast structure is seen along the shaft, as are striations from a smoothing operation. The hole in the head is slanted at a 25° angle.

YPM Catalog Number ANT.017834
Description Shawl pin
Dimensions 165 × 10 mm; *Weight* 13.1 g
Material Bronze
Source No data

The heavy layer of corrosion retains a bit of fiber and strong impressions of cloth.

YPM Catalog Number ANT.017835
Description Shawl pin
Dimensions 161 × 35 mm; *Weight* 25.9 g
Material Silver alloy
Source Cave 7A

This pin has a somewhat flattened top.

YPM Catalog Number ANT.017836
Description Shawl pin with celestial motif
Dimensions 58 × 17 mm; *Weight* 4.1 g
Material Bronze (87.55% copper, 12.5% tin)
Source No data

This pin, with its sun and moon decoration, is from the colonial period in Peru. The high tin content (see Table 1.5) gives it a distinctive yellow color.

YPM Catalog Number ANT.017837; *Exhibit Catalog Number* 139
Description Shawl pin
Dimensions Estimated 280 × 24 mm; *Weight* 40 g
Material Bronze
Source Alvistur collection

This pin appears to be nearly identical to ANT.017823 and ANT.017829.

YPM Catalog Number ANT.017838
Description Shawl pin
Dimensions 199 × 60 mm; *Weight* 22 g
Material Silver alloy
Source No data

The end of the stem of this pin has been broken off, so its original length was longer than 199 mm.

YPM Catalog Number ANT.017839; *Exhibit Catalog Number* 135
Description Shawl pin
Dimensions 300 × 80 mm; *Weight* 81.5 g
Material Silver alloy
Source Alvistur collection

Abrasions marks on the head suggest sharpening.

YPM Catalog Number ANT.017840; *Exhibit Catalog Number* 135
Description Shawl pin
Dimensions 222 × 46 mm; *Weight* 31 g
Material Silver alloy
Source No data

Facets left from the rounding of the shaft are well preserved. The upper end of the shaft near the head, which is circular, has an unusual decorative element worked into it.

YPM Catalog Number ANT.017841
Description Star-head pin
Dimensions 285 × 2.8 mm; *Weight* 33.9 g
Material Bronze
Source See Erdis (1912:37)

This pin is No. 3 in Mathewson's Table I. He removed a section of the stem at 115 mm from the point for chemical analysis (see Table 1.5), and subsequently reattached the pieces with a threaded joint. His micrographs show that the as-cast dendritic structure is retained at the head, while the metal in the stem has been forged and annealed. The pin and stem were cast as one piece. Like the shawl pins, the stem was subsequently shaped by hammering.

YPM Catalog Number ANT.017842; *Exhibit Catalog Number* 140
Description Shawl pin
Dimensions 150 × 20 mm; *Weight* No data
Material Bronze
Source Alvistur collection

The head of this pin is shaped as an *aryballos*. Data on it are lacking in the Rutledge (1984) compilation.

YPM Catalog Number ANT.017843; *Exhibit Catalog Number* 136
Description Shawl pin
Dimensions 162 × 68 mm; *Weight* 37.5 g
Material Silver alloy
Source Alvistur collection

The design of this pin, with its flat top and three triangular openings, is unique among the shawl pins. The shaft was made by rounding the original square, as-cast shape; the rounding is incomplete in several places.

YPM Catalog Number ANT.017844; *Exhibit Catalog Number* 139
Description Shawl pin
Dimensions 172 × 27 mm; *Weight* 45.4 g
Material Bronze
Source Alvistur collection

Numerous forge marks, the tapered hole, and a groove running the length of the shaft suggest that the artisan doing the final forge work on the casting for this rather heavy and unusual shawl pin left the task incomplete.

YPM Catalog Number ANT.017845; *Exhibit Catalog Number* 138
Description Large shawl pin
Dimensions 474 × 135 mm; *Weight* 336 g
Material Bronze
Source No data

This, along with ANT.017846, make a pair of nearly identical, unusually large shawl pins that show an exceptionally high standard of workmanship.

YPM Catalog Number ANT.017846; *Exhibit Catalog Number* 138
Description Large shawl pin
Dimensions 479 × 145 mm; *Weight* 373 g
Material Bronze
Source No data

See ANT.017845.

YPM Catalog Number ANT.017847; *Exhibit Catalog Number* 137
Description Shawl pin
Dimensions 234 × 110 mm; *Weight* 99 g
Material Bronze
Source Alvistur collection

The shaft of this pin, which has an unusually large head, retains marks from shaping by forging; the hole in the head is nearly semicircular and is off-center.

YPM Catalog Number ANT.017848; *Exhibit Catalog Number* 135
Description Shawl pin
Dimensions 321 × 78 mm; *Weight* 57 g
Material Silver alloy
Source No data

This pin has a spade-shaped head. Evidence of the manufacturing process remains at the junction of the head and shaft, where the metal has not been completely rounded and smoothed.

YPM Catalog Number ANT.017849; *Exhibit Catalog Number* 147
Description Pendant disc
Dimensions 110 × 95 mm; *Weight* 123 g
Material Bronze
Source No data

Although severely damaged by corrosion, this can be recognized as a disc similar to, but larger than, ANT.018480, and therefore may have been silver-plated.

YPM Catalog Number ANT.017850; *Exhibit Catalog Number* 144
Description Disc
Dimensions 90 × 90 mm; *Weight* 16 g
Material Silver alloy
Source Section 41A (Erdis 1912:57)

The hole in this thin disc suggests that it may have been made to attach to clothing. The silver alloy was sufficiently ductile to withstand folding and unfolding.

YPM Catalog Number ANT.017851
Description Tool, possibly unfinished
Dimensions 207 × 20 mm; *Weight* 35 g
Material Bronze
Source No data

This could be either a tool useful in shaping clay, as for molds for bronze or silver alloy castings, or an unfinished work piece.

YPM Catalog Number ANT.017852
Description Knife
Dimensions 97 × 91 mm; *Weight* 17 g
Material Bronze
Source Cave 10A

Unlike most of the knives found at Machu Picchu the shaft of this one ends in a hook rather than a loop.

YPM Catalog Number ANT.017853
Description Knife
Dimensions 125 × 107 mm; *Weight* 31 g
Material Bronze
Source Cave 6A

This is No. 23 in Mathewson's Table I. He took drillings from the side of the shaft for chemical analysis (see Table 1.5). Striations on the blade suggest it was sharpened; nicks in the edge suggest use.

YPM Catalog Number ANT.017854
Description Knife
Dimensions 80 × 45 mm; *Weight* 14.5 g
Material Bronze
Source Section 44A (Erdis 1912:59)

This knife has an unusually short handle.

YPM Catalog Number ANT.017855; *Exhibit Catalog Number* 154
Description Knife
Dimensions 110 × 110 mm; *Weight* 45.2 g
Material Bronze
Source No data

This is No. 26 in Mathewson's Table I. He used metal drilled from two holes in the shaft for chemical analysis (see Table 1.5). Surface markings indicate that substantial forge work was done on the shaft.

YPM Catalog Number ANT.017856
Description Knife
Dimensions 72 × 62 mm; *Weight* 7.4 g
Material Bronze
Source Cave 3A

Abrasion on the blade indicates extensive use of this knife.

YPM Catalog Number ANT.017857
Description Knife
Dimensions 86 × 80 mm; *Weight* 11.7 g
Material Bronze
Source Cave 5A

The blade has been sharpened. Indentations on the top of the blade suggest that it was pounded on while cutting some tough substance.

YPM Catalog Number ANT.017858
Description Knife
Dimensions 102 × 92 mm; *Weight* 26.4 g
Material Bronze
Source No data

The porous structure revealed by a diagonal crack in the blade shows the presence of a casting defect in the blank used to make this knife.

YPM Catalog Number ANT.017859
Description Knife
Dimensions 100 × 92 mm; *Weight* 17 g
Material Bronze
Source No data

This is No. 27 in Mathewson's Table I. He removed metal for chemical analysis (see Table 1.5).

YPM Catalog Number ANT.017860
Description Knife fragment
Dimensions 75 × 35 mm; *Weight* 18 g
Material Bronze
Source North side main stairway

Both the blade and shaft of this knife are broken off and missing.

YPM Catalog Number ANT.017861
Description Knife
Dimensions 110 × 65 mm; *Weight* 20.5 g
Material Bronze
Source South end amphitheater

The shaft is cracked and one end of the blade broken off.

YPM Catalog Number ANT.017862; *Exhibit Catalog Number* 154
Description Knife
Dimensions 129 × 118 mm; *Weight* 46 g
Material No data
Source No data

The loop for suspension usually found on knives is missing.

YPM Catalog Number ANT.017863
Description Knife
Dimensions 7 × 6 mm; *Weight* 9 g
Material Bronze
Source Station 9A (Erdis 1912)

Deep corrosion obscures surface detail on this knife.

YPM Catalog Number ANT.017864; *Exhibit Catalog Number* 154
Description Knife

Dimensions 110 × 109 mm; *Weight* 48.5 g
Material Bronze
Source No data

This is No. 25 in Mathewson's Table I, identified as such on the basis of its weight and yellow color, which suggests a high tin content (see Table 1.5 for analysis). The handle is decorated with transverse lines, Xs, and rhomboids. Deep indentations in the blade suggest this knife had hard use.

YPM Catalog Number ANT.017865
Description Knife
Dimensions 85 × 50 mm; *Weight* 5.8 g
Material Bronze
Source Room 24A

Striations perpendicular to the edge of the blade suggest this knife was used for heavy cutting.

YPM Catalog Number ANT.017866
Description Knife
Dimensions 60 × 52 mm; *Weight* 3.5 g
Material Bronze
Source Cave 10A

The blade of this knife is unusually thin and sharp.

YPM Catalog Number ANT.017867
Description Knife
Dimensions 41 × 36 mm; *Weight* 3 g
Material Bronze
Source No data

The blade of this small knife appears to have been sharpened.

YPM Catalog Number ANT.017868; *Exhibit Catalog Number* 154
Description Knife
Dimensions 48 × 46 mm; *Weight* 6.5 g
Material Bronze
Source Cave 3A

This small knife was cast with a llama-head finial that includes a loop through which string may be passed. The blade as been sharpened.

YPM Catalog Number ANT.017869
Description Shawl pin
Dimensions 88 × 20 mm; *Weight* 3.9 g
Material Bronze
Source No data

The top of the head of this pin is flat. Rounding at the edge of the hole on one side shows that it was punched through the metal. Forging marks from rounding the shaft are retained.

YPM Catalog Number ANT.017870
Description Shawl pin
Dimensions 80 × 18 mm; *Weight* 2 g
Material Silver alloy
Source Cave 81

The very thin head of this pin is cracked. Near the join with the shaft the metal has been bent back. Forge marks are retained on the shaft.

YPM Catalog Number ANT.017871
Description Necklace
Dimensions Each disc 12–13 mm diameter; *Weight* 5.2 g
Material Bronze
Source Cave 2A (Erdis 1912:14)

This necklace consists of 38 discs with thickness of 0.1 to 0.3 mm.

YPM Catalog Number ANT.017872; *Exhibit Catalog Number* 142
Description Headband
Dimensions 658 × 37 mm; *Weight* 47.2 g
Material Silver alloy
Source No data

This headband was found coiled and appeared not to have been unrolled between the time it was recovered and 1983. One end has three holes through which string could be passed and looped around a tab on the other end to secure the band. Corrosion had caused the tab to break loose from the band.

YPM Catalog Number ANT.017873; *Exhibit Catalog Number* 133
Description Bracelet
Dimensions 153 × 13 mm; *Weight* 10.1 g
Material Silver alloy
Source Room 39A (Erdis 1912)

The metal is less than 1 mm thick. A loop at one end was made by turning the metal back on itself. A pattern of lines cut into the surface makes this one of the few decorated artifacts found at Machu Picchu.

YPM Catalog Number ANT.017874; *Exhibit Catalog Number* 134
Description Finger ring
Dimensions 85 × 5 mm; *Weight* 3 g
Material Silver alloy
Source Cave 53 (Erdis 1912:53)

This is a strip of silver-copper alloy wrapped roughly into a circle with overlap of the ends so that the wearer could adjust it to finger size.

YPM Catalog Number ANT.017875
Description Finger ring
Dimensions 21 × 18 mm; *Weight* 1 g

Material Silver alloy
Source Terrace north of main stairway (Erdis 1912:13)

This is one of the few mechanically fabricated objects in the collection. The artisan who made this ring first cut a sheet of silver alloy into a thin strip with slits at each end and a tab on one end. After bending it into a circle, he engaged the slits to make a secure joint and bent the tab up and around to make the small cup on the top of the ring.

YPM Catalog Number ANT.017876; *Exhibit Catalog Number* 157
Description Pendant
Dimensions 97 × 56 mm; *Weight* 54.5 g
Material Bronze
Source No data

The high tin content of the bronze (28%) gives the metal a yellow color. It also means that this artifact had to be cast to its final shape, because bronze containing this much tin is brittle. The brittleness would also make it unsuitable for use as a knife. Therefore it seems to have been intended as a decoration to be worn suspended from the loop included at the center of the casting.

YPM Catalog Number ANT.017877; *Exhibit Catalog Number* 147
Description Pendant
Dimensions 73 × 70 mm; *Weight* 34 g
Material Bronze
Source Station 9A (Eaton 1916)

This bronze disc has an asymmetrical shape and is unusual among the items in the collection in having a chevron design cut into its stem.

YPM Catalog Number ANT.017878; *Exhibit Catalog Number* 143
Description Headdress ornament
Dimensions 70 × 45 mm; *Weight* 35.2 g
Material Silver alloy
Source No data

This ornament was cut out of a sheet of silver alloy and is not quite perfectly symmetrical because the artisan who made it had some difficulty cutting the interior openings. Two holes at the bottom allowed it to be attached to a cloth band for wear.

YPM Catalog Number ANT.017879
Description Molder's or potter's slick
Dimensions 125 × 21 mm; *Weight* 16.6 g
Material Bronze
Source No data

This bronze tool with a point at one end and a flat edge at the other would have been useful in shaping clay molds or pottery.

YPM Catalog Number ANT.017880
Description Shawl pin
Dimensions 82 × 18 mm; *Weight* 35 g

Material Silver alloy
Source Cave 103 (Eaton 1916)

This shawl pin has an unusually large hole in its head and retains forging marks along its shaft.

YPM Catalog Number ANT.017881; *Exhibit Catalog Number* 135
Description Shawl pin
Dimensions 137 × 33 mm; *Weight* 31.5 g
Material Silver alloy
Source No data

This fragment is a piece broken from a shawl pin, ANT.017955, ANT.017959.

YPM Catalog Number ANT.017882
Description Rod or bar
Dimensions 99 × 4 mm; *Weight* 8 g
Material Bronze
Source No data

One end of this bar was sawn off by Mathewson (No. 29 in his Table I); for chemical analysis, see Table 1.5. The hammer marks along its length and the variation in thickness from 3.4 to 4.5 mm along its length suggest that it was work in progress.

YPM Catalog Number ANT.017884
Description Finial of a textile tool
Dimensions 44 × 28 mm; *Weight* 38.5 g
Material Bronze
Source No data

This cast bronze representation of a head is remarkable for its large, pointed ears.

YPM Catalog Number ANT.017885
Description Remnant of a shawl pin
Dimensions 50 × 18 mm; *Weight* 16 g
Material Bronze
Source No data

This seems to be a fragment of a pendant.

YPM Catalog Number ANT.017886, ANT.017888; *Exhibit Catalog Number* 144
Description Discs
Dimensions 2.2 × 2.2 mm; *Weight* 0.5–1 g
Material Silver alloy
Source Section 40A

The indentation of the metal adjacent to the holes in these two thin silver alloy discs shows that the holes were punched after the discs were cut out of silver alloy sheet.

YPM Catalog Number ANT.017890; *Exhibit Catalog Number* 141
Description Lime spoon
Dimensions 55 × 19 mm; *Weight* 2.8 g

Material Bronze
Source Grave 26 (Eaton 1916)

The stem and the figure of a bird on its upper end were cast as one piece.

YPM Catalog Number ANT.017891; *Exhibit Catalog Number* 131
Description Pendant or tweezers
Dimensions 38 × 28 mm; *Weight* No data
Material Silver alloy
Source Room 64A (Erdis 1912)

This has been interpreted as either a pendant or half of a tweezers broken at its hinge, which would have been unusually small for this service.

YPM Catalog Number ANT.017892
Description Bell
Dimensions 35 × 15 mm; *Weight* 10.5 g
Material Bronze
Source No data

A core was required to make the hollow end of this bronze casting. Traces in the dendritic structure formed as the bronze solidified are still visible in the surface.

YPM Catalog Number ANT.017893; *Exhibit Catalog Number* 132
Description Tweezers
Dimensions 13 × 10 mm; *Weight* 3.7 g
Material Bronze
Source Grave 26 (Eaton 1916)

These tweezers, one of several of the same design in the collection, are larger than the other examples. Illustration: Eaton (1916, pl. I, item 2)

YPM Catalog Number ANT.017895, *Exhibit Catalog Number* 132
Description Tweezers
Dimensions 25 × 10 mm; *Weight* 1.4 g
Material Bronze
Source No data

This falls in the middle of the size range of tweezers found at Machu Picchu.

YPM Catalog Number ANT.017896; *Exhibit Catalog Number* 132
Description Tweezers
Dimensions 19 × 11 mm; *Weight* 1.0 g
Material Bronze
Source Cave 73

This is one of the smaller tweezers in the collection.

YPM Catalog Number ANT.017897; *Exhibit Catalog Number* 153
Description Plate handle
Dimensions 48 × 15 mm; *Weight* 10 g

Material Gold-silver alloy
Source No data

This handle, probably for a silver alloy plate, was fabricated from several sheets formed around a central tube. It was broken off at its juncture with the plate. It is one of the few artifacts from the royal or religious elite to be found at Machu Picchu.

YPM Catalog Number ANT.017898; *Exhibit Catalog Number* 150
Description "T" axe
Dimensions 130 × 170 mm; *Weight* 391 g
Material Bronze
Source Espiritu Pampa on the Conservidayoc River (Foote and Buell 1912)

Bingham purchased this axe in 1911 after leaving Machu Picchu, and subsequently turned it over to Foote and Buell for detailed study. Samples from the end of one arm and the blade were examined in 1983; see Appendix A.

YPM Catalog Number ANT.017899; *Exhibit Catalog Number* 151
Description "T" axe
Dimensions 95 × 91 mm; *Weight* 557 g
Material Bronze
Source No data

The clumsy shape and low tin content of the alloy would have limited the utility of this axe as a tool for working on stone or wood. Nevertheless, the heavy indentations on the top of the crossbar show that it was pounded on. A section taken at the end of the crossbar was prepared for metallographic examination in 1982; see Appendix A.

YPM Catalog Number ANT.017900; *Exhibit Catalog Number* 150
Description "T" axe
Dimensions 120 × 116; *Weight* 506 g
Material Bronze
Source Near Rosalina on the Urabamba River, 90 km from Machu Picchu (Foote and Buell 1912)

This axe was purchased by Bingham in 1911 about 100 km from Machu Picchu. Foote and Buell machined three recesses on one side to gain access to uncorroded metal. In 1982 sections from the end of one arm and the blade were examined; see Appendix A.

YPM Catalog Number ANT.017902; *Exhibit Catalog Number* 150
Description "T" axe
Dimensions 130 × 109 mm; *Weight* 718 g
Material Bronze
Source No data

Surface markings on the blade and top of this axe show that it was used for heavy work, probably on stone. In 1982 the microstructure of a section at the end of the crossbar was examined; see Appendix A.

YPM Catalog Number ANT.017903
Description "T" axe
Dimensions 130 × 110 mm; *Weight* 832 g

Material Bronze
Source Modern reproduction made by Foote and Buell

YPM Catalog Number ANT.017904; *Exhibit Catalog Number* 151
Description Axe or knife
Dimensions 150 × 92 mm; *Weight* 203 g
Material Bronze
Source No data

This crescent-shaped axe could be hafted or used as a handheld knife. An apparent parting line visible on the underside of the handle suggests the axe was cast in a bivalve mold. Part of the blade has been broken off; the fracture reveals substantial porosity in the bronze.

YPM Catalog Number ANT.017905; *Exhibit Catalog Number* 151
Description Axe
Dimensions 95 × 80 mm; *Weight* 203.1 g
Material Bronze
Source No data

This crescent-shaped axe could be hafted or used as a handheld knife. The cutting edge has been sharpened by rubbing against stone.

YPM Catalog Number ANT.017906; *Exhibit Catalog Number* 152
Description "T" axe
Dimensions 150 × 140 mm; *Weight* No data
Material Bronze
Source Alvistur collection

This item was not examined in 1984.

YPM Catalog Number ANT.017907; *Exhibit Catalog Number* 151
Description Chisel
Dimensions 65 × 40 mm; *Weight* 84 g
Material Bronze
Source No data

This bronze chisel has been heavily indented on its top by hammer blows. The hammering has opened a small crack on the top. The cutting edge is blunt and flattened by contact with a hard material, probably stone. A metallographic examination was made of a section at the top in 1984; see Appendix A.

YPM Catalog Number ANT.017908; *Exhibit Catalog Number* 151
Description Axe head
Dimensions 120 × 61 mm; *Weight* 342 g
Material Copper
Source No data

There are a few nicks on the cutting edge, but this axe, unlike the bronze axes and chisels, seems to have had very little use. This axe is unusual in shape—unlike any other found at Machu Picchu—and in being made of nearly pure copper rather than bronze. The shape and composition are similar to those of the many copper flat axes found throughout Europe, the Near East, and

Southwest Asia. Axes of the same design cast in bronze were later adopted in the Early Bronze Age before being replaced by the flanged axe design (Allen, Britton, and Coghlan 1970:55–84).

YPM Catalog Number ANT.017909
Description Plumb bob
Dimensions 77 × 25 mm; *Weight* 167 g
Material Bronze
Source Yale Peruvian Expedition, 1912

The recess in the top of this modern plumb bob has a cast-in crossbar around which a string can be fastened. Dendritic structure characteristic of as-cast bronze is visible at some of the clear areas on the surface. Facets on the lower section suggest that this may have been partially shaped by hammering.

YPM Catalog Number ANT.017910
Description Knife
Dimensions 92 × 82 mm; *Weight* 50.3 g
Material Bronze
Source Alvistur collection

The near-perfect symmetry and thick, round shaft of this knife—features unlike any other knife in the collection—coupled with lack of corrosion and the quality of the casting suggest that this may be a modern product.

YPM Catalog Number ANT.017911
Description Knife or awl
Dimensions 143 × 15 mm; *Weight* 90 g
Material Bronze
Source No data

The sharpened end of the stem and the damage to the blade from pounding suggest that this tool was used as an awl rather than as a knife.

YPM Catalog Number ANT.017912; *Exhibit Catalog Number* 148
Description Plume holder
Dimensions 90 × 50 mm; *Weight* 54.4 g
Material Silver alloy
Source Section 40A between Room 24A and Caves 4A, 5A, and 6A and just south of the stairway at the east corner of a house on the southeast side of Sacred Plaza (Erdis 1912)

A silver alloy sheet has been wrapped into a frustum of a cone and the edges secured with tabs. Substantial damage obscures the finer details of this artifact. Bingham interpreted this as an armlet. It has also been interpreted as a decoration placed on the top of a tool used in ritual activities, or as a plume holder.

YPM Catalog Number ANT.017913
Description Bar
Dimensions 197 × 10 mm; *Weight* 31 g
Material Bronze
Source Room 48A (Erdis 1912:59)

This bronze bar has well-preserved indentations made by hammerstones. Examination of the microstructure shows that the bronze had developed long cracks due to concentrations of sulfide inclusions in the process of forging; see Appendix A. The processing of this piece may have been abandoned because of the poor quality of the bronze.

YPM Catalog Number ANT.017914
Description Knife blade
Dimensions 6.6 × 1.9 mm; *Weight* 5.7 g
Material Bronze
Source No data

This seems to be No. 31 in Mathewson's Table I. It contains hole left where metal was taken for chemical analysis.

YPM Catalog Number ANT.017957
Description Tweezers blade fragment
Dimensions 22 × 15 mm; *Weight* 0.4 g
Material Bronze
Source No data

This may be a tweezers fragment.

YPM Catalog Number ANT.017962; *Exhibit Catalog Number* 155
Description Llama-head knife
Dimensions 76 × 20 mm; *Weight* 13.2 g
Material Bronze and bismuth bronze
Source Cave 54 (Erdis 1912:41)

This composite knife has a stem and blade of 3% tin bronze and a cast-on llama head made of copper-bismuth-tin alloy. The head was sectioned by Mathewson, and this section was reexamined in 1984; see Appendix A.

YPM Catalog Number ANT.017963
Description Knife
Dimensions 98 × 50 mm; *Weight* 14.2 g
Material Bronze
Source No data

Mathewson listed this knife as No. 14 in his Table I. The section he cut through the handle parallel to its axis shows that the sulfide inclusions in the bronze were elongated by forging, that the loop at the end was made by bending, and that the knife was annealed after these operations were completed. The scleroscope hardness of the blade was 27 (HV 98) and of the handle, 14 (HV 75). Unless the handle only was heated to annealing temperature, which seems unlikely, the blade must have been hardened by further hammering after the anneal.

YPM Catalog Number ANT.017964
Description Chisel
Dimensions 134 × 30 mm; *Weight* 153 g
Material Bronze
Source No data

Mathewson used a strip cut from the side of this chisel in a series of forging experiments to determine the effect of forging bronze at different temperatures on the microstructure. He used these observations to show that the tip of the chisel was shaped by hot working. The tip section was reexamined in 1984, and microhardness data were taken along the axis back from the tip. See Appendix A.

YPM Catalog Number ANT.017965
Description Ball
Dimensions 20 × 20 mm; *Weight* 35 g
Material Bronze
Source No data

This is No. 4 in Mathewson's Table I; see Table 1.5 for his chemical analysis. The cross section cut by Mathewson shows that this approximately spherical ball has a cast-in cavity and crossbar that would accommodate a string up to 3 mm in diameter. The surface of the ball is indented, presumably by hammering, but the as-cast microstructure is retained.

YPM Catalog Number ANT.017966
Description Chisel
Dimensions 69 × 40 mm; *Weight* 98 g
Material Bronze
Source Section 40A (Erdis 1912:54)

The twist of about 12° in this chisel along its length and its broken top show that it had hard use. It is No. 16 in Mathewson's Table I; see Table 1.5 for his analysis. Mathewson polished one edge of the chisel for study of the microstructure. This section was reexamined in 1984; see Appendix A. The chisel was cast, forged, and subsequently annealed. It was probably used to split rock.

YPM Catalog Number ANT.017967; *Exhibit Catalog Number* 150
Description "T" axe
Dimensions 103 × 100 mm; *Weight* 409.5 g
Material Bronze
Source Room 24A (Erdis 1912)

This seems to be No. 15 in Mathewson's Table I, although his drawing does not show the broken corner. He removed metal from the end of the crossbar for analysis. The remaining section of the metal he removed was reexamined in 1984; see Appendix A. The axe was cast, forged, and subsequently annealed. It was hammered on and the blade broken by a brittle fracture in subsequent use.

YPM Catalog Number ANT.017968
Description Shawl pin
Dimensions 108 × 20 mm; *Weight* 6.8 g
Material Bronze
Source No data

The shaft of this pin has been broken and a sample removed at some time in the past.

YPM Catalog Number ANT.017969
Description Axe blade, broken

Dimensions 75 × 73 mm; *Weight* 219 g
Material Bronze
Source No data

This broken axe blade is No. 8 in Mathewson's Table I. To test the ductility of the metal he removed a 7 × 9 × 16 mm piece near the fracture, which he was able to roll into a bar 4 mm in diameter by 38 mm long, in several passes before it broke up. Sections from the fractured end and the blade were examined in 1982; see Appendix A. The high level of porosity observed may be the cause of the brittle fracture of the blade. The tip of this blade is too blunt for cutting wood, but it could have been used for splitting. Strain lines in the metal show that it has been subjected to impacts.

YPM Catalog Number ANT.017970
Description Lime spoon
Dimensions No data; *Weight* No data
Material Bronze
Source Cave 66 (Erdis 1912:56; Eaton 1916:63)

This is No. 2 in Mathewson's Table I. His analysis (see Table 1.5) showed a high tin content: 13%. Since he found that this alloy contains the brittle δ phase, he decided to demonstrate that it could nevertheless be forged by hammering out a piece cut from the stem. Mathewson's sections were reexamined in 1982; see Appendix A. The head retains its as-cast structure; the stem has been forged and annealed.

YPM Catalog Number ANT.017971
Description Knife
Dimensions 67 × 52 mm; *Weight* 16.4 g
Material Copper
Source No data

This knife is No. 9 in Mathewson's Table I. His analysis showed it to be made of unalloyed copper. He examined a section cut through the stem and blade and found from the extensive elongation of the Cu_2O inclusion that the blade had been heavily forged.

YPM Catalog Number ANT.017972
Description Tweezers blank
Dimensions 65 × 12 mm; *Weight* 7.2 g
Material Bronze
Source Room 24A

This is No. 13 in Mathewson's Table I. He cut a longitudinal section for study, finding that the structure consists of recrystallized grains with residual coring. Apparently forging was started, the piece annealed, and then abandoned. We do not know how close to this shape the original blank may have been cast.

YPM Catalog Number ANT.017973; *Exhibit Catalog Number* 156
Description Knife, with modeled handle
Dimensions 130 mm; *Weight* 42.3 g
Material Bronze
Source Room 24A (Erdis 1912:31)

This knife with the cast-in figure of a fisherman on its top is one of the best known items in the collection. Mathewson's examination showed a cast bronze structure in the head of the figure. The metal in the blade is recrystallized, indicating that some forge work was done followed by an anneal.

YPM Catalog Number ANT.017974
Description Axe blade, broken
Dimensions 56 × 26 mm; *Weight* 54.5 g
Material Bronze
Source Room 34A (Erdis 1912: entry for 11 Sept. 1912)

This blade fragment is No. 10 in Mathewson's Table I. A section of the blade parallel to the one cut by Mathewson was examined in 1982; see Appendix A. This did not confirm his suggestion that the blade had been used in heavy work, perhaps on stone. Instead, serious casting defects were found; see Appendix A.

YPM Catalog Number ANT.017975
Description Chisel, broken
Dimensions 60 × 40 mm; *Weight* 61.9 g
Material Bronze
Source Section 40A (Erdis 1912:55, entry for 19 Sept. 1912)

The top end of this chisel had been broken off at the time it was found. Although at some time prior to 1982 a sample had been removed at one corner of the top, it cannot be identified with any of the artifacts described in Mathewson's report. In 1982, metallographic sections at the blade and at the fracture surface were examined; see Appendix A. Surface markings suggest that this chisel was used for splitting wood.

YPM Catalog Number ANT.017978
Description Metal stock, crumpled
Dimensions 50 mm; *Weight* 52.4 g
Material Tin
Source Section 41A (Erdis 1912:57, entry for 19 Sept. 1912)

These are two pieces of pure sheet tin that had been crumpled into ball-like shapes. The sheet has deep score marks such as would be made by a chisel used to cut off small pieces. The microstructure consists of fully recrystallized metal with a medium to coarse grain size and traces of mechanical twins.

YPM Catalog Number ANT.017979
Description Metal stock
Dimensions 225 × 53 mm; *Weight* 156 g
Material Tin
Source Room 26A (Erdis 1912: entry for 4 Sept. 1912)

This sheet of tin was found to have been folded and subsequently unfolded sometime before 1982. The edge shows the indentations of a chisel used to cut off pieces, such as might be needed in formulating an alloy. The microstructure indicates that the sheet was cast. At the edge, fine grains suggest the chill margin of a mold. These are followed by columnar grains and, in the interior, equiaxed grains. Mechanical twins are common, a result of the folding and unfolding.

YPM Catalog Number ANT.017980
Description Bar, possibly stock

Dimensions 35 × 11 mm; *Weight* 18 g
Material Bronze
Source No data

This 5 mm thick piece of bronze is No. 21 in Mathewson's Table I. The surfaces prepared by Mathewson were reexamined in 1982; the metal structure consists of fully recrystallized, fine grains free of strain lines. It was annealed after some preliminary forge work and abandoned.

YPM Catalog Number ANT.017982a, ANT.017982b
Description Metal stock
Dimensions 80 × 75 mm; *Weight* 134.5 g
Material Tin
Source Section 40A (Erdis 1912: entry for 18 Sept. 1912)

These two lumps of pure tin retain impressions of coarse organic matter such as straw, suggesting that molten tin may have been poured onto a cavity in the ground.

YPM Catalog Number ANT.017988
Description Metal spill
Dimensions 25 × 20 mm; *Weight* 4 g
Material Bronze
Source No data

This small scrap of bronze seems to be metal left over from a casting operation that was poured from a crucible or was spilled.

YPM Catalog Number ANT.018400, ANT.018420
Description Spangles
Dimensions No data; *Weight* No data
Material Silver alloy
Source Alvistur collection

These are fragments of silver alloy sheet that seem to have been used as decorations attached to clothing.

YPM Catalog Number ANT.018425; *Exhibit Catalog Number* 149
Description Mace head
Dimensions 88 × 24 mm; *Weight* No data
Material Bronze
Source Alvistur collection

Indentation and abrasions suggest that this mace head saw service as a weapon.

YPM Catalog Number ANT.018426; *Exhibit Catalog Number* 146
Description Ball
Dimensions 33 × 33 mm; *Weight* No data
Material Silver alloy
Source No data

This is similar in shape to the other balls in the collection, but made of silver alloy instead of bronze. The use of silver alloy suggests the possibility that it was intended for some ritual use as a plummet.

YPM Catalog Number ANT.018427, ANT.018428; *Exhibit Catalog Number* 145
Description Bronze pendants, possibly bells
Dimensions 35/39 mm; *Weight* 4.5/3 g
Material Bronze
Source Cave 57 and Cave 58 (Eaton 1916)

These bronze objects have been interpreted as either ear pendants or small bells.

YPM Catalog Number ANT.018429
Description Finial
Dimensions 37 × 25 mm; *Weight* 20.5 g
Material Bronze
Source Cave 106 (Erdis 1912:75, entry for 13 Nov. 1912)

This hollow bronze casting, deeply corroded, may have been intended to surmount a staff.

YPM Catalog Number ANT.018430
Description Shawl pin
Dimensions 111 × 16 mm; *Weight* 8.3 g
Material Bronze
Source No data

This pin carries deep grooves suggestive of polishing against a rough stone surface.

YPM Catalog Number ANT.018431
Description Shawl pin
Dimensions 94 × 21 mm; *Weight* 2.8 g
Material Silver alloy
Source Grave 26

YPM Catalog Number ANT.018432
Description Shawl pin
Dimensions 100 × 16 mm; *Weight* 38 g
Material Silver alloy
Source No data

This pin has been heavily damaged by corrosion.

YPM Catalog Number ANT.018433
Description Small needle
Dimensions 75 × 4 mm; *Weight* 2.2 g
Material Bronze
Source Cave 91 (Eaton 1916)

The eye of this needle was made by folding over its end.

YPM Catalog Number ANT.018434
Description Needle?
Dimensions 93 × 1.5 mm; *Weight* 1 g
Material Bronze
Source No data

On this needle most of the eye is missing, but the remnant indicates that it was formed by bending the rod back on itself.

YPM Catalog Number ANT.018436
Description Bracelet fragment
Dimensions 40 × 21 mm; *Weight* 2 g
Material Bronze
Source Room 64A (Erdis 1912)

The thickness of this bronze fragment is approximately 1 mm.

YPM Catalog Number ANT.018437
Description Earspool
Dimensions 20 × 13 mm; *Weight* 1.4 g
Material Bronze
Source Cave 97 (Eaton 1916)

This fragment may be the surviving part of an earspool or bell similar to ANT.018427.

YPM Catalog Number ANT.018438
Description Pin fragment
Dimensions 39 × 1 mm; *Weight* 0.2 g
Material Bronze
Source No data

Corrosion has destroyed most of this length of bronze rod.

YPM Catalog Number ANT.018439
Description Pendant
Dimensions 23 × 15 mm; *Weight* 4.5 g
Material Bronze
Source Cave 63 (Eaton 1916)

This small pendant or bell is heavily damaged by corrosion.

YPM Catalog Number ANT.018440
Description Tweezers
Dimensions 25 × 20 mm; *Weight* 2 g
Material Bronze
Source No data

This is a typical tweezers, but in poor condition.

YPM Catalog Number ANT.018441
Description Shawl pin fragment
Dimensions 33 × 2 mm; *Weight* 1 g
Material Bronze
Source No data

This may be the end of a shawl pin stem.

YPM Catalog Number ANT.018442
Description Tweezers
Dimensions 14 × 5 mm; *Weight* 1 g
Material Bronze
Source No data

This tweezers is small and lacks the sophisticated shape of the other example found.

YPM Catalog Number ANT.018443
Description Possible knife blade fragment
Dimensions 28 × 12 mm; *Weight* 0.4 g
Material Bronze
Source No data

This may be the end of a broken knife blade.

YPM Catalog Number ANT.018444
Description Possible knife blade fragment
Dimensions 19 × 15 mm; *Weight* 0.5 g
Material Bronze
Source No data

There is insufficient material left to reliably identify this item.

YPM Catalog Number ANT.018447
Description Ball
Dimensions 21 × 21 mm; *Weight* 36 g
Material Bronze
Source No data

This ball is similar to ANT.017965.

YPM Catalog Number ANT.018448
Description Shawl pin
Dimensions 150 × 30 mm; *Weight* 6.6 g
Material Bronze
Source No data

Nearly all the head is missing from this pin.

YPM Catalog Number ANT.018449
Description Work piece or metal stock
Dimensions 110 × 3.3 mm; *Weight* 8.6 g
Material Silver alloy
Source No data

Facets on the surface show that this bar was being forged when it was abandoned. The microstructure shows that this is a forged and annealed hypereutectic alloy of silver and copper; see discussion in Section One under "Surface Treatments and Decoration."

YPM Catalog Number ANT.018450
Description Pendant disc
Dimensions 31 × 31 mm; *Weight* 3.3 g
Material Bronze
Source No data

The stem that would have carried a hole for suspending this disc has been broken off. The concave-convex shape would have limited its use as a mirror. The edge at the upper rim has been flattened.

YPM Catalog Number ANT.018451
Description Shawl pin head
Dimensions 21 × 21 mm; *Weight* 1.3 g
Material Bronze
Source No data

Only the head, deeply corroded, remains from this pin.

YPM Catalog Number ANT.018452
Description Shawl pin head
Dimensions 35 × 17 mm; *Weight* 1.6 g
Material Silver alloy
Source No data

Only the upper half of the head remains. The break passed through the hole in the pin head, possibly because cracks were initiated at the time the hole was punched.

YPM Catalog Number ANT.018453
Description Small tool or work in progress
Dimensions 68 × 13 mm; *Weight* 5 g
Material Copper
Source No data

This piece, shaped like a slim isosceles triangle, was hammered on both ends.

YPM Catalog Number ANT.018454; *Exhibit Catalog Number* 147
Description Pendant disc
Dimensions 45 × 36 mm; *Weight* 6 g
Material Bronze
Source Station 9A (Erdis 1912:84)

The concave-convex shape of this disc eliminates its possible use as a mirror. It has a stem with a hole that would allow it to be worn as a pendant.

YPM Catalog Number ANT.018460
Description Metal stock
Dimensions 77 × 35 mm; *Weight* 14.8 g
Material Bronze
Source No data

An artisan hammered this sheet of bronze to a thickness of less than 1 mm. The wavy profile suggests either crumpling of the sheet or that the maker had difficulty keeping it flat as he hammered it out.

YPM Catalog Number ANT.018461
Description Metal spill
Dimensions 70 × 45 mm; *Weight* 18 g
Material Bronze
Source No data

This is metal that was spilled from a crucible, perhaps at the end of pouring a casting; see Appendix A. Examination of the microstructure shows the large grain size and dendritic structure associated with slow cooling, as on a warm stone surface.

YPM Catalog Number ANT.018477
Description Shawl pin
Dimensions 238 × 51 mm; *Weight* 21.1 g
Material Bronze
Source No data

This pin has a semicircular head and is deeply corroded.

YPM Catalog Number ANT.018478, ANT.018479
Description Crowbar
Dimensions 1063 × 427 mm; *Weight* 1063 g
Material Bronze
Source Section 44A (Erdis 1912:58, entry for 21 Sept. 1912)

This bar is No. 20 in Mathewson's Table I. He did a tensile test by placing the entire bar in the testing machine; marks left by the machine grips remained in the bar in 1982. He found the tensile strength to be 192 MPa and the elongation 6% in 50 mm. Gross porosity is responsible for the very low ductility and low strength.

YPM Catalog Number ANT.018480; *Exhibit Catalog Number* 147
Description Pendant disc
Dimensions 97 × 80 mm; *Weight* 69.4 g
Material Bronze with trace of silver plating
Source Grave 26 (Eaton 1916)

This disc is No. 12 in Mathewson's Table I. He sectioned the disc along its plane of symmetry. The handle retains its as-cast structure, but the rest of the disc must have been lightly forged, since the sulfide inclusions show no evidence of deformation by the metal is fully recrystallized. See Section One under "Surface Treatments and Decoration" for the evidence of silver plating. The concave-convex shape clearly shown in the cross section would make this useless as a viewing mirror; it must have been intended to be worn as a pendant.

YPM Catalog Number ANT.018481
Description Metal residue
Dimensions 80 × 53 mm; *Weight* 267 g

Material Bronze
Source Cave 52 (Eaton 1916)

This is No. 25 in Mathewson's Table I. The convex bottom and flat but rough top suggest that this is bronze that solidified in the bottom of a crucible. The microstructure at the section cut by Mathewson was examined in 1984; see Appendix A.

YPM Catalog Number ANT.018482
Description Shawl pin shaft
Dimensions 95 × 2 mm; *Weight* 2 g
Material Bronze
Source Cave 37 (Eaton 1916)

The eye at the head of this needle is missing.

YPM Catalog Number ANT.018626
Description Large needle
Dimensions 456 × 7 mm; *Weight* 59.5 g
Material Bronze
Source Section 41A (Erdis 1912)

This needle is No. 18 in Mathewson's Table I. It has been forged along its length and the end turned back on itself to make the eye. The facets left by forging are about 5 mm long and are interpreted as left by the blunt end of a hammerstone.

APPENDIX D

Artifact Descriptions

Metal Artifacts from Machu Picchu Included in Section Two

This inventory is based on inspection of the collection in 1985, with a few additions from Rutledge (1984) and personal communications from Lucy Salazar (2010, 2011).

Catalog number	Type code	Description
ANT.016677	1121	Tweezer: miscellaneous symmetrical valve style
ANT.016678	5115	Flat tumi: T variant
ANT.016679a	1012	Tupu: half-round, > semicircular
ANT.016679b	1010	Tupu: half-round
ANT.016679c	1012	Tupu: half-round, > semicircular
ANT.016680	1007	Tupu: half-round transitional
ANT.016681	1001	Tupu: round
ANT.016682	1900	Cone "bell": indeterminate
ANT.016683	2439	Tiny tupu or lime dipper: other head cast in the round (ball and loop)
ANT.016684	1109	Tweezer: straight transitional
ANT.016685	2840	T-shaped tumi: straight back; globular join
ANT.017819	1014	Tupu: drooping
ANT.017821	1012	Tupu: half-round, > semicircular
ANT.017822	1010	Tupu: half-round
ANT.017823	1011	Tupu: half-round, head thick as shaft
ANT.017824	1010	Tupu: half-round
ANT.017825	1010	Tupu: half-round
ANT.017826	1015	Tupu: half-round or drooping thin, indeterminate
ANT.017827	1010	Tupu: half-round
ANT.017828	2430	Tiny tupu or lime dipper: biconical club-shaped head, no hole
ANT.017829	1011	Tupu: half-round, head thick as shaft
ANT.017830	1037	Tupu: thin head, indeterminate shape
ANT.017831	1010	Tupu: half-round
ANT.017832	1010	Tupu: half-round
ANT.017833	1010	Tupu: half-round
ANT.017834	1001	Tupu: round, head thick as shaft
ANT.017835	1010	Tupu: half-round; possibly sharpened top edge

Continued.

Catalog number	Type code	Description
ANT.017838	1010	Tupu: half-round
ANT.017840	1001	Tupu: round
ANT.017841	1083	Tupu: small star mace head, no hole
ANT.017845	1001	Tupu: round; very large, matches ANT.017846
ANT.017846	1001	Tupu: round; very large, matches ANT.017845
ANT.017848	1012	Tupu: half-round, > semicircular; large, thin, bent head
ANT.017850	5423	Disc: plain, flat, one hole near edge, 40–100 mm diameter (90 mm diameter, folded into rectangular packet, later unfolded)
ANT.017851	2700	Chisel: fine; probably hafted; working edge battered and bent over
ANT.017852	2840	T-shaped tumi: straight back; flat loop
ANT.017853	2840	T-shaped tumi: straight back; flat loop
ANT.017854	2840	T-shaped tumi: straight back; flat loop on short handle, probably a repair
ANT.017855	2840	T-shaped tumi: straight back; round shaft with loop
ANT.017856	2840	T-shaped tumi: straight back; flat loop
ANT.017857	2840	T-shaped tumi: straight back; flat loop with neck step, as on tweezers
ANT.017858	2840	T-shaped tumi: straight back; flat loop
ANT.017859	2840	T-shaped tumi: straight back; flat loop
ANT.017860	2840	T-shaped tumi: straight back; most of handle missing; possibly serrated
ANT.017861	2840	T-shaped tumi: straight back; no loop
ANT.017862	2841	T-shaped tumi: slightly flaring back; no loop
ANT.017863	2841	T-shaped tumi: slightly flaring back; end of handle missing
ANT.017864	2840	T-shaped tumi: straight back; no loop; traced designs on handle
ANT.017865	2840	T-shaped tumi: straight back; no loop
ANT.017866	2841	T-shaped tumi: slightly flaring back; flat loop
ANT.017867	2841	T-shaped tumi: slightly flaring back; flat loop
ANT.017868	2840	T-shaped tumi: straight back; cast camelid head
ANT.017869	1001	Tupu: round
ANT.017870	1001	Tupu: round
ANT.017871	5422	38 discs: plain, flat, one hole near edge, <40 mm diameter (12–13 mm diameter; Bingham [1930:123] reported 39 discs)
ANT.017872	3190	Other: strip; 656 mm long, 37 mm wide, 3 holes at one squared end, thin and flexible, bent into 135 mm diameter circle, possibly a headband or belt
ANT.017873	3190	Other: strip; 165 mm long, 13 mm wide, squared ends, thick stiff sheet, traced design on outside, bent into 52 mm diameter circle, possibly a bracelet
ANT.017874	1601	Ring: plain sheet (lies flat on finger); 6.3 mm wide
ANT.017875	1603	Ring: edgewise strip appliqué; 3.3 mm wide band, 9 mm wide bulge for appliqué

Continued.

Catalog number	Type code	Description
ANT.017876	3364	Plaque: cast ornamented crescent; may be a crescent knife, but edge appears thick and rounded
ANT.017877	5610	Lirpu: disc with pierced tab for suspension; 70 mm diameter; traced design on suspension tab
ANT.017878	3020	Ornament: bangle or pendant; may be a headdress ornament
ANT.017879	2700	Chisel: fine; probably hafted; tang bent
ANT.017880	1037	Tupu: thin head, indeterminate shape
ANT.017881, 017955, 017959	1010	Tupu: half-round (3 joining fragments)
ANT.017882	3170	Other: bar
ANT.017884	1565	Figurine: anthropomorphic head with horns, possibly head of a distaff
ANT.017885	1062	Tupu: cone, double, with loop
ANT.017886	5422	Disc: plain, flat, one hole near edge, <40 mm diameter (20.8 mm diameter)
ANT.017888	5422	Disc: plain, flat, one hole near edge, <40 mm diameter
ANT.017890	1701	Tiny spoon: bird finial
ANT.017891	1103	Tweezer: teardrop (only one valve present)
ANT.017892	2001	Split bell: cast; 17 mm diameter; 21 mm suspension shaft with cast loop
ANT.017893	1101	Tweezer: triangular; neck step
ANT.017895	1104	Tweezer: teardrop transitional
ANT.017896	1104	Tweezer: teardrop transitional
ANT.017897	1412	Vessel: handled plate; probable bird head handle formed from sheet
ANT.017899	4270	Axe: rectangular tangs, no hole, wide crescent blade
ANT.017901	4250	Axe: rectangular tangs, no hole, trapezoidal blade ("classic")
ANT.017904	4470	Axe: curved tangs, no hole, wide crescent blade ("ancla"); edge damaged
ANT.017907	2710	Chisel: heavy; butt upset; probably sharpened
ANT.017908	4030	Possible celt: lenticular section, rounded, flared; probably sharpened
ANT.017909	2740	Tool: plumb bob; cast bar in hole for suspension
ANT.017911	2840	T-shaped tumi: straight back; no loop; edge damaged; blade bent
ANT.017912	3110	Miscellaneous: plume holder cone; fabricated from sheet
ANT.017913	3170	Miscellaneous: bar
ANT.017914	2839	Knife: possible knife blade, long oval, resembles blade of a T-shaped tumi with no handle
ANT.017962	2849	T-shaped tumi: tiny cast blade; cast-on animal head
ANT.017963	2840	T-shaped tumi: straight back; flat loop
ANT.017964	4020	Celt: straight or slightly flared sides, with flared end
ANT.017965	1801	Bola: spheroid with suspension hole; 20 mm diameter
ANT.017966	4010	Celt: straight or slightly flared sides

Continued.

Catalog number	Type code	Description
ANT.017967	4250	Axe: rectangular tangs, no hole, trapezoidal blade ("classic")
ANT.017968	1001	Tupu: round; possibly sharpened
ANT.017969	4750	Axe: indeterminate haft, trapezoidal blade
ANT.017970	1701	Tiny spoon: bird finial
ANT.017971	2840	T-shaped tumi: straight back; flat handle, loop indeterminate
ANT.017972	1101	Tweezer: triangular; unfinished
ANT.017973	2830	Knife: handleless transverse; cast scene of boy fishing
ANT.017974	4701	Axe: indeterminate haft, indeterminate blade shape
ANT.017975	4020	Celt: straight or slightly flared sides, with flared end
ANT.017978	2933	Production: sheet scrap; tin; thick wadded-up irregular sheet with cutmarks
ANT.017979	2933	Production: sheet scrap; tin; thick folded irregular sheet with cutmarks
ANT.017980	2930	Production: probable ingot
ANT.017982a	2920	Production: smelting or refining product, excess from melting; tin
ANT.017982b	2920	Production: smelting or refining product, excess from melting; tin
ANT.017988a	2002	Split bell: forged; small flattened split spherical, 12 mm diameter
ANT.017988b	2920	Production: smelting or refining product, excess from melting
ANT.018400–018420	3035	Ornament: sheet ornament; fragments; labeled "pieces of thin silver dress ornament"
ANT.018426	1801	Bola: spheroid with suspension hole; 33 mm diameter
ANT.018427	1902	Conical "bell": with arms
ANT.018428	1902	Conical "bell": with arms
ANT.018429	3059	Ornament: rod/staff end cap
ANT.018430	1011	Tupu: half-round, thick as shaft
ANT.018431	1010	Tupu: half-round
ANT.018432	1037	Tupu: thin head, indeterminate shape
ANT.018433	1207	Needle: simple bent loop (flapless loop eye)
ANT.018434	1203	Needle: loop eye, indeterminate section
ANT.018436	3190	Other: strip, 20 mm wide with hole at squared end
ANT.018437	1900	Cone "bell": indeterminate
ANT.018438	3200	Indeterminate: shaft
ANT.018439	2001	Split bell: cast; 15 mm diameter; 14 mm suspension shaft with cast hole
ANT.018440	1111	Tweezer: flaring
ANT.018441	3200	Indeterminate: shaft
ANT.018442	1115	Tweezer: pointed
ANT.018443	3210	Indeterminate: sheet fragment
ANT.018444	3210	Indeterminate: sheet fragments
ANT.018447	1801	Bola: spheroid with suspension hole; 21.8 mm diameter

Continued.

Catalog number	Type code	Description
ANT.018448	1015	Tupu: half-round or drooping, indeterminate
ANT.018449	1206	Needle: pierced eye, indeterminate; broken at eye, end missing
ANT.018450	3215	Miscellaneous fragment; may be round tupu head or round tweezer valve
ANT.018451	1010	Tupu: half-round
ANT.018452	1037	Tupu: thin head, indeterminate shape
ANT.018453	2700	Chisel: fine
ANT.018454	5610	Lirpu: disc with pierced tab for suspension; 37 mm diameter
ANT.018460	2933	Production: sheet scrap (irregularly cut and bent sheet)
ANT.018461	2920	Production: smelting or refining product, excess from melting
ANT.018477	1010	Tupu: half-round
ANT.018478, 018479	2750	Tool: crowbar (in two pieces)
ANT.018480	5610	Lirpu: disc with pierced tab for suspension; 77 mm diameter
ANT.018481	2920	Production: smelting or refining product, excess from melting
ANT.018482	1206	Needle: pierced eye, indeterminate; broken at eye, end missing
ANT.018626	1202	Needle: loop eye, rectangular section

Metal Artifacts from the Bingham Collection at Yale University Not Included in Section Two

Attributions of artifacts to the Alvistur collection purchase were provided by Lucy Salazar (personal communications 2010, 2011). While these artifacts are not included in the tables, maps, or most discussion in Section Two, some are discussed in Section One and Appendices A, B, and C.

Catalog number	Type code	Description	Reason for exclusion
ANT.017820	1010	Tupu: half-round	Alvistur collection purchase
ANT.017836	1001	Tupu: round with cast sun and moon decoration	Presumed colonial
ANT.017837	1011	Tupu: half-round, head thick as shaft	Lucy Salazar pers. comm.
ANT.017839	1010	Tupu: half-round	Alvistur collection purchase
ANT.017842	2425	Tiny tupu or lime dipper: cast aryballoid with openwork strips	Alvistur collection purchase
ANT.017843	1036	Tupu: miscellaneous thin head, elaborated outline	Alvistur collection purchase
ANT.017844	1023	Tupu: round, flaring bump	Lucy Salazar pers. comm.
ANT.017847	1001	Tupu: round	Alvistur collection purchase
ANT.017849	5610	Lirpu: disc with pierced tab for suspension; 95 mm diameter	Alvistur collection purchase
ANT.017898	4250	Axe: rectangular tangs, no hole, trapezoidal blade ("classic")	From "an old Inca settlement near the Pampaconas River..."[a]
ANT.017900	4250	Axe: rectangular tangs, no hole, trapezoidal blade ("classic")	From the "valley of the Urubamba River near Rosalina"[b]
ANT.017902	4250	Axe: rectangular tangs, no hole, trapezoidal blade ("classic")	Lucy Salazar pers. comm.
ANT.017903	4250	Axe: rectangular tangs, no hole, trapezoidal blade ("classic")	Modern reproduction for metallurgical testing[c]
ANT.017905	4470	Axe: curved tangs, no hole, wide crescent blade	Alvistur collection purchase
ANT.017906	4270	Axe: rectangular tangs, no hole, wide crescent blade	Alvistur collection purchase
ANT.017910	2840	T-shaped tumi: straight back, globular join, disc head, very fine casting	Alvistur collection purchase
ANT.017988[d]	2104	Bead: rolled sheet	Beads are excluded from this analysis
ANT.018425	2760	Weapon: star-shaped mace head	Alvistur collection purchase
ANT.022060	1097	Tupu: cast viscacha, twisted shaft	Colonial
No number	1061	Tupu: cone, single, with loop	Object without catalog number, sketched by Owen in 1985; no record of this object is currently available

[a] Foote and Buell 1912; Figure 2.1.
[b] Foote and Buell 1912; Figure 2.2.
[c] Foote and Buell 1912:129
[d] This is a different object from ANT.017988 in Section One and Appendix C. That object is catalogued in Section Two as ANT.017988b.

APPENDIX E

Artifact Data Sources

Sources of Metal Artifact Data and the Number of Items Contributed by Each

Number of artifacts	Source
1,881	AMERICAN MUSEUM OF NATURAL HISTORY, NEW YORK, NY, USA 1986. Personal inspection of collection and documents, courtesy of Peter Kvietok (Bandelier 1910, n.d.; Chapin 1961).
1,218	MAYER, EUGEN FRIEDRICH 1998. *Vorspanische Metallwaffen und –werkzeuge in Peru/Armas y herramientas de metal prehispánicas en Perú.* Mainz: Philipp Von Zabern. (Materialien zur Allgemeinen und Vergleichenden Archäologie 55.)
933	MAYER, EUGEN FRIEDRICH 1992. *Vorspanische Metallwaffen und -werkzeuge in Ecuador/Armas y herramientas de metal prehispánicas en Ecuador.* Mainz: Philipp Von Zabern. (Materialien zur Allgemeinen und Vergleichenden Archäologie 47.)
931	MAYER, EUGEN FRIEDRICH 1986. *Vorspanische Metallwaffen und -werkzeuge in Argentinien und Chile/Armas y herramientas de metal prehispánicas en Argentina y Chile.* Munich: C.H. Beck. (Materialien zur Allgemeinen und Vergleichenden Archäologie 38.)
793	FIELD MUSEUM OF NATURAL HISTORY, CHICAGO, IL, USA 2004. Digital photographs of metals and context database, courtesy of Patrick Ryan Williams (Dorsey 1901). Complemented by objects recorded in 1986, listed separately below.
722	PHOEBE A. HEARST (FORMERLY LOWIE) MUSEUM, UNIVERSITY OF CALIFORNIA, BERKELEY, CA, USA 1986. Personal inspection of part of Uhle collection and documents, courtesy of Larry Dawson (Kroeber and Strong 1924a, 1924b; Bennett 1939, 1944; Root 1949; Menzel 1966, 1976).
559	BAESSLER, ARTHUR 1906. *Altperuanische Metallgerate.* Berlin: von Georg Reimer.
479	ANTZE, GUSTAV 1930. *Metallarbeiten aus dem Nördlichen Peru. Ein Beitrag zur Kenntnis ihrer Formen.* Hamburg: Friederichsen, De Gruyter. (Mitteilungen aus dem Museum für Völkerkunde in Hamburg 15.)

Continued.

364	MAYER, EUGEN FRIEDRICH 1994. *Vorspanische Metallwaffen und -werkzeuge in Bolivia/Armas y herramientas de metal prehispánicas en Bolivia*. Mainz: Philipp Von Zabern. (Materialien zur Allgemeinen und Vergleichenden Archäologie 53.)
261	TOPIC, JOHN R. 1977. *The Lower Class at Chan Chan: A Qualitative Approach* [dissertation]. Cambridge: Harvard University, Department of Anthropology.
247	AMBROSETTI, JUAN B. 1904. Arqueología Argentina—El Bronce en la Región Calchaquí. *Anales del Museo Nacional de Buenos Aires*, Series 3, 4(11):163–314.
225	UPPER MANTARO ARCHAEOLOGICAL RESEARCH PROJECT, JAUJA, PERU 1983–1986. Personal inspection of collections in Jauja and at the objects conservation department of The Metropolitan Museum of Art, courtesy of Ellen Howe; field descriptions by Timothy Earle and Bruce Owen (Earle et al. 1980, 1987; Owen 1986, 2001; Costin et al. 1989; D'Altroy 1992; Bezur and Owen 1996; D'Altroy and Hastorf 2001).
187	LATCHAM, RICARDO 1938. *Arqueología de la Región Atacameña*. Santiago: Prensa de la Universidad de Chile.
180	MACHU PICCHU COLLECTION, YALE PEABODY MUSEUM OF NATURAL HISTORY, NEW HAVEN, CT, USA 1985. Personal inspection of the collection, courtesy of Richard Burger and Leopold Pospisil, with a few additions from Rutledge (1984) and personal communications from Lucy Salazar (2010, 2011) (Mathewson 1915; Eaton 1916; Bingham 1930; Rutledge 1984; Rutledge and Gordon 1987).
156	MUSEO CONTISUYO, MOQUEGUA, PERU 2004. Personal inspection of objects from Estuquiña (courtesy of Niki Clark), San Antonio (courtesy of Geoff Conrad), Sabaya, Capanto, and Camata (courtesy of Peter Bürgi); these objects complement those recorded in 1988 as Programa Contisuyo holdings, listed separately below.
118	FIELD MUSEUM OF NATURAL HISTORY, CHICAGO, IL, USA 1986. Personal inspection of part of collection and documents, courtesy of Robert Welsh. Complemented by photographs and database provided in 2004, listed separately above.
104	VERNEAU, RENÉ AND PAUL RIVET 1912. *Ethnographie Ancienne de L'Equateur*. Paris: Du Bureau des Longitudes, de l'Ecole Polytechnique. (Mission du Service Geographique de L'Armee pour la Mesure d'un Arc de Méridien Equatorial en Amérique du Sud 6.)
78	SUTLIFF, MARIE J. 1989. Domestic production of small copper artifacts during the Milagro occupation at Peñon del Río (Guayas Basin). Paper presented at: the 54th Annual Meeting of the Society for American Archaeology; April 5–9, 1989; Atlanta, GA, USA.

Continued.

75	SMITHSONIAN INSTITUTION, WASHINGTON, DC, USA 1986. Data from duplicates of catalog cards provided by Bruce Smith; many objects not recorded because of insufficiently specific notes.
67	VALCÁRCEL, LUIS E. 1935b. Sajsawaman redescubierto. (IV). *Revista del Museo Nacional* 4(2):163–204.
61	JIJÓN Y CAAMAÑO, JACINTO 1920. Los Tincullpas y Notas acerca de la Metalurgia de los Aborigenes del Ecuador. *Boletín de la Sociedad Ecuatoriana* 5(13–14):4–43.
58	RÍOS MARCELA, AND ENRIQUE RETAMOZO 1978. *Objetos de Metal Procedentes de la Isla de San Lorenzo*. Lima: Instituto Nacional de Cultura, Museo Nacional de Antropología y Arqueología. (Arqueológicas 17.)
58	PEDERSEN, ASBJORN 1952. Objetos de Bronce de la Zona del Rio Salado (Región Chaco-Santiagueña). In: ICA. *Proceedings of the Thirtieth International Congress of Americanists: Held at Cambridge, 18–23 August 1952*. London: Royal Anthropological Institute.
42	MCCOWN, THEODORE D. 1945. Pre-Incaic Huamachuco: Survey and Excavations in the Region of Huamachuco and Cajabamba. *University of California Publications in American Archaeology and Ethnology* 39(4):223–400.
41	PROGRAMA CONTISUYO, MOQUEGUA, PERU 1988. Personal inspection of part of the project's collections stored in Moquegua, Peru, courtesy of Don Rice and Geoff Conrad; complemented by objects recorded at the Museo Contisuyo in 2004, listed separately above.
30	LLANOS, LUIS A. 1936. Trabajos Arqueologicos en el Dep. del Cuzco Bajo la Dirección del Dr. Luis E. Valcárcel: Informe Sobre Ollantaitambo. *Revista del Museo Nacional* 38:93–108.
29	VALCÁRCEL, LUIS E. 1934a. Sajsawaman Redescubierto. *Revista del Museo Nacional* 3(1–2):3–36.
25	RUIZ ESTRADA, ARTURO 1976. *Hallazgos de oro, Sillustani (Puno)*. Lima: [Museo Nacional de Antropología y Arqueología]. (Serie Metalurgia 1.) A large lot of 391 uniform gold bangles, 23 gold beads, and 54 gold discs are not included in this analysis.
24	NORDENSKIÖLD, ERLAND 1921. *The Copper and Bronze Ages in South America*. Göteborg: Elanders Boktryckeri Aktiebolag. (Comparative Ethnographical Studies 4.)
20	JIJÓN Y CAAMAÑO, JACINTO 1949. *Maranga: Contribución al Conocimiento de los Aborígenes del Valle del Rimac, Perú*. Quito: La Prensa Católica.
18	ALVAREZ M., LUIS 1959. Descripción de los implementos metalurgicos y liticos obtenidos de una tumba de La Lisera. *Boletín del Museo Regional de Arica* 1:13–15, 21–22.

Continued.

15	YALE PEABODY MUSEUM OF NATURAL HISTORY, NEW HAVEN, CT, USA 1985. Personal inspection of the Hiram Bingham collections and purchases from sites other than Machu Picchu, courtesy of Richard Burger and Leopold Pospisil. Attributions of artifacts to the Alvistur collection purchase were provided by Lucy Salazar (personal communications 2010, 2011) (Foote and Buell 1912; Salazar and Burger 2004a).
13	BAUER, BRIAN S. 2004. Archaeological investigations at Maukallaqta and Puma Orco, Department of Cuzco, Peru. *Nawpa Pacha* 25–27:207–250.
13	JIJÓN Y CAAMAÑO, JACINTO 1922. La Edad del Bronce en America del Sur. *Boletín de la Academia Nacional de Historia, Quito* 4(9):119–126.
12	MUSEO AREQUEOLÓGICO DE LA UNIVERSIDAD NACIONAL SAN AGUSTIN, AREQUIPA, PERU 2004. Personal inspection of a small sample of the UNSA museum's metal holdings that were on display in August 2004, courtesy of Pablo de la Vera Cruz and Mario Vera.
10	DISSELHOFF, HANS D. 1971. *Vicús: Eine Neu Entdeckte Altperuanische Kulture*. Berlin: Gebr. Mann. (Monumenta Americana 7.)
9	CAPDEVILLE, AUGUSTO 1921. Notas acerca de la Arqueología de Taltal III. *Boletín de la Academia Nacional Historia, Quito* 3(7–8):229–233.
9	VALCÁRCEL, LUIS E. 1935a. Los trabajos arqueológicos en el Departamentos del Cusco. Sajsawaman redescubierto. (III). *Revista del Museo Nacional* 4(1):1–24.
9	VALDEZ, LIDIO 2002. Y la tradición continua: la alfarería de la época inka en el valle de Ayacucho, Peru. *Boletín de Arqueología PUCP* 6:395–410.
7	VALCÁRCEL, LUIS E. 1934b. Los trabajos arqueológicos en el Departamentos del Cusco. II. Sajsawaman redescubierto. *Revista del Museo Nacional* 3(3):211–233.
7	AMPUERO BRITO, GONZALO 1969. Excavaciones arqueológicas en el fundo "Coquimbo," Departamento de La Serena. In: Chile, Dirección General de Bibliotecas, Archivos y Museos, Museo Arqueológico de La Serena. *Actas del V Congreso Nacional de Arqueología: 16–20 de Octubre 1969*. La Serena, Chile: Museo Arqueológico de La Serena. pp. 153–166.
5	LARREA, JUAN 1941. El Yauri, Insignia Incaica. *Revista del Museo Nacional* 10(1):25–50.
5	MARSHALL, GEORGE 1964. *Notes on the Examination of Some pre-Columbian Metal Samples; Examen de Algunas Muestras Pre-Colombinas de Metal*. Lima: Museo Nacional de Antropologia y Arqueologia. (Arqueologicas 7.)

Continued.

4	DORSEY, GEORGE A. 1901. *Archaeological Investigations on the Island of La Plata, Ecuador.* Chicago: Field Columbian Museum. (Publication 56, Anthropological Series 2(5).)
4	NASH, DONNA 2005, 2012. Personal communication and photograph of cone "bells" and a "cowbell" found at Cerro Baúl.
4	SCHWOERBEL, GABRIELA H. 1969. Armas de Cobre en la Necropolis de Tablada de Lurín. *Boletín del Seminario de Arqueología, Pontifica Universidad Catolica del Peru* 1(3):46–51.
3	HELSLEY-MARCHBANKS, ANNE M. 2004. The Inca presence in Chayanta, Bolivia: The metallurgical component. *Nawpa Pacha* 25–27:251–260.
2	GIBAJA O. AND M. ARMINDA 2004. Dos ofrendas al agua de Ollantaytambo. *Nawpa Pacha* 25–27:177–188.
2	SCHIAPPACASSE, VIRGILIO AND HANS NIEMEYER 1989. Avances y sugerencias para el conocimiento de la prehistoria tardía en el desembocadura del valle de Camarones (Region de Tarapaca). *Chungará* 22:63–84.
1	DÍAZ, LUISA AND FRANCISCO VALLEJO 2002. Armatambo y el dominio incaico en el valle de Lima. *Boletin de Arqueología PUCP* 6:355–374.
1	JULIEN, CATHERINE J. 1982. A late burial from Cerro Azoguini, Puno. *Nawpa Pacha* 19:129–154.
1	PILLISTAY SITE VISIT, VALLEY OF CAMANÁ, PERU 2004. Hafted star-shaped mace curated by Sr. Valediano, resident of Pillistay, Camaná, Peru.
10,120	Total

APPENDIX F

Metal Artifact Typology

This typology attempts to encompass the full range of metal artifacts in the database. Nevertheless, it emphasizes variation in common metal objects that seemed likely to be of interest for questions concerning the Late Horizon and Late Intermediate periods, with less detail for elaborate, rare, or apparently early forms. These categories are types only in a loose sense, since many are arbitrary divisions of continuous ranges of variations of forms, made in the hope of capturing some patterning in the same way that an excavator uses arbitrary levels when there is no visible stratigraphy. There is no reason to assume that the features used here to divide different forms of tweezers, tumis, axes, and so on were necessarily salient to the people who made and used them. These "types" are purely exploratory analytical tools, and other ways of dividing the variation in metal forms might be more effective or culturally correct. The four-digit codes are arbitrary labels to concisely identify each type. There is no significance to the codes or their order other than convenience for data entry and analysis. The types are presented here to give greater specificity to the discussion in Section Two, "The Meanings of Metals," and as a starting point for description and comparisons in other cases. Many of the types are illustrated in Appendix G. A number of variables that cross-cut multiple types were also recorded for each object in the database. These variables and their possible values follow the list of types below.

Metal Object Types

Type code	Description of type
Tupu	
1001	Round
1002	Round, neck step
1003	Squat ovoid head, tapered neck
1004	Vertically elongated ovoid/flat spoon
1005	Round, crude
1006	Long taper
1007	Half-round transitional
1010	Half-round
1011	Half-round, head thick as shaft
1012	Half-round, >semicircular
1014	Drooping
1015	Half-round or drooping (indeterminate)
1020	Round to half-round, neck lobe

Continued.

Type code	Description of type
1021	Half-round with cast figure, corner holes
1022	Round, small bump
1023	Round, flaring bump
1024	Round, spirals
1025	Round, neck step and spirals
1026	Drooping, spirals
1027	Two spirals
1028	Y head, possibly broken "two spirals" head
1029	Flat narrow head (may be needle)
1035	Miscellaneous thin heads, plain outline
1036	Miscellaneous thin heads, elaborated outline, may have cutouts, etc.
1037	Thin head, indeterminate shape
1040	Nail head, thick, with cross-hole
1041	Nail head, thin, with cross-hole
1042	Axial solid, raised rings, no cross-hole
1043	Axial solid, plain, no cross-hole
1044	Axial solid, slight nail head, cross-hole
1048	Loop
1050	2-piece flat mold, llama head
1051	2-piece flat mold, other
1055	Cast animal head: llama with ears
1056	Cast animal head: earless animal
1057	Cast animal head: feline
1058	Cast animal head: indeterminate animal with ears
1060	Cast standing anthropomorphic figure
1061	Cone, single, with loop
1062	Cone, double, with loop
1080	Cast "yauri" head
1083	Star-shaped mace head, whorl-sized, no hole
1086	Rattles (one to three, plain or elaborate)
1087	Bolivian bifurcated cast types
1089	Miscellaneous cast in the round
1090	Flat figural wire-relief
1091	Applied spirals
1092	Flaring squared, possibly worn or broken
1097	Probably colonial
1098	Other
1099	Completely indeterminate type
Tweezer	
1100	Indeterminate type
1101	Triangular
1102	Triangular transitional
1103	Teardrop
1104	Teardrop transitional

Continued.

Type code	Description of type
1105	Circular, flaring neck
1106	Circular, straight neck
1107	Circular transitional
1108	Straight
1109	Straight transitional
1110	Miscellaneous straight style
1111	Flaring
1112	Fish-shaped
1113	Narrow-necked
1114	Oyster-shaped
1115	Pointed
1116	Compound curved strip
1117	Bifurcated
1118	Series
1119	Headed long-necked
1120	Notched
1121	Miscellaneous symmetrical valve style
1122	Spiral-armed
1123	Twisted-neck
1124	Figural valve
1125	Spiral valve
1126	Other asymmetrical valve
1127	Crescent
1128	Wide ovoid with long straight hinge
Needle	
1200	Indeterminate type
1201	Loop-eye, round section
1202	Loop-eye, rectangular section
1203	Loop-eye, indeterminate section
1208	Loop-eye, semicircular section
1204	Pierced-eye, closed end
1205	Pierced-eye, trough end (open or pinched shut)
1206	Pierced-eye, indeterminate
1207	Simple flapless bent loop-eye
Earspool	
1300	Indeterminate
1301	Small straight tube, expanded face, recurved rim
1302	Small straight tube, other expanded face
1303	Small straight tube, small face
1304	Small straight tube, indeterminate
1305	Large tube, closed
1306	Large tube, open
1307	Large tube, indeterminate face

Continued.

Type code	Description of type
1308	Indeterminate tube, indeterminate face
1309	Small concave tube, closed at least one end
1310	Chiclayo style: flaring, closed tube
1311	Straight tube, closed both ends
Vessel	
1400	Indeterminate type
1401	Kero (including tall plain *vaso sin retrato*)
1402	Sculptural (*vaso retrato*)
1403	"Peanut" plan (gourd-shaped)
1404	Carinated pan
1405	Rounded bowl
1406	Tiny shallow vessel or lid
1407	Cast
1408	Indeterminate/other
1410	Tiny deep, necked vessel, possibly lime container
1411	Sculptural other than *vaso retrato*
1412	Handled plate
Figurine	
1509	Fragment, human, no other detail clear
1512	Human, standing, hands on torso, Inca style, dressed, indeterminate sex
1513	Human, standing, hands on torso, Inca style, undressed, male
1514	Human, standing, hands on torso, Inca style, undressed, female
1515	Human, standing, hands on torso, Inca style, undressed, indeterminate sex
1516	Human, standing, hands on torso, other style
1517	Human, standing, hands on torso, Inca style, undressed, male, pot on back
1518	Human, standing, hands on torso, Inca style, undressed, female, pot on back
1532	Human, standing, arms not on torso, Inca style, undressed
1536	Human, standing, hands on torso, other style
1537	Human, standing, rest indeterminate
1538	Human, standing, male with corn
1549	Human, other position, indeterminate style
1551	Titicaca human pendant, female
1552	Titicaca human pendant, indeterminate sex
1560	Human with camelid
1564	Mummy? with face, feet, hunchback
1565	Anthropomorphic nonhuman, head only
1566	Human head only, non-Inca style
1570	Camelid, standing
1575	Camelid, openwork like rattle head tupu 1086
1577	Camelid, other position or style
1590	Bird (possibly from tupu or lime spoon)
1594	Other animal
1595	Monkey and probably camelid
1598	Indeterminate animal

Continued.

Type code	Description of type
Finger ring	
1600	Indeterminate type
1601	Plain sheet (lies flat on finger)
1602	Traced design
1603	Edgewise strip appliqué
1604	Cast-in-the-round ornament
1605	Flat-cast (probably colonial)
1606	Narrow or wire, possibly nose ornament
1607	Twisted pair of wires
1608	Doughnut cut from thick sheet (perpendicular to finger)
1609	Other type
Tiny spoon	
1700	Indeterminate finial
1701	Bird finial
1702	Other finial
Bola weight	
1800	Indeterminate
1801	Spheroid with suspension hole with crossbar
1802	Elaborated shape with suspension hole with crossbar
1803	Circumferential groove, no hole (all are lead)
1804	Spheroid with simple or U-shaped hole (all are lead, typically fairly irregular)
1808	Spheroid with cast circumferential band and suspension hole with crossbar
1809	Bird with suspension hole and crossbar
1820	Spiked flail weight with suspension hole with crossbar
1830	Other form with suspension hole with crossbar
1831	Other bola weight
Conical "bell" (probably hair ornament)	
1900	Indeterminate
1901	Plain
1902	With arms
1903	With other elaborations
Split bell	
2000	Indeterminate
2001	Cast
2002	Forged
Bead (recorded, but excluded from this analysis)	
2100	Indeterminate or other type
2101	Solid (a few may be whorls)
2102	Sheet star bead or bangle
2103	Hollow sphere
2104	Rolled sheet (including rolled around string)
2105	Hollow sphere with suspension loop

Continued.

Type code	Description of type
Nose ornament	
2201	Solid
2202	Sheet
Sheet sheathing	
2300	Indeterminate
2301	Spiral
2302	Plates
2303	Annular strip
2304	Spiral with nails
2305	Plates with nails
2306	Annular with nails
2307	Indeterminate with nails
Tiny tupu or lime dipper	
2410	Cast cone head with loop, single
2421	Cast "noose," 2-piece flat mold
2422	Cast "noose," in the round
2425	Cast aryballoid with openwork strips like rattle tupu 1086
2430	Biconical club-shaped head, no hole
2439	Other head cast in the round, various forms
Fat-shafted implement, possibly lime dipper	
2501	Flat round head, similar to tupu 1001
2503	Flat lobed head, similar to tupu 1020
2505	Flat round head with neck-step, similar to tupu 1002
2521	Bolivian simple llama head
2523	Rattle head, openwork strip design, similar to tupu 1086
2525	Bolivian bifurcated cast head, similar to tupu 1087
2529	Other head
Chisel	
2700	Fine
2701	Fine, with elaborate ornamentation
2705	Large, long, flaring
2710	Heavy (grading into celts, types 4010 and 4020)
2711	Heavy with solid cylinder head
2713	"Formón" like type 2716, with elaborate ornament at end
2716	"Formón": flat blade that narrows abruptly to the hafting tang
Other tool	
2712	Long, narrow bar with rounded work end
2715	Other cutting tool, punch, spatula, etc.
2717	Diamond-head "spatula"
2718	Two flat heads, both ends of handle (possible "mizmina," type 2719)
2719	"Mizmina" or "mizima": two-headed "spinning tool used by men" (from label)

Continued.

Type code	Description of type
2720	Spindle whorl (some may be beads)
2735	Ladle
2740	Plumb bob
2750	Crowbar

Weapon

2760	Star-shaped mace head (5 to 8 points), no central cylinder, medium length rounded points ("classic" form)
2761	Star-shaped mace head, no central cylinder, long, narrow points
2762	Star-shaped mace head, no central cylinder, vertical fin points
2763	Star-shaped mace head, no central cylinder, other points or form
2765	Star-shaped mace head, central cylinder, short to medium points
2766	Star-shaped mace head, central cylinder, long, narrow points
2767	Star-shaped mace head, central cylinder, vertical fin points
2768	Star-shaped mace head, central cylinder, other points or form
2769	"Axe-mace" (Lechtman 2007): star-shaped mace head with axe blade
2770	Spherical to cylindrical mace head or haft weight
2775	Disc-shaped mace head, with or without central cylinder, including toothed and other variants
2780	Other weapon head
2790	Atlatl hook
2800	Atlatl grip
2805	Atlatl with both hook and grip

Projectile point

2814	Flat, with socketed base
2815	Flat, with concave base
2816	Flat, with straight base (triangular form)
2817	Long, usually square-sectioned bar, pointed at both ends
2818	Long, with "whistle" (hollow spherical section with one hole)
2819	Long, with barbs

Fishing implement

2820	Fishhook
2822	Harpoon head barb

Knife

2830	Handleless transverse
2835	Crescent to rectangular to trapezoidal probable knife, hole(s) near back edge
2837	Rectangular probable knife with flaring corners, hole(s) near back edge
2836	Tall trapezoidal to flaring knife with elaborate ornament at back
2838	Tall trapezoidal to flaring knife with hole at back edge
2839	Possible knife blade, long oval, resembles blade of a T-shaped tumi with no handle

T-shaped tumi

2840	Straight back

Continued.

Type code	Description of type
2841	Slightly flaring back
2842	Elaborated blade
2846	Backswept blade
2849	Tiny cast blade
2848	Indeterminate blade shape

Flat tumi (grading into axe monies and North Coast tumis)

5100	Flaring back edge
5105	Crescent to quadrant blade variant, grades into type 5031
5106	Crescent to quadrant blade with elaborate ornament at end of handle
5110	Pointed-blade variant
5115	"T" variant: shape similar to T-shaped tumi, but flat, as if cut from sheet
5116	Small backswept blade
5117	Piura variant, offset hole
5119	Blade shape indeterminate

Guayas tumi

5120	Guayas type: pointed deep crescent blade, thick flat to rounded handle (Mayer 1992)

North Coast tumi

5000	Form indeterminate
5010	Rectangular handle, semicircular blade, plain head
5020	Rectangular handle, semicircular blade, elaborated head
5011	Curved join, less than semicircle
5012	Flaring handle, semicircle blade
5031	Quadrant blade, plain head (grades into type 5105; small ones may show use wear)
5040	Quadrant blade, elaborated head
5080	Straight flaring, elaborated head

Unsplit bell

2900	Cup form
2905	"Cowbell" with cast designs
2906	Tantan or censero ("cowbell")
2907	Full-size star-shaped bell apparently forged from disc
2908	Clapper? with star-shaped "bell"

Production

2920	Smelting or refining product, excess melt, forging blank (may include some slag)
2922	Prill (poorly separated from 2920)
2930	Probable ingot
2933	Sheet scrap: cut-marked, jagged, folded, stacked, packets, etc.
2935	Slag (not included in this analysis)
2938	Stone metalworking tool (not included in this analysis)

Continued.

Type code	Description of type
Ornament	
3020	Bangle or pendant (some may have been used as small cutting tools)
3025	Fish bangle
3027	Two-headed animal pendant
3035	Sheet ornament
3037	Pierced sheet ornament (flat)
3040	Sheet tubes on cloth
3055	Atacama-type "earrings," may be atlatl finger loops
3056	Tarqui-type bimetallic bracelets
3057	Sheet gauntlet
3059	End cap for rod or staff
3070	Elaborated staff head or mace head
Plaque	
3360	Rectangular plaque with pierced bulge for suspension, possible knife 2835
3361	Rectangular plaque with decoration, other type, possible knife
3362	Cast disc with spiral-tailed animals
3363	Cast disc with designs: "caille"
3364	Cast ornamented crescent, suggests a knife, but with blunt, rounded "cutting" edge
3368	Cast other flat shape with decoration
3369	Other shape with pierced bulge for suspension
Headdress	
5310	Frontal: one or more long plumes, including a variety of shapes
5311	Frontal: concave-sided
5312	Frontal: stacked crescents
5313	Frontal: plume base, form indeterminate
5315	Frontal: short tufted plume (lower portion is for mounting)
5316	Frontal: crescent and plume
5317	Frontal: wide or elaborate, various forms
5320	Frontal: trapezoid on rectangle
5325	Cylindrical or conical headdress structure, with or without frontal
Axe monies and related wealth stores	
3103	Hosler, Lechtman, and Holm (1990), hide
3104	Rounded Ecuadorian style
3105	Hosler, Lechtman, and Holm (1990), types 1a, 1b, 2
3106	Hosler, Lechtman, and Holm (1990), naipe
3107	Hosler, Lechtman, and Holm (1990), feather
3108	Piura type (Mayer 1998, items 1631 to 1661)
Miscellaneous	
3110	Plume holder cone
3112	Long-handled plume holder
3114	Sculpture, figurine, vessel, and others fabricated from formed sheet metal parts

Continued.

Type code	Description of type
3116	Chisel-handled "rattle"
3117	Tumi-handled "rattle"
3120	Rectangular folded-up object, possibly tray, plaque, bead, or ornament
3122	Quena or zampoña
3130	Mummy mask
3132	Sheet metal from mouth of mummy or burial
3138	Cone on long loop
3140	"Yo-yo"
3142	"Washer" (may have irregular outer shape)
3145	"Brazal" (Mayer 1986)
3150	"Manopla" or "knuckle duster" (Mayer 1986)
3153	Object vaguely resembling a miniature sea anchor
3156	Possible snuff tablet
3157	Ecuadorian "placa ceremonial" (Mayer 1992)
3159	Elaborated cast representation of axe and handle: "toki" (Ambrosetti 1904)
3160	Elaborated cast representation of axe head with ornament: handleless "toki"
3161	Elaborated cast representation of T-shaped axe head with ornaments, Vicus style
3162	Large tupu-like object with broad flat or thick, massive handle, not pin shaft
3165	Decorated nail/spike object, possibly a lime dipper
3168	Tiwanaku architectural clamp
3170	Bar
3175	Bar pointed on one or both ends, square section, possible projectile point
3176	Bar pointed on one or both ends, square section, curved, possible harpoon barb
3180	Wire
3187	Wire hoop
3185	Wire or rod loops joined as chain
3190	Strip (some may be bracelets, headbands, or similar items)
3195	Strip with hooks (some may be bracelets, headbands, or similar items)
3197	Wire with hooks (some may be bracelets, headbands, or similar items)

Indeterminate

3200	Indeterminate shaft
3210	Sheet fragment
3215	Miscellaneous fragment

Other

3220	Miscellaneous metal object
3240	Miscellaneous cast object

Lead used to plug or mend a ceramic vessel

3290	Mend (usually two hourglass shapes joined by an irregular bar)
3295	Plug (oval shape with concave edges)
3297	Mend or plug, indeterminate

Celt (probably agricultural tool tip, possibly axe or other uses)

4010	Straight or slightly flared sides (grading into heavy chisels, type 2710)

Continued.

Type code	Description of type
4020	Straight or slightly flared sides, with flared end (grading into type 2710)
4030	Possible celt: lenticular section, rounded, flared
4040	Celt or chisel: long curved flare, narrow shaft
4050	Possible celt: rectangular with both ends flared
4090	Other celt or hoe form
Axe	
4140	One large hole, short rectangular to slightly flared blade
4145	One large hole, short rectangular small abrupt flaring blade
4150	One large hole, trapezoidal to curved flaring blade
4170	One large hole, wide crescent blade
4195	One large hole, other variant blade
4200	Rectangular tangs, no hole, long narrowing blade (ranges from axe to pike forms)
4220	Rectangular tangs, no hole, long rectangular blade
4225	Rectangular tangs, no hole, long rectangular blade with side bars
4250	Rectangular tangs, no hole, trapezoidal blade ("classic")
4255	Rectangular tangs, no hole, trapezoidal blade with side bars
4270	Rectangular tangs, no hole, wide crescent blade
4275	Rectangular tangs, no hole, wide crescent blade with side bars
4290	Rectangular tangs, no hole, other blade form
4300	Rectangular tangs, one hole, long narrowing blade (ranges from axe to pike forms)
4320	Rectangular tangs, one hole, long rectangular blade
4350	Rectangular tangs, one hole, trapezoidal blade
4370	Rectangular tangs, one hole, wide crescent blade
4380	Rectangular tangs, multiple holes or piercing, wide crescent blade
4390	Rectangular tangs, indeterminate blade form
4420	Curved tangs, no hole, long rectangular blade
4440	Curved tangs, no hole, short rectangular blade
4450	Curved tangs, no hole, trapezoidal blade
4470	Curved tangs, no hole, wide crescent blade ("forma de ancla," Mayer 1986, 1992, 1994, 1998)
4480	Curved tangs, no hole, transverse rectangular blade
4490	Curved tangs, one hole, long narrowing blade (ranges from axe to pike forms)
4510	Variant tangs, no hole, long narrowing blade (ranges from axe to pike forms), hook
4512	Variant tangs, no hole, long narrowing blade (ranges from axe to pike forms)
4520	Variant tangs, no hole, long rectangular blade
4522	Variant tangs, no hole, long flaring blade
4523	Variant tangs, no hole, long flaring blade, hook
4525	Variant tangs, no hole, long rectangular blade with side bars
4540	Variant tangs, no hole, short rectangular blade
4550	Variant tangs, no hole, trapezoidal blade
4570	Variant tangs, no hole, wide crescent blade
4575	Variant tangs, no hole, wide crescent blade with side bars
4580	Variant tangs, no hole, transverse rectangular blade
4585	Variant tangs, no hole, other blade form
4586	Variant tangs, no hole, other blade form with sidebars

Continued.

Type code	Description of type
4587	Variant tangs, one hole, long rectangular blade
4588	Variant tangs, one hole, trapezoidal to flaring blade
4589	Variant tangs, one hole, wide crescent blade
4590	Variant tangs, two holes, long rectangular blade
4591	Variant tangs, one hole, long narrowing blade (ranges from axe to pike forms)
4599	Other tanged axe or pike form
4620	Socket, tail, long rectangular blade
4630	Socket, tail, long rectangular blade, hook
4640	Socket, tail, long narrowing rectangular blade
4651	Socket, tail, trapezoidal blade, side spikes suggesting an axe-mace
4660	Socket, tail, trapezoidal blade, hook
4682	Socket, tail, curved flaring blade, hook
4689	Socket, tail, flat blade of indeterminate form
4690	Socket, tail, rod blade ("yauri," Larrea 1941)
4700	Indeterminate haft, long narrowing blade
4701	Indeterminate haft, indeterminate blade shape
4720	Indeterminate haft, long rectangular blade
4730	Indeterminate haft, long rectangular blade, hook
4740	Indeterminate haft, short rectangular blade
4750	Indeterminate haft, trapezoidal blade
4760	Indeterminate haft, trapezoidal blade, hook
4770	Indeterminate haft, wide crescent blade
4850	Side notches and hole, rectangular to trapezoidal to concave-sided blade
4859	Side notches, no hole, rectangular to trapezoidal to concave-sided blade
4880	Two holes only, trapezoidal blade
4881	Two holes, other type
4882	Two holes, flaring to wide crescent blade
4883	Two holes only, long narrowing blade, hook
4887	Three or more holes, wide crescent blade
4888	Tang fragment, indeterminate form
4990	Socket, no tail, rod blade
4992	Socket, no tail, long rectangular to slightly flaring blade
4950	Socket, no tail, trapezoidal blade
4952	Socket, no tail, trapezoidal blade, face or other sculpture on back of haft
4995	Socket, no tail, wide crescent blade
4996	Socket, no tail, other blade form

Socketed point: agricultural tool tip and/or store of wealth

5130	Slotted socket, indeterminate blade
5131	Slotted socket, long point
5132	Slotted socket, chisel point
5133	Slotted socket, flaring blade
5134	Slotted socket, wide blade
5135	Flap socket, sheet or skin
5136	Flap socket, narrow blade
5137	Flap socket, wide crescent blade

Continued.

Type code	Description of type
5142	Cast full socket, chisel point
5144	Cast full socket, wide blade
5145	Cast full socket, wide tip
5146	Other socketed point

Thin sheet metal disc

5401	Plain, flat, indeterminate hole, indeterminate diameter
5402	Plain, flat, indeterminate hole, <40 mm diameter
5403	Plain, flat, indeterminate hole, 40–100 mm diameter
5404	Plain, flat, indeterminate hole, >100 mm diameter
5411	Plain, flat, no hole, indeterminate diameter
5412	Plain, flat, no hole, <40 mm diameter
5413	Plain, flat, no hole, 40–100 mm diameter
5422	Plain, flat, one hole near edge, <40 mm diameter
5423	Plain, flat, one hole near edge, 40–100 mm diameter
5424	Plain, flat, one hole near edge, >100 mm diameter
5425	Plain, flat, one hole near center, indeterminate diameter
5426	Plain, flat, one hole near center, <40 mm diameter
5428	Plain, flat, one hole near center, >100 mm diameter
5432	Plain, flat, two close holes near edge, <40 mm diameter
5433	Plain, flat, two close holes near edge, 40–100 mm diameter
5437	Plain, flat, two opposed holes near edge, 40–100 mm diameter
5442	Plain, convex, indeterminate hole, <40 mm diameter
5462	Plain, convex, one hole near edge, <40 mm diameter
5465	Plain, convex, one hole near center, indeterminate diameter
5466	Plain, convex, one hole near center, >100 mm diameter
5472	Plain, convex, two close holes near edge, <40 mm diameter
5473	Plain, convex, two close holes near edge, 40–100 mm diameter
5474	Plain, convex, two close holes near edge, >100 mm diameter
5482	Plain, convex, two opposed holes near edge, <40 mm diameter
5486	Plain, convex, more than two holes, <40 mm diameter
5512	Repoussé or decoratively pierced, <40 mm diameter
5513	Repoussé or decoratively pierced, 40–100 mm diameter
5514	Repoussé or decoratively pierced, >100 mm diameter
5553	Other combination, 40–100 mm diameter
5554	Other combination, >100 mm diameter

Lirpu (disc with pierced tab or stem for suspension)

5610	Lirpu: disc with pierced tab for suspension
5620	Lirpu: disc with stem and globular head for suspension

Other disc variants

5630	With large center hole (donut disc)
5640	With ring through hole
5650	Large with central raised face: "tincullpa" (Jijón y Caamaño 1920)
5670	Multiple (conjoined discs in one piece)

Metal Variables

Variable	Values	
Recorded for all entries		
Provenience		
Collection or source		
Museum number		
Notes page number		
Location code	Arbitrary number that links to table of latitude and longitude	
Phase code	0	Unknown
	1	Middle Horizon
	2	Early Late Intermediate period (Wanka I in Upper Mantaro)
	3	Late Intermediate period (middle and general) (Wanka IIA in Mantaro)
	4	Late Late Intermediate period (Wanka II in Upper Mantaro)
	5	Late Horizon (Wanka III in Upper Mantaro)
	6	Colonial (Wanka IV in Upper Mantaro)
	7	Late Late Intermediate period and/or Late Horizon
	8	Late Horizon and/or Colonial
	9	Late Intermediate period and/or Late Horizon and/or Colonial
Type	Four-digit type code; see type list	
Count	Number of original objects or N (Not applicable) if cannot be counted	
Number	Number of original objects or 1 if count is N	
Percent complete	Number or I (Indeterminate)	
Mass	Total of all pieces, in grams, to tenths	
Sampled	Y (Yes) or .	
Material (visual estimate)	CU	Copper or copper alloy only
	CU ± AG	Copper or copper alloy with possible silver content
	CU ± AGU	Copper or copper alloy with possible silver and/or gold content
	CU/AG	Copper with some silver
	AG	Silver
	AG ON CU	Copper or copper alloy with silver-enriched surface
	AG ± CU	Silver with possible copper content
	AG ± PB	Silver with possible lead content
	AG/CU	Silver with some copper
	AG/PB	Silver and/or lead
	AG/AU	Silver and/or gold
	PB	Lead
	AU	Gold
	AU/AG	Gold with some silver
	AU/CU	Gold with some copper
	AU ON CU	Copper or copper alloy with gold-enriched surface

Continued.

Variable	Values	
	SN	Tin
	SLAG	Slag (excluded from this analysis)
	STONE	Stone (metalworking tool; excluded from this analysis)
	CERAMIC	Mold (for metal artifact; excluded from this analysis)
From sheet	Y	(Yes) or .
Cast	Y	(Yes), P (Probably), or .
Forged	Y	(Yes) or .
Shaft section	R	(Round)
	O	(Ovoid)
	S	(Square)
	F	(Flat)
	T	(flat To rounded)
	I	(I-beam)
	D	(lengthwise Depression)
	J	(lengthwise Join)
	C	(reCtangular)
	U	(roUnded rectangular)
	W	(flat With lengthwise depression)
	.	(Not applicable)
Shaft twisted	Y	(Yes) or .
Maximum midshaft diameter*		
Minimum midshaft diameter*		
Point	S	(Sharp)
	M	(Medium)
	D	(Dull)
	V	(Very blunt)
	C	(Chisel)
	.	(Indeterminate, not applicable, or not observed)
Holes	0–99	
	M	(Many)
	I	(Indeterminate)
	.	(Not applicable or not observed)
Hole type	P	(Poked, with rim stretched up and often folded over on one side)
	C	(Cut, with material removed)
	S	(Slot, opening made by cut or slit without material removed)
	E	(Eccentric or off-center, typically on tupus)
	.	(Indeterminate or none of the above)
Concave-convex	Y (Yes), N (No), P (Probably), or .	
Repoussé design	Y (Yes), P (Probably), or .	
Traced design	Y (Yes), C (probably Colonial), or .	
Traced design type	(combination of a design code and a fill code below; multiple pairs allowed, separated by spaces)	

Continued.

Variable	Values	
Design codes	S	(Simple geometric—lines, angles, triangles, rhomboids)
	C	(Complex geometric—stair steps, complex polygons)
	B	(Birds)
	F	(other Figural forms—unidentifiable, supernatural, feline, and others)
	Z	(plain Zigzags)
	W	(row of nested angles, similar to Wari chevron bands)
	D	(Detail lines on repoussé, cutout, or complex silhouette design)
	L	(Line or lines of punctations, but no traced lines)
	P	(complex design formed with Punctations, but no traced lines)
	H	(probably Historical—floral, man on horse, on Colonial object, etc.)
	U	(crosshatching in Undelimited areas, as on thickened vessel rims)
	I	(Indeterminate)
	O	(Other)
Fill codes	N	(None)
	P	(Punctation in areas delimited by traced lines or lines of punctations)
	C	(Cross hatching in areas delimited by traced lines)
	H	(parallel Hatching in areas delimited by traced lines)
	S	(Single dot in center of rhomboid or other area delimited by traced lines)
	T	(parallel Ticks in narrow band)
	I	(Indeterminate)
	O	(Other)
Pierced design	Y (Yes) or .	
Miniature	Y (Yes), P (Probably), or .	
Unfinished	Y (Yes), P (Probably), or .	
Intentionally destroyed	Y (Yes), P (Probably), or .	
Mushrooming	H	(Heavy)
	M	(Moderate)
	S	(Slight)
	P	(Possible)
	.	(No mushrooming or indeterminate)
Sharpening	Y	(Yes)
	P	(Probably)
	N	(No, well-preserved edge definitely not sharpened)
	S	(Serrated)
	.	(Indeterminate, not applicable, or not observed)
Use wear	H	(Heavy)
	M	(Moderate)
	S	(Slight)
	P	(Possible)
	.	(no use wear or indeterminate)

Continued.

Variable	Values
Spiral decoration	Y (Yes) or .
Yarn associated	Y (Yes) or .

Discs
Diameter*

Hole location	M	(Middle)
	C	(near the edge, Close together if multiple holes)
	O	(near the edge, Opposite each other if multiple holes)
	I	(Interior, neither middle nor near edge)
	B	(Both middle and edge)

Tweezers

Neck step	Y (Yes), P (Probably), N (No, definitely not present) or .
Elaborated	Y (Yes) or .
Length*	

Tupus

Neck V	Y (Yes) or . (V-shaped depression at neck from working shaft inward)
Neck steps	Y (Yes), P (Probably), or .
Cast-type neck	Y (Yes, globular neck join)
	P (Probably)
	W (Webbed as if from 2-piece mold, but not globular)
	. (No or not applicable)
Other accentuated neck	Y (Yes), P (Probably), or .
Head thickness*	K (thick, but not as thick as the shaft)
	F (as Fat as the shaft)
	. (Thin or not applicable)
Head shape looks worn	Y (Yes), P (Probably), or .
Fat-type shaft	Y (Yes) or .
Shaft length*	
Total length*	
Head length*	
Head width*	

Strips
Width*

End	S	(Square)
	R	(Round)
	I	(Intermediate)
	.	(not applicable or not observed)

Continued.

Variable	Values
Vessels	
Max diameter*	
Min diameter*	
Depth*	
Rim	P (Plain, rim has same orientation and thickness as upper body)
	S (rim turns outward, forming external horizontal Shelf)
	T (Thickened square rim section)
	O (thickened Other rim section)
	I (rim turns Inward, forming internal horizontal shelf)
Tumis	
Blade length*	
Blade width*	
Cast-type join	Y (Yes, globular join between handle and blade), N (No), or .
Head	P (Plain)
	L (Loop)
	H (animal Head)
	S (cast sculptural Scene or figure)
	D (Disc that shares axis with handle, like the head of a nail)
	F (Flat handle and head, similar to flat tumi types 5100–5119, but any blade shape)
	W (Widened flat, as in Mayer 1992 items 1747–1771)
	O (Other)
Axes	
Axe elaborated	Y (Yes) or .
Needles	
Shaft length*	
Total length*	
Head length*	

*Measurements are in millimeters, to tenths where possible.

APPENDIX G

ILLUSTRATIONS OF SELECTED METAL ARTIFACT TYPES

These illustrations depict specific objects in the spatial GIS database of 10,120 metal objects found at known places in the Inca empire (see Section Two, "The Meanings of Metals"), but are intentionally schematic to emphasize the formal, abstracted nature of the categories. Where a type is illustrated by multiple examples, the illustrations are selected to indicate the range of variation in form, but not always of size, since very small and very large examples are difficult to present in a consistent scale. The examples are also intended to imply the features that define the type, and to highlight the areas of ambiguity between similar types. Some objects could reasonably be classified in either of two types, as some of the illustrations show. This problem is simply inherent in the continuous and multidimensional variability of the artifacts and necessarily imparts some fuzziness to the typological analysis.

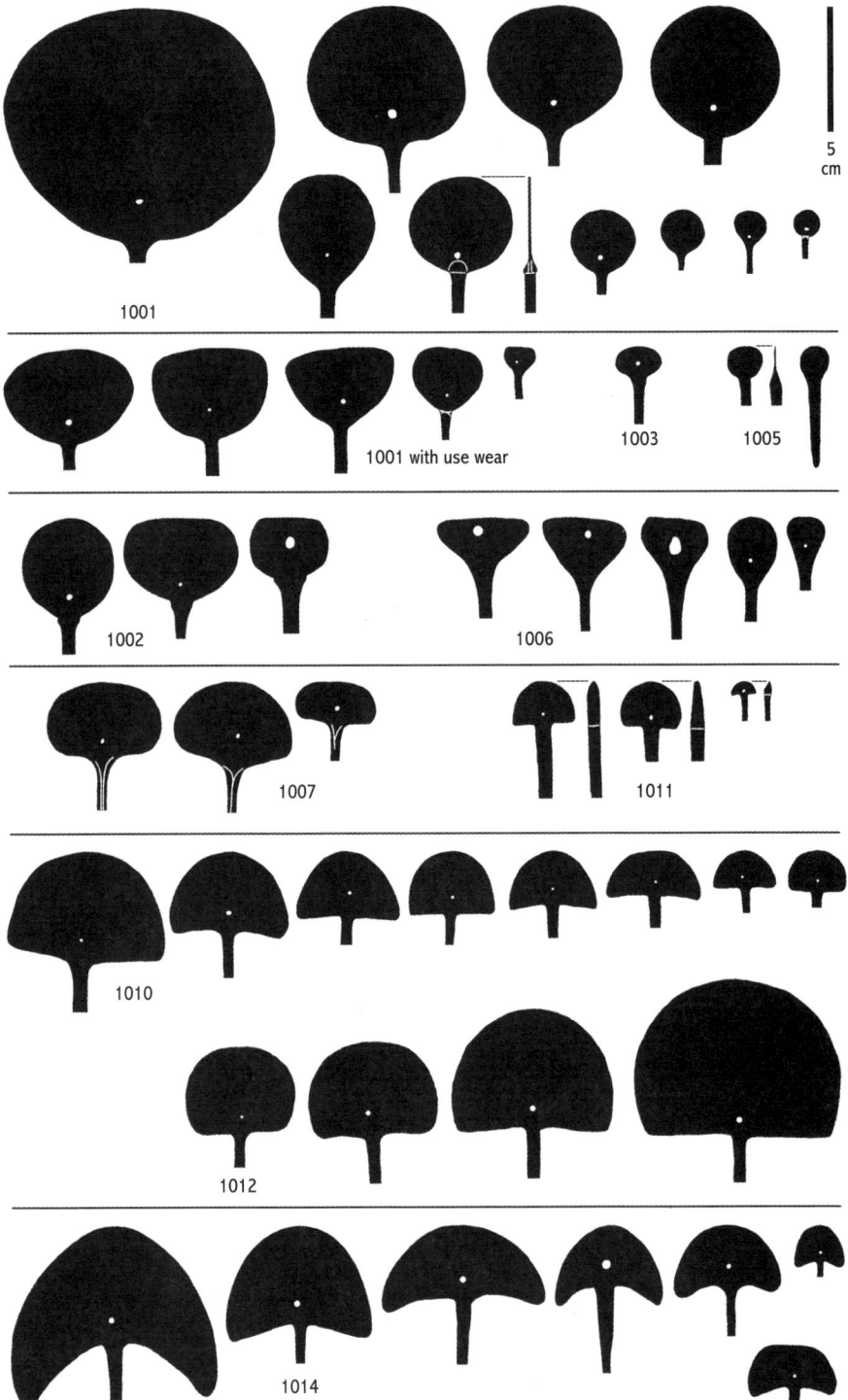

Figure G1

Appendix G

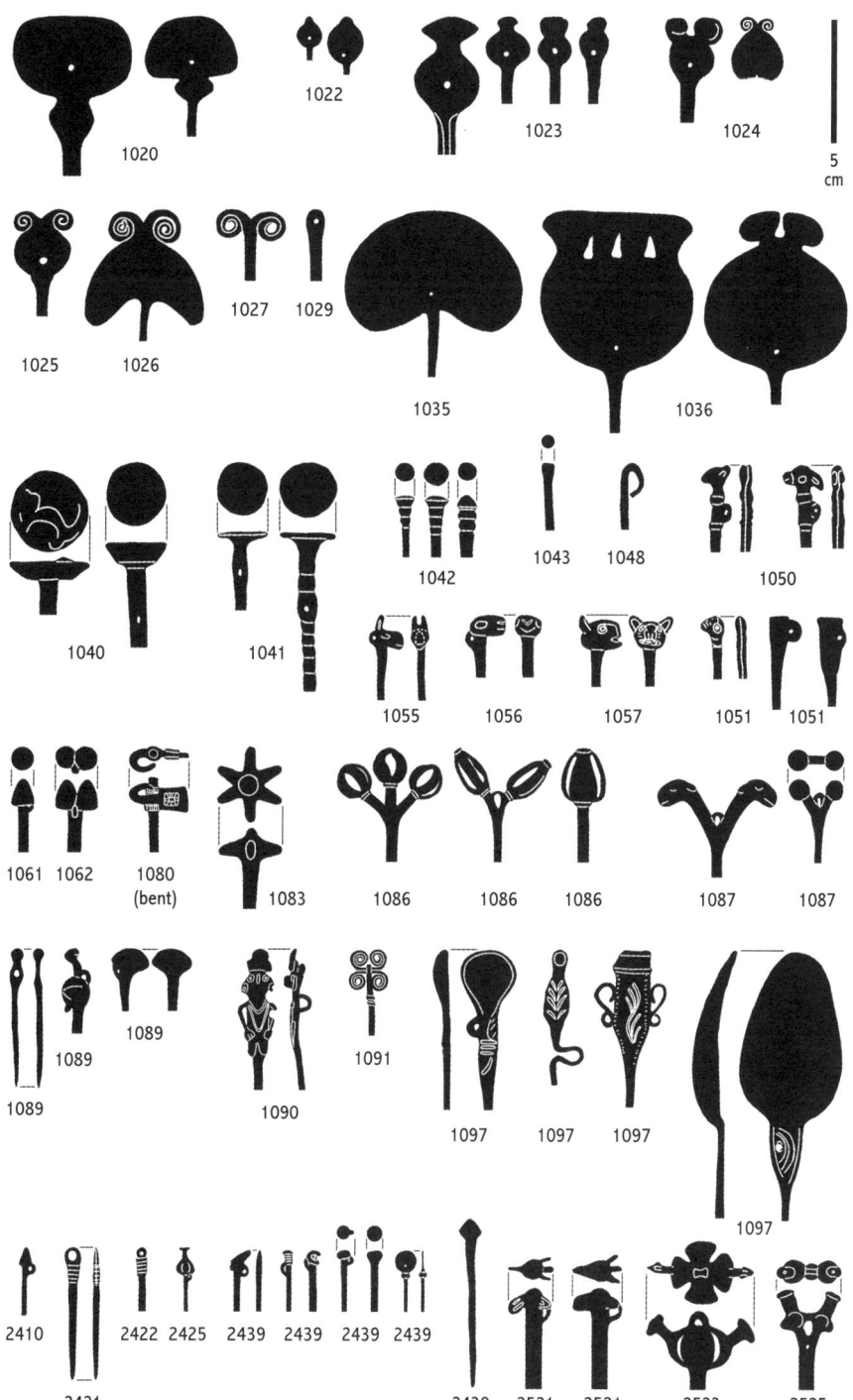

Figure G2

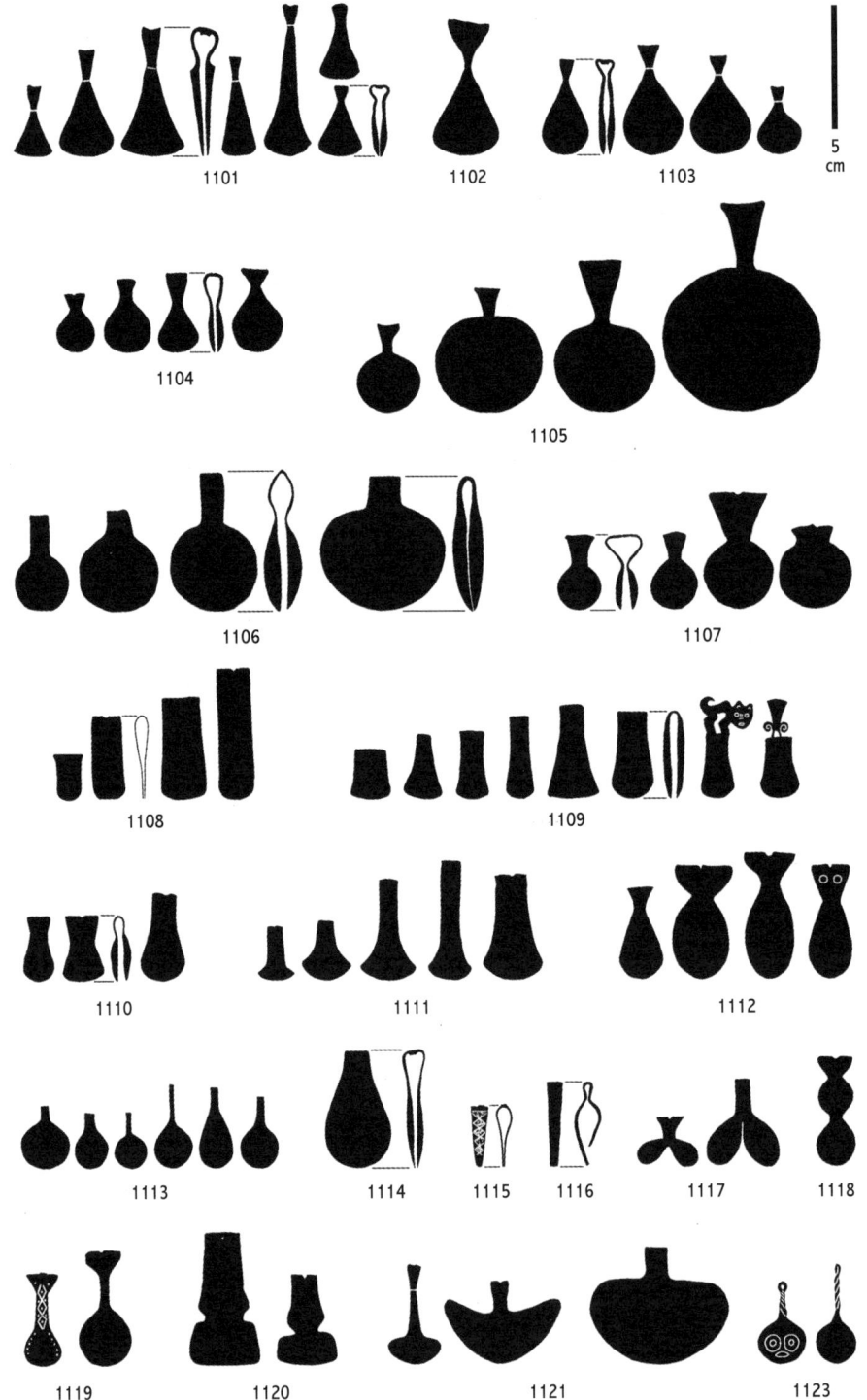

Figure G3

APPENDIX G

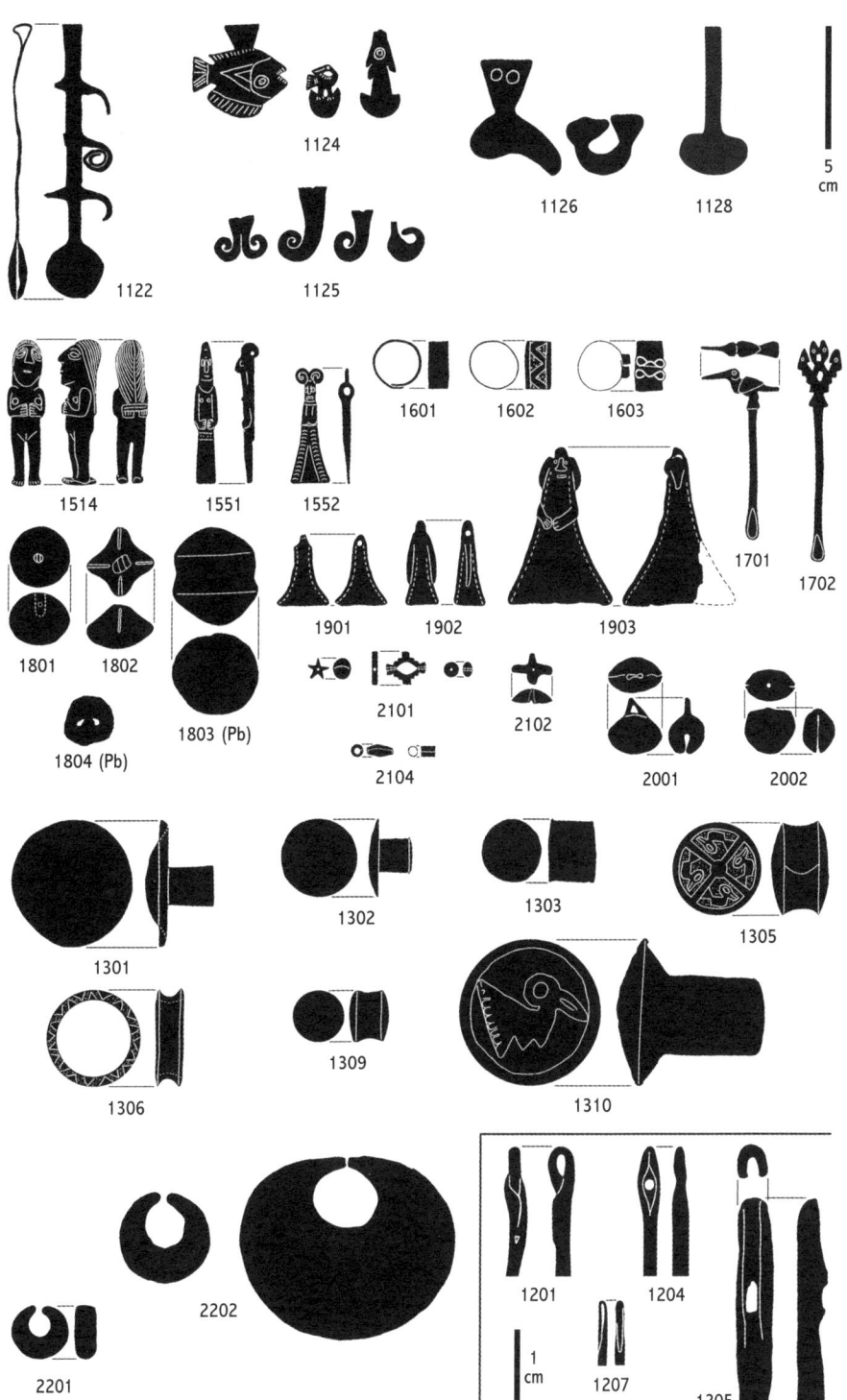

FIGURE G4

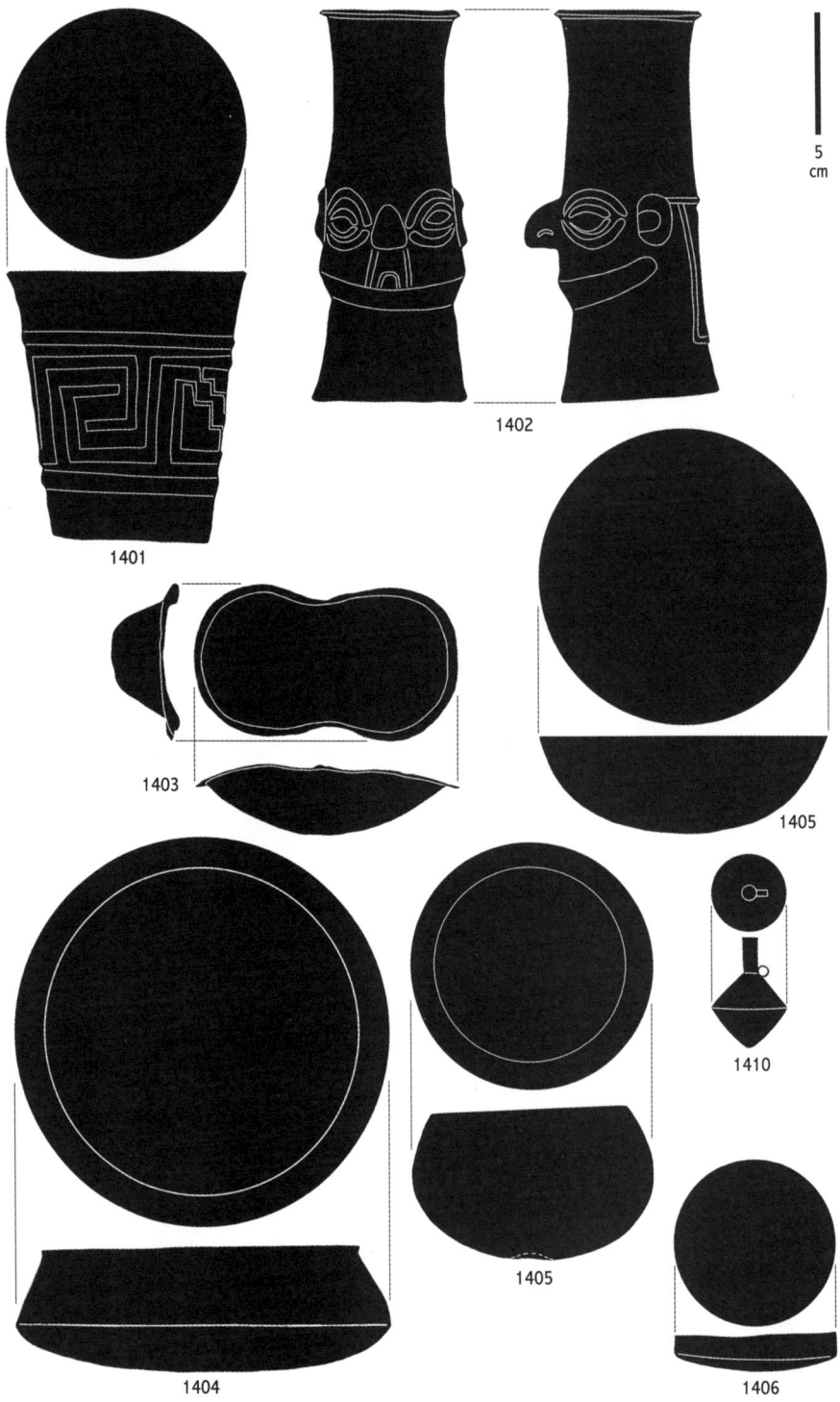

Figure G5

APPENDIX G

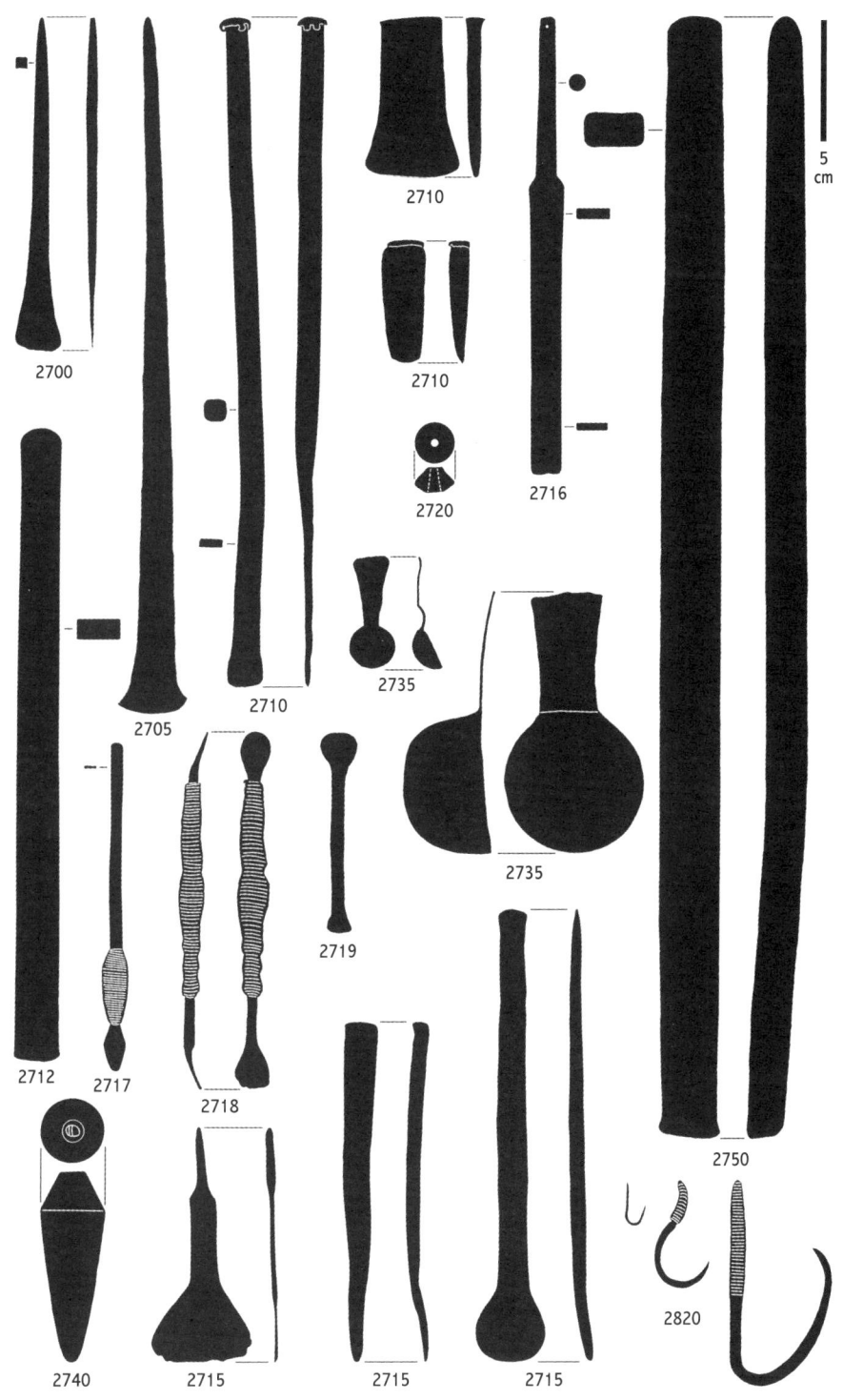

FIGURE G6

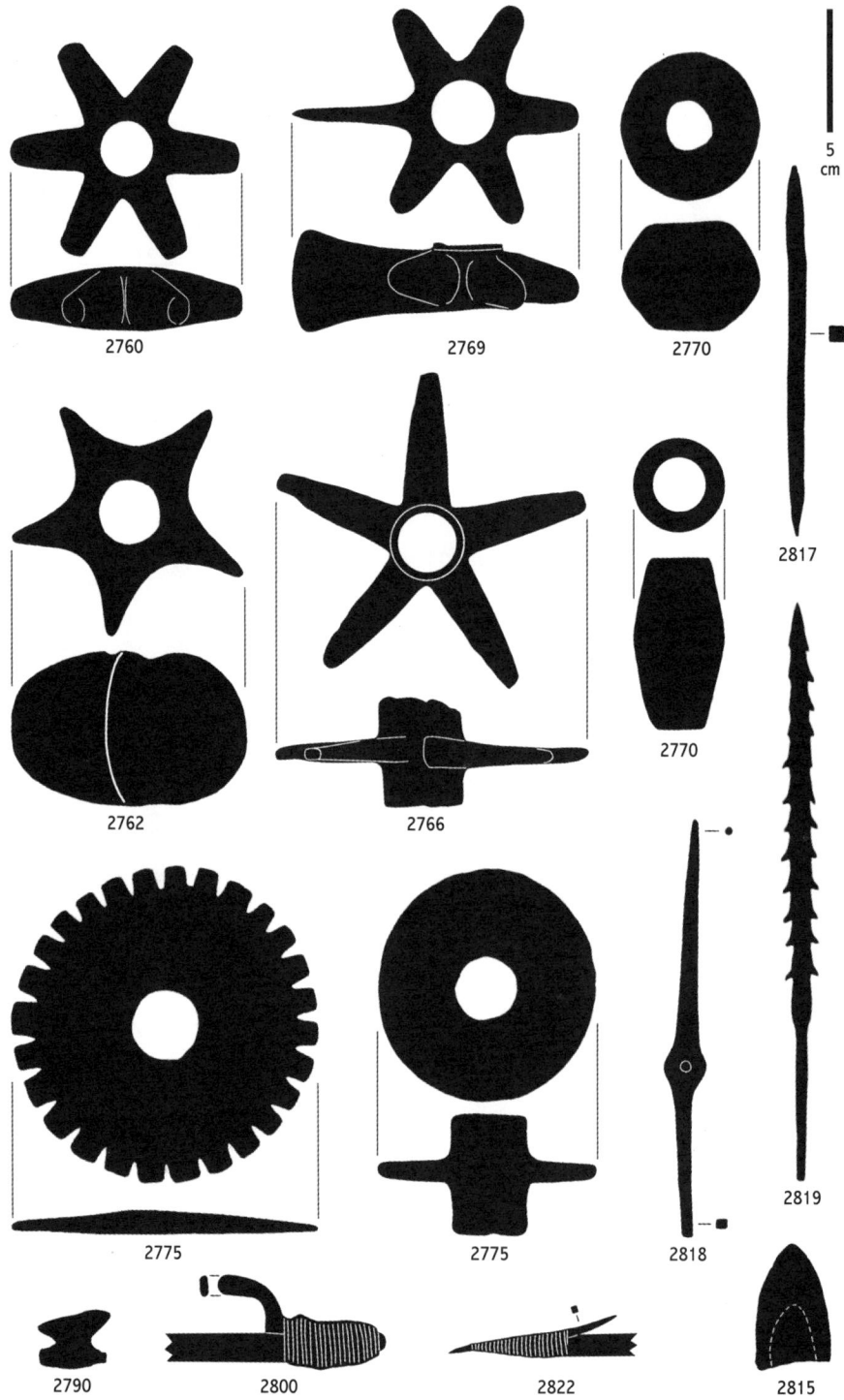

FIGURE G7

Appendix G

Figure G8

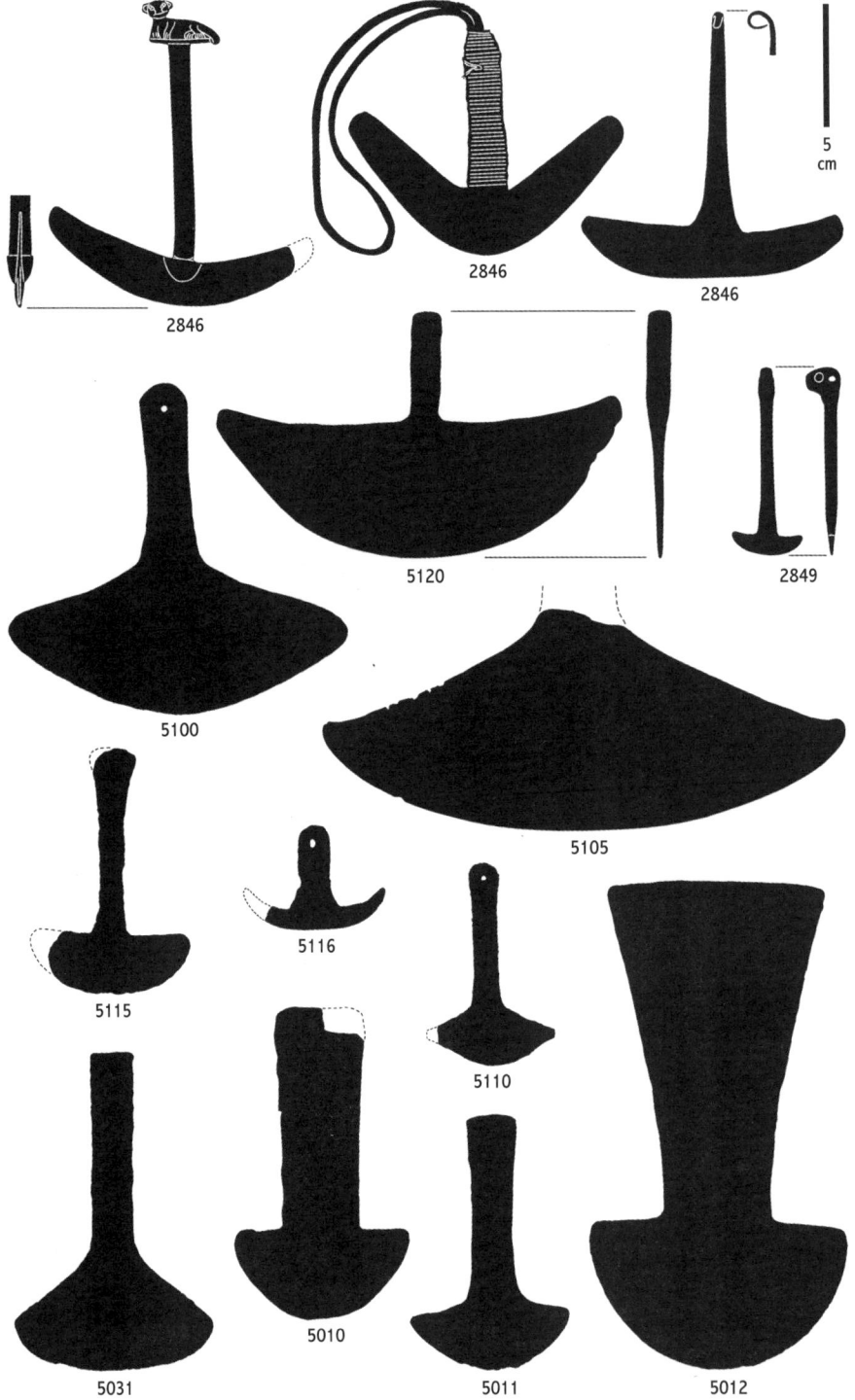

FIGURE G9

APPENDIX G

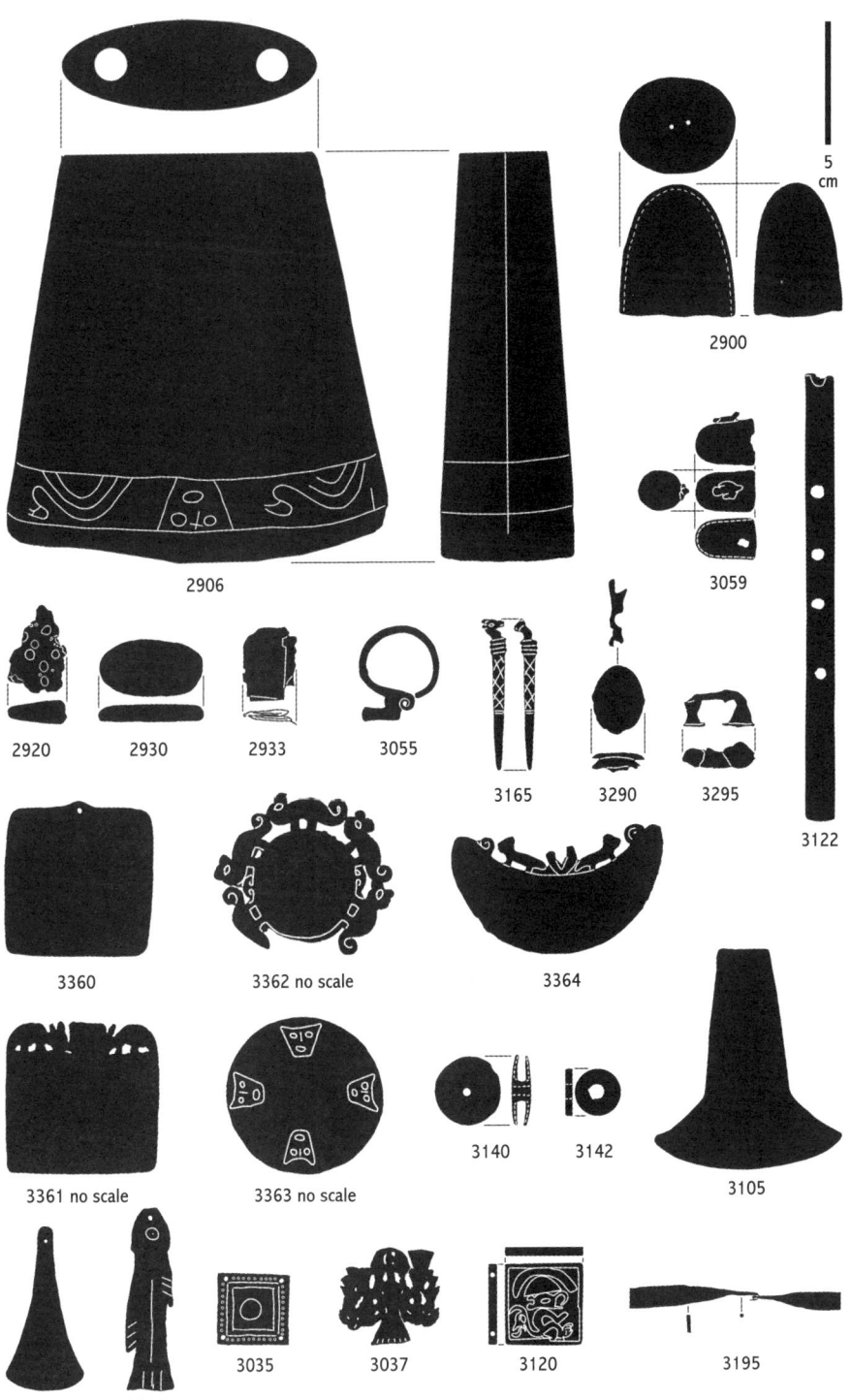

FIGURE G10

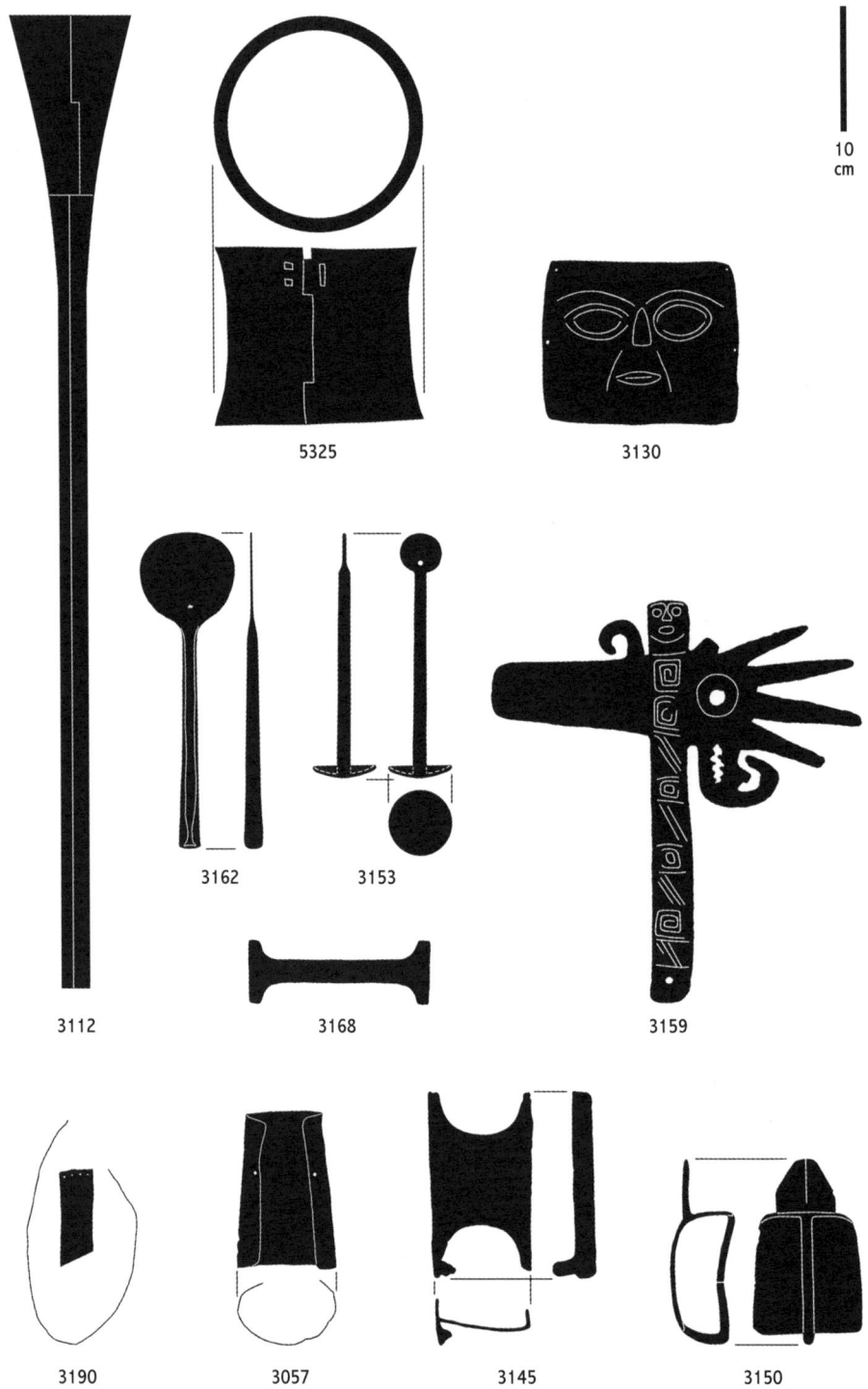

Figure G11

Appendix G

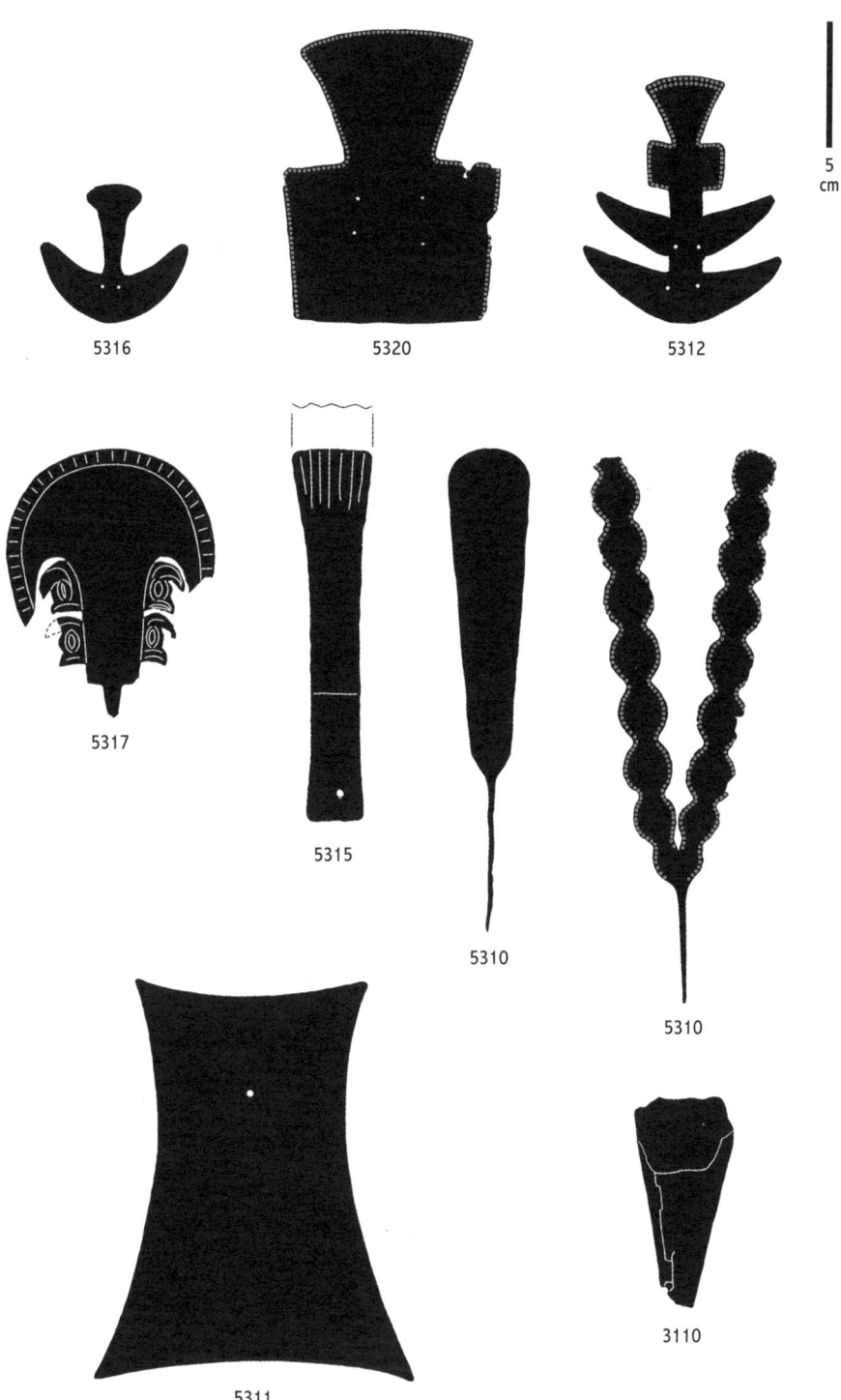

Figure G12

FIGURE G13

Appendix G

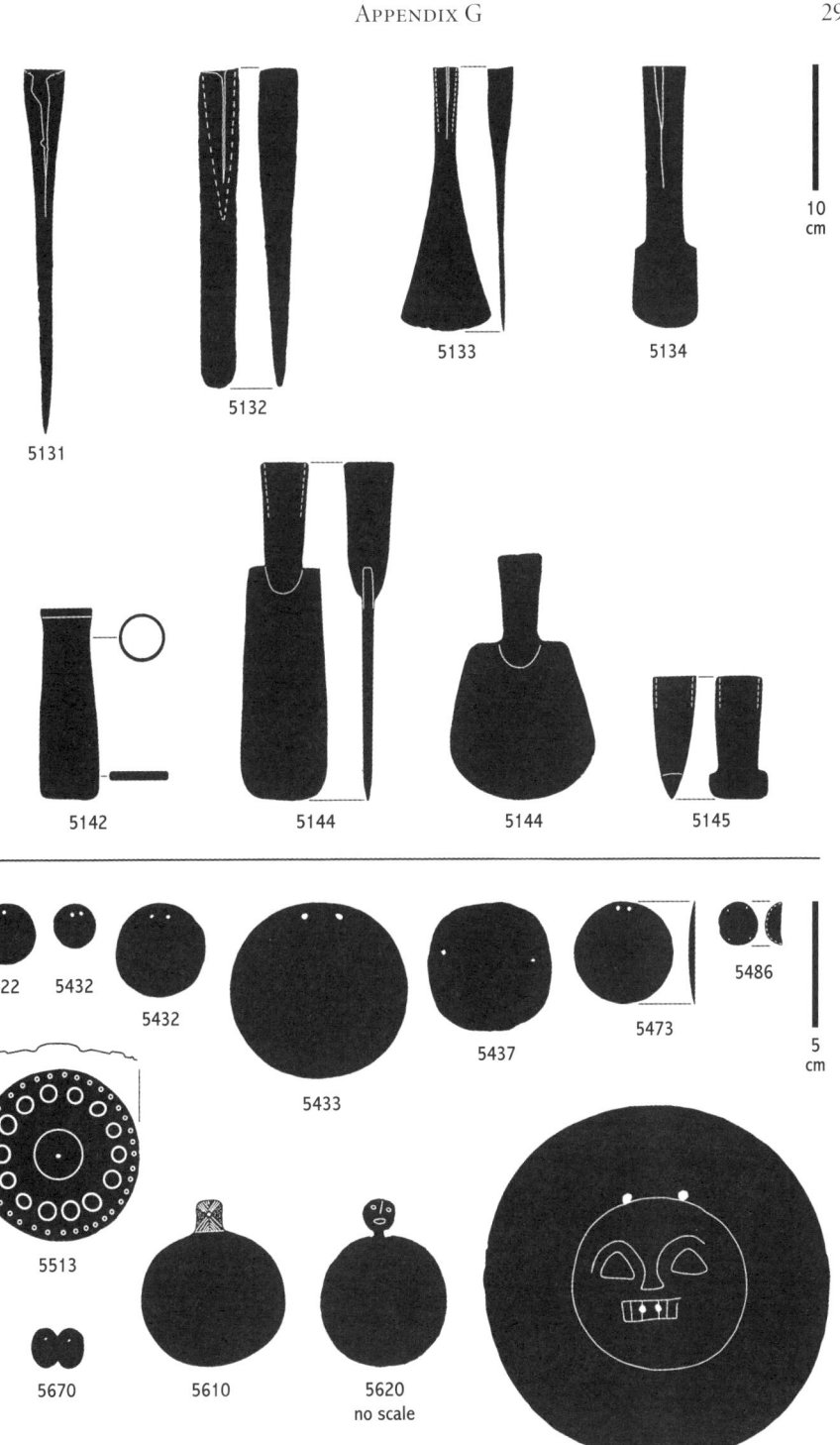

Figure G14

References

Abbott, Mark B. and Alexander P. Wolfe. 2003. Intensive pre-Inca metallurgy recorded by lake sediments from the Bolivian Andes. *Science* 301(5641):1893–1895.

Allen, Ivor M., Dennis Britton, and Herbert H. Coghlan. 1970. *Metallurgical Reports on British and Irish Bronze Age Implements and Weapons in the Pitt Rivers Museum*. Oxford: Pitt Rivers Museum. (Occasional Papers on Technology 10.)

Allen, James and Brian Gilmour. 2000. *Persian Steel: The Tavanoli Collection*. Oxford: Oxford University Press.

Alvarez M., Luis. 1959. Descripción de los implementos metalurgicos y liticos obtenidos de una tumba de La Lisera. *Boletín del Museo Regional de Arica* 1:13–15, 21–22.

Ambrosetti, Juan B. 1904. Arqueología Argentina—El Bronce en la Región Calchaquí. *Anales del Museo Nacional de Buenos Aires*, Series 3, 4(11):163–314.

Ampuero Brito, Gonzalo. 1969. Excavaciones arqueológicas en el fundo "Coquimbo," Departamento de La Serena. In: Chile, Dirección General de Bibliotecas, Archivos y Museos, Museo Arqueológico de La Serena. *Actas del V Congreso Nacional de Arqueología: 16–20 de Octubre 1969*. La Serena, Chile: Museo Arqueológico de La Serena. pp. 153–166.

Antze, Gustav. 1930. *Metallarbeiten aus dem Nördlichen Peru. Ein Beitrag zur Kenntnis ihrer Formen*. Hamburg: Friederichsen, De Gruyter. (Mitteilungen aus dem Museum für Völkerkunde in Hamburg 15.)

Astete, Fernando. 2001. Aportes e Investigaciones en Machupicchu (1994–2000). *Vision Cultural* 4:103–106.

Baessler, Arthur. 1906. *Altperuanische Metallgerate*. Berlin: von Georg Reimer.

Baker, W. A. and F. C. Child. 1944. The removal of gases from molten bronzes. *Journal of the Institute of Metals* 70:349–371.

Baker, W. A., F. C. Child, and W. H. Glaisher. 1944. The effect of shrinkage and gas porosity on the pressure tightness and mechanical properties of bronze sand castings. *Journal of the Institute of Metals* 70:373–406.

Bakewell, Peter. 1984. *Miners of the Red Mountain*. Albuquerque: University of New Mexico Press.

Bandelier, Adolph F. A. 1910. *The Islands of Titicaca and Koati*. New York: The Hispanic Society of America.

Barba, Alvaro A. 1923. *El Arte de los Metales (Metallurgy)*. Ross E. Douglass and Edward P. Mathewson, trans. New York: J. Wiley.

Bauer, Brian S. 2004. Archaeological investigations at Maukallaqta and Puma Orco, Department of Cuzco, Peru. *Nawpa Pacha* 25–27:207–250.

Bennett, Wendel C. 1939. *Archaeology of the North Coast of Peru*. New York: American Museum of Natural History. (Anthropological Papers of the American Museum of Natural History 37, pt. 1.)

—1944. *The Northern Highlands of Peru: Excavations in the Callejón de Huaylas and at Chavín de Huántar*. New York: [American Museum of Natural History]. (Anthropological Papers of the American Museum of Natural History 39, pt. 1.)

Bezur, Aniko and Bruce D. Owen. 1996. Abandoning arsenic? Technological and cultural changes in the Mantaro Valley, Perú. *Boletín Museo del Oro* 41:119–129.

Bingham, Hiram III. 1915a Dec. Manuscript Notes on Metallurgy at Machu Picchu. Yale Peruvian Expedition Papers, MS 664. Manuscripts and Archives, Yale University Library.

—1915b. Types of Machu Picchu pottery. *American Anthropologist* 7(2):257–271.

—1915c. The Story of Machu Picchu, The Peruvian Expeditions of the National Geographic Society and Yale University. *National Geographic* 27:172–186, 203–217.

—1930. *Machu Picchu: A Citadel of the Incas*. New Haven: Yale University Press.

—1948. *Lost City of the Incas: The Story of Machu Picchu and Its Builders*. New York: Duell, Sloan, and Pearce.

Burger, Richard L. 1996. Chavín. In: Elizabeth Boone, editor. *Andean Art at Dumbarton Oaks*, Volume 1. Washington: Dumbarton Oaks Research Library and Collection. pp. 45–86.

—2004. Scientific insights into daily life at Machu Picchu. In: Richard L. Burger and Lucy C. Salazar, editors. *Machu Picchu: Unveiling the Mystery of the Incas*. New Haven: Yale University Press. pp. 85-108.

Burger, Richard L. and Robert B. Gordon. 1998. Early Andean metalworking from Mina Perdida, Peru. *Science* 282:1108–1111.

Burger, Richard L. and Lucy C. Salazar, editors. 2004. *Machu Picchu: Unveiling the Mystery of the Incas*. New Haven: Yale University Press.

Capdeville, Augusto. 1921. Notas acerca de la Arqueología de Taltal III. *Boletín de la Academia Nacional de Historia, Quito* 3(7–8):229–233.

Carpenter, Harold and J. M. Robertson. 1930. The metallography of some ancient Egyptian implements. *Nature* 125(3162):859–862.

Chapin, Heath McBain. 1961. *The Bandelier Archaeological Collection from Pelechuco and Charassani, Bolivia*. Rosario, Argentina: Impreta de la Universidad Nacional del Litoral, Santa Fe.

Childs, Susan T. 1991. Transformations: Iron and copper production in Central Africa. *MASCA Research Papers in Science and Archaeology* 8(1):33–46.

Cieza de León, Pedro de. 1959. *The Incas* [1553]. Harriet de Onis, trans.; Victor Wolfgang von Hagen, editor. Norman: University of Oklahoma Press.

Cobo, Bernabe. 1983. *History of the Inca Empire* [Historia del Nuevo Mundo, 1653]. Roland Hamilton, trans. Austin: University of Texas Press.

Coghlan, Herbert H. 1975. *Notes on the Prehistoric Metallurgy of Copper and Bronze in the Old World*. 2nd ed. T. K. Penniman and B. M. Blackwood, editors. Oxford: Oxford University Press. (Occasional Papers on Technology 4.)

Cook, Maurice and W. G. Tallis. 1941. The physical properties and annealing characteristics of standard phosphor-bronze alloys. *Journal of the Institute of Metals* 67:49–65.

Cordy-Collins, Alana. 1996. Chimu. In: Elizabeth H. Boone, editor. *Andean Art at Dumbarton Oaks*, Volume 1. Washington, D.C.: Dumbarton Oaks Research Library and Collection. pp. 223–276.

Costin, Cathy, Timothy Earle, Bruce D. Owen, and Glenn Russell. 1989. The impact of Inca conquest on local technology in the Upper Mantaro Valley, Peru. In: Sander E. van der Leeuw and Robin Torrence, editors. *What's New? A Closer Look at the Process of Innovation*. London: Unwin Hyman. pp. 107–139. (One World Archaeology 14.)

Craddock, Peter T. and N. D. Meeks. 1987. Iron in ancient copper. *Archaeometry* 29(2):187–204.

Cummins, Tom. 2007. Queros, Aquillas, Uncus, and Chulpas: The composition of Inka artistic expression and power. In: Richard L. Burger, Craig Morris, and Ramiro Matos Mendieta, editors. *Variations in the Expression of Inka Power:* a symposium at Dumbarton Oaks, 18 and 19 October 1997. Washington, D.C.: Dumbarton Oaks. pp. 267–311.

D'Altroy, Terence N. 1992. *Provincial Power in the Inka Empire.* Washington, D.C.: Smithsonian Institution Press.

D'Altroy, Terence N. and Christine A. Hastorf, editors. 2001. *Empire and Domestic Economy.* New York: Kluwer Academic/Plenum Publishers.

DeMarrais, Elizabeth, Luis Jaime Castillo, and Timothy Earle. 1996. Ideology, materialization, and power strategies. *Current Anthropology* 37(1):15–31.

Díaz, Luisa and Francisco Vallejo. 2002. Armatambo y el dominio incaico en el valle de Lima. *Boletín de Arqueología PUCP* 6:355–374.

Disselhoff, Hans D. 1971. *Vicús: Eine Neu Entdeckte Altperuanische Kulture.* Berlin: Gebr. Mann. (Monumenta Americana 7.)

Dorsey, George A. 1901. *Archaeological Investigations on the Island of La Plata, Ecuador.* Chicago: Field Columbian Museum. (Publication 56, Anthropological Series 2(5).)

Earle, Timothy K., Terence N. D'Altroy, Christine A. Hastorf, Catherine Scott, Cathy Costin, Glenn Russell, and Elsie Sandufer. 1987. *Archaeological Field Research in the Upper Mantaro, Peru, 1982–1983: Investigations of Inka Expansion and Exchange.* Los Angeles: Institute of Archaeology, University of California, Los Angeles. (Monograph 28.)

Earle, Timothy K., Terence N. D'Altroy, Catherine J. LeBlanc, Christine A. Hastorf, and Terry Y. LeVine. 1980. Changing settlement patterns in the Upper Mantaro Valley, Peru. Preliminary Report for the 1977, 1978, and 1979 Seasons of the Upper Mantaro Archaeological Research Project. *Journal of New World Archaeology* 4(1):1–49.

Eaton, George F. 1910. Egypt. In: *Encyclopaedia Britannica.* 11th ed. New York: Encyclopaedia Britannica. p. 71.

—1912. Notes on Yale Peruvian Expedition. Yale Peruvian Expedition Papers, MS 664, box 19, folders 14–26; Manuscripts and Archives, Yale University Library.

—1916. *The Collection of Osteological Material from Machu Picchu.* New Haven: Tuttle, Morehouse and Taylor. (Memoirs of the Connecticut Academy of Arts and Sciences 5.)

Erdis, Ellwood C. 1912. Journal. Yale Peruvian Expedition Papers, MS 664, box 19. Manuscripts and Archives, Yale University Library.

Foote, Harry W. and W. H. Buell. 1912. The composition, structure, and hardness of some Peruvian axes. *American Journal of Science,* Series 4, 34:128–132.

Garcilaso de la Vega. 1961. *The Incas: The Royal Commentaries of the Inca. Garcilaso de la Vega, 1539–1616* [Comentarios Reales, 1609]. Maria Jolas, trans., from the critical, annotated French edition of Alain Gheerbrant. New York: Orion Press.

Gibaja O. and M. Arminda. 2004. Dos ofrendas al agua de Ollantaytambo. *Nawpa Pacha* 25–27:177–188.

Gonzales Holguín, Diego. 1608 [1952]. *Vocabulario de la Lengua General de Todo el Perú, Llamada Lengua Qqichua o del Inca*; Edición del Instituto de Historia. Lima: Imprenta Santa Maria. (Universidad Nacional Mayor de San Marcos, Publicaciones del cuarto centenario.)

Gordon, Robert B. 1985. Laboratory evidence of the use of metal tools in Machu Picchu and environs. *Journal of Archaeological Science* 12(4):311–327.

GORDON, ROBERT B. AND R. KNOPF. 2006. Metallurgy of bronze used in tools from Machu Picchu, Peru. *Archaeometry* 48(1):57–76.

—2007. Late Horizon silver, copper, and tin from Machu Picchu, Peru. *Journal of Archaeological Science* 34(1):38–47.

GORDON, ROBERT B. AND JOHN W. RUTLEDGE. 1984. Bismuth bronze from Machu Picchu. *Science* 223(4636):585–586.

GORDON, ROBERT B. AND NIKOLAAS J. VAN DER MERWE. 1984. Metallographic study of iron artifacts from the Eastern Transvaal, South Africa. *Archaeometry* 26(1):63–87.

GOWLAND, WILLIAM. 1910. The art of working metals in Japan. *Journal of the Institute of Metals* 4:4–41.

GRANT, M. R. 1994. Iron in ancient tin from Rooiberg, South Africa. *Journal of Archaeological Science* 21(4):455–460.

GROSSMAN, JOEL W. 1972. An ancient goldworker's tool kit. *Archaeology* 25:270–275.

GUAMAN POMA DE AYALA, FELIPE [HUAMÁN POMA]. 1615. *El Primer Nueva Corónica y Buen Gobierno*; GKS 2232 4°; autograph manuscript facsimile and annotated transcription by Rolena Adorno, John V. Murra, and Jorge L. Urioste [electronic resource]. The Guaman Poma Website [2001; accessed July 18, 2009]. Copenhagen: The Royal Library. Available at: http://www.kb.dk/permalink/2006/poma/info/en/frontpage.htm

HELSLEY-MARCHBANKS, ANNE M. 2004. The Inca presence in Chayanta, Bolivia: The metallurgical component. *Nawpa Pacha* 25–27:251–260.

HOFFMAN, CHRISTOPHER R. 1999. Intentional damage as technological agency: Breaking metals in Late Prehistoric Mallorca, Spain. In: Marcia-Anne Dobres and Christopher R. Hoffman, editors. *The Social Dynamics of Technology: Practice, Politics, and World Views*. Washington, D.C.: Smithsonian Institution Press. pp. 103–123.

HOSLER, DOROTHY, HEATHER LECHTMAN, AND OLAF HOLM. 1990. *Axe-monies and their Relatives*. Washington, D.C.: Dumbarton Oaks Research Library and Collection. (Studies in Pre-Columbian Art and Archaeology 30.)

HOWE, ELLEN G. AND ULRICH PETERSON. 1994. Silver and lead in the late prehistory of the Mantaro Valley, Peru. In: David A. Scott and Pieter Meyers, editors. *Archaeometry of Pre-Columbian Sites and Artifacts*. Los Angeles: Getty Conservation Institute. pp. 183–198.

HULL, DANIEL R. 1950. *Casting of Brass and Bronze: Some Practical Aspects of Brass and Bronze Casting in America, 1900 to 1950*. Cleveland: American Society for Metals.

IDROVO URIGÜEN, JAIME. 2000. *Tomebamba: Arqueología e Historia de una Ciudad Imperial*. Quito: Ediciones del Banco Central del Ecuador, Dirección Cultural Regional Cuenca.

ISBELL, WILLIAM H. 1985. Conchopata, ideological innovator in Middle Horizon 1A. Paper presented at: 25th annual meeting of the Institute for Andean Studies; January 4–5, 1985; Berkeley, CA, USA.

JIJÓN Y CAAMAÑO, JACINTO. 1920. Los Tincullpas y Notas acerca de la Metalurgia de los Aborigenes del Ecuador. *Boletín de la Sociedad Ecuatoriana* 5(13–14):4–43.

—1922. La Edad del Bronce en America del Sur. *Boletín de la Academia Nacional de Historia, Quito* 4(9):119–126.

—1949. *Maranga: Contribución al Conocimiento de los Aborígenes del Valle del Rimac, Perú*. Quito: La Prensa Católica.

JULIEN, CATHERINE J. 1982. A late burial from Cerro Azoguini, Puno. *Nawpa Pacha* 19:129–154.

—1983. *Hatunqolla: A View of Inca Rule from the Lake Titicaca Region.* Berkeley: University of California Press. (University of California Publications in Anthropology 15.)

—2004. Las Tumbas de Sacsahuaman y el Estilo Cuzco-Inca. *Nawpa Pacha* 25–27:1–125.

KEHL, GEORGE L. 1949. *Principles of Metallographic Laboratory Practice.* 3rd ed. New York: McGraw-Hill.

KROEBER, ALFRED L. AND WILLIAM D. STRONG. 1924a. The Uhle Collections from Chincha. *University of California Publications in American Archaeology and Ethnology* 21(1):1–54.

—1924b. The Uhle Pottery Collections from Ica. *University of California Publications in American Archaeology and Ethnology* 21(3):[95]–133.

LARREA, JUAN. 1941. El Yauri, Insignia Incaica. *Revista del Museo Nacional* 10(1):25–50.

LATCHAM, RICARDO. 1938. *Arqueologia de la Región Atacameña.* Santiago: Prensa de la Universidad de Chile.

LECHTMAN, HEATHER. 1973. The gilding of metal in pre-Columbian Peru. In: William J. Young, editor. *Application of Science in Examination of Works of Art; proceedings of the seminar: June 15–19, 1970.* Boston: Museum of Fine Arts. pp. 38–51.

—1976. A metallurgical site survey in the Peruvian Andes. *Journal of Field Archaeology* 3(1):1–42.

—1979. Issues in Andean metallurgy. In: Elizabeth Benson, editor. *Pre-Columbian Metallurgy in South America.* Washington, D.C.: Dumbarton Oaks. pp. 1–40.

—1980. The Central Andes: Metallurgy without iron. In: Theodore A. Wertime and James D. Muhly, editors. *The Coming of the Age of Iron.* New Haven: Yale University Press. pp. 267–334.

—1984. Andean value systems and the development of prehistoric metallurgy. *Technology and Culture* 25:1–36.

—1988. Traditions and styles in Central Andean metalworking. In: Robert Maddin, editor. *The Beginning of the Use of Metals and Alloys.* Cambridge: MIT Press. pp. 344–378.

—1991. The production of copper-arsenic alloys in the Central Andes: Highland ores and coastal smelters? *Journal of Field Archaeology* 18:43–76.

—1993. Technologies of power: The Andean case. In: John S. Henderson and Patricia J. Netherly, editors. *Configurations of Power: Holistic Anthropology in Theory and Practice.* Ithaca: Cornell University Press. pp. 244–280.

—1996a. Arsenic bronze: Dirty copper or chosen alloy? A view from the Americas. *Journal of Field Archaeology* 23:477–514.

—1996b. Cloth and metal: The culture of technology. In: Elizabeth H. Boone, editor. *Andean Art at Dumbarton Oaks*, Volume 1. Washington, D.C.: Dumbarton Oaks Research Library and Collection. pp. 33–44.

—1998. Architectural cramps at Titwanaku, copper-arsenic-nickel bronze. In: Thilo Rehren, Andreas Hauptmann, James D. Muhly, Hans-Gert Bachmann, and Robert Maddin, editors. *Metallurgica Antiqua: in honour of Hans-Gert Bachmann and Robert Maddin.* Bochum: Deutsches Bergbau-Museum. pp. 77–92.

—1999. Afterword. In: Marcia-Anne Dobres and Christopher R. Hoffman, editors. *The Social Dynamics of Technology: Practice, Politics, and World Views.* Washington, D.C.: Smithsonian Institution Press. pp. 223–232.

—2003. Middle Horizon bronze: Centers and outliers. In: Lambertus van Zelst, editor. *Patterns and Process: A Festschrift in Honor of Dr. Edward V. Sayre.* Suitland, MD: Smithsonian Center for Materials Research and Education. pp. 248–268.

—2005. Arsenic bronze at Pikillacta. In: *Pikillacta, the Wari Empire in Cuzco*. Gordon F. McEwan, ed. Iowa City: University of Iowa Press. pp. 131–146.

—2007. The Inka, and Andean metallurgical tradition. In: Richard L. Burger, Craig Morris, and Ramiro Matos Mendieta, editors. *Variations in the Expression of Inka Power*. Washington, D.C.: Dumbarton Oaks. pp. 313–355.

LECHTMAN, HEATHER, ANTONIETA ERLIJ, AND EDWARD BARRY, JR. 1982. New perspectives on Moche metallurgy: Techniques of gilding copper at Loma Negra, Northern Peru. *American Antiquity* 47-1:3–30.

LE PAIGE, GUSTAVO. 1961. Cultura de tiahuanaco en San Pedro de Atacama. Antofagasta, Chile: Universidad del Norte. (Anales de la Universidad del Norte 1.)

LLANOS, LUIS A. 1936. Trabajos Arqueologicos en el Dep. del Cuzco Bajo la Dirección del Dr. Luis E. Valcárcel: Informe Sobre Ollantaitambo. *Revista del Museo Nacional* 38:93–108.

LUMBRERAS, LOUIS. 1974. *The Peoples and Cultures of Ancient Peru*. Betty J. Meggers, trans. Washington, D.C.: Smithsonian Institution Press.

MACKAY, W. IAN. 1995. Gold extraction equipment at Maukallqta: The merging of indigenous and Spanish technology. In: Duncan R. Hook and David R. M. Gaimster, editors. *Trade and Discovery*. London: Department of Scientific Research, British Museum. pp. 159–170. (British Museum Occasional Paper 109.)

MARSHALL, GEORGE. 1964. *Notes on the Examination of Some pre-Columbian Metal Samples; Examen de Algunas Muestras Pre-Colombinas de Metal*. Lima: Museo Nacional de Antropologia y Arqueologia. (*Arqueologicas* 7.)

MATHEWSON, CHAMPION H. 1915. A metallographic description of some ancient Peruvian bronzes from Machu Picchu. *American Journal of Science*, 4th series, 40:525–616.

MAYER, EUGEN FRIEDRICH. 1986. *Vorspanische Metallwaffen und -werkzeuge in Argentinien und Chile / Armas y herramientas de metal prehispánicas en Argentina y Chile*. Munich: C. H. Beck. (Materialien zur Allgemeinen und Vergleichenden Archäologie 38.)

—1992. *Vorspanische Metallwaffen und -werkzeuge in Ecuador / Armas y herramientas de metal prehispánicas en Ecuador*. Mainz: Philipp Von Zabern. (Materialien zur Allgemeinen und Vergleichenden Archäologie 47.)

—1994. *Vorspanische Metallwaffen und -werkzeuge in Bolivia / Armas y herramientas de metal prehispánicas en Bolivia*. Mainz: Philipp Von Zabern. (Materialien zur Allgemeinen und Vergleichenden Archäologie 53.)

—1998. *Vorspanische Metallwaffen und -werkzeuge in Peru / Armas y herramientas de metal prehispánicas en Perú*. Mainz: Philipp Von Zabern. (Materialien zur Allgemeinen und Vergleichenden Archäologie 55.)

McCOWN, THEODORE D. 1945. Pre-Incaic Huamachuco: Survey and excavations in the region of Huamachuco and Cajabamba. *University of California Publications in American Archaeology and Ethnology* 39(4):223–400.

MENOTTI, FRANCESCO. 1998. *The Inkas: Last Stages of Stone Masonry Development in the Andes*. Oxford: Archaeopress. (BAR International Series 735.)

MENZEL, DOROTHY. 1966. The Pottery of Chincha. *Nawpa Pacha* 4:77–144.

—1976. *Pottery Style and Society in Ancient Peru*. Berkeley: University of California Press.

MEYERS, PIETER. 2003. The production of silver in antiquity: ore types identified based on elemental compositions of ancient silver artifacts. In: Lambertus van Zelst, editor. *Patterns and Process: A Festschrift in Honor of Dr. Edward V. Sayre*. Suitland, MD: Smithsonian Center for Materials Research and Education. pp. 271–288.

MOSELEY, MICHAEL E. 2001. *The Incas and their Ancestors: The Archaeology of Peru*. Rev. ed. London: Thames and Hudson.

MURRA, JOHN V. 1980. *The Economic Organization of the Inka State*. Greenwich, CT: JAI Press. (Research in Economic Anthropology, Suppl. 1).

NIELSEN, AXEL E. 2007. Significant arms: cultural plots, war and social change in the pre-hispanic southern Andes. *Boletín del Museo Chileno de Arte Precolombino* 12(1):9–41.

NILES, SUSAN A. 2004. The nature of Inca royal estates. In: Richard L. Burger and Lucy C. Salazar, editors. *Machu Picchu: Unveiling the Mystery of the Incas*. New Haven: Yale University Press. pp. 49–70.

NORCONK, MARILYN A. 1987. Analysis of the UMARP burials, 1983 field season: Paleopathology report, Appendix 2. In: Timothy K. Earle, Terence N. D'Altroy, Christine Hastorf, Catherine Scott, Cathy Costin, Glenn Russell, and Elsie Sandufer, editors. *Archaeological Field Research in the Upper Mantaro, Peru, 1982–1983: Investigations of Inka Expansion and Exchange*. Los Angeles: Institute of Archaeology, University of California, Los Angeles. (Monograph 28.)

NORDENSKIÖLD, ERLAND. 1921. *The Copper and Bronze Ages in South America*. Göteborg: Elanders Boktryckeri Aktiebolag. (Comparative Ethnographical Studies 4.)

NORTHOVER, J. P. AND C. GILLIS. 1999. Questions in the analysis of ancient tin. In: Suzanne M. M. Young, A. Mark Pollard, Paul Budd, and Robert A. Ixer, editors. *Metals in Antiquity*. Oxford: Archaeopress. pp. 78–85. (BAR International Series 792.)

OCHATOMA PARAVICINO, JOSE AND MARTHA CABRERA ROMERO. 2001. *Poblados Rurales Huari, Una Visión desde Aqo Wayqo*. Lima: Cano Asociados.

OWEN, BRUCE D. 1983. Re-analysis of a Peruvian bronze axe [senior thesis]. Typescript, Machu Picchu Collection. Division of Anthropology, Peabody Museum of Natural History, Yale University.

—1986. *The Role of Common Metal Objects in the Inka State* [master's thesis]. Los Angeles: University of California, Los Angeles.

—1998. Bows and spearthrowers in southern Peru and northern Chile: evidence, dating, and why it matters. Paper presented at: 63rd Annual Meeting of the Society for American Archaeology; 1998 March 25–29; Seattle WA. Available at: http://bruceowen.com/research/Owen1998-SAA-BowsAndSpearthrowersInSouthernPeruAndNorthernChile.pdf

—2001. The economy of metal and shell wealth goods. In: Terence N. D'Altroy and Christine A. Hastorf, editors. 2001. *Empire and Domestic Economy*. New York: Kluwer Academic/Plenum Publishers.

OWEN, BRUCE D. AND MARILYN A. NORCONK. 1987. Analysis of the human burials, 1977–1983 field seasons: Demographic profiles and burial practices, Appendix 1. In: Timothy K. Earle, Terence N. D'Altroy, Christine Hastorf, Catherine Scott, Cathy Costin, Glenn Russell, and Elsie Sandufer, editors. *Archaeological Field Research in the Upper Mantaro, Peru, 1982–1983: Investigations of Inka Expansion and Exchange*. Los Angeles: Institute of Archaeology, University of California, Los Angeles. (Monograph 28.)

PEDERSEN, ASBJORN. 1952. Objetos de Bronce de la Zona del Rio Salado (Región Chaco-Santiagueña). In: ICA. *Proceedings of the Thirtieth International Congress of Americanists: Held at Cambridge, 18–23 August 1952*. London: Royal Anthropological Institute. pp. 92–100.

PERCY, JOHN. 1880. *Metallurgy, Silver and Gold—Part I*. London: John Murray.

PETERSEN G., GEORG. 1970. *Minería y Metalurgía en el Antiguo Perú*. Lima: Museo Nacional de Antropología y Arqueología. (Arqueológicas 12.)

PROTZEN, JEAN-PIERRE. 1985. Inca quarrying and stonecutting. *Journal of the Society of Architectural Historians* 44(2):161–182.

—1986. Inca stonemasonry. *Scientific American* 254(2):94–103.

—1993. *Inca Architecture and Construction at Ollantaytambo*. New York: Oxford University Press.

REHDER, J. E. 1994. Blowpipes versus bellows in ancient metallurgy. *Journal of Field Archaeology* 21(3):345–350.

REHREN, T. AND M. TEMME. 1994. Pre-Columbian gold processing at Putushio, South Ecuador: The archaeometallurgical evidence. In: David A. Scott and Pieter Meyers, editors. *Archaeometry of Pre-Columbian Sites and Artifacts: proceedings of a symposium organized by the UCLA Institute of Archaeology and the Getty Conservation Institute, Los Angeles, California, March 23-27, 1992*. Marina Del Rey, CA : Getty Conservation Institute. pp. 267–284.

RÍOS, MARCELA AND ENRIQUE RETAMOZO. 1978. *Objetos de Metal Procedentes de la Isla de San Lorenzo*. Lima: Instituto Nacional de Cultura, Museo Nacional de Antropología y Arqueología. (Arqueológicas 17.)

ROOT, WILLIAM C. 1949. The metallurgy of the southern coast of Peru. *American Antiquity* 15:10–37.

ROSTWOROWSKI DE DIEZ CANSECO, MARÍA. 1999. *History of the Inca Realm*. Harry B. Iceland, trans. Cambridge: Cambridge University Press.

ROWE, JOHN HOWLAND. 1996. Inca. In: Elizabeth H. Boone, editor. *Andean Art at Dumbarton Oaks*, Volume 1. Washington, D.C.: Dumbarton Oaks Research Library and Collection. pp. 301–320.

RUIZ ESTRADA, ARTURO. 1976. *Hallazgos de oro, Sillustani (Puno)*. Lima: [Museo Nacional de Antropología y Arqueología]. (Serie Metalurgia 1.)

RUTLEDGE, JOHN W. 1984. *The Metal Artifacts from the Yale Peruvian Expedition of 1912, Catalog and Commentary* [master's thesis]. New Haven: Yale University.

RUTLEDGE, JOHN W. AND ROBERT B. GORDON. 1987. The work of metallurgical artificers at Machu Picchu, Peru. *American Antiquity* 52(3):578–594.

SALAZAR, LUCY C. 2001. Religious ideology and mortuary ritual at Machu Picchu. In: John E. Staller and Elizabeth J. Currie, editors. *Mortuary Practices and Ritual Associations: Shamanic Elements in Prehistoric Funerary Contexts in South America*. Oxford: Archaeopress. pp. 117–127. (BAR International Series 982.)

—2004. Machu Picchu: Mysterious royal estate in the cloud forest. In: Richard L. Burger and Lucy C. Salazar, editors. *Machu Picchu: Unveiling the Mystery of the Incas*. New Haven: Yale University Press. pp. 21–47.

—2007. Machu Picchu's silent majority: A consideration of the Inka cemeteries. In: Richard L. Burger, Craig Morris, and Ramiro Matos Mendieta, editors. *Variations in the Expression of Inka Power*. Washington, D.C.: Dumbarton Oaks. pp. 165–183.

SALAZAR, LUCY C. AND RICHARD L. BURGER. 2004a. Catalogue. In: Richard L. Burger and Lucy C. Salazar, editors. *Machu Picchu: Unveiling the Mystery of the Incas*. New Haven: Yale University Press. pp. 125–217.

—2004b. Lifestyles of the rich and famous: Luxury and daily life in the households of Machu Picchu's elite. In: Susan T. Evans and Joanne Pillsbury, editors. *Palaces of the Ancient New World*. Washington, D.C.: Dumbarton Oaks. pp. 325–357.

Salazar, Lucy C. and Vuka Roussakis. 2002. Textiles and weavers of Tahuantinsuyo. In: Antoine B. Daniel, Franklin Pease G. Y., et al. *The Incas: Art and Symbols*. Lima: Banco de Credito. pp. 263–297.

Schiappacasse, Virgilio and Hans Niemeyer. 1989. Avances y sugerencias para el conocimiento de la prehistoria tardía en el desembocadura del valle de Camarones (Region de Tarapaca). *Chungará* 22:63–84.

Schwoerbel, Gabriela H. 1969. Armas de Cobre en la Necropolis de Tablada de Lurín. *Boletín del Seminario de Arqueología, Pontifica Universidad Catolica del Peru* 1(3):46–51.

Shimada, Izumi. 1994. Pre-Hispanic metallurgy and mining in the Andes: Recent advances and future tasks. In: Alan K. Craig and Robert C. West, editors. *In Quest of Mineral Wealth: Aboriginal Mining and Colonial Mining and Metallurgy in Spanish America*. Baton Rouge: Geoscience Publications, Dept. of Geography and Anthropology, Louisiana State University. pp. 37–73. (Geoscience and Man 33.)

Shimada, Izumi, Stephen Epstein, and Alan K. Craig. 1982. Batan Grande: A prehistoric metallurgical center in Peru. *Science* 216:952–959.

Smith, Cyril S. 1960. *A History of Metallography: The Development of Ideas on the Structure of Metals Before 1890*. Chicago: University of Chicago Press.

Sutliff, Marie J. 1989. Domestic production of small copper artifacts during the Milagro occupation at Peñon del Río (Guayas Basin). Paper presented at: 54th Annual Meeting of the Society for American Archaeology; April 5–9, 1989; Atlanta, Georgia, USA.

Timberlake, Simon. 1994. An experimental tin smelt at Flag Fen. *Journal of the Historical Metallurgy Society* 28(2):121–128.

Topic, John R. 1977. *The Lower Class at Chan Chan: A Qualitative Approach* [dissertation]. Cambridge: Harvard University. Available from: ProQuest Dissertations & Theses [database online]; http://www.proquest.com (publication no. AAT 033508).

Topic, Theresa Lange and John R. Topic. 1984. *Huamachuco Archaeological Project: Preliminary Report on the Third Season, June–August 1983*. Peterborough, ON, Canada: Dept. of Anthropology, Trent University. (Occasional Papers in Anthropology 1.)

Tushingham, A. Douglas, Ursula M. Franklin, and Christopher Toogood. 1979. *Studies in Ancient Peruvian Metalworking: an investigation of objects from the Museo Oro del Peru exhibited in Canada in 1976-77 under the title "Gold for the Gods."* Toronto: Royal Ontario Museum. (History, Technology and Art Monograph 3.)

Tylecote, Ronald F. 1976. *A History of Metallurgy*. London: Metals Society.

—1986. *The Prehistory of Metallurgy in the British Isles*. London: The Institute of Metals.

Tylecote, Ronald F., H. A. Ghaznani, and P. J. Boydell.1977. Partitioning of trace elements between ores fluxes, slags and metal during the smelting of copper. *Journal of Archaeological Science* 4(4):305–333.

Uhle, Max. 1912. *Las Relaciones Prehistóricas Entre el Perú y la Argentina, Extracto de las Actas del XVII° Congreso Internacional de Americanistas, pág. 509 y siguentes*. Buenos Aires: Imprenta de Coni Hermanos. pp. 1–34.

Valcárcel, Luis E. 1934a. Sajsawaman redescubierto. *Revista del Museo Nacional* 3(1–2):3–36.

—1934b. Los trabajos arqueológicos en el Departamentos del Cusco. II. Sajsawaman redescubierto. *Revista del Museo Nacional* 3(3):211–233.

—1935a. Los trabajos arqueológicos en el Departamentos del Cusco. Sajsawaman redescubierto. (III). *Revista del Museo Nacional* 4(1):1–24.

—1935b. Sajsawaman redescubierto. (IV). *Revista del Museo Nacional* 4(2):163–204.

VALDEZ, LIDIO. 2002. Y la tradición continua: la alfarería de la época inka en el valle de Ayacucho, Peru. *Boletín de Arqueología PUCP* 6:395–410.

VALENCIA ZEGARRA, ALFREDO. 1970. Dos tumbas de Saqsaywaman. *Revista Española de Antropología Americana* 4:67–75.

VAN BUREN, MARY AND BARBARA H. MILLS. 2005. *Huayrachinas* and *Tocochimbos*: Traditional smelting technology of the southern Andes. *Latin American Antiquity* 16(1):3–25.

VERNEAU, RENÉ AND PAUL RIVET. 1912. *Ethnographie Ancienne de L'Equateur.* Paris: Du Bureau des Longitudes, de l'Ecole Polytechnique. (Mission du Service Geographique de L'Armee pour la Mesure d'un Arc de Méridien Equatorial en Amérique du Sud 6.)

WILLIAMSON, HAROLD F. 1952. *Winchester*. Washington, D.C.: Combat Forces Press.

WRIGHT, KENNETH AND ALFREDO ZEGARRA. 2000. *Machu Picchu: A Civil Engineering Marvel.* Reston, VA: American Society of Civil Engineers.

Index

A

African Iron Age, 29
African metallurgies, 57
alloy preparation and smelting
  alloy compositions, 13
  bronze alloys
    chemical composition, 13–14
    impurities and inclusions, 14–15, 17
    trace elements, 17
  evidentiary research, 11–12
  pre-Columbian metallurgies, 70
  preparation methods, 12–13
  prill smelting technique, 61
  silver-copper alloys, 17, 19, 21, 60–61
  Spanish artisans, 70–71
altiplano exotic artifacts, 114
altiplano region, 89
Alvistur collection, 96, 106
amalgamation techniques, 71
ambiguous objects, 109, 115, 121
American Journal of Science, xiii, 2
American Museum of Natural History (AMNH), 75, 99, 130
ancla axes, 87, 93–94, 107, 128, 138, 139
Ancon, 98, 111
Andean metalworking
  discs, 102
  Late Horizon period, 77–85
  Machu Picchu
    axes, 106–107
    bola weights, 103, 106
    celts, 107
    chisels, 107–108
    construction tools, 106
    general Andean-style artifacts, 102–108, 140
    half-round-headed tupus, 102
    lirpus, 103
    pierced-eye needles, 103
    sources, 102
    T-shaped tumis, 103, 138
  projectile points, 117–118
  regional patterns
    axe-maces, 96
    axes, 92–95
    bola weights, 91–92
    discs, 92
    earspools, 97
    geographic distribution, 85, 101–102
    headdress ornamentals/frontals, 97–98
    Inca-style artifacts, 86–87, 101, 106–107
    lime dippers, 90
    lirpus, 96–97
    shawl pins (*tupus*), 87, 89–90, 101–103
    southern Titicaca metalsmiths, 101–102
    star-shaped mace heads, 95
    T-shaped tumis, 90–91
    tumis, 101
    yauri pikes, 94–95
  southern Titicaca metalsmiths, 101–103, 140
Andes
  metallurgical history, 56–63
  silver ore, 19
animal-headed tumis, 87, 91, 114
animal-headed tupus, 87, 89
ankle bells, 130
annealing techniques
  See forging and annealing techniques
antimony (Sb)
  bronze alloy impurities, 15, 17
  chemical composition determination techniques, 22
  silver alloy impurities, 19
  tin antimonide (Sn_2Sb), 22
  tin impurities, 22
Aqo Wayqo, 89
arc-shaped knife blades (*tumis*), 7
Argentina
  altiplano exotic artifacts, 114
  axes, 93, 94
  brazales, 99, 117
  celts, 107
  chisels, 107, 129
  metallurgical history, 62
  oval artifacts, 115
  projectile points, 118
  tin bronze technology, 122
argentite (Ag_2S), 19
Arica, Chile, 109
armlets, 99, 112, 236
arrastra, 71
arsenic (As)
  bronze alloy impurities, 17
  chemical composition determination techniques, 13, 195
  copper-arsenic alloys, 9, 15, 60, 62
  silver alloy impurities, 19, 21
artifact fabrication, 22
artifact function and use
  form and function, 52–53
  tool design, 53–55
  tool use evidence, 55–56
artisan tools, 53–55
aryballos, 225
Atacama earrings, 117
atlatls, 118
Auca Runa, 96, 97
awls, 118, 236
axe-maces, 73, 87, 96, 138
axe-monies, 117
axes
  axe blade fragment, 209–210
  axe heads, 197, 199, 235–236
  blade forms, 92–93
  blade tip, 209–210
  broken axe blades, 4, 35, 202, 205, 238–239, 240
  casting defects, 35, 210
  casting techniques, 24, 28, 33
  catalog description, 235
  chemical composition determination techniques, 13, 15
  collection percentage, 7, 8
  cutting edge damage, 128
  design standardization, 10
  forging and annealing techniques, 37, 41, 44, 69–70
  functional role, 54, 125–129
  geographic distribution, 92–95, 106–107, 137, 139
  haft and tang styles, 92, 93–94
  hoja-hoz blade shape, 93
  impurities and inclusions, 17
  Inca-style artifacts, 87, 92, 93, 138
  intentional destruction, 131–132
  Late Horizon period, 78, 106–107, 140
  lost or discarded artifacts, 135
  meanings and significance, 73
  metallographic examinations, 4
  physical metallurgical research, 1–2
  quotidian metal artifacts, 92–95
  tool use evidence, 55–56
  T-shaped axe heads
    broken axe blades, 202, 205
    catalog description, 234–235, 238
    chemical composition, 195, 197, 202
    crossbars, 191–192, 195, 197, 202, 234, 238
    forging and annealing techniques, 41, 44, 191–192, 197, 238
    geographic distribution, 87, 94, 121, 138

meanings and significance, 74
microstructures, 195, 202
technical description, 191–192, 195, 197
tin content, 14
use evidence, 54, 55, 234
use evidence, 55–56, 235
axially symmetrical tupus, 90

B

balls
  casting techniques, 24, 66
  catalog description, 238, 241, 244
  microstructures, 25, 27, 238
Bandelier, Adolph, 91
bangles, 111
bars, 35, 46, 199, 232, 236–237, 240–241
Batán Grande, 61
beads, 76
bells
  catalog description, 233, 242, 243
  collection percentage, 8
  geographic distribution, 100–101, 109, 114, 119, 139
  microstructures, 25, 27, 233
  split bells, 109
bell-shaped ornaments, 84
Bessemer, Henry, 2
Bingham, Hiram, xiii, 1, 2, 7, 17, 191, 195, 234
bird-head lime spoons
  burial artifacts, 118
  casting and molding skills, 66
  casting defects, 35
  composition gradient, 25
  geographic distribution, 111, 116, 139
  metallographic examinations, 4
  surface treatments and decoration, 48
  tin content, 14
  use evidence, 111
bismuth (Bi)
  bronze alloy impurities, 17
  copper-tin-bismuth alloy, 200, 237
  llama-head knife, 200, 237
  surface coloration, 67
blowpipes, 70, 71
bola weights
  Cuzqueño artifacts, 103, 106
  geographic distribution, 91–92, 101, 139
  Inca-style artifacts, 87
  Late Horizon period, 84
  Machu Picchu, 103, 106
  nonmortuary contexts, 135
  regional metalworking patterns, 91–92, 101
Bolivia
  axes, 93
  headdress ornamentals/frontals, 98

mace heads, 95
metallurgical history, 58, 62, 70
projectile points, 117
silver production, 71
tin bronze technology, 122
tin production, 63
bracelets, 7, 49, 114, 230, 243
brazales, 99, 117
broken axe blades, 4, 35, 202, 205, 238–239, 240
broken chisels, 210, 240
bronze
  bronze alloys
    alloy preparation and smelting, 13–14
    casting techniques, 23–24
    forging and annealing techniques, 36–44
    impurities and inclusions, 14–15, 17
    trace elements, 17
  bronze artifacts
    alloy preparation, 12
    artisan skills, 64–66
    awls, 236
    axes, 1, 235
    balls, 238, 244
    bars, 232, 236–237, 240–241
    bells, 233
    bracelets, 243
    broken axe blades, 238–239, 240
    casting techniques, 25, 27–28, 34
    chisels, 235, 237–238, 240
    crowbars, 246
    earspools, 220, 243
    finials, 232, 242
    forging and annealing techniques, 28–29, 36–44
    high-tin bronzes, 1, 3, 13–14
    innovative techniques, 66–67
    knife blades, 244
    knives, 13, 219, 220–221, 227–229, 236, 237, 239–240
    lime dippers/spoons, 220, 232–233, 239
    llama-head knife, 237
    mace heads, 241
    metal residue, 246–247
    metal spill, 241, 246
    metal stock, 245–246
    microstructures, 25, 27, 50–52
    molder's slick, 231
    necklaces, 230
    needles, 242–243, 247
    pendant disc, 226, 245, 246
    pendants, 231, 242, 243
    physical metallurgical research, 1–2
    pins, 243
    plumb bobs, 236
    shawl pins (tupus), 221–223, 224, 225–226, 229, 232, 238,

242, 243, 244, 245, 246, 247
    star-head pin, 225
    surface coloration, 50–51, 66–67
    tin concentrations, 13–14
    tool design and use, 53–55
    tools, 69, 226
    T-shaped axe heads, 234–235, 238
    tweezers, 220, 233, 237, 239, 243, 244
  chemical composition, 195
  copper-tin bronzes, 2, 13, 67, 122, 191
  metal spill, 241
  tin bronzes
    casting defects, 34
    color significance, 14, 49
    composition gradient, 25
    copper-tin bronzes, 2, 13, 67, 122, 191
    forging and annealing techniques, 36
    Inca-style artifacts, 74–75, 78, 89
    lead alloys, 13, 70
    Machu Picchu artifacts, 67
    metallurgical properties, 1, 2, 3
    microstructures, 24
    southern Titicaca metalsmiths, 62–63, 101, 122, 138
    spoons, 116
Bronze Age Europe, 69–70
Buell, William H., 1, 191, 195, 234
Burger, Richard, 8, 71
burial artifacts
  axes, 93
  corporate- versus imperial-style artifacts, 84–85
  Cuzqueño artifacts, 118–119, 121, 140–141
  heavy cast copper alloy objects, 99
  intentional destruction, 132, 134
  lirpus, 96–97
  quotidian metal artifacts, 135, 138
  star-shaped mace heads, 95

C

Calchaqui region, 131
camayoc craft producers, 102
campanillas, 130
Cañarí culture, 103, 114
Capac, Manco, 84
Carnegie Institute of Technology, 1
casting techniques
  artisan skills, 65–66
  basic processes, 23–24, 32–34
  Bronze Age Europe, 69–70
  historical background, 2–3
  Mochica culture, 59
  problems and difficulties, 34–35, 66

cave 37, 119
cave 38, 121
cave 57, 130
cave 63, 119
cave 109, 132
caves, 8–9
celts, 107, 129, 135
ceramics, 78, 118, 119, 121
cerargyrite (AgCl), 19
Cerro Amaru, 89
Cerro Baúl, 130
Cerro Junin, Manabi, Ecuador, 117
cerussite (PbCO2), 19
chalcopyrite, 15
Challco Chima, 96
champi, 84
Chan Chan, 98, 109, 121
Chavín culture, 58–59
Chepen, 76, 112
Chief Courier, 95
Chile
  chisels, 129
  projectile points, 117, 118
  tweezers, 100, 117
Chimú culture, 60, 101, 108
Chincha
  finger rings, 111
  metalsmiths, 101
Chipaya culture, 130–131
chisels
  broken chisels, 210, 240
  casting techniques, 28
  catalog description, 235, 237–238
  chemical composition, 197, 200, 201, 210
  collection percentage, 7, 8
  forging and annealing techniques, 37, 41, 42, 44, 69, 197, 200–202, 238
  functional role, 129–130, 202
  geographic distribution, 107–108
  microstructures, 197, 201, 210, 238
  nonmortuary contexts, 135
  physical metallurgical research, 1
  tool use evidence, 55–56, 210
Chuquitanta, 111
clod breakers, 95
coastal exotic artifacts, 108–109, 111–114
Cochabamba province, 98
collection significance
  artisan skills, 64–66
  contextual perspectives, 67, 69
  innovative techniques, 66–67
  pre-Machu Picchu metallurgy, 56–63
Colonial period
  intentionally destroyed metal artifacts, 134
  lost, discarded, or interred artifacts, 135
  round-headed tupus, 103
  T-shaped tumis, 91

color significance, 73
Colten, Roger, 71
comparative data criteria
  geographic provenience, 75–76, 78, 83–85
  tumi knives, 77
  typology, 76–77
compound curved strip tweezers, 100
concave-sided frontal ornamentation, 97, 98
Conchopata, 89
conical bells/conical-shaped ornaments
  burial artifacts, 135
  geographic distribution, 100–101, 114, 119, 139
  Late Horizon period, 84
  use evidence, 130–131
construction tools, 106
copper (Cu)
  alloy preparation, 12
  axe heads, 235–236
  bola weights, 91
  chemical composition determination techniques, 4, 13, 195
  copper alloys
    discs, 106
    ingots, 109, 121
    strips, 113–114
    suppliers, 1
  copper-arsenic alloys, 9, 15, 60, 62
  copper oxide (Cu_2O), 15
  copper sulfide (Cu_2S), 14–15, 191, 195
  copper-tin-bismuth alloy, 200, 237
  copper-tin bronzes, 2, 13, 67, 122, 191
  heavy cast copper alloy objects, 99
  impurities and inclusions, 15
  knives, 239
  metallurgical history, 58
  silver-copper alloys
    alloy preparation and smelting, 17, 19, 21, 60–61
    artisan skills, 64–66
    casting techniques, 29–32
    depletion silvering technique, 2, 50–52, 60, 63
    forging and annealing techniques, 44–46
    innovative techniques, 66–67
    metallographic examinations, 4, 5
    microstructures, 44–46
    Mochica culture, 59–60
    shawl pins (*tupus*), 219–220
    silver content, 51–52
    surface coloration, 50–52, 66–67

  Wanka culture, 61
  smelting techniques, 60–62
  surface coloration, 49, 66–67
  tools, 245
corporate-style artifacts, 74–75
Corregidor de Provincias, 97
Coya Raymi, 96
coyas, 112
crescent moon-shaped frontal ornamentation, 97
crosshatching decorations, 113
crowbars, 35, 69, 106, 135, 246
crucibles and molds, 12–13, 32–33, 65–66, 71
crumpled metal stock, 240
crushing techniques, 71
cutting tools, 98, 123–124
Cuzco, 55, 73, 74, 86
Cuzco–Inca ceramic vessels, 118, 119, 121
Cuzqueño artifacts
  axes, 93, 106–107
  bola weights, 103, 106
  burial artifacts, 118–119, 121, 140–141
  construction tools, 106
  corporate- versus imperial-style artifacts, 74–75
  discs, 102
  geographic distribution, 139
  human figurines, 99
  Inca-style artifacts, 86–87, 106–107, 138–139
  Machu Picchu, 102–108
  metalworking traditions, 138–139
  plate handles, 116
  socketed points, 117
  T-shaped tumis, 103, 138
  tupus, 123
cymbals, 8

D

daggers, 7
decorated artifacts, 121
decorated rings, 111
decorated strips, 113–114
defective castings, 34–35
defects and imperfections, 2
depletion silvering technique, 2, 50–52, 60, 63, 246
diamond pyramid hardness (DPH), 5
dirks, 69
disc frontal ornamentation, 97–98
disc-headed T-shaped tumis, 91
discs
  casting techniques, 34
  catalog description, 226, 232, 245
  depletion silvering technique, 50–52
  fabrication technique, 232
  intentional destruction, 131, 132

Late Horizon period, 84, 92, 102, 106
nonmortuary contexts, 135
pendant disc, 226, 245, 246
repair practices, 134
repoussé technique, 112
use evidence, 226
disc-shaped mace heads, 95
dishes, 116
double-cone tupus, 102
drooping tupus, 84, 101, 114

E

Early Horizon period, 57, 58–59
Early Intermediate Horizon period, 49
Early Intermediate period, 19, 57, 59–60
Early Iron Age Europe, 29, 43
Early Iron Age Persia, 29
earrings, 130
earspools
  catalog description, 220, 243
  geographic distribution, 85, 97, 116
  Late Horizon period, 78, 84, 85, 97
Eastern Urban sector, 7
Eckert, James, 5, 71
Ecuador
  altiplano exotic artifacts, 114
  axes, 93
  bells, 100
  celts, 107
  projectile points, 117
  tweezers, 100
energy dispersive X-ray spectrometry, 4
engraved decorations, 113
Espiritu Pampa, 5, 17
ethnicity, 73
European Bronze Age, 33
exotic artifacts
  altiplano exotic artifacts, 114
  coastal exotic artifacts, 108–109, 111–114
  geographic distribution, 140

F

feather stacks, 117
ferric chloride etches, 4, 195
Field Museum of Natural History (FMNH), 75
fine chisels, 129
finger rings, 47, 111, 230–231
finials, 49, 232, 242
fisherman handleless transverse knife, 108, 121, 239–240
fishhooks, 139
flapless bent loop-eye needles, 115
flaring-backed T-shaped tumis, 101
flaring tweezers, 113

flat axes, 129, 235–236
flat tumis, 77, 114
floral motifs, 113
Foote, Harry W., xiii, 1, 191, 195, 234
forging and annealing techniques
  Bronze Age Europe, 69–70
  bronze artifacts
    α–δ eutectoid structure, 42–43
    annealing temperatures, 42–43
    basic processes, 28–29, 36–38
    forging temperatures, 42
    strain hardening, 43–44, 48, 69
  chisels, 197, 200–202, 238
  hammered bronze bar, 199
  historical background, 2–3
  knives, 37–39, 220–221, 227, 237, 239
  lime dippers/spoons, 239
  llama-head knife, 199–200
  metalworking tools, 46–47
  physical metallurgical research, 1
  shawl pins (*tupus*), 36–39, 45, 221–223, 225–226, 230
  sheet metal fabrication, 47–48, 112
  silver-copper alloys, 44–46
  T-shaped axe heads, 41, 191–192, 197, 238
  tweezers, 239
formón chisels, 108

G

galena (PbS), 19
Galli, Heather, 71
gauntlets, 99
geographic distribution
  axe-maces, 96
  axes, 92–95
  bola weights, 91–92
  discs, 92
  earspools, 97
  headdress ornamentals/frontals, 97–98
  Inca-style artifacts, 86–87, 101, 106–107, 138–139
  lime dippers, 90
  lirpus, 96–97
  metalworking traditions, 138–141
  regional metalworking patterns, 85
  shawl pins (*tupus*), 87, 89–90, 101–103
  southern Titicaca metalsmiths, 101–102
  star-shaped mace heads, 95
  T-shaped tumis, 90–91
  tumis, 101
  yauri pikes, 94–95
geographic place, 73
glow discharge mass spectrometry, 5

gold artifacts, 7, 49, 58–60, 70, 233–234
gongs, 8
Göttingen University, 1
Governador de los Caminos Reales, 97
graves, 8–9
guairas, 62, 70–71
Guaman Poma de Ayala, Felipe (drawings and observations)
  earspools, 84, 97
  headdress ornamentals/frontals, 97, 98
  lirpus, 96, 103
  plume holders, 112
  Rumiñavi, 123, 126
  star-shaped mace heads, 84, 95
  tumis, 123
  tupus, 53
  weapons, 94, 126
Guayas tumis, 77, 117
Guidoboni, Richard, 71

H

haft weights, 95
hair ornaments, 130–131
halberds
  collection percentage, 7
  forging and annealing techniques, 69
half-round-headed tupus, 84, 87, 102, 118, 119, 138, 139
hammered bronze bar, 35, 46, 199
hammering technique
  balls, 238
  bars, 232, 237
  forging and annealing process, 27–28, 36–39, 42, 44–45
  gold artifacts, 58–59
  hammerstones, 8, 11, 46, 53–55, 61, 237, 247
  Inca artisans, 65, 67
  knives, 237
  lime dippers/spoons, 239
  metal stock, 245–246
  needles, 247
  plumb bobs, 236
  shawl pins (*tupus*), 221–223
  sheet metal fabrication, 47–48
  silver-copper alloys, 51, 52, 61
  star-head pin, 225
  tool design, 53–55
  T-shaped axe heads, 54, 238
  work-in-progess artifacts, 245
Hammond Laboratory (Yale University), 1
handleless transverse knife, 108, 121, 239–240
hardhead, 22
hardness determination, 5
Hatun Chasqui, 95
headbands
  casting techniques, 31

catalog description, 230
coastal artifacts, 113
forging and annealing
  techniques, 45, 47
Late Horizon period, 84, 99, 113
silver content, 51–52
headdress ornamentals/frontals
  catalog description, 231
  forging and annealing
    techniques, 47
  geographic distribution, 85,
    97–98, 116
  Inca-style artifacts, 138
  Late Horizon period, 78, 85
heavy cast copper alloy objects, 99
heavy chisels, 129–130
high-tin bronzes, 1, 3, 13–14
historical metallurgical sequence,
  56–57
hoja-hoz blade shape, 93
Holmes, William H., 2
horseshoe-shaped frontal
  ornamentation, 97
Huando, 115
Huari, 86
Huascar, 96
huayrachina, 62, 70–71
human figurines, 99
hydrogen peroxide etches, 4, 25,
  195

I
Ica
  bangles, 111
  earspools, 97
  Late Horizon metal assemblages,
    78, 83, 84, 85
  metalsmiths, 101
  plume holders, 112
  sheet metal objects, 76
  star-shaped mace heads, 95
  T-shaped tumis, 103
imperial-style artifacts, 74–75
Inca heartland, 86
Incan ceramics, 78
Inca-style artifacts
  celts, 107
  geographic distribution, 86–87,
    101, 106–107, 138–139
  quotidian metal artifacts,
    101–103, 106–107
  See also specific artifact
ingots, 109, 121
Initial period, 57
iron (Fe)
  bronze alloy impurities, 14–15
  chemical composition
    determination techniques,
    4, 13
  pre-Columbian metallurgies, 70
  silver alloy impurities, 19
  strength property
    determinations, 7

Island of San Lorenzo, 111
Island of the Sun, 98, 101, 106

J
Jauja
bola weights, 106
  chisels, 107
  decorated strips, 114
  intentionally destroyed metal
    artifacts, 132
  Late Horizon metal assemblages,
    78, 83
  lost, discarded, or interred
    artifacts, 135, 138
  needles, 115
  T-shaped tumis, 103
  tweezers, 100, 115
JEOL JKA-8600 microprobe, 5

K
Katanga region, Africa, 29
Killick, David, 71
knives
  bronze knife, 13
  casting defects, 35, 228
  casting techniques, 24, 27–28, 33
  catalog description, 219, 220–
    221, 227–229, 236–237, 239
  coastal exotic artifacts, 108–109
  collection percentage, 7
  comparative data criteria, 77
  contextual perspectives, 67
  copper knife, 13, 15
  design standardization, 9–10
  forging and annealing
    techniques, 37–39, 220–221,
    227, 237, 239
  functional role, 53
  geographic distribution, 138, 139
  globular join features, 101–102
  Inca-style artifacts, 87, 101, 138
  innovative techniques, 66–67
  intentional destruction, 131, 132
  knife blades, 237, 244
  Late Horizon period, 83, 84
  meanings and significance, 74
  microstructures, 239
  neck-stepped tumis, 116
  provenience, 9
  repair practices, 134
  selection criteria, 10–11
  southern Titicaca metalsmiths,
    101
  surface treatments and
    decoration, 48–49, 229
  tin content, 229
  tool use evidence, 219, 227, 229
  T-shaped tumis
    burial artifacts, 135
    coastal exotic artifacts, 114
    comparative data criteria, 77
    functional role, 123–124
    geographic distribution, 87,
      90–91, 103, 122, 138, 139
    globular join features, 102, 121
    intentional destruction, 131,
      132
    Late Horizon period, 83, 84,
      116
Knopf, Robert, 71

L
Lake Titicaca, 62, 87, 89–90, 98,
  114
Lambayeque, 78, 112
La Paz, Bolivia, 71
La Plata Island, 100, 103, 130
large shawl pin, 226
Late Bronze Age, 13, 69–70
Late Horizon period
  alloy preparation and smelting,
    13, 19, 21
  Andean metalworking patterns,
    85–87, 89–102
  approximate dates, 57
  axes, 78, 106–107
  coastal exotic artifacts, 108–109,
    111–114
  Cuzqueño-style artifacts/general
    Andean-style artifacts,
    102–108
  discs, 92, 106
  earspools, 97
  intentionally destroyed metal
    artifacts, 134
  Late Horizon metal assemblages,
    77–85
  lirpus, 96–97
  lost, discarded, or interred
    artifacts, 135
  metal strips, 99
  quotidian metal artifacts, 76, 140
  star-shaped mace heads, 95
  T-shaped tumis, 91, 103, 116, 138
  tweezers, 112–113
Late Intermediate period
  alloy preparation and smelting,
    19, 21, 60
  approximate dates, 57
  intentionally destroyed metal
    artifacts, 132, 134
  lost, discarded, or interred
    artifacts, 135
  quotidian metal artifacts, 76
  regional metalworking patterns,
    85
Laurake pendants, 130
lead (Pb)
  bola weights, 91–92
  bronze alloy impurities, 17
  casting techniques, 70
  cerussite ($PbCO_3$), 19
  galena (PbS), 19
  silver alloy impurities, 19, 21
  silver-lead ores, 70–71
  tin bronzes, 13, 70

Lima region, 111, 115
lime dippers/spoons
    altiplano exotic artifacts, 114
    burial artifacts, 118, 119
    casting techniques, 232–233
    catalog description, 220, 232–233, 239
    chemical composition, 205
    forging and annealing techniques, 239
    geographic distribution, 111
    microstructures, 209
    regional metalworking patterns, 90, 101
    use evidence, 111
lirpus
    burial artifacts, 118, 119, 121, 135
    geographic distribution, 139
    Late Horizon period, 84
    Machu Picchu, 103, 114
    meanings and significance, 103
    regional metalworking patterns, 96–97
little bells, 130
llama-head knife
    casting techniques, 34
    catalog description, 237
    chemical composition, 199, 237
    forging and annealing techniques, 199–200
    microstructures, 199–200
    surface coloration, 67
    surface treatments and decoration, 48
    tin content, 14
llama-head pins, 33
long-eared finial, 49
long spike points, 117–118
long-taper tupus, 101
loop-eye needles, 115, 117, 132
loop-headed tumis, 101
lost-wax casting technique, 33–34, 59, 116

M

mace heads
    catalog description, 241
    collection percentage, 7
    Late Horizon period, 78, 83, 84–85
Machu Picchu artifacts
    alloy preparation and smelting, 11–15
    Andean metalworking patterns, 102–108
    axes, 93
    burial artifacts, 118–119, 121, 140–141
    classification and characteristics, 7–11
    conical bells, 100, 119
    Cuzqueño artifacts, 102–108
    design standardization, 9–10

discs, 102
false leads, 100
headbands, 99
historical background, 1–3
lirpus, 96–97
meanings and significance, xiii
metallurgical research, xiii–xiv
1912 expedition, xiii
provenience, 8–9
quotidian metal artifacts
    altiplano exotic artifacts, 114
    Andean metalworking patterns, 85–87, 89–102
    axes, 106–107, 125–129, 140
    bangles, 111
    bola weights, 103, 106
    burial artifacts, 118–119, 121
    celts, 107, 129
    chisels, 107–108, 129–130
    coastal exotic artifacts, 108–109, 111–114
    comparative data criteria, 75–77
    conical bells, 130–131
    construction tools, 106
    Cuzqueño-style artifacts, 102–108
    finger rings, 111
    general Andean-style artifacts, 102–108, 140
    geographic distribution, 138–141
    half-round-headed tupus, 102
    intentional destruction, 131–134
    Late Horizon metal assemblages, 77–85, 140
    life histories, 121–135, 138
    lirpus, 103, 114
    lost, discarded, or interred artifacts, 135, 138
    meanings and significance, 140–141
    metalsmiths, 121–122, 140
    needles, 115, 117
    notable absences, 116–118
    oval artifacts, 115
    pierced-eye needles, 103
    projectile points, 117–118
    repair practices, 134–135
    sheet metal objects, 112
    split bells, 109
    spoons, 111
    summary, 138–141
    technological and stylistic characteristics, 115–116
    T-shaped tumis, 103, 123–124, 138
    tupus, 123
    tweezers, 112–113, 115
    research methods, 3–5, 7
    selection criteria, 10–11
    sources, 102
    star-shaped mace heads, 95

Mallorca, 131
Manco Capac (Manco Inca), 84
manoplas, 117
Mantaro Valley, 19
Massachusetts Institute of Technology, 1
Mathewson, Champion H., xiii, 1–3, 4, 17, 35, 237–238, 246
Matsumoto, Yuichi, 71
Mayer, Eugen, 75
Merrimack, New Hampshire, 5
metal dishes, 116
metal earspools, 84, 85
metallurgical sequence, 56–57
metal residue, 246–247
metals and alloys
    alloy preparation and smelting
        artifact fabrication, 22
        bronze alloys, 13–15, 17
        metal sources, 23, 60–61
        preparation methods, 12–13
        silver alloys, 17, 19, 21, 60–61
        tin alloys, 22
    artifact function and use
        form and function, 52–53
        tool design, 53–55
        tool use evidence, 55–56
    artisan skills, 64–66
    casting techniques
        basic processes, 23–24, 32–34
        bronze artifacts, 25, 27–28, 34
        Mochica culture, 59
        problems and difficulties, 34–35, 66
        silver-copper artifacts, 29–32
    Chavín culture, 58–59
    composition controls, 64
    forging and annealing techniques
        α–δ eutectoid structure, 42–43
        annealing temperatures, 42–43
        basic processes, 36–38
        bronze artifacts, 28–29, 36–44
        forging temperatures, 42
        metalworking tools, 46–47
        sheet metal fabrication, 47–48, 112
        silver-copper alloys, 44–46
        strain hardening, 43–44, 48, 69
    innovative techniques, 66–67
    metallurgical history, 2–3
    metal sources, 11–12, 23
    quotidian metal artifacts
        altiplano exotic artifacts, 114
        Andean metalworking patterns, 85–87, 89–102
        axes, 125–129
        celts, 129
        chisels, 129–130
        coastal exotic artifacts, 108–109, 111–114
        comparative data criteria, 75–77
        conical bells, 130–131

corporate- versus imperial-
    style artifacts, 74–75
Cuzqueño-style artifacts,
    102–108
general Andean-style artifacts,
    102–108, 140
geographic distribution,
    138–141
intentional destruction,
    131–134
Late Horizon metal
    assemblages, 77–85, 140
life histories, 121–135, 138
lost, discarded, or interred
    artifacts, 135, 138
meanings and significance,
    73–75, 108, 140–141
metalsmiths, 121–122, 140
repair practices, 134–135
summary, 138–141
T-shaped tumis, 123–124
tupus, 123
surface treatments and
    decoration
    characteristics, 48–49
    surface coloration, 49–52,
        66–67
metalsmiths, 101–103, 121–122,
    140
metal spill, 241, 246
metal stock
    catalog description, 240–241,
        244, 245–246
    collection percentage, 8
    forging and annealing
        techniques, 12
    geographic provenience, 9
    impurities and inclusions, 15
    microstructures, 31, 39
    sources, 23
metal strips, 99, 113–114
metalworking tools, 46–47, 135
microprobe analyses, 4, 13
Middle Bronze Age, 13
Middle Horizon period, 51–52, 57
mirrors, 74, 96–97
misruns, 66
mitimaes, 86, 107
Mochica culture, 59–60
molder's slick, 231
Moquegua, Peru, 75, 90, 98, 99,
    113, 130
muffles, 71
mummy masks, 112
Museo Contisuyo, 75
mushrooming damage, 107, 123,
    126, 129–130
Mutquin, 114
Muyuntasita, Bolivia, 131

N
Naugatuck Valley (Connecticut), 1
necklaces, 230
neck-stepped tumis, 116

needles
    burial artifacts, 119
    catalog description, 242–243, 247
    collection percentage, 7
    geographic distribution, 115, 117
    intentional destruction, 131, 132
    Machu Picchu artifacts, 103
    nonmortuary contexts, 135
    pierced-eye needles, 103, 115,
        119
Nesbitt, Jason, 71
New Haven, Connecticut, 1
New World metallurgies, 57
North Coast tumis, 77, 117, 131,
    132
Northern Analytical Laboratory,
    Inc., 5, 71
nose ornaments, 117
notched tweezers, 100, 117

O
Old World metallurgies, 57, 69–70
Ollantaytambo
    axes, 55, 93, 129, 140
    bola weights, 106
    celts, 107
    construction tools, 106
    half-round-headed tupus, 102
    headdress ornamentals/frontals,
        98
    Late Horizon metal assemblages,
        78
    quotidian metal artifacts, 140
    star-shaped mace heads, 95
    T-shaped tumis, 103
optical microscopy, 2
orejones, 73
oval artifacts, 115
Owen, Bruce, xiii, 71

P
Pacasmayo, 112
Pachacamac, 98, 101, 111
Pachacuti Inca Yupanqui, 73, 78,
    102, 139, 140
palstaves, 69
Peabody Museum of Natural
    History, 4, 71, 75
pelike-shaped jug, 119
pendants
    catalog description, 220, 226,
        231, 233, 242, 243, 245
    geographic distribution, 111, 114
    pendant disc, 226, 245, 246
    surface treatments and
        decoration, 49, 231
    tin content, 14, 231
Percy, John, 2
personal adornments, 130
Phoebe A. Hearst Museum, 75
physical metallurgy, 1–2
pierced-eye needles, 103, 115, 119
Pikillacta, 89, 106

pins, 10, 101, 243
    See also shawl pins (*tupus*)
plain-headed tumis, 101
plain round-headed tupus, 84
plain sheet strip ring, 111
plaques, 98
plate handles, 47, 112, 115–116,
    233–234
plumb bobs, 106, 236
plumed artifacts, 98
plume holders, 112, 135, 236
pointed tweezers, 100, 115
Polaroid film, 3, 4
Pooley, Alan, 4, 71
Porco, Bolivia, 70
Potosí, 62, 63, 70
potter's slick, 231
pottery, 78, 118, 119, 121
precious metal objects, 99
pre-Columbian metallurgies, xiii,
    69–70
pre-Machu Picchu metallurgy,
    56–63
prill smelting technique, 61
projectile points, 117–118
punches, 118
punctate dots, 113–114

Q
Quebrada de la Vaca, 85, 95
quimbelate, 71
quotidian metal artifacts
    comparative data criteria
        geographic provenience,
            75–76, 78, 83–85
        tumi knives, 77
        typology, 76–77
    corporate- versus imperial-style
        artifacts, 74–75, 84–85
    geographic distribution, 85,
        101–102
    geographic provenience, 75–76,
        78, 83–85
    Late Horizon metal assemblages,
        77–85
    Machu Picchu
        altiplano exotic artifacts, 114
        Andean metalworking
            patterns, 85–87, 89–102
        axes, 106–107, 125–129, 140
        bangles, 111
        bola weights, 103, 106
        burial artifacts, 118–119, 121
        celts, 107, 129
        chisels, 107–108, 129–130
        coastal exotic artifacts,
            108–109, 111–114
        comparative data criteria,
            75–77
        conical bells, 130–131
        construction tools, 106
        Cuzqueño-style artifacts,
            102–108
        finger rings, 111

general Andean-style artifacts, 102–108, 140
geographic distribution, 138–141
half-round-headed tupus, 102
intentional destruction, 131–134
Late Horizon metal assemblages, 77–85, 140
life histories, 121–135, 138
lirpus, 103, 114
lost, discarded, or interred artifacts, 135, 138
meanings and significance, 140–141
metalsmiths, 121–122, 140
needles, 115, 117
notable absences, 116–118
oval artifacts, 115
pierced-eye needles, 103
projectile points, 117–118
repair practices, 134–135
sheet metal objects, 112
sources, 102
split bells, 109
spoons, 111
summary, 138–141
technological and stylistic characteristics, 115–116
T-shaped tumis, 103, 123–124, 138
tupus, 123
tweezers, 112–113, 115
meanings and significance, 73–75, 108, 140–141
Ollantaytambo, 140
regional metalworking patterns
axe-maces, 96
axes, 92–95
bola weights, 91–92
discs, 92
earspools, 97
geographic distribution, 85, 101–102
headdress ornamentals/ frontals, 97–98
Inca-style artifacts, 86–87, 101, 106–107
lime-dippers, 90
lirpus, 96–97
shawl pins (*tupus*), 87, 89–90, 101–103
southern Titicaca metalsmiths, 101–102
star-shaped mace heads, 95
T-shaped tumis, 90–91
tumis, 101
yauri pikes, 94–95

R
rapiers, 69
rattles, 130
rectangular plaques, 98

repoussé technique, 112, 113
research methods
chemical composition determination, 4–5
cleaning process, 3
experimental metallurgy, 5, 7
Machu Picchu artifacts, 3–5, 7
metallographic examinations, 3
Vickers hardness determination, 5
rhyolite, 55
Rosalina, 4, 17, 195, 234
rounded mace heads, 95
round-headed tupus, 89, 101–103, 115, 138
Rumiñavi, 123, 126
Rutledge, John W., xiii, 71

S
Sacsawaman
axes, 128–129
bola weights, 106
celts, 107
construction tools, 106
half-round-headed tupus, 102
headbands, 99
headdress ornamentals/frontals, 98
Late Horizon metal assemblages, 78, 83, 85, 140
lirpus, 96
star-shaped mace heads, 95
T-shaped tumis, 103
tweezers, 112
Salazar, Lucy, 8, 71
San Pedro de Atacama, 99, 122
scanning electron microscopy, 4–5
scleroscope, 5
scrap materials, 9
shaping techniques, 2
shawl pins (*tupus*)
altiplano exotic artifacts, 114
burial artifacts, 118, 135
casting techniques, 27–28, 223
catalog description, 219–225, 229–232, 238, 242, 243, 244, 245, 246, 247
chemical composition, 221
collection percentage, 7, 8
contextual perspectives, 67
design standardization, 9–10
fasteners, 222
forging and annealing techniques, 36–39, 45, 221–223, 225–226, 230
functional role, 123
geographic distribution, 87, 89–90, 101–103, 118–119, 139
Inca-style artifacts, 87, 101, 138
innovative techniques, 66–67
intentional destruction, 131, 132
Late Horizon period, 78, 84

Machu Picchu artifacts, 102
meanings and significance, 73, 74
microstructures, 222
nonmortuary contexts, 135
provenience, 8–9
repair practices, 134
selection criteria, 10–11
shawl pin stem, 31
spade-shaped head, 226
surface treatments and decoration, 224, 225
tin content, 224
sheet metal fabrication, 47–48, 112
sheet metal objects, 76, 97–98, 99, 112, 121, 132, 240–241
sheet strips, 84
Sheffield, England, 2
Sheffield Scientific School (Yale University), 1
Sillustani, 76, 99
silver (Ag)
alloy preparation, 12
argentite (Ag_2S), 19
bronze alloy impurities, 17
cerargyrite (AgCl), 19
chemical composition determination techniques, 4, 13, 195
silver alloys
alloy preparation and smelting, 17, 70–71
balls, 241
bracelets, 230
Chavín culture, 59
discs, 226, 232
finger rings, 230–231
headbands, 230
headdress ornamentals/ frontals, 231
metal stock, 244
pendants, 233
plate handles, 233–234
plume holders, 236
shawl pins (*tupus*), 221, 222, 223, 224, 225, 226, 230, 231–232, 242, 245
spangles, 241
tweezers, 219, 233
silver artifacts
collection percentage, 7–8
depletion silvering technique, 2, 50–52, 60, 63, 246
Spanish artisans, 70
silver-copper alloys
alloy preparation and smelting, 17, 19, 21, 60–61
artisan skills, 64–66
casting techniques, 29–32
depletion silvering technique, 2, 50–52, 60, 63
forging and annealing techniques, 44–46

innovative techniques, 66–67
metallographic examinations, 4, 5, 195
microstructures, 44–46
Mochica culture, 59–60
shawl pins (*tupus*), 219–220
silver content, 51–52
surface coloration, 50–52, 66–67
Wanka culture, 61
silver-lead ores, 70–71
single-cone tupus, 102
Sipán, 76
small knife, 220–221
small pin, 220
Smith, Bruce, 75
Smithsonian Institution, 75
socketed points, 117
Sorby, Henry C., 2
sounding devices, 8
South American metallurgies, 57–58
southern Titicaca metalsmiths, 61–63, 101–103, 122, 138, 140
spangles, 17, 45, 241
Spanish artisans, 70–71
spearheads, 69
spear points, 7
spearthrowers, 118
spherical ball, 238
spheroid bola weights, 84, 87, 91–92
spindle whorls, 117
split bells, 109
spoons
burial artifacts, 100, 118, 135
geographic distribution, 111, 116, 139
See also bird-head lime spoons; lime dippers/spoons
squashed conical sheet metal object, 112
staff ornaments, 47
stair-stepped knives, 108–109
Standard Model, 57
star-head pins, 14, 33, 49, 225
star-shaped axes, 73
star-shaped mace heads
Cuzqueño artifacts, 102–103
geographic distribution, 95, 138
Inca-style artifacts, 87
Late Horizon period, 78, 83, 84–85
station 9A, 121
stone bola weights, 91–92
stonecutting tools, 54–55, 106, 197
straight-backed T-shaped tumis, 101
straight-transitional tweezers, 113
strain hardening, 43–44, 48, 69
strength properties, 2
strip rings, 111

sulfur (S)
argentite (Ag_2S), 19
bronze alloy impurities, 14–15
casting defects, 35
chemical composition determination techniques, 4, 13, 195
copper sulfide (Cu_2S), 14–15, 191, 195
galena (PbS), 19
strength property determinations, 7
surface treatments and decoration characteristics, 48–49
surface coloration, 49–52, 66–67
See also specific artifact
swords, 7

T

Tammann, Gustav, 1
teardrop-shaped tweezers, 84, 113
textile tool finial, 232
thin half-round tupus, 101
Thomsen, Christian, 56
Tiahuanaco, 130
Tiawanaku, 62, 70
tin (Sn)
alloy preparation, 12
antimony impurities, 22
bronze alloys, 13–14
chemical composition determination techniques, 4, 13, 22, 195
copper-tin-bismuth alloy, 200, 237
copper-tin bronzes, 2, 13, 67, 122, 191
geographic distribution, 122
high-tin bronzes, 1, 3, 13–14
impurities and inclusions, 22
metal stock, 240, 241
metalworking effects, 47
sheet metal objects, 47
silver alloy impurities, 19, 21
tin antimonide (Sn2Sb), 22
tin belt, 61–62
tin bronzes
casting defects, 34
color significance, 14, 49
composition gradient, 25
copper-tin bronzes, 2, 13, 67, 122
forging and annealing techniques, 36
Inca-style artifacts, 74–75, 78, 89
lead alloys, 13, 70
Machu Picchu artifacts, 67
metallurgical properties, 1, 2, 3
microstructures, 24
southern Titicaca metalsmiths, 62–63, 101, 122, 138
spoons, 116

tiny spoons, 100, 116
Titicaca region
altiplano exotic artifacts, 114
axes, 93
bola weights, 91
burial artifacts, 121
conical bells, 100–101, 119, 130, 139
decorated strips, 114
headdress ornamentals/frontals, 98
Late Horizon metal assemblages, 62, 78
lime dippers/spoons, 119
metallurgical innovations, 101
pierced-eye needles, 103
precious metal objects, 99
southern Titicaca metalsmiths, 101–103, 140
split bells, 109
tin bronze technology, 122
T-shaped tumis, 103, 116, 123–124, 139
tupus, 87, 89–90, 123, 139
Tiwanaku, 86, 89, 106, 114, 116
tokis, 117
tools
casting and molding, 32–33
catalog description, 226, 245
collection percentage, 8
metalworking tools, 46–47
provenience, 9
tool design, 53–55
tool-making artisans, 69
tool use evidence, 55–56
traced decorations, 113–114, 121
Tracor-Northern Standardless Semiquantitative (SSQ) analysis program, 4–5, 13
trapezoid-shaped frontal ornamentation, 97
triangular neck-step tweezer, 121–122
triangular tweezers, 84, 100, 113, 119, 122, 139
T-shaped axe heads
broken axe blades, 202, 205
catalog description, 234–235, 238
chemical composition, 195, 197, 202
crossbars, 191–192, 195, 197, 202, 234, 238
forging and annealing techniques, 41, 44, 191–192, 197, 238
geographic distribution, 94, 121, 138
Inca-style artifacts, 87, 138
meanings and significance, 74
microstructures, 195, 202
technical description, 191–192, 195, 197
tin content, 14

use evidence, 54, 55, 56, 234
T-shaped tumis
  burial artifacts, 135
  coastal exotic artifacts, 114
  comparative data criteria, 77
  functional role, 123–124
  geographic distribution, 87, 90–91, 103, 122, 138, 139
  globular join features, 102, 121
  Inca-style artifacts, 87, 138
  intentional destruction, 131, 132
  Late Horizon period, 83, 84, 116
  regional metalworking patterns, 90–91
tumis
  casting defects, 228
  casting techniques, 27–28
  catalog description, 219, 220–221, 227–229, 236–237, 239
  collection percentage, 7
  comparative data criteria, 77
  contextual perspectives, 67
  forging and annealing techniques, 37–39, 220–221, 227, 237, 239
  geographic distribution, 138, 139
  globular join features, 101–102
  Inca-style artifacts, 87, 101, 138
  innovative techniques, 66–67
  intentional destruction, 131, 132
  knife blades, 237, 244
  Late Horizon period, 83, 84
  meanings and significance, 74
  microstructures, 239
  neck-stepped tumis, 116
  repair practices, 134
  southern Titicaca metalsmiths, 101
  surface treatments and decoration, 48–49, 229
  tin content, 229
  tool use evidence, 219, 227, 229
  T-shaped tumis
    burial artifacts, 135
    coastal exotic artifacts, 114
    comparative data criteria, 77
    functional role, 123–124
    geographic distribution, 87, 90–91, 103, 122, 138, 139
    globular join features, 102, 121
    intentional destruction, 131, 132
    Late Horizon period, 83, 84, 116
Tupac Amaru, 95
tupus
  altiplano exotic artifacts, 114
  burial artifacts, 118, 135
  casting techniques, 27–28, 223
  catalog description, 219–225, 229–232, 238, 242, 243, 244, 245, 246, 247
  chemical composition, 221

collection percentage, 7, 8
contextual perspectives, 67
design standardization, 9–10
fasteners, 222
forging and annealing techniques, 36–39, 45, 221–223, 225–226, 230
functional role, 123
geographic distribution, 87, 89–90, 101–103, 118–119, 139
Inca-style artifacts, 87, 101, 138
innovative techniques, 66–67
intentional destruction, 131, 132
Late Horizon period, 78, 84
Machu Picchu artifacts, 102
meanings and significance, 73, 74
microstructures, 222
nonmortuary contexts, 135
provenience, 8–9
repair practices, 134
selection criteria, 10–11
shawl pin stem, 31
spade-shaped head, 226
surface treatments and decoration, 224, 225
tin content, 224
tweezers
  burial artifacts, 118, 119, 135
  catalog description, 219, 220, 233, 237, 239, 243, 244
  coastal artifacts, 100, 112–113
  collection percentage, 7
  exotic artifacts, 115
  forging and annealing techniques, 38, 40–41, 239
  functional role, 52
  geographic distribution, 118–119, 139
  Late Horizon period, 84
  meanings and significance, 74
  microstructures, 239
  misclassification, 219
  nonmortuary contexts, 135
  notched tweezers, 100, 117
  selection criteria, 11
  skills and innovation, 65
  tin content, 14
  triangular neck-step tweezer, 121–122
  triangular tweezers, 84, 100, 113, 119, 122, 139

U

United States National Museum, 2
universal metallurgical sequence, 56–57
University of California at Berkeley, 75
Upper Mantaro Archaeological Research Project (UMARP), 75, 132, 135

Upper Mantaro Valley, 61
upsetting damage, 107, 123, 126, 129–130, 131
Urubamba River, xiii, 195, 234
Urubamba Valley, 15, 140

V

Vecitador y Vedor de Estos Reinos, 97
vessels, 8
Vickers hardness determination, 5
Vicus, 76, 93, 95, 109, 118
Vilcabamba, xiii

W

waistbands, 99
Wanka culture, 61
Wanka II period, 132, 134
Wari culture, 89
wavelength spectroscopy, 5
weapons, 7
wet chemical, quantitative analyses, 4–5, 13
Williams, Patrick, 75
Winchester Repeating Arms Company, 1
wind-blown shaft furnaces, 62, 70–71
withies, 13, 32
woodcutting tools, 53–54, 129–130
work-in-progess artifacts
  casting techniques, 31
  catalog description, 226, 240–241, 245
  collection percentage, 7, 8
  surface-depletion process, 52

Y

Yale Peabody Museum of Natural History, xiii, 4, 71, 75
Yale Peruvian Scientific Expedition, xiii
Yale University Department of Geology and Geophysics, 5
yanacona retainers, 73, 84, 86, 89, 102, 107
yauri pikes, 85, 94–95, 138
Yupanqui, 73, 78, 102, 139, 140

Z

Zeiss Neophot metallographs, 3, 4
zinc impurities, 15